T5-CVU-036

Recent Developments in Antitrust

CESifo Seminar Series
Edited by Hans-Werner Sinn

Inequality and Growth: Theory and Policy Implications, Theo S. Eicher and Stephen J. Turnovsky, editors

Public Finance and Public Policy in the New Century, Sijbren Cnossen and Hans-Werner Sinn, editors

Spectrum Auctions and Competition in Telecommunications, Gerhard Illing and Ulrich Klüh, editors

Managing European Union Enlargement, Helge Berger and Thomas Moutos, editors

European Monetary Integration, Hans-Werner Sinn, Mika Widgrén, and Marko Köthenbürger, editors

Measuring the Tax Burden on Capital and Labor, Peter Birch Sørensen, editor

A Constitution for the European Union, Charles B. Blankart and Dennis C. Mueller, editors

Labor Market Institutions and Public Regulation, Jonas Agell, Michael Keen, and Alfons J. Weichenrieder, editors

Venture Capital, Entrepreneurship, and Public Policy, Vesa Kanniainen and Christian Keuschnigg, editors

Exchange Rate Economics: Where Do We Stand?, Paul De Grauwe, editor

Prospects for Monetary Unions after the Euro, Paul De Grauwe and Jacques Mélitz, editors

Structural Unemployment in Western Europe: Reasons and Remedies, Martin Werding, editor

Institutions, Development, and Economic Growth, Theo S. Eicher and Cecilia García-Peñalosa, editors

Competitive Failures in Insurance Markets: Theory and Policy Implications, Pierre-André Chiappori and Christian Gollier, editors

Japan's Great Stagnation: Financial and Monetary Policy Lessons for Advanced Economies, Michael M. Hutchison and Frank Westermann, editors

Tax Policy and Labor Market Performance, Jonas Agell and Peter Birch Sørensen, editors

Privatization Experiences in the European Union, Marko Köthenbürger, Hans-Werner Sinn, and John Whalley, editors

Recent Developments in Antitrust: Theory and Evidence, Jay Pil Choi, editor

See http://mitpress.mit.edu for a complete list of titles in this series.

Recent Developments in Antitrust

Theory and Evidence

edited by Jay Pil Choi

CESifo Seminar Series

The MIT Press
Cambridge, Massachusetts
London, England

MIT Press books may be purchased at special quantity discounts for business or sales promotional use. For information, please e-mail special_sales@mitpress.mit.edu or write to Special Sales Department, The MIT Press, 55 Hayward Street, Cambridge, MA 02142.

This book was set in Palatino by SNP Best-set Typesetter Ltd., Hong Kong, and printed and bound in the United States of America.

Library of Congress Cataloging-in-Publication Data

Recent developments in antitrust : theory and evidence / edited by Jay Pil Choi.
p. cm.—(CESifo seminar studies)
Includes bibliographical references and index.
ISBN-13: 978-0-262-03356-5 (alk. paper)
ISBN-10: 0-262-03356-9 (alk. paper)
1. Competition. 2. Antitrust law. 3. Economic policy. I. Choi, Jay Pil.

HF1414.R425 2007
338.8—dc22

2006049442

10 9 8 7 6 5 4 3 2 1

Contents

Series Foreword

This book is part of the CESifo Seminar Series. The series aims to cover topical policy issues in economics from a largely European perspective. The books in this series are the products of the papers and intensive debates that took place during the seminars hosted by CESifo, an international research network of renowned economists organized jointly by the Center for Economic Studies at Ludwig-Maximilians-Universität, Munich, and the Ifo Institute for Economic Research. All publications in this series have been carefully selected and refereed by members of the CESifo research network.

Introduction

Economic analysis now plays a crucial role in formulating antitrust policy (referred as competition policy in Europe) across the Atlantic, and courts have endorsed a central role for economic theory and empirical analysis in rendering their decisions. For instance, economic concepts are widely adopted in the U.S. Merger Guidelines, and the recent discussion of European merger reform also mirrors this trend, with more emphasis on economics-based merger enforcement. In addition, antitrust court cases are increasingly argued with sophisticated economic analysis by all parties concerned. In major cases such as *Eastman Kodak Co. v. Image Technical Services, Inc.* and the *US v. Microsoft*, both plaintiffs and defendants made extensive use of game theory, the economics of information, and transaction cost economics in advancing their arguments.[1]

The need for sophisticated economic reasoning is reflected in the substantial presence of economists in antitrust agencies and major consulting firms. Two U.S. antitrust agencies, the Department of Justice and the Federal Trade Commission, each employ fifty to sixty PhD-level economists headed by Chief Economists who are usually respected academics. As part of the reform process, the European Commission also recently created the position of Chief Economist.

Against this background, this book brings together a panel of specialists to discuss the conceptual and empirical issues involved in the formulation and enforcement of competition policy. The chapters in the book reflect the wide range of issues in antitrust analysis and provide a broad picture of recent developments by discussing the current state of the art and identifying avenues for further research.

The first set of three chapters deals with theoretical issues that have played important roles in recent antitrust cases such as *Eastman Kodak Co. v. Image Technical Services, Inc.*, et al., the Visa and MasterCard antitrust suit initially filed by Wal-Mart, Sears, and a few other large chains, and the European Commission's case against Microsoft.

I.1 Antitrust Analysis in Durable-Goods Markets (Chapter 1)

In chapter 1, Michael Waldman points out that there are a number of issues that only arise in durable-goods markets, or at least arise more frequently in such markets that have important implications for antitrust policy. For instance, issues concerning secondhand or used-good markets are important for durable goods, whereas such issues are virtually nonexistent for nondurable goods. The durable goods also typically require maintenance service, which creates an aftermarket that is complementary to a durable-goods producer's primary product. In fact, the issue of whether a durable-goods producer should be allowed to monopolize aftermarkets for its own durable products has been the most contentious point in the cases involving Kodak, Data General, Unisys, and Xerox. Recognizing the peculiarities of the durable-goods markets for sensible antitrust policy is important, considering the role of such markets in the economy. In the United States, personal-consumption expenditures on durable goods exceeded $800 billion in 2000. Waldman reviews and discusses a number of recent advances in the durable-goods-theory literature that have important implications for several prominent antitrust issues concerning durable-goods markets.

In particular, he points out that the classic Swan approach to durable-goods modeling has the unrealistic feature that consumers can combine a number of used units to make a perfect substitute for a new unit. Waldman and other authors, such as Igal Hendel and Alessandro Lizzeri, have recently explored an alternative approach to modeling durable-goods markets that is not characterized by this feature. In this new approach, each individual is assumed to consume either zero or one physical unit per period, where the quality of a unit deteriorates as the unit ages. The assumption that each individual consumes either zero or one physical unit per period thus escapes the same criticism as the Swan approach concerning the ability to combine used units to create a perfect substitute for a new unit. Another key assumption is that consumers vary in terms of their valuations of product quality, as in the standard Mussa and Rosen analysis. Waldman convincingly argues for the importance of such an approach by showing that optimal antitrust merger policy for durable-goods markets is significantly different in an analysis that employs this new approach, than in the more traditional but less realistic Swan approach.

I.2 Two-Sided Markets and Platform Competition (Chapter 2)

There are many markets where two or more groups of participants interact via intermediaries or platforms. Such markets have been called *two-sided* markets (or more generally, multisided markets) and have recently been one of the most active areas of research. The defining characteristic of multisided markets is the existence of at least two distinct groups of customers with *intergroup network externalities*: members of each group benefit from interacting with members from the other side of the market. A favorite example to illustrate two-sided markets is dating services or nightclubs where each member of two distinct groups of people (men and women) derives value from interacting with members of the other group. In this example, members of each group obviously derive higher utility as more people from the other group patronize the same dating service or nightclub. This type of intergroup network externality is not limited to dating services. Other examples with more significant economic importance include auction sites, such as eBay and Yahoo, where buyers and sellers get together to consummate a deal; credit card payment systems such as Visa and MasterCard, where both merchants and consumers need to participate in the same system; video game platforms such as PlayStation, X-box, and GameCube, where game developers and consumers constitute the two distinct sides, and so on.[2] In such markets, the need to get all sides of the market to get on board creates a so-called chicken-and-egg problem in that members of each group are willing to participate in the market only if they expect many members from the other side to participate. The literature on two-sided markets has been mainly concerned with the optimal pricing structure to coordinate the demands of distinct groups of customers who need each other in some way.

More recently, the importance of studying antitrust issues in two-sided markets has been recognized by several authors (Evans 2003; Wright 2003). In particular, the recent literature has called for caution in applying the traditional one-sided logic to two-sided markets in the antitrust arena. In chapter 2, Mark Armstrong takes up this important issue and investigates whether intergroup network externalities in such markets require new insight and thus render previous analyses based on one-sided logic less applicable.

I.3 Antitrust Analysis of Tying Arrangements (Chapter 3)

Tying arrangements recently have been a major and contentious issue in many high-profile antitrust cases in the United States and Europe. Examples include the Microsoft case, the Visa and MasterCard case, and the proposed GE-Honeywell merger, to name a few. Chapter 3 (by Jay Pil Choi) conducts a selective review of developments in the analysis of tying arrangements and discusses relevant antitrust cases concerned with tying arrangements in light of theoretical advances in this area. Because recent antitrust cases are concerned increasingly with firms operating in industries where innovation is central to a firm's success, however, there has been a question of whether antitrust analysis is up to the challenge. More specifically, with the emergence of the "new economy," it is unclear whether traditional antitrust analysis—which was developed to address concerns about price practices in the railroad and smokestack industries, and has typically ignored issues of innovation almost entirely—is appropriate in the context of the rapidly evolving technology based industries like computing and the Internet. Thus, chapter 3 describes models of tying that incorporate incentives to innovate. In particular, it demonstrates that even in the absence of exit by the rival firm (hence, no changes in the market structure in the tied-good market), tying can be a profitable strategy via its long-term effects on competition through innovation.

The welfare implications of tying arrangements are, in general, ambiguous because tying could have efficiency effects even when it has harmful exclusionary effects. Microsoft's tying of Internet Explorer and Media Player with its operating system is a case in point. The literature suggests that such technical tying can be exclusionary under certain conditions. At the same time, however, there may be offsetting effects of tying, such as enhanced performance due to a seamless integration of products and reduced costs of distribution if the tying good and the tied good are often used. As such, there seems to be a consensus emerging among economists that tying should not be treated as *per se* violation of antitrust laws, and that the rule of reason should be adopted in the assessment of tying arrangements.[3] However, beyond the general principle that any sensible antitrust policy should balance possible efficiency effects against potential anticompetitive effects, it seems to be an elusive goal to come up with a simple legal standard to apply in antitrust cases, since the appropriate antitrust policy will depend on the specifics of the case.

The next set (chapters 4–7) is a series of chapters that are empirical in nature.

I.4 Empirical Analysis of Bundling and Tying (Chapter 4)

As summarized in chapter 3, bundling can have both anticompetitive effects and efficiency benefits, and the motivations for such practices can be diverse. Despite theoretical advances in understanding the practice of bundling, empirical analysis in this area has been lagging. This is especially problematic because the central policy issue in this area is to distinguish empirically anticompetitive cases of bundling and tying from those that arise commonly under competition, presumably because the practice is efficient. David S. Evans and Michael Salinger's piece in chapter 4 is a first step toward developing a better empirical analysis of the effects of bundling. More specifically, they apply and extend the cost-based approach to bundling and tying under competition developed in their companion paper on over-the-counter pain relievers and cold medicines.[4] They document that consumers pay much less for tablets with multiple ingredients than they would to buy tablets containing each ingredient separately. They then decompose the sources of these savings into marginal cost savings and a component that reflects fixed costs of product offerings. The analysis both documents substantial economies of bundling and illustrates the sort of cost analysis necessary for understanding tying.

I.5 The Political Economy of Merger Control (Chapter 5)

Vivek Ghosal examines the political-economy aspects of merger enforcement in chapter 5. More specifically, he empirically models the short-run switches of the political party in power, models the longer-run deep-seated ideological regime shifts, and quantifies their impact on enforcement by the Antitrust Division of the U.S. Department of Justice from 1958 to 2002.

For the political and ideological effects, Ghosal's key empirical results are as follows. First, he finds evidence of a distinct downward regime shift in the intensity of merger enforcement after 1974. He posits several factors that could have contributed to the trend, such as the emphasis on pro-competitive and efficiency aspects of corporate conduct, the increasingly conservative composition of the U.S. Supreme Court, and some administrative changes that affected merger evaluation, such as introduction of the Merger Guidelines in 1968 and the HSR Act of 1976. Second, Ghosal shows that, contrary to popular belief, Republicans do not initiate fewer merger challenges than Democrats. This is true both with respect to merger enforcement under the older antitrust doctrine prevailing in the 1950s and 1960s, and with respect to the newer regime that increasingly placed emphasis on market forces and pro-competitive effects. Third, to look at the bigger picture, Ghosal examines the Antitrust Division's overall civil enforcement. Similar to the findings on merger enforcement, these data show a regime shift in the early 1970s. In contrast to merger challenges, data on total civil enforcement show that, post–regime shift, the Republicans have initiated fewer cases than Democrats.

I.6 Market Definition in Differentiated Product Markets (Chapter 6)

Antitrust agencies and courts have shifted from relying primarily on market-share evidence to more sophisticated simulation analysis in predicting the effects of various business practices on competition. For a variety of reasons, however, it is likely that the market-definition approach will remain an important tool in competition policy analysis for some time, despite the increased importance of other tools such as the simulation approach. The European Commission's new block exemption on vertical restraints in the car market, for instance, relies heavily on the computation of market shares. Against this background, in chapter 6, Randy Brenkers and Frank Verboven suggest an econometric approach to define the relevant markets with differentiated products. They show that their approach is directly consistent with the SSNIP test, and it is in fact more satisfactory than previous approaches such as critical elasticity analysis or the simple use of standard industry classifications. In addition, their approach shares a lot of features with the simulation approach (similar data requirements, and similar assumptions about current market power).

To draw lessons from a rigorous application of the market definition, Brenkers and Verboven apply their method in analyzing the European car market and find that the relevant market for minivan cars is defined at the widest level—that is, at the aggregate country level. Furthermore, in Italy the relevant markets for domestic cars are defined at an intermediate level—the segment level. In all other cases, the relevant markets for cars may be defined at the narrowest level—the subsegment level. Based on these results, Brenkers and Verboven identify the firms that may violate the market-share thresholds stipulated in the block-exemption regulation. They find that if an approach based on standard industry classifications instead of their econometric approach has been used, their conclusions would have been different, and in fact, inconclusive. They also draw attention to other issues in market definition that may be of use to practitioners.

I.7 Merger Control in Differentiated Product Markets (Chapter 7)

Merger policy is an important element of antitrust policy. In the enforcement of merger policy, thresholds defined on the level and change in the market shares reflected in the Herfindahl-Hirschmann Index (HHI) seem to be the main instrument for selecting notified mergers for investigation in both the European and United States. Franco Mariuzzo, Patrick Paul Walsh, and Ciara Whelan question the use of such a selection rule in differentiated product industries in chapter 7. They propose the use of a structural approach to apply HHI thresholds based on profit shares rather than market shares. To illustrate their point, they use product data for Retail Carbonated Soft Drinks (Price, Market Share, and Characteristics). They estimate company (product) markups consistent with a structural model of equilibrium using demand primitives from a nested logit model and a random coefficient model. They demonstrate the importance of their approach by providing an example where the HHI thresholds based on profit shares identify potentially damaging mergers not captured by applying thresholds to output shares, or conversely, identify mergers of no concern that would be selected for investigation on the basis of output shares.

The next set of chapters (chapters 8 and 9) deals with antitrust and regulatory issues in markets with imperfect information.

I.8 Comparative Advertising (Chapter 8)

Advertising is an important strategic tool in competition with large firms spending up to billions of dollars annually to promote their products. There are two contrasting views on advertising: persuasive and informative. The *persuasive* view holds that advertising alters consumer tastes and creates product differentiation in consumers' minds that leads to brand loyalty. As a result, the advertising firm's product becomes less price-elastic, which allows the firm to charge a higher price. The *informative* view, in contrast, views advertising as a mitigating factor with respect to imperfect consumer information and consumer search cost. As a result, advertising makes the firm's demand curve more price-elastic and promotes competition.[5]

Francesca Barigozzi and Martin Peitz take the informative view of advertising in chapter 8. In particular, they investigate implications of comparative advertising for competition and the role of competition policy in regulating it. In many European countries, competition authorities have tended to view comparative advertising with skepticism. The attitudes are changing and they now see it as helpful in promoting competition and even encourage firms to use it. They reason that comparative advertising, if fair and not misleading, increases consumer information about alternative brands. For this to work, comparative claims must be credible. Competition policy and legal practice are essential in making comparative advertising (directly and indirectly) informative. In chapter 8, Barigozzi and Peitz address issues associated with this important, but hitherto underexplored, practice. They provide useful legal background on comparative advertising in Europe and the United States. In addition, they discuss some recent legal cases in both regions. They also provide an economic analysis of comparative advertising in which they discuss the ways comparative advertising can affect market outcomes. In the analysis, they emphasize the scope of information transmission through comparative advertising and the way antitrust laws affect it. They find that the effects of comparative advertising depend on the nature of the products involved. More specifically, comparative advertising can relax price competition by differentiating products in the case of search goods. However, in the case of experience and credence goods, it can intensify competition by signaling the sponsoring brand's quality.

I.9 Regulation of Information Disclosure (Chapter 9)

In markets with asymmetric information, informed parties have incentives to strategically transmit their private information to uninformed parties. Jos Jansen analyzes such a situation in the context of process innovation in chapter 9. More specifically, he considers a Cournot duopoly model in which the innovating firm has private information on the size of its process innovation. The strategic advantage of revealing it in an efficient firm is to limit a rival firm's output level. The disadvantage is knowledge spillover associated with the disclosure of the information. Jansen analyzes disclosure incentives by comparing the expected profit of Cournot duopolists under precommitment, in which the disclosure rule of a firm is fixed before the firm learns the size of its innovation, with the expected profit under strategic disclosure. He shows that for intermediate values of the knowledge spillover, an antitrust authority needs to prohibit the innovative firm from precommitting to information-sharing rules.

I.10 Competition in Local Access (Chapter 10)

Traditionally, local telephone companies were allowed to remain monopolists in their respective local markets. The competitive landscape, however, has recently changed dramatically. The Telecommunications Act of 1996 in the United States, for instance, allows anyone to enter any communications business—to let any communications business compete in any market against any other. To facilitate entry to the local-access market, the Telecommunications Act of 1996 also ordered the local telephone companies to lease parts of their network to new entrants. One potential source of competition in the local-access market is a cable network that could offer local service through the existing high-capacity coaxial cables that run into homes. For instance, AT&T spent billions of dollars acquiring the cable television companies TCI and MediaOne, as well as a stake in Time Warner, to get into the local telephone markets through broadband cable television connections.

In the final chapter, Duarte Brito and Pedro Pereira discuss the role of cable television networks and their ownership structure in promoting competition in the local-access market. They show that the dual ownership of a local telephone network and a cable network, compared with separate ownership, may increase or decrease incentives to invest in upgrading the cable television network. They also argue that separate ownership of the two networks is important to promote competition in local access.

Most of the contributions to this book were presented and discussed at the Venice Summer Institute held during the summer of 2004. The remaining chapters were invited from leading contributors in the specific areas to complement the conference papers. All chapters went through the normal refereeing process that adheres to the MIT Press guidelines. I am grateful to all the referees for their valuable comments and to contributors for their responsiveness to the comments. Finally, I thank the staff at CESifo for logistical support in organizing the conference.

Notes

1. Kovacic and Shapiro 2000.

2. See Evans 2003 and Rochet and Tirole 2003 for more examples of two-sided markets.

3. See Motta 2004; Tirole 2005.

4. Evans and Salinger 2004.

5. For an excellent survey of advertising, see Bagwell 2003.

References

Bagwell, Kyle. 2003. "The Economic Analysis of Advertising." Unpublished manuscript.

Evans, David S. 2003. "The Antitrust Economics of Multi-Sided Platform Markets." *Yale Journal on Regulation* 20:325–381.

Evans, David S., and Michael A. Salinger. 2004. "The Role of Cost in Determining When Firms Offer Bundles and Ties." http://ssrn.com/abstract=555818.

Kovacic, William, and Carl Shapiro. 2000. "A Century of Antitrust and Legal Thinking." *Journal of Economic Perspectives* 14:43–60.

Motta, Massimo. 2004. *Competition Policy: Theory and Practice.* Cambridge: Cambridge University Press.

Rochet, Jean-Charles, and Jean Tirole. 2003. "Platform Competition in Two-Sided Markets." *Journal of the European Economic Association* 1:990–1029.

Tirole, Jean. 2005. "The Analysis of Tying Cases: A Primer." *Competition Policy International* 1:1–25.

Wright, Julian. 2003. *One-Sided Logic in Two-Sided Markets.* Washington, DC: AEI-Brookings Joint Center for Regulatory Studies.

Antitrust Perspectives for Durable-Goods Markets

Michael Waldman

1.1 Introduction

Markets for durable goods constitute an important part of the economy. For example, in the United States in the year 2000 personal-consumption expenditures on durable goods exceeded $800 billion. Further, in the manufacturing sector in the United States in 2000 durable goods constituted roughly 60 percent of aggregate production. This importance in the overall economy has resulted in an extensive theoretical literature on the microeconomics of durable-goods markets, where this literature has witnessed significant progress in the last ten years. In this chapter I first briefly review the microeconomic-theory literature on durable-goods markets, where much of my focus is on the last ten years. I then discuss a number of my own recent analyses concerning optimal antitrust policy in durable-goods markets that mostly build on ideas in the larger literature.

One might ask, why is there a literature devoted solely to the operation of durable-goods markets? The answer is that there are a number of issues that only arise in durable-goods markets or arise more frequently in such markets. For example, issues concerning secondhand or used-goods markets are important for durable goods but arise infrequently for nondurables. Another issue that arises frequently in durable-goods markets but rarely for nondurables is that of time inconsistency. That is, as first pointed out by Coase (1972), a monopolist selling a durable good in the absence of commitment does not have optimal incentives concerning actions taken after it first sells new units, with the result that its own profitability can be reduced by its choice of such actions. Finally, in durable-goods markets there is the issue of product upgrades, by which I mean the introduction of new products that improve on existing products or products that consumers can add on to such existing products to improve them.

From the standpoint of this chapter, what is of particular importance is that the various issues that arise frequently in durable-goods markets but infrequently elsewhere lead to antitrust issues unique to durable-goods markets. For example, it has been argued by various authors such as Carlton and Gertner (1989) that in durable-goods markets the stock of used units constrains the exercise of market power by new-unit sellers with large markets shares (such as a monopolist). This naturally leads to a question concerning optimal antitrust merger policy for durable-goods markets. That is, since the stock of used units constrains the exercise of market power in durable-goods markets, one could argue as Carlton and Gertner do that antitrust authorities should be less concerned about mergers that increase market power in durable-goods markets. Another important issue concerns aftermarket monopolization. Because durable goods by definition have long economic lives, there is greater scope in such markets for important aftermarket products such as maintenance and other types of complementary products. In such markets durable-goods sellers frequently have the ability to stop other firms from selling aftermarket products important for their own durable units and in this way monopolize these aftermarkets. The antitrust issue is then the extent to which the antitrust authorities should prohibit this behavior.

The point of this chapter is that there have been a number of recent advances in the literature on durable-goods theory that have important implications for several prominent antitrust issues concerning durable-goods markets. Consider again the issue of optimal antitrust merger policy in durable-goods markets. Carlton and Gertner (1989) formally analyze this issue. They first show that the existence of a stock of used units in durable-goods industries dramatically lowers the social-welfare losses associated with a merger that moves a durable-goods industry from competition to monopoly. They then conclude by arguing that the antitrust authorities should be much less concerned in durable-goods industries than in nondurable-goods industries about blocking mergers that increase market concentration. But Carlton and Gertner employ the approach to modeling durable goods made popular by Swan in the early 1970s, which has an important unrealistic feature—that is, consumers can combine a number of used units to make a perfect substitute for a new unit. Clearly, in most real-world durable-goods markets such as those for automobiles and refrigerators this is not the case.

Waldman (1996a) and Hendel and Lizzeri (1999b) have developed a more realistic way of modeling durable-goods markets. In their approach each individual consumes either zero or one physical unit per period and a unit's quality decays as it ages, so there is no number of used units that serves as a perfect substitute for a new unit. As discussed in detail in section 1.4, Gerstle and Waldman (2004) reconsider the Carlton and Gertner analysis by employing this new approach to durable-goods modeling. They show that with this more realistic way of modeling durable-goods markets, it is still the case that an existing stock of used units limits the social-welfare losses associated with a merger that increases market concentration, but much less so than in the Carlton and Gertner analysis. Their conclusion is that there should be a reduced level of scrutiny by the antitrust authorities of mergers in durable-goods industries relative to nondurable-goods markets, but the size of this reduction should be significantly less than suggested by the Carlton and Gertner analysis.

Another issue I consider in this chapter is that of bundling in durable-goods markets characterized by complementary goods. Because of Microsoft's tying behavior, there has been significant recent attention in the theoretical literature to tying in complementary-goods markets. Papers such as Choi and Stefanadis 2001 and Carlton and Waldman 2002 have helped us understand the idea that some of Microsoft's tying behavior is likely motivated by a desire to preserve its Windows monopoly. As argued most clearly in Carlton and Waldman's paper, this motivation for tying will arise when the alternative producer's complementary good—for example, Netscape Navigator—has the potential to evolve into a substitute for Windows. But I find it implausible that this explains all of Microsoft's tying behavior, such as Microsoft's tying of Windows and digital media technology. In addition, Whinston (1990) shows that a monopolist of an "essential" primary good—one that is required for all uses of the complementary good—has no incentive to tie. Given the high market share of Windows in the PC market, this leaves as a puzzle some of Microsoft's more recent tying actions.

Whinston considers a one-period model in his analysis. In section 1.6 I discuss Carlton and Waldman 2005b, which considers the robustness of Whinston's result in multiple-period settings. In particular, Carlton and I consider two-period durable-goods settings in which the monopolist's primary good is essential and the alternative producer has a superior complementary good. Further, building on recent analyses such as Fudenberg and Tirole 1998, an important feature of our model is that in the second period we allow for upgrades of the complementary good. Also, consistent with the Microsoft case, we allow consumer switching costs for the complementary good—that is, a consumer in the second period receives higher gross utility by consuming a complementary unit produced by the same firm that produced the complementary unit the individual consumed in the first period.[1] Our basic finding is that Whinston's result concerning essential primary products no longer holds. That is, even though the monopolist's primary product is essential, the firm sometimes ties in order to foreclose competition in the complementary market and in this way monopolize the complementary market. The conclusion I draw from this result is that antitrust intervention concerning tying in complementary markets may be justified more frequently than the existing literature on the topic suggests.

As a final introductory point, it is worthwhile noting that much of the following discussion concerns monopoly producers of durable goods that sell directly to consumers. The correct interpretation of this is not that these analyses only apply to such settings. First, although most durable-goods producers are not monopolists, many if not most do have some market power and monopoly analyses should provide useful insights into the behavior of such firms. Second, the problems faced by durable-goods producers selling to firms should be similar to the problems faced by durable-goods producers that sell directly to consumers. Thus, the analyses that follow should help us better understand some of the important issues faced by producers of durable intermediate products.[2]

The outline for the chapter is as follows. Sections 1.2 and 1.3 present a brief history of the microeconomic-theory literature on durable goods that starts with three classic contributions of the early 1970s, but that focuses quite a bit on the last ten years of this literature. Sections 1.4 through 1.7 then present recent antitrust-related analyses of mine that build to a great extent on ideas from the last ten years of this larger literature. Section 1.4 concerns optimal antitrust merger policy for durable-goods markets. Section 1.5 concerns the incentive for durable-goods producers to "eliminate secondhand markets" and whether this should be prohibited by antitrust authorities. Section 1.6 discusses some recent ideas concerning the bundling of complementary goods in the presence of complementary-goods upgrades and switching costs. Section 1.7 discusses antitrust policy for the monopolization of aftermarkets in durable-goods industries. Section 1.8 presents concluding remarks.

1.2 A Brief History of Durable-Goods Theory—Part I

In this section I discuss the literature on durable-goods theory from the early 1970s through the early 1990s. I start with three classic contributions to this literature, each of which first appeared in the early 1970s. I then discuss more broadly the literature up through the early 1990s. In the next section I discuss the last ten years of this literature.[3]

1.2.1 Three Classic Contributions

As just mentioned, the early 1970s witnessed three classic contributions to durable-goods theory. From the standpoint of today's literature, probably the best known of these three from the standpoint of durable-goods theory is Coase's (1972) influential analysis of time inconsistency. Because Coase's initial analysis was informal, I will start by discussing Bulow's (1982) formalization of the underlying idea. Consider a durable-goods monopolist operating in a two-period setting in which units are perfectly durable and the monopolist must choose an output level for each period. The basic time-inconsistency problem is that the commitment and noncommitment outcomes are different. That is, if in the first period the monopolist is unable to commit to an output level for the second period, then the monopolist sells "too much" in the second period, with a resulting decrease in overall monopoly profitability. The decrease occurs because consumers in the first period anticipate this behavior, and are thus willing to pay less for new units in the first period than in the commitment case in which the firm sells fewer second-period new units.

As indicated, what I have just described is not actually the argument that appeared in Coase's initial paper, but rather the formalization of Coase's idea that appears in Bulow 1982. What Coase actually argued, which is called the *Coase conjecture*, is that a durable-goods monopolist selling a perfectly durable good in an infinite-period setting will not be able to exercise any market power. That is, because consumers will anticipate that the price will quickly fall to marginal cost due to the basic idea of time inconsistency described above, even in the first period consumers will be unwilling to pay more than marginal cost, so the equilibrium is marginal-cost pricing in every period. The other main part of Coase's argument is that leasing or renting avoids the time-inconsistency problem. The logic here is that time inconsistency arises when the monopolist sells its output because the monopolist does not take into account in later periods how current output decisions affect the value of units previously sold. Since leasing means that in those later periods the monopolist owns those previously produced units, under leasing there is no externality and thus time inconsistency is avoided.

The second classic contribution of the early 1970s is the analysis of optimal durability choice that appeared in a series of papers by Swan (see Swan 1970, 1971; Sieper and Swan 1973). In the late 1960s and early 1970s, a number of authors argued that a durable-goods monopolist would choose a durability level below the first-best efficient level or that which would be chosen by a competitive industry (see Kleiman and Ophir 1966; Levhari and Srinivasan 1969; Schmalensee 1970). In the series of papers mentioned Swan showed that these authors were in fact incorrect, or, in other words, in the type of setting considered by these authors a durable-goods monopolist would choose the socially optimal level of durability.

To understand Swan's argument, consider a durable-goods monopoly setting in which consumers value "service units," and from the standpoint of current consumption a unit, whether new or used, can be described as some number of service units (this way of modeling durable goods dates back to Wicksell 1934). Further, assume that depreciation simply means that the number of service units contained in a single physical unit declines as the unit ages, where durability controls the speed of decline. Now think about monopoly behavior in the steady state. Since consumers only care about the service units consumed in any period, the monopolist will choose output and durability such that the steady-state number of service units is produced at minimum cost. In other words, although the standard monopoly distortion means the firm produces less than the socially optimal steady-state number of service units, there is no distortion in terms of durability since the monopolist will produce this number at minimum cost. But this is the same as saying that, taking as fixed the steady-state number of service units available per period, the monopolist chooses the socially optimal durability level, and also that, in many cases, it makes the same durability choice as would a competitive industry.

The last classic contribution to durable-goods theory of the early 1970s is the influential analysis of Akerlof (1970) concerning adverse selection or the market for lemons. This paper is clearly recognized as one of the key papers that launched the asymmetric-information revolution in economics, but it has not traditionally been described as an important contribution to durable-goods theory. However, given that the main analysis in that paper concerns the secondhand market for a durable good, the paper in fact has important implications for durable-goods markets.

Although I am sure that all the readers know the argument, let me repeat it here briefly. In Akerlof's model there are potential sellers each of whom owns a single used car, where cars vary in quality and each potential seller knows the quality of his or her own car. There are also potential buyers each of whom does not initially own a used car, where each potential buyer does not know the quality of any specific used car but rather only knows the average quality of the used cars offered for sale. The other key assumption is that buyers value cars more than sellers do, so full information or first-best efficiency requires that all cars be traded. The main point of the analysis is that under asymmetric information not all cars are traded in equilibrium. The reason is that the asymmetry of information means that the secondhand-market price for any specific used car reflects the average quality of the cars offered for sale, so potential sellers with high-quality used cars keep them rather than sell them.[4]

1.2.2 The 1970s through the Early 1990s and Overview

Proceeding chronologically, let me begin this subsection by reviewing work from the 1970s. The durable-goods literature of the 1970s was primarily focused on investigation of the robustness of Swan's results (see Schmalensee 1979 for a survey of this literature). This literature considered relaxing various assumptions of the basic Swan framework. For example, Barro (1972) allowed firms and consumers to have different discount rates, Schmalensee (1974) and Su (1975) introduced a maintenance decision on the part of consumers, while Auernheimer and Saving (1977) allowed for short-run nonconstant returns to scale. The bottom line is not surprising. Relaxation of certain assumptions causes durability choice to remain efficient, while relaxation of other assumptions results in inefficient durability choices. Note here that certain parts of this literature are a bit confusing because a demonstration that monopoly and competitive durability levels are different and a showing of inefficiency are not the same. That is, a demonstration that a monopolist chooses different durability than a competitive industry does not mean that durability is inefficient (or at least not second-best efficient). The reason is that, since output varies across the two cases, the second-best efficient durability choice can be different for monopoly and competition.

What I find surprising about this literature is that very little attention was paid to what seems to me clearly the most questionable assumption in Swan's approach, which is the basic way that he modeled durability. As discussed earlier, in Swan's approach a unit can be defined as a number of "service units," which means that it is always possible to combine a number of used units to create a perfect substitute for a new unit. Although this assumption has advantages from a tractability standpoint, the assumption is clearly unrealistic. For most real-world durable-goods markets, such as the markets for automobiles, refrigerators, and toasters, a consumer cannot combine a number of used units to create a perfect substitute for a new unit. In these markets, instead, new and used units vary in quality, and ownership of a new unit provides utility from consumption that cannot be matched by any number of used units. As will be discussed in the next section, relaxation of this assumption clearly changes Swan's conclusion that monopoly durability choice is socially optimal.

Whereas the 1970s focused on Swan's contribution, the 1980s and early 1990s focused on Coase's contribution. Bulow (1982, 1986) formalized the basic idea of time inconsistency in durable-goods-monopoly output choice, where his focus was simple settings in which the logic of the idea is easy to see. In addition to showing the existence of a time-inconsistency problem that can be avoided by leasing, Bulow in his second paper showed that the time-inconsistency problem can result in a durable-goods monopolist building less than the socially optimal level of durability into its output. The logic is that because of time inconsistency, the monopolist is hurt by the durable nature of the product, so reducing durability is a way to reduce the loss in profits due to time inconsistency.

The rest of this literature focused on three topics. The first was whether the Coase conjecture briefly discussed earlier is correct—that is, would a durable-goods monopolist operating in an infinite-period setting drop price to marginal cost almost immediately? This idea was investigated in a number of papers, including Stokey 1981, Gul,

Sonnenschein, and Wilson 1986, and Ausubel and Deneckere 1989. There are two main related results here. The first is that, if buyers' strategies do not depend on past behavior so that reputation formation by the firm is not possible, then Coase is correct as long as the consumer valuation distribution exhibits no gaps—that is, the valuation of the lowest-valuation consumer is less than or equal to the firm's marginal cost. The second result contained in Ausubel and Deneckere's analysis is that if buyers' strategies can depend on past behavior so reputation formation is possible, then even retaining the no-gap assumption, there are equilibria in which the monopolist regains some or all of its market power.

The other two issues considered are the robustness of Coase's results to changes in his assumptions, and tactics that the firm can employ to avoid the time-inconsistency problem other than leasing. In terms of the first issue, Bond and Samuelson (1984) demonstrate that depreciation and replacement sales serve to ameliorate the time-inconsistency problem, Kahn (1986) in a similar vein shows that time inconsistency is reduced if the monopolist's marginal cost is upward sloping rather than constant, while Bagnoli, Salant, and Swierzbinski (1989) and Levine and Pesendorfer (1995) consider how the analysis changes when the monopolist's output is discrete. In terms of the second issue, as already discussed, Bulow (1986) demonstrates that the monopolist can reduce time inconsistency by reducing the durability of its output, Butz (1990) shows that contractual provisions such as best-price provisions can be used to avoid the problem, while Karp and Perloff (1996) investigate the extent to which the monopolist can avoid the problem by initially employing an inferior high-cost technology.[5]

As a final point, although I feel that Coase's insight that a durable-goods monopolist faces a time-inconsistency problem concerning actions in later periods is one of the fundamental insights concerning durable-goods markets, I also feel that his and others' focus on time inconsistency concerning output choice was somewhat misplaced. Consistent with Butz's analysis, contractual commitments concerning future outputs and prices are frequently feasible (and it is also frequently possible to establish a reputation concerning price). Hence, my feeling is that the specific time-inconsistency problem identified by Coase is infrequently observed in real-world markets, although knowledge of the problem can help us better understand real-world contractual provisions that are used to avoid the problem. In contrast, I believe there are other choice variables such as R&D expenditures and new-product introductions for which contracting is much more difficult, and thus time inconsistency concerning these variables is much more likely to be observed in real-world markets. Some possibilities along this line are discussed in later sections.

1.3 A Brief History of Durable-Goods Theory—Part II

In section 1.2 I described durable-goods theory from roughly 1970 through the early 1990s. In this section I describe what I regard as the important contributions to durable-goods theory over roughly the last ten years. I focus on three lines of research: (1) development of a more realistic approach to modeling durability choice, (2) models of new-product introductions, and (3) exploring the role of adverse selection in durable-goods markets. The main point of the discussion is that, whereas the literature up through the early 1990s developed some important key insights concerning durable-goods markets but was somewhat lacking in terms of the realism of the main models analyzed, the last ten years of research has built on those earlier key insights to create much more realistic models of durable-goods markets.

As discussed in the previous section, there is a significant drawback with the Swan approach to modeling durability choice, which is that for most real-world durable products a consumer cannot combine a number of used units to create a perfect substitute for a new unit. Recent papers have focused on this drawback and developed an alternative approach based on the classic monopoly product-line pricing analysis of Mussa and Rosen 1978. I will first discuss that paper and then consider how these recent papers have adapted that analysis for the modeling of durable-goods markets.

Mussa and Rosen consider a single-period monopoly model in which the monopolist sells new units of varying quality levels to consumers who vary in terms of their valuation for quality. They additionally assume that the monopolist does not know each individual's valuation for quality, but does know the distribution of these valuations in the population (equivalently, they could have assumed that the monopolist knows each individual's valuation but is unable to prevent resale). Their main result concerns the quality levels the firm sells to the various groups. In particular, for the high-valuation group the monopolist sells the first-best efficient quality level, but for lower-valuation groups the monopolist sells quality levels below the first-best levels. The reason is that a higher-valuation group always has the option of choosing the quality level the firm is selling to a lower-valuation group. This, in turn, links the prices in such a way that the firm has an incentive to reduce the qualities sold to lower-valuation groups below the efficient levels because of the resulting increases in the prices of higher-quality units.

Waldman (1996a) and Hendel and Lizzeri (1999b) develop an approach to durable-goods modeling closely related to the Mussa and Rosen framework (see also Kim 1989 and Anderson and Ginsburgh 1994). In their approach each individual consumes either zero or one physical unit per period, where the quality of a unit deteriorates as the unit ages. The fact that each individual consumes either zero or one physical unit per period means that this approach is not subject to the same criticism as the Swan approach concerning the ability to combine used units to create a perfect substitute for a new unit. The other key assumptions are that consumers vary in terms of their valuations for product quality just like they do in the Mussa and Rosen analysis, that durability choice is the speed at which used units deteriorate in quality, and that there is a frictionless secondhand market on which used units can be traded.

These two papers demonstrate that models along this line are similar in many respects to the Mussa and Rosen analysis just described.[6] For example, one important result that comes out of this type of model is that, in contrast to what was true in Swan's approach to modeling durable goods, a durable-goods monopolist chooses a durability level below the socially efficient level, where the logic for this result is similar to why in the Mussa and Rosen analysis lower-valuation individuals are sold quality levels below the efficient levels. That is, similar to the Mussa and Rosen analysis, in each period there is a linkage between the prices of high- and low-quality units (or equivalently, new and used units), and this linkage provides the monopolist with an incentive to distort the quality consumed by low-valuation groups down in order to increase the price for high-quality or new units. In turn, the way the monopolist accomplishes this is by reducing durability below the first-best level. Note that in sections 1.4 and 1.5 I discuss other applications of this way of modeling durable-goods markets.

The second recent innovation I will describe is the emphasis on models concerning new-product introductions such as found in Waldman 1993, 1996b; Choi 1994; Fudenberg and Tirole 1998; Lee and Lee 1998; Ellison and Fudenberg 2000; Fishman and Rob 2000; and Nahm 2004. Clearly, new-product introductions are an important part of many, if not most, real-world durable-goods markets. By focusing on new-product introductions, these recent papers have been able to address various aspects of real-world durable-goods markets that previous literature had ignored or had not sufficiently emphasized.

One topic that has received significant attention is that of pricing in durable-goods markets given new-product introductions. Of the papers that have focused on this issue, the most important is Fudenberg and Tirole's paper. In their two-period model units are perfectly durable, but new units in the second period are of higher quality than used units. They also assume that consumers vary in terms of their valuations for quality. Although there is no durability choice and products do not deteriorate as they age, there is a close relationship here with the Mussa and Rosen product-line pricing analysis, as is the case for the durability analyses just described. As a result, Fudenberg and Tirole show the same type of linkage between new- and used-unit prices as found in those durability analyses. In addition to demonstrating this linkage, Fudenberg and Tirole also demonstrate a number of implications of this linkage to issues such as the use of trade-ins and buybacks in firms' marketing strategies (see section 1.5 for a discussion related to their buyback result).

The other main issue that has been investigated here is that of planned obsolescence or equivalently time inconsistency concerning new-product introductions (see, for example, Waldman 1993, 1996b; Choi 1994; Ellison and Fudenberg 2000; Nahm 2004). Earlier papers such as Swan 1972 and Bulow 1986 discuss the issue of planned obsolescence from the standpoint of durability choice, but as Bulow (1986, 747) states, "planned obsolescence is much more than a matter of durability, it is also and perhaps primarily about how often a firm will introduce a new product and how compatible the new product will be with older versions." The recent papers listed above follow Bulow's suggestion of defining planned obsolescence in terms of new-product introductions, and show how Coase's initial insight concerning output choice can be used to provide a theory of planned obsolescence.

Coase's initial insight described broadly is that in later periods a durable-goods monopolist has an incentive to take actions that lower the value of units it previously sold, where these actions serve to lower the firm's overall profitability. These recent papers apply this idea to new-product introductions and show that, both in terms of compatibility choice and quality improvement, a durable-goods monopolist sometimes has an incentive to introduce new products in later periods that lower the value of units it previously sold, which lowers the firm's overall profitability. Also, similar to what was true in analyses of the original Coase time-inconsistency problem concerning output choice, the time-inconsistency problem concerning new-product introductions can typically be avoided by leasing rather than selling output.[7]

The last recent innovation in the durable-goods-theory literature I will describe in this section is the recent literature that further investigates the role of adverse selection in durable-goods markets. As discussed in section 1.2, in my view Akerlof's (1970) influential analysis of adverse selection and asymmetric information is also a classic contribution to durable-goods theory. However, although I feel this position is easy to justify given that the main analysis in that paper was of a secondhand market, the paper's implications for durable-goods markets was basically ignored for almost thirty years. Only recently have papers such as Hendel and Lizzeri 1999a, 2002, as well as Johnson and Waldman 2003, started to further investigate Akerlof's argument of adverse selection in durable-goods markets.

One drawback of Akerlof's original analysis is that it is a very partial analysis in the sense that it focuses on the secondhand market and completely ignores the market for new units. Hendel and Lizzeri (1999a) address this issue by considering an asymmetric-information durable-goods model that incorporates both new- and used-goods markets. Their main result is that adverse selection continues to be important even after the new-unit market is incorporated into the analysis. The other main result is that the model captures a richer picture of why secondhand trade is efficient than is found in Akerlof's analysis. In Akerlof's analysis it is directly assumed that used-unit buyers have higher valuations for used units than sellers and so trade is efficient. Hendel and Lizzeri enrich this view by incorporating the new-unit market. In Hendel and Lizzeri's analysis each individual has a valuation for a single unit that depends on the unit's quality. The result is that in equilibrium high-valuation consumers buy new units and sell used units to low-valuation consumers. The way to interpret this is that it is still the case as in Akerlof's analysis that buyers have higher valuations for the used units than the sellers, but now it is the "net" valuations that are higher—that is, the valuations for used units taking into account the possibility of buying a new unit of output from a new-unit seller.

More recently, Hendel and Lizzeri (2002) and Johnson and Waldman (2003) have shown that this approach can be employed to provide an explanation for leasing in the new-car market. Although Hendel and Lizzeri focus on a monopoly model while Johnson and Waldman consider competition, both papers rely on basically the same argument. The argument in both cases is that the adverse-selection inefficiency arises because of the presence of asymmetric information in the secondhand market, so leasing in the new-car market avoids the inefficiency because with leasing, used cars are returned to the manufacturers and the manufacturers have no private information. This results in leasing in the monopoly case because avoiding inefficiency increases consumer willingness to pay, which in turn increases monopoly profitability, while in the competitive case there is leasing because competition causes firms to market their products in the manner that reduces inefficiency or, in other words, maximizes consumer welfare. In addition to showing this basic argument, both the Hendel and Lizzeri analysis and the Johnson and Waldman analysis show that this approach explains various features of real-world new- and used-car markets.[8]

1.4 Optimal Merger Policy for Durable-Goods Markets

An important antitrust issue concerning durable-goods markets is that of the optimal policy concerning mergers. The reason that optimal merger policy might be different for durable-goods industries than for nondurable-goods industries is the presence of a stock of used units that exists at any point in time in durable-goods industries. That is, as has been argued previously by others, this existing stock potentially constrains the exercise of market power after a merger, which should in turn have implications for optimal antitrust policy concerning mergers. In this section I first briefly discuss the classic analysis of Carlton and Gertner 1989 concerning this issue, and then discuss in more detail the recent analysis that appears in Gerstle and Waldman 2004.

The classic analysis on this topic is the paper by Carlton and Gertner.[9] They consider a durable-goods setting in which there is a merger at some point in time that transforms a competitive industry into a monopoly, and then some number of periods later unanticipated entry moves the industry back to competition. Their focus is on a comparison of the social-welfare loss associated with this scenario with the social-welfare loss associated with the same scenario in a nondurable-goods industry. They show that for reasonable parameterizations of their model the social-welfare loss in the durable-goods case is a small fraction of the loss in the analogous nondurable-goods setting. For example, assuming a slow depreciation rate of .95 and entry after five periods yields that the deadweight loss in the durable-goods case is 2 percent of the deadweight loss in the nondurable-goods case. Carlton and Gertner's conclusion is that in durable-goods industries the existing stock of used units constrains the existence of market power so much after a merger that the antitrust authorities need worry very little about mergers in durable-goods industries.

Gerstle and Waldman (2004) reconsider this issue. Carlton and Gertner employ the approach to modeling durable goods popularized by Swan in the early 1970s. As discussed in detail in sections 1.2 and 1.3, there is a drawback with that approach. Briefly, in the Swan approach to modeling durable goods, a unit, whether new or used, is equivalent to some number of "service units," so in that type of world it is always possible to combine a number of used units to create a perfect substitute for a new unit. Although appealing from a tractability standpoint, the problem is that it is clearly unrealistic in the sense that in most durable-goods markets—such as those for automobiles, refrigerators, and toasters—it is not possible to combine a number of used units to create a perfect substitute for a new unit. In my paper with Gerstle, instead of employing the Swan approach to durable-goods modeling, we employ the approach to durable-goods modeling developed in Waldman 1996a and Hendel and Lizzeri 1999b, which was discussed in detail in section 1.3. In that approach new and used units vary in terms of quality and each individual consumes either zero or one physical unit per period. One important feature of modeling durable goods in this way is that used units cannot be combined to create a perfect substitute for a new unit.

In our paper we redo the basic analysis of Carlton and Gertner using this alternative approach to modeling durable goods. That is, we investigate what happens when a competitive situation is transformed into a monopoly by merger, and then some number of periods later unanticipated entry moves the industry back to a competitive situation. Also, our focus is on a comparison of the social-welfare loss associated with this scenario with the social-welfare loss associated with the same scenario in a nondurable-goods industry. What we show is that modeling durability in this alternative fashion in some respects yields similar results to those found in the Carlton and Gertner analysis, while in other respects the results are quite different.

To be precise, we find two main results. First, if entry occurs a small number of periods after the merger, then consistent with Carlton and Gertner's analysis we find that the social-welfare loss associated with merger to monopoly in the durable-goods case is significantly smaller than the social-welfare loss in the analogous nondurable-goods case. However, although it is smaller than in the analogous nondurable-goods case, it is significantly larger than in Carlton and Gertner's analysis. For example, focusing on the same parameterizations discussed above in which in Carlton and Gertner's analysis the social-welfare loss given durable goods was 2 percent of the social-welfare loss in the analogous nondurable-goods case, we find a figure of roughly 15 percent. Similarly, for the same parameterization we decrease the depreciation rate to .9 and show that in the Carlton and Gertner approach the figure increases to 8 percent, while in our approach the figure increases to 30 percent.

The second main result is that an increase in the number of periods until unanticipated entry takes place causes the social-welfare loss in the durable-goods case to get closer to the social-welfare loss in the analogous nondurable-goods case. For example, starting with the parameterization mentioned above in which in our model the durable-goods loss was roughly 15 percent of the nondurable-goods loss given entry after five periods, we find that this figure goes up to roughly 33 percent given entry after ten periods, up to roughly 50 percent given entry after fifteen periods, and up to roughly 80 percent given entry after one hundred periods. Also, we find that for some parameterizations, if the number of periods until entry is sufficiently high, the durable-goods loss can even exceed the analogous nondurable-goods loss. Note that qualitatively the comparative static result on this parameter is the same as in the Carlton and Gertner analysis—that is, in their approach it is also the case that increasing the number of periods until entry occurs moves the social-welfare loss in the durable-goods case closer to the social-welfare loss in the analogous nondurable-goods case. But in the Carlton and Gertner analysis the two figures are far apart for a much broader set of parameterizations than in our analysis.

The obvious question is, what is driving the different results between our analysis and Carlton and Gertner's, and the answer is the difference in the basic approach to modeling durable goods described above. As stated, Carlton and Gertner employ the Swan approach to modeling durable goods, which has the property that consumers can combine used units to create a perfect substitute for a new unit.

Suppose that in that world depreciation is slow and the merger to monopoly is followed by entry after just a few periods. Any consumer with a high valuation for the durable product will either purchase a new unit or combine used units to consume the equivalent of a new unit. The result is that the social-welfare loss comes solely from consumers who receive little surplus from consuming under competition and do not consume the good during the monopoly periods. Since these consumers derive little surplus from consuming during competition, the aggregate social-welfare loss from having these individuals not consume during the monopoly periods is small.

Now consider what happens in our model when depreciation is slow and the merger to monopoly is followed by entry after just a few periods. In contrast to what happens in the Carlton and Gertner model, it is not just the individuals who receive little surplus under competition who are affected. Rather, because each individual is restricted to consuming a single physical unit per period, when the monopolist exercises its market power by decreasing output below the competitive level the result is that individuals scattered throughout the valuation distribution wind up consuming older and thus lower-quality units than they consume under competition. This, in turn, is exactly why we find a larger social-welfare loss than is found in the Carlton and Gertner analysis. Rather than the aggregate loss being due to no consumption by individuals who receive little surplus from consumption under competition to begin with, in our model many individuals—some of whom have very high valuations for the product—are hurt either because they do not consume or consume a unit of lower quality than they would under competition.

Note that we believe our analysis makes sense not just because the modeling approach is more realistic than the Swan approach employed by Carlton and Gertner, but also because the outcome is more realistic in terms of who is hurt by a merger that increases market power. As stated above, in the Carlton and Gertner analysis the social-welfare loss comes solely from low-valuation individuals who consume the good under competition but not under monopoly. But suppose, for example, that all of the world's automobile manufacturers were, in fact, to merge, and then the merged firm exercised its market power by reducing output. In contrast to the Carlton and Gertner analysis, the resulting social-welfare loss would not just come from low-valuation individuals who wind up without a car. Rather, there would also be a loss because of higher-valuation individuals who wind up consuming older and thus lower-quality cars than they would have in the absence of any mergers. In other words, the social-welfare loss would look much more like the loss in our analysis than the loss in Carlton and Gertner's analysis.

Let me end the section by briefly discussing the antitrust implications of the analysis. I believe there are three main points. First, the analysis supports the Carlton and Gertner view that, because the presence of an existing stock of used units limits the exercise of market power after a merger, the antitrust authorities need to be less concerned with mergers that increase market power in durable-goods industries than in nondurable-goods industries. Second, since we find social-welfare losses due to mergers in durable-goods industries to be much closer to the losses in nondurable-goods industries than do Carlton and Gertner, the reduction in scrutiny for durable-goods industries suggested by our analysis is smaller than that suggested by Carlton and Gertner's analysis. Third, because our results indicate that the social-welfare loss associated with a merger in durable-goods industries is closer to the nondurable-goods social-welfare loss when future entry is likely to be slow, we would emphasize more than Carlton and Gertner the importance of expected speed of entry in judging whether a durable-goods merger should be allowed.

1.5 "Eliminating" Secondhand Markets

A classic antitrust issue concerning durable goods is whether a new-unit seller would ever have an incentive to "eliminate" the secondhand market for its own product. One complication concerning this issue is that the term *eliminate* could have a variety of meanings in this context. For example, it could mean that the firm prohibits the trade of used units, or it could mean that it behaves in a manner that makes used units unavailable for consumption. Although both issues are of potential real-world importance and from a theory standpoint can be closely related, I believe the latter issue comes up more frequently in real-world cases, so I will focus the discussion on that issue.

Until recently the standard thinking on this issue was due to Swan 1980 (see also Rust 1986). Swan's argument was that since the new-unit price reflects the expected prices that the unit will sell for on the secondhand market in future periods, a new-unit seller has no incentive to behave in a manner that makes used units unavailable for consumption. For example, in his 1980 article Swan states:

> Clearly it is not the existence of a secondhand market per se which need imply any restraint on the profitability or the pricing decision of a monopolist. . . . The pure monopolist selling such a durable item as an automobile is paid an amount which reflects the net present value of the stream of automobile services to possibly a whole host of future owners. Competitive secondhand auto dealers (or scrap merchants and recyclers in the case of aluminum) can then buy and sell the item indefinitely without in any way restricting the power of the monopolist as the original seller. (p. 77)

In Waldman 1997, I show that this logic is incorrect (see also Waldman 1996a and Hendel and Lizzeri 1999b).[10] My argument builds on the approach to modeling durable goods discussed in section 1.3 in which consumers cannot combine a number of used units to create a perfect substitute for a new unit. Suppose that, as is discussed in section 1.3, in each period each individual consumes either zero or one physical unit of the product, a unit's quality deteriorates as the unit ages, and consumers vary in terms of their valuation for quality. Further, suppose that the new-unit seller has market power because, for example, the firm is a monopolist. Then, as I show in my 1997 paper, the firm will sometimes have an incentive to behave in a fashion that makes used units unavailable for consumption. For example, a new-unit seller may use a lease-only policy and then scrap the used units that are returned.

The basic logic here is closely related to the analysis of durability choice discussed in section 1.3. There it was argued that in this type of model a new-unit seller with market power will have an incentive to reduce durability below the socially optimal level because the resulting decrease in used-unit quality allows the firm to charge a higher price for new units in later periods. There are two ways this result can translate into the new-unit seller wanting to behave in a fashion that makes used units unavailable for consumption. First, if in the argument just given the incentive for a new-unit seller to reduce used-unit quality is sufficiently strong—that is, optimal used-unit quality equals zero—then we immediately get the result that the firm has an incentive to make used units unavailable for consumption. Second, the new-unit seller may have limited ability to change the production process in a manner that lowers used-unit quality without reducing new-unit quality. In such a case the firm might have an incentive not to directly reduce the durability built into new units, but rather market the product in a way that allows the firm to make functional used units unavailable for consumption.

There are a number of ways that a firm could make functional used units unavailable for consumption. One way is the practice of lease-only mentioned earlier that was a major focus of the 1953 United Shoe Machinery Case in the United States and that was the focus of my 1997 paper.[11] The basic idea here is that the firm offers to lease and refuses to sell new units of output, and then makes used units unavailable for consumption by scrapping the used units when they are returned. Note that one question that arises concerning this practice is why is lease-only required—that is, why can't the firm achieve the same result by selling its output and repurchasing and scrapping used units? As I show in my 1997 paper, the problem with this alternative strategy is that it is time inconsistent. In other words, in the leasing strategy the firm does not need to commit to scrap the used units when they are returned because scrapping is optimal at that point in time. In contrast, the repurchase strategy is not time consistent. At the repurchase date the firm has an incentive not to repurchase, so given any limit on commitment ability such as would be the case given a positive probability of bankruptcy, lease-only will be preferred over sales and repurchases.

Another example of a practice firms employ to make used units unavailable for consumption occurs in the textbook market. In that market firms kill off the secondhand market through the frequent introduction of new editions, which make used copies nearly worthless. One might object at this point that the above analysis is one in which new-unit sellers have significant market power, but the textbook market is one typically with many sellers, so that market power is limited. But this argument misses an important feature of that market. There may be significant competition in terms of the professor choosing which textbook to use for his or her course. However, once the professor has made a choice, the publisher is basically in a monopoly position in terms of selling copies to students, so the above argument is quite applicable.[12]

The antitrust issue here is whether the antitrust authorities should intervene to eliminate practices that serve to make used units unavailable for consumption. The perspective put forth here is that the answer is frequently yes. According to the argument here such practices eliminate the consumption of low-quality used units by low-valuation consumers, so that the firm can raise the price for new units. The result is a reduction in social welfare in that there is no social-welfare benefit, but a social-welfare loss due to individuals who consume used units in the first best but do not consume used units when such a practice is employed. Thus, the analysis supports the U.S. antitrust authorities' behavior in cases concerning United Shoe, IBM, and Xerox where the authorities stopped the firms from pursuing lease-only policies.[13]

As a final point, one qualification to this conclusion is that such a prohibition may not be optimal in certain cases because of other distortions that would be created. For example, I do not think it is feasible for the government to intervene in the textbook market and require firms to introduce new products less frequently. There are a number of factors that come into play in terms of the decision to introduce a new version of a textbook, and government intervention concerning this decision is likely to cause more problems than it would solve. Another example concerns the lease-only policy. Although as stated above I believe that intervening in the United Shoe, IBM, and Xerox cases was the correct decision in each case, there was a potential downside with those interventions. That is, to the extent that a firm unable to use lease-only responds by building less durability into its new units (this is a potential response since in this argument lease-only and reduced durability are substitute ways to reduce the availability of used units), it is possible that a prohibition on lease-only could result in decreased rather than increased social welfare.

1.6 Tying Given Durability, Upgrades, and Switching Costs

Because of the attention paid to Microsoft's behavior and, in particular, its tying of various products including Internet Explorer with Windows, there has been significant theoretical attention paid to the tying of complementary goods by firms with significant market power. Most of these analyses do not focus on the durable nature of Microsoft's products and the fact that Microsoft introduces upgraded products over time. In this section I describe the analysis in Carlton and Waldman 2005b, which focuses on the tying of complementary goods in durable-goods settings characterized by upgrades and switching costs, where our analysis of upgrades builds on analyses of new-product introductions such as the analysis of Fudenberg and Tirole 1998 discussed in section 1.3. As I will describe, the basic conclusion of our analysis is that, in the presence of product durability, switching costs, and product upgrades, tying in order to foreclose competition in the tied market is profitable in a broader set of circumstances than the previous literature suggests.

The classic analysis of tying used to foreclose competition in the tied market is Whinston 1990. Whinston shows that in contrast to what had been argued previously by a number of authors connected to the "Chicago school," there are situations in which a monopolist of a primary product will tie a second product to the primary product in order to foreclose competition in the tied market and in this way increase the firm's profitability in that market.[14] Focusing on his analysis of complementary goods, however, Whinston shows that this result never holds when the monopolist's primary good is "essential"—that is, when the monopolist's primary product is required for all uses of the complementary good. This is problematic from the standpoint of understanding Microsoft's behavior because, to the extent that Microsoft has or had a monopoly in the operating systems market, Whinston's analysis indicates little or no return to Microsoft from a foreclosure standpoint for bundling applications programs with Windows.

One approach to resolving this puzzle is to move attention away from the primary-good monopolist capturing profits in the complementary market to the primary-good monopolist preserving its primary-market monopoly and extending this monopoly to newly emerging markets.[15] This possibility was analyzed in Carlton and Waldman 2002 (see also Choi and Stefanadis 2001). That paper considered a series of models that show how a primary-good monopolist can use tying to both preserve and extend its primary-good monopoly. For example, we considered a two-period model in which an alternative producer has a superior complementary product, can enter the complementary market in either period, but can only enter the primary market in the second period. We showed that, if the alternative producer has costs of entering both the primary and complementary markets, then there are parameterizations in which the monopolist ties in order to preserve its primary-good monopoly in the second period. The logic is that tying reduces the incentive for the alternative producer to enter the complementary market by eliminating any first-period sales, and this reduced incentive for the alternative producer to enter the complementary market results in the alternative producer not entering either market in either period.

We believe that our previous analysis just described provides a plausible explanation for why Microsoft integrated Explorer into Windows—that is, many experts thought that a successful browser had the potential to evolve into a substitute for Windows and thus it is plausible that tying was used by Microsoft to preserve its operating systems monopoly. But we also feel that this explanation is not that plausible for some of Microsoft's other tying decisions. For example, Microsoft recently chose to bundle digital media technology with Windows, but digital media technology does not seem to pose the same long-term threat to Windows as Netscape Navigator did. With this in mind, we decided to reconsider the question originally asked by Whinston: Under what circumstances will a monopolist of a primary good tie its complementary good in order to foreclose competition in the tied market and earn monopoly profits in that market? The difference, however, is that in contrast to Whinston we consider a durable-goods setting in which product upgrades are possible, and we also consider the possibility of consumer switching costs—that is, in upgrading a consumer derives a higher gross benefit by not switching brands (see note 1 for references to articles concerning consumer switching costs).

Before proceeding to the results of our analysis, it is useful to consider the logic behind Whinston's finding that tying is never used to extract rents from the complementary market when the monopolist's primary good is essential. Consider a one-period model in which the monopolist's primary good is essential and in which the alternative producer has a superior complementary product. Let P^* denote the monopolist's optimal bundle price and π^* monopoly profitability if the monopolist bundles. Now suppose the monopolist does not bundle and sets the price of the primary good at P^*-c_c and the price of the complementary good at c_c, where c_c is the marginal cost of the complementary good. Doing this must result in monopoly profitability equal to π^*. Hence, since optimal pricing when the monopolist does not tie must result in profits at least equal to this level, we have that selling individual products yields profits greater than or equal to that with tying so the monopolist has no incentive to tie.

I will now discuss what happens in my analysis with Carlton, which considers a two-period setting characterized by product upgrades for the complementary good in the second period and potentially consumer switching costs. Also, consistent with the above discussion, we assume that the alternative producer has a superior complementary good. We show that in this setting Whinston's result that tying is never optimal when the monopolist's primary good is essential breaks down for various reasons. We first consider the case in which there are no consumer switching costs and firms must sell as opposed to lease or rent their products. In this case the argument breaks down because the monopolist does not sell the primary good in the second period, and thus there is no way for the monopolist to capture the second-period profits associated with the complementary-good upgrade through the pricing of the primary good. The result is that, if the increased product quality associated with the complementary-good upgrade is sufficiently high, then the monopolist ties because this allows the firm to capture the second-period profits associated with upgrading.

Our second analysis then considers what happens when firms can lease as well as sell their products. We first show that the option to lease eliminates the result just described. That is, if the monopolist can lease, then in the absence of consumer switching costs there is no return to the monopolist to tying. The reason is that leasing allows the monopolist to capture second-period-upgrade profits through the second-period lease price for the primary product. We then introduce consumer switching costs and show that, even with leasing, the monopolist may tie its products. The logic here is that the second-period lease price allows the monopolist to capture second-period profits due to the upgrade but does not necessarily allow the monopolist to capture second-period profits associated with the switching costs. The result is that, if switching costs are sufficiently large, the monopolist may tie in order to capture the profits due to the switching costs.

Both of the analyses described above depend on ties being irreversible—that is, a consumer cannot use the alternative producer's complementary product if the monopolist sells or leases a tied product consisting of primary and complementary goods. Since in the Microsoft situation ties are at least partly reversible, an interesting extension is to consider what happens with irreversible ties. Along this line, we consider what happens to our results when we relax the full-irreversibility assumption. Our conclusion is that the qualitative nature of our results is unchanged given various types of partial reversibility, but our results are not robust to the assumption of full reversibility. We believe this result helps explain instances in which Microsoft not only tied an applications program to Windows, but also behaved in a fashion that either increased the cost or decreased the functionality of alternative producers' complementary products.

Let me end the section with a brief discussion of the antitrust implications of the analysis. What the analysis suggests is that there is a sense in which the antitrust authorities should be more concerned about the tying of complementary goods than the previous literature suggests.[16] In particular, Whinston's classic paper finds that, if the primary good is essential, then a primary-good monopolist would not have an incentive to tie a complementary good in order to capture profits associated with the complementary market. To the extent Windows is an essential product, this result suggests that many of Microsoft's tying decisions are not driven by a foreclosure motivation, so these actions are likely benign from a social-welfare standpoint and should thus be allowed. But Carlton and I show that Whinston's finding is not robust to the introduction of durability, product upgrades, and consumer switching costs—all important features of the Microsoft situation. In particular, in such a situation, even if the monopolist's primary good is essential, a monopolist may tie and foreclose a superior complementary product in order to capture profits associated with the complementary-good market. Hence, if these features are present, then tying even when the primary good is essential may be used to foreclose competition in the tied market and thus merits the scrutiny of the antitrust authorities.

1.7 Aftermarket Monopolization in Competitive Industries

A series of court cases in the United States concerning firms such as Kodak, Data General, Unisys, and Xerox concern the issue of aftermarket monopolization. Aftermarket here refers to the market for a product that is complementary to a durable-goods producer's primary product such as the market for maintaining a particular brand of automobile. The basic issue is whether a durable-goods producer should be allowed to behave in a manner that monopolizes aftermarkets for its own durable products. For example, in *Eastman Kodak Co. v. Image Technical Services, Inc.*, et al. (1992), Kodak was alleged to have monopolized the maintenance markets for its own copiers and micrographic equipment by refusing to sell spare parts to alternative maintenance suppliers. In-depth discussions of aftermarket monopolization appear in Shapiro 1995, Chen, Ross, and Stanbury 1998, and Carlton 2001. Here I discuss recent research I have conducted on this topic.

The issue of aftermarket monopolization has received significant theoretical attention during the last fifteen years because of interest in the Kodak case mentioned above. In that case the U.S. Supreme Court ruled that, even if Kodak had no market power in the market for new copiers and micrographic equipment, Kodak could still be guilty of having illegally monopolized the maintenance markets for these products. This was a surprising decision because earlier decisions would have suggested that the efficiency properties associated with competitive markets would have resulted in Kodak's behavior in the maintenance markets being ruled legal rather than illegal. The case and the decision prompted a number of industrial-organization economists to consider why a competitive durable-goods seller might monopolize an aftermarket for its own product, and the related question of whether the antitrust authorities should or should not allow the behavior.

The previous literature on the subject has focused mostly on a set of related arguments that regard the behavior as some variant of the holdup problem (see, e.g., Borenstein, Mackie-Mason, and Netz 1995).[17] In these arguments consumers are locked into purchasing maintenance once they purchase a new durable unit, and aftermarket monopolization is a way that the durable-goods producer exploits these locked-in positions to extract ex post rents. In these analyses there is a social-welfare loss due to the monopoly pricing of maintenance, so these analyses serve to justify the Supreme Court's decision.

The problem with this argument is that it requires either that consumers do not consider the maintenance price in their original decisions to purchase new units, that consumers are surprised, or that contracting to avoid the holdup problem is not feasible. The reason this is problematic is that none of these possibilities seem likely. On the one hand, the first two possibilities are not likely because in a number of the cases consumers were sophisticated businesses and the cost of maintenance was a significant proportion of the total cost of using the product. On the other hand, the last possibility is not likely because long-term maintenance contracts are quite common in many of the industries in which the monopolization of maintenance markets has been observed.

In Carlton and Waldman 2003 and Morita and Waldman 2003, I put forth along with coauthors a new explanation for the behavior that is based on an important aspect of the Kodak case (and that has been mentioned as a possible feature in a number of other important cases). That is, a feature of a number of the cases, including the Kodak case, is that the market is characterized by the presence of consumer switching costs. Similar to the usage in the previous section, consumer switching costs here means that when a consumer wants to replace an old durable unit with a new unit there are costs to the consumer of switching from one firm's product to another's. These costs could arise for a number of reasons such as the presence of learning-by-doing and investments in durable complementary goods that become worthless when a consumer changes brands.[18]

The first step of the argument builds on a result found in earlier papers such as Schmalensee 1974, Su 1975, and Rust 1986. Those papers consider durable-goods-monopoly models in which the maintenance market is competititve. Their main finding is that, because the monopolist charges a price for its output that is above its marginal cost of production while maintenance is priced competitively, consumers do not behave in an efficient fashion. Rather, when faced with these prices, consumers sometimes maintain used units when it would be efficient to replace those units with new units. The result is typically a reduction in monopoly profitability because the maintenance-versus-replacement inefficiency reduces consumer willingness to pay.

The first step of our argument is to show that the basic finding described above for durable-goods-monopoly models also holds when the new-unit market is competitive but there are consumer switching costs. The logic here is that, due to the switching costs, a firm selling new replacement durable units has market power when selling to individuals who consumed a unit of the firm's product in the previous period. Hence, if the maintenance market is competitive, the presence of this market power at the date of the replacement decision causes consumers to maintain rather than replace their used units more often than is socially efficient. Note that one difference between this result and the monopoly result discussed above concerns who is hurt by this social-welfare distortion. As indicated, in the monopoly case typically much or all of the reduction in social surplus takes the form of decreased monopoly profits. In contrast, because competitive firms earn zero profits in equilibrium, here all of the decreased social surplus takes the form of decreased consumer welfare.

The second step of the argument is to show that the social-welfare distortion concerning the maintenance-versus-replacement decision is avoided if the seller monopolizes the maintenance market for its own product. If the firm monopolizes the maintenance market, then it will charge a price above marginal cost for both replacement units and maintenance and, more importantly, it maximizes profits at the maintenance-versus-replacement decision date by pricing in such a way that this decision is made efficiently. Note, however, even though the firm can be thought of as monopolizing the maintenance market in order to maximize profits at the maintenance-versus-replacement decision date, it is in fact consumers who are made better off when firms are allowed to monopolize the maintenance markets for their own products. That is, since competition means that over the whole course of the game the firms must earn zero expected profits, when firms monopolize the maintenance markets for their own products and eliminate the maintenance-versus-replacement distortion, it is the consumers who are made better off.

From a social-welfare perspective, our analysis yields exactly the opposite conclusion of that associated with the holdup analyses described above, which currently constitute the standard explanation for the phenomenon.[19] As discussed, in the holdup explanation the monopoly pricing of maintenance creates a standard monopoly deadweight loss so monopolization of maintenance markets serves to decrease social wefare. In contrast, in the explanation just described monopolizing the maintenance market serves to increase both consumer welfare and social welfare. Clearly, our analysis suggests that whether or not the courts should allow the behavior depends on which of the explanations one thinks is more likely to be correct.

As discussed briefly above, there are various reasons why I find the holdup arguments not completely plausible in many of the cases in which the behavior has been observed. To be more specific, my feeling is that there is a strong argument that in cases like the Kodak case in which there is clear evidence of consumer switching costs the behavior should be allowed. In such cases theory indicates that competitive maintenance markets do not yield efficient outcomes, so a prohibition that keeps maintenance markets competitive does not seem justified. I would further argue more generally that the antitrust authorities should be hesitant to intervene whenever the market for new durable units is competitive. Theory indicates that competitive-durable-goods producers have a strong incentive to market their products in the fashion that maximizes both consumer welfare and social welfare. So intervention in such markets should only occur when the authorities have a strong and clear case that behavior is not serving societal interests.

1.8 Conclusion

Markets for durable goods raise a number of issues that do not arise or arise less frequently in nondurable-goods markets. In turn, these differences between durable- and nondurable-goods markets lead to antitrust issues that are specific to durable-goods markets. For example, a feature specific to durable-goods markets is that of secondhand markets for used units, which leads to the following antitrust issue: To what extent should antitrust authorities allow new-unit producers to behave in ways that eliminate secondhand markets by making used units unavailable for consumption? Another example concerns the issue of aftermarket monopolization. Aftermarkets such as markets for maintenance are much more common and important for durable goods than for nondurables. The important antitrust issue here is to what extent should durable-goods sellers be allowed to behave in ways that monopolize the aftermarkets for their own products.

In this chapter I first briefly reviewed the theoretical literature on durable-goods markets, and then described a number of my own recent analyses concerning optimal antitrust policy for durable-goods markets that mostly build on ideas that have appeared in the last few years of the larger literature. For example, the classic Swan approach to durable-goods modeling has the unrealistic feature that consumers can combine a number of used units to make a perfect substitute for a new unit. Waldman (1996a) and Hendel and Lizzeri (1999b) have recently explored an alternative approach to modeling durable-goods markets that is not characterized by this feature. In their approach each individual consumes zero or one physical unit per period and durable-good quality decays as a unit ages. In section 1.4 I discussed the recent paper of Gerstle and Waldman (2004), who show that optimal antitrust merger policy for durable-goods markets is significantly different in an analysis that employs this new approach rather than the more traditional but less realistic Swan approach.

Another analysis concerns the issue of tying in complementary markets. In a classic paper, Whinston (1990) considers a monopolist of a primary product and shows that, if the primary product is essential—that is, needed for all uses of a complementary product—then the monopolist would have no incentive to tie its primary and complementary products in order to extend its monopoly to the complementary market. But Whinston considers a one-period setting. In section 1.6 I describe Carlton and Waldman 2005b, which considers this issue in a durable-goods setting, where our analysis builds on recent contributions concerning new-product introductions in durable-goods markets such as Fudenberg and Tirole 1998. In particular, we consider a two-period setting in which the monopolist's primary good is essential in both periods, but in the second period both the monopolist and the alternative producer have the ability to sell a complementary-good upgrade. We show that in this model Whinston's result concerning essential primary goods breaks down for various reasons—that is, tying may be used to foreclose competition in the tied market even when the monopolist's primary good is essential. The conclusion I draw from this finding is that antitrust intervention to stop the tying of complementary goods may be justified in more cases than the previous literature suggests.

In summary, there have been significant advances in the theoretical literature on durable goods in recent years, where these advances have significantly moved the literature toward greater realism. The main focus of this chapter has been on discussing a number of my own recent analyses that show how one can employ these advances to further our understanding of optimal antitrust policy on various important antitrust issues concerning durable-goods markets. But I feel that the analyses described do not come close to exhausting the implications of these advances for antitrust policy. My hope, therefore, is that in addition to communicating some recent ideas concerning antitrust policy for durable-goods markets, the chapter convinces other researchers to focus more on what the recent durable-goods-theory literature tells us about optimal antitrust policy.

Notes

I would like to thank Dennis Carlton, Ari Gerstle, Justin Johnson, and Hodaka Morita for conversations on the topics discussed in this chapter.

1. There is an extensive literature that investigates models characterized by consumer switching costs. Papers in this literature include Klemperer 1987, 1989; Farrell and Shapiro 1988, 1989. See also the earlier work of Williamson 1975, 1985. Klemperer 1995 surveys the literature.

2. For example, a paper I am currently working on with Ken Sokoloff investigates how the durable-goods time-inconsistency problem can be used to think about firm-boundary issues in settings characterized by durable intermediate products. I believe this is just one of many possible applications of durable-goods theory to the production of durable intermediate products.

3. See Waldman 2003 for a more in-depth discussion of this literature

4. In Akerlof's analysis there is no trade under asymmetric information. But this result is due to specific assumptions he made concerning the relative valuations of buyers and sellers, rather than the result being a general property of such models.

5. More recently, Morita and Waldman (2004) show that time inconsistency can be avoided if the firm monopolizes the maintenance market for its own product, where the logic here is similar to the original leasing result.

6. Waldman (1996a) discusses in detail the similarities between this approach to modeling durable goods and the Mussa and Rosen product-line-pricing analysis.

7. One can also construct a theory of planned obsolescence and new-product introductions using an analysis closely related to the durability discussion earlier in this section. See section 1.5 for a discussion.

8. Johnson and Waldman (2004) extend their earlier analysis by incorporating moral hazard and show that this allows the analysis to even better match the evidence concerning real-world new- and used-car markets.

9. Other papers on the topic include Froeb 1989 and Reitman 2001.

10. A similar argument appears in earlier papers, such as Benjamin and Kormendi 1974, Miller 1974, Liebowitz 1982, and Levinthal and Purohit 1989. Those papers start by specifying demand functions and show that, given certain assumptions concerning how the demand for new units is affected by the availability of used units, a durable-goods seller could have an incentive to behave in a manner that makes used units unavailable for consumption. But this leaves as an open question whether such a demand specification is reasonable. In contrast, my paper starts with utility functions and production functions and shows that indeed such a demand specification is reasonable.

11. There are a number of alternative explanations for United's lease-only practice. For example, Posner (1976) suggests that the behavior was a response to the time-inconsistency argument put forth originally by Coase (see the discussion in section 1.2). However, as pointed out by DeGraba (1994), avoiding the Coase time-inconsistency problem requires short-term leases, so given that United employed seventeen-year leases, it does not seem that the Coase argument is correct in this case. Another perspective is put forth in Wiley, Rasmusen, and Ramseyer 1990 and in Masten and Snyder 1993, which both ignore the monopoly aspect of the case and put forth efficiency rationales more consistent with a competitive market. However, since the practice is not widely observed but has been observed in a few cases of firms with significant market power (United Shoe, IBM, and Xerox), I find this perspective unconvincing.

12. As I argued in Waldman 1993 (see the related discussion in section 1.3), another possible explanation for the frequent introduction of new editions in the textbook market is that it is the result of a time-inconsistency problem that new-unit sellers face in terms of the introduction of new products. In contrast to the argument above, in this argument the practice hurts rather than helps the firm's profitability. Given that textbook publishers are in the market for many periods and so can establish a reputation for how frequently they introduce new editions, I now believe that this time-inconsistency argument is not the correct explanation for the frequent introduction of new editions in the textbook market.

13. In 1953 the courts ruled a variety of United Shoe's practices illegal, including its use of a lease-only policy (see Kaysen 1956 for discussion). In 1956 IBM agreed to a Justice Department consent decree requiring it to discontinue its lease-only policy (see Soma 1976 and Fisher, McGowan, and Greenwood 1983 for discussions). In 1975 Xerox and the Federal Trade Commission entered into a consent decree that stated that Xerox was violating the antitrust laws through its use of a lease-only policy.

14. In particular, Director and Levi (1956), Bowman (1957), Posner (1976), and Bork (1978) all argued that a monopolist of a primary product never has an incentive to tie a complementary product in order to monopolize the complementary market. Their argument was that the primary-good monopolist could capture all the potential monopoly profits in the complementary market through its sales of the primary good. Whinston's paper formalizes this argument but also shows that it is not valid in all cases—that is, it is not correct when the tied good is not characterized by constant returns to scale and competition and when the primary or tying good is not essential (see also the earlier work of Ordover, Sykes, and Willig 1985).

15. Another possibility is that Microsoft ties for efficiency reasons. See, for example, Carlton and Perloff 1999 for efficiency rationales for tying.

16. See Carlton and Waldman 2005ab for a discussion of why from other perspectives the antitrust authorities should be less aggressive in intervening when tying is the issue.

17. An alternative argument that has been put forth is that the behavior is used to price discriminate (see Chen and Ross 1993; Klein 1993). In this argument, consumers with higher valuations for the durable-goods producer's product are heavy users of maintenance, with the result that the seller more effectively price discriminates by monopolizing the maintenance market and increasing the maintenance price. Although Klein argues otherwise, the natural interpretation of this argument is that it provides a clear rationale for aftermarket monopolization by firms with significant market power but has trouble explaining why firms with little or no market power would adopt the practice.

18. The allegations against Kodak in the 1992 case contained a number of detailed accounts of switching costs faced by consumers of Kodak's products. An example follows: "The system at CSC includes a combination of micrographics machines, and of computer hardware and software tailored specifically to CSC's needs. Trading its entire equipment for an 'interbrand' competitor of Kodak, due to supra-competitive prices, it would be financially unfeasible for CSC. The special software would have to be retailored at a cost of several hundred thousand dollars. Data would have to be reformatted and operators would have to be retrained, again, at a cost of hundreds of thousands of dollars" (Plaintiff's Memorandum in *Eastman Kodak Co. v. Image Technical Services, Inc.*, et al., 1992, 19–20). The allegations also state that similar systems to the one described were found in a variety of places such as "Blue Cross/Blue Shield, insurance companies, banks, and other large financial institutions in many states" (Plaintiff's Memorandum in *Eastman Kodak Co. v. Image Technical Services, Inc.*, et al., 1992, 19–20).

19. Schwartz and Werden 1996, Chen and Ross 1999, and Elzinga and Mills 2001 are previous papers that provide efficiency explanations for the behavior. First, Schwartz and Werden develop a signaling explanation for aftermarket monopolization in which high-quality durable units require more of the aftermarket product. Second, Chen and Ross develop an explanation in which free maintenance is bundled with the sale of new durable units, where this stops subsidization of light users of the product by heavy users and thus improves efficiency by moving maintenance toward efficient levels. Third, Elzinga and Mills provide an efficiency role for aftermarket monopoly in an industry in which there are increasing returns to scale in the production of new durable units so that competition is not feasible. I believe that, at least in terms of the Kodak case, the explanation put forth above better matches the evidence, and, in particular, the first and third of these alternatives seem to be a weak fit. In terms of the Schwartz and Werden argument, this is because high-quality durable units typically require less rather than more maintenance, while the Elzinga and Mills argument is inconsistent with the court's focus on Kodak being a competitive producer. More generally, the above argument is the only

one that relies on consumer switching costs, which was clearly an important aspect of the Kodak case and which has also been mentioned as an important aspect of a number of other cases.

References

Akerlof, G. 1970. "The Market for 'Lemons': Quality Uncertainty and the Market Mechanism." *Quarterly Journal of Economics* 84:488–500.

Anderson, S., and V. Ginsburgh. 1994. "Price Discrimination via Second-Hand Markets." *European Economic Review* 38:23–44.

Auernheimer, L., and T. Saving. 1977. "Market Organization and the Durability of Durable Goods." *Econometrica* 45:219–228.

Ausubel, L., and R. Deneckere. 1989. "Reputation in Bargaining and Durable Goods Monopoly." *Econometrica* 57:511–531.

Bagnoli, M., S. Salant, and J. Swierzbinski. 1989. "Durable-Goods Monopoly with Discrete Demand." *Journal of Political Economy* 97:1459–1478.

Barro, R. 1972. "Monopoly and Contrived Depreciation." *Journal of Political Economy* 80:589–607.

Benjamin, D., and R. Kormendi. 1974. "The Interrelationship between the Markets for New and Used Durable Goods." *Journal of Law and Economics* 17:381–401.

Bond, E., and L. Samuelson. 1984. "Durable Good Monopolies with Rational Expectations and Replacement Sales." *Rand Journal of Economics* 15:336–345.

Borenstein, S., J. Mackie-Mason, and J. Netz. 1995. "Antitrust Policy in Aftermarkets." *Antitrust Law Journal* 63:455–482.

Bork, R. 1978. *The Antitrust Paradox: A Policy at War with Itself* New York: Basic Books.

Bowman, W. 1957. "Tying Arrangements and the Leverage Problem." *Yale Law Review* 67:19–36.

Bulow, J. 1982. "Durable Goods Monopolists." *Journal of Political Economy* 90:314–332.

Bulow, J. 1986. "An Economic Theory of Planned Obsolescence." *Quarterly Journal of Economics* 101:729–749.

Butz, D. 1990. "Durable-Good Monopoly and Best-Price Provision." *American Economic Review* 80:1062–1076.

Carlton, D. 2001. "A General Analysis of Exclusionary Conduct and Refusal to Deal—Why Aspen and Kodak Are Misguided." *Antitrust Law Journal* 68:659–683.

Carlton, D., and R. Gertner. 1989. "Market Power and Mergers in Durable Goods Industries." *Journal of Law and Economics* 32:203–226.

Carlton, D., and J. Perloff. 1999. *Modern Industrial Organization*. 3rd ed. New York: Addison-Wesley.

Carlton, D., and M. Waldman. 2002. "The Strategic Use of Tying to Preserve and Create Market Power in Evolving Industries." *Rand Journal of Economics* 33:194–220.

Carlton, D., and M. Waldman. 2003. "Competition, Monopoly, and Aftermarkets." Photocopy, Cornell University.

Carlton, D., and M. Waldman. 2005a. "How Economics Can Improve Antitrust Doctrine towards Tie-In Sales." *Competition Policy International* 1:27–40.

Carlton, D., and M. Waldman. 2005b. "Tying, Upgrades, and Switching Costs in Durable-Goods Markets." Photocopy, Cornell University.

Chen, Z., and T. Ross. 1993. "Refusals to Deal, Price Discrimination and Independent Service Organizations." *Journal of Economics and Management Strategy* 2:593–614.

Chen, Z., and T. Ross. 1999. "Refusals to Deal and Orders to Supply in Competitive Markets." *International Journal of Industrial Organization* 17:399–417.

Chen, Z., T. Ross, and W. Stanbury. 1998. "Refusals to Deal and Aftermarkets." *Review of Industrial Organization* 13:131–151.

Choi, J. 1994. "Network Externality, Compatibility Choice, and Planned Obsolescence." *Journal of Industrial Economics* 42:167–182.

Choi, J., and C. Stefanadis. 2001. "Tying, Investment, and the Dynamic Leverage Theory." *Rand Journal of Economics* 32:52–71.

Coase, R. 1972. "Durability and Monopoly." *Journal of Law and Economics* 15:143–149.

DeGraba, P. 1994. "No Lease Is Short Enough to Solve the Time Inconsistency Problem." *Journal of Industrial Economics* 42:361–374.

Director, A., and E. Levi. 1956. "Law and the Future: Trade Regulation." *Northwestern University Law Review* 51:281–296.

Ellison, G., and D. Fudenberg. 2000. "The Neo-Luddite's Lament: Excessive Upgrades in the Software Industry." *Rand Journal of Economics* 31:253–277.

Elzinga, K., and D. Mills. 2001. "Independent Service Organizations and Economic Efficiency." *Economic Inquiry* 39:549–560.

Farrell, J., and C. Shapiro. 1988. "Dynamic Competition with Switching Costs." *Rand Journal of Economics* 19:123–137.

Farrell, J., and C. Shapiro. 1989. "Optimal Contracts with Lock-In." *American Economic Review* 79:51–68.

Fisher, F., J. McGowan, and J. Greenwood. 1983. *Folded, Spindled, and Mutilated: Economic Analysis and U.S. v. IBM*. Cambridge, MA: MIT Press.

Fishman, A., and R. Rob. 2000. "Product Innovation by a Durable-Good Monopoly." *Rand Journal of Economics* 31:237–252.

Froeb, L. 1989. "Evaluating Mergers in Durable Good Industries." *Antitrust Bulletin* 34:99–119.

Fudenberg, D., and J. Tirole. 1998. "Upgrades, Tradeins, and Buybacks." *Rand Journal of Economics* 29:235–258.

Gerstle, A., and M. Waldman. 2004. "Mergers in Durable-Good Industries: A Re-Examination of Market Power and Welfare Effects." Photocopy, Cornell University.

Gul, F., H. Sonnenschein, and R. Wilson. 1986. "Foundations of Dynamic Monopoly and the Coase Conjecture." *Journal of Economic Theory* 39:155–190.

Hendel, I., and A. Lizzeri. 1999a. "Adverse Selection in Durable Goods Markets." *American Economic Review* 89:1097–1115.

Hendel, I., and A. Lizzeri. 1999b. "Interfering with Secondary Markets." *Rand Journal of Economics* 30:1–21.

Hendel, I., and A. Lizzeri. 2002. "The Role of Leasing under Adverse Selection." *Journal of Political Economy* 110:113–143.

Johnson, J., and M. Waldman. 2003. "Leasing, Lemons, and Buybacks." *Rand Journal of Economics* 34:247–265.

Johnson, J., and M. Waldman. 2004. "Leasing, Lemons, and Moral Hazard." Photocopy, Cornell University.

Kahn, C. 1986. "The Durable Goods Monopolist and Consistency with Increasing Costs." *Econometrica* 42:289–301.

Karp, L., and J. Perloff. 1996. "The Optimal Suppression of a Low-Cost Technology by a Durable-Good Monopoly." *Rand Journal of Economics* 27:346–364.

Kaysen, C. 1956. *United States v. United Shoe Machinery Corporation: An Economic Analysis of an Antitrust Case*. Cambridge, MA: Harvard University Press.

Kim, J. 1989. "Trade in Used Goods and Durability Choice." *International Economic Journal* 3:53–63.

Kleiman, E., and T. Ophir. 1966. "The Durability of Durable Goods." *Review of Economic Studies* 33:165–178.

Klein, B. 1993. "Market Power in Antitrust: Economic Analysis After *Kodak*." *Supreme Court Economic Review* 3:43–92.

Klemperer, P. 1987. "Markets with Consumer Switching Costs." *Quarterly Journal of Economics* 102:375–394.

Klemperer, P. 1989. "Price Wars Caused by Switching Costs." *Review of Economic Studies* 56:405–420.

Klemperer, P. 1995. "Competition When Consumers Have Switching Costs: An Overview with Applications to Industrial Organization, Macroeconomics, and International Trade." *Review of Economic Studies* 62:515–539.

Lee, I., and J. Lee. 1998. "A Theory of Economic Obsolescence." *Journal of Industrial Economics* 46:383–401.

Levhari, D., and T. Srinivasan. 1969. "Durability of Consumption Goods: Competition versus Monopoly." *American Economic Review* 59:102–107.

Levine, D., and W. Pesendorfer. 1995. "When Are Agents Negligible?" *American Economic Review* 85:1160–1170.

Levinthal, D., and D. Purohit. 1989. "Durable Goods and Product Obsolescence." *Marketing Science* 8:35–56.

Liebowitz, S. 1982. "Durability, Market Structure, and New-Used Goods Models." *American Economic Review* 72:816–824.

Masten, S., and E. Snyder. 1993. "United States versus United Shoe Machinery Corporation: On the Merits." *Journal of Law and Economics* 36:33–70.

Miller, H. 1974. "On Killing Off the Market for Used Textbooks and the Relationship between Markets for New and Used Secondhand Goods." *Journal of Political Economy* 82:612–619.

Morita, H., and M. Waldman. 2003. "Competition, Monopoly Maintenance, and Consumer Switching Costs." Photocopy, Cornell University.

Morita, H., and M. Waldman. 2004. "Durable Goods, Monopoly Maintenance, and Time Inconsistency." *Journal of Economics and Management Strategy* 13:273–302.

Mussa, M., and S. Rosen. 1978. "Monopoly and Product Quality." *Journal of Economic Theory* 18:301–317.

Nahm, J. 2004. "Durable Goods Monopoly with Endogenous Innovation." *Journal of Economics and Management Strategy* 13:303–319.

Ordover, J., A. Sykes, and R. Willig. 1985. "Nonprice Anticompetitive Behavior by Dominant Firms toward the Producers of Complementary Products." In F. Fisher, ed., *Antitrust and Regulation: Essays in Memory of John J. McGowan*. Cambridge, MA: MIT Press.

Plaintiff's Memorandum in *Eastman Kodak Co. v. Image Technical Services, Inc.*, et al. 1992.

Posner, R. 1976. *Antitrust Law: An Economic Perspective*. Chicago: University of Chicago Press.

Reitman, D. 2001. "Mergers in Durable Good Markets with Rational Consumers." U.S. Department of Justice, Antitrust Division, Economic Analysis Group Discussion Paper, EAG 01-8. Washington, DC: U.S. Department of Justice.

Rust, J. 1986. "When Is It Optimal to Kill Off the Market for Used Durable Goods?" *Econometrica* 54:65–86.

Schmalensee, R. 1970. "Regulation and the Durability of Goods." *Bell Journal of Economics* 1:54–64.

Schmalensee, R. 1974. "Market Structure, Durability, and Maintenance Effort." *Review of Economic Studies* 41:277–287.

Schmalensee, R. 1979. "Market Structure, Durability, and Quality: A Selective Survey." *Economic Inquiry* 17:177–196.

Schwartz, M., and G. Werden. 1996. "A Quality Signalling Rationale for Aftermarket Tying." *Antitrust Law Journal* 64:387–404.

Shapiro, C. 1995. "Aftermarkets and Consumer Welfare: Making Sense of *Kodak*." *Antitrust Law Journal* 63:483–511.

Sieper, E., and P. Swan. 1973. "Monopoly and Competition in the Market for Durable Goods." *Review of Economic Studies* 40:333–351.

Soma, J. 1976. *The Computer Industry*. Lexington, MA: Lexington Books.

Stokey, N. 1981. "Rational Expectations and Durable Goods Pricing." *Bell Journal of Economics* 12:112–128.

Su, T. 1975. "Durability of Consumption Goods Reconsidered." *American Economic Review* 65:148–157.

Swan, P. 1970. "Durability of Consumption Goods." *American Economic Review* 60:884–894.

Swan, P. 1971. "The Durability of Goods and Regulation of Monopoly." *Bell Journal of Economics* 2:347–357.

Swan, P. 1972. "Optimum Durability, Second Hand Markets, and Planned Obsolescence." *Journal of Political Economy* 80:575–585.

Swan, P. 1980. "Alcoa: The Influence of Recycling on Monopoly Power." *Journal of Political Economy* 88:76–99.

Waldman, M. 1993. "A New Perspective on Planned Obsolescence." *Quarterly Journal of Economics* 108:273–283.

Waldman, M. 1996a. "Durable Goods Pricing When Quality Matters." *Journal of Business* 69:489–510.

Waldman, M. 1996b. "Planned Obsolescence and the R&D Decision." *Rand Journal of Economics* 27:583–595.

Waldman, M. 1997. "Eliminating the Market for Secondhand Goods." *Journal of Law and Economics* 40:61–92.

Waldman, M. 2003. "Durable Goods Theory for Real World Markets." *Journal of Economic Perspectives* 17:131–154.

Whinston, M. 1990. "Tying, Foreclosure, and Exclusion." *American Economic Review* 80:837–859.

Wicksell, K. 1934. *Lectures on Political Economy*. Vol. 1. London: Routledge & Kegan Paul.

Wiley, J., E. Rasmusen, and M. Ramseyer. 1990. "The Leasing Monopoly." *UCLA Law Review* 37:693–731.

Williamson, O. 1975. *Markets and Hierarchies: Analysis and Antitrust Implications*. New York: Free Press.

Williamson, O. 1985. *The Economic Institutions of Capitalism: Firms, Markets, Relational Contracting*. New York: Free Press.

2 Two-Sided Markets: Economic Theory and Policy Implications

Mark Armstrong

2.1 Introduction and Examples

There are many examples of markets where two or more groups of participants interact via intermediaries or "platforms." Surplus is created—or perhaps destroyed in the case of negative externalities—when the groups interact. Of course, there are countless examples where firms compete to deal with two or more groups. Firms compete for labor and compete to sell output to customers, for instance. Or an exercise gym is likely to do better if it appeals to both men and women. However, in a set of interesting cases, cross-group network effects are present, and the benefit enjoyed by a member of one group depends on how well the platform does in attracting custom from the other group. For instance, a (heterosexual) dating agency or nightclub can *only* do well if it succeeds in attracting business from both men and women (unlike the gym example). This chapter is about such markets.

Some examples include:

- *Academic journals* Journals compete both for authors and for readers. Keeping submission and subscription charges constant, authors are more likely to submit their best work to a journal that is widely read, while readers (and libraries) are more likely to subscribe to a journal with higher-quality articles. A common (though not universal) way to organize the interaction is for readers and libraries to pay and for authors to publish for free.
- *Content in media markets* People are more likely to buy a newspaper or watch a TV channel the greater the variety of content it contains. In the newspaper context, this content would be "columnists" and the like. Most usually, columnists are contracted on an exclusive basis to the newspaper. Clearly, the more such content the paper attracts, the

easier it will be able to attract readers. Also, it is plausible that columnists will, in addition to receiving a salary, enjoy communicating their opinions to a wide readership.

• *Advertising in media markets* Advertisers wish to gain access to potential consumers to tempt them to buy their products. Often advertising is bundled with other services, such as newspapers, magazines, radio, or TV, which act as intermediaries between advertisers and consumers. Revenues from advertising are often used to subsidize the media product for readers/viewers. In some special cases, viewers/readers might not benefit directly from advertising, or might actually dislike intrusive advertising (which would then be a negative cross-group externality). But, for instance in the case of informative advertising, viewers/readers will benefit from the presence of advertising, as is the case in the next example.

• *Yellow pages* Yellow-pages directories are a form of mediated advertising that is not bundled with other content. Typically, consumers receive one or more directories for free, while advertisers pay to be listed. When there are several competing directories, if there are effort costs involved in consulting more than one directory, consumers are perhaps more likely to use the directory with more ads, while an advertiser will be prepared to pay more to be included in a directory with a wider readership. On the other hand, keeping readership fixed, an advertiser might prefer to be in a directory with fewer other ads. This might be for two reasons: its ad might become lost in the "clutter" of other ads, or a reader might see an ad for a competing product and call that number instead.[1] This is an example of a negative *intra*group externality.

• *Shopping malls* Continuing with the theme of matching consumers to retailers, an example where this is done physically is the shopping mall. Often, there are several malls in the relevant area that compete both for consumers and for retailers. Typically, retailers pay rent to malls while consumers gain entry for free (and might also have additional features, such as free convenient parking, offered to attract them). Typically, consumers care about the number of retailers when they decide which mall to visit, and obviously retailers care about the number of consumers coming through the mall. Like the previous yellow-pages example, business-stealing effects might mean that, all else equal, a retailer will prefer to be in a mall containing no other similar retailers.

• *Supermarkets* A closely related example is that of supermarkets, which deal with suppliers on one side and which compete to attract consumers on the other side. The principal difference between shopping malls and supermarkets is that in the former case the "platform owner" does not directly control the retail prices (which are chosen by the individual shops), whereas a supermarket sets all its retail prices. A common perception is that supermarkets often offer rather low prices to consumers, but deal quite aggressively with their suppliers (paying them only a low charge for their supplies).

• *Payment systems* Still continuing with the theme of facilitating interactions between consumers and retailers, consider the various methods of paying for products, including cash and various kinds of card payment. Both consumers and retailers may derive direct benefits (in terms of convenience or security) from using one method over another. (This is the relevant surplus created from the interaction, not the surplus created by the consumer buying the product itself, which will, in many cases, occur regardless of the chosen payment method.) To the extent that a consumer only chooses a limited number of payment instruments, he or she will care about the number of retailers who choose to accept a given payment method. Similarly, if there are setup costs in being able to accept a given payment method, a retailer will take into account the number of consumers who wish to use that method. A common contractual arrangement is for consumers to be able to use a credit or debit card with little or no charge (or even to be paid a subsidy), and for retailers to cover the costs of the transaction.

• *Airline reservation systems* Plane tickets are usually reserved and paid for via computerized reservation systems. A travel agent will typically use a single system of this type, and airlines will wish to be listed on all major systems in order for all travel agents to be able to purchase their tickets. The equilibrium is often that travel agents are charged little or nothing for the service, while airlines often complain about the high charges they must pay to gain access to the systems.[2]

• *Telecommunications with call externalities* Both callers and recipients of calls typically derive some benefit from telephone calls, which are mediated by telecommunications networks. There is often vigorous competition between networks for subscribers. Subscribers generally make and receive calls, and so it is less clear that there are "two sides" in this market. However, if one thinks of "subscription to a network" as one side and "number of calls made to a network" as the other side, then this industry fits into this framework. The more calls a network receives (for instance, because it sets a low charge for delivering calls), the more attractive the network is for subscribers; and naturally, the more subscribers a network has, the more calls it will receive. An inefficient pattern of pricing can sometimes be seen, with networks exploiting their monopoly position over delivering calls to their subscribers and using the proceeds to subsidize connections to the network (perhaps in the form of subsidized handsets).

• *Dating services and nightclubs* Similar features are present in the market for (heterosexual) dating services. Each side of the market cares positively about the number of people on the other side (and perhaps they care negatively about the number of people on their own side). It is sometimes the case that one side of the market is subsidized (e.g., no entry fee for women), and used to "attract" the other side from whom surplus can then be extracted. (Such discriminatory policies might be illegal in some jurisdictions, however.)

• *Smokers and nonsmokers* In a restaurant or aircraft, nonsmokers (and even smokers) typically care about the number of people smoking in the space. Unlike many of the previous examples, this is a negative intergroup externality. Another difference from the previous examples is that the "platform" can affect the extent of the externality, namely, by instituting a nonsmoking policy. Such a policy presumably entails a utility loss for smokers, and in a competitive environment, the platform must trade off this disutility against the extra attraction it now holds for the nonsmokers. In the case of airlines (outside of Asia at least), the equilibrium is clearly to have a nonsmoking policy, whereas for restaurants the pattern is more mixed.

This list of examples is mainly taken from "traditional" industries, partly to counteract the occasional view that two-sided markets are principally concerned with high-tech products such as software and the Internet. For further examples of two-sided markets, see Evans 2003a, 2003b; Rochet and Tirole 2006.

The main questions addressed in this chapter are (1) what determines the structure of relative prices offered to the two groups, and (2) when is the resulting allocation socially efficient? Once we understand these issues we are in a better position to think about policy toward these industries. For instance, we will also consider the effects of a merger between two platforms on the two groups.

In the next section I outline the main determinants of market performance.

2.2 Basic Issues

2.2.1 Effect of Cross-Group Externalities

Suppose there are two groups of agents that interact via one or more "platforms." If a member of group 1 exerts a large positive externality on each member of group 2, then it is natural to expect that group 1 will be targeted aggressively (i.e., offered a low price relative to the cost of supply) by platforms. In broad terms, and especially in competitive markets, it is group 1's benefit to the other group that determines group 1's price, not how much group 1 benefits from the presence of group 2.[3]

Consider for instance the case of the imaging software, Adobe Acrobat. Two versions of Acrobat software are available: the Acrobat "reader" is available free of charge, whereas the Acrobat "writer" (needed to create files) requires payment. A possible rationale for this policy might be that authors of documents are very keen for their documents to be read, but that people do not particularly enjoy reading these documents. In this case, the way to extract the maximum revenue from the two sides is to distribute the reading software for free in order to maximize the number of people who can read documents, and to extract all the revenue from the people who write documents. (Of course, something like the reverse happens with, say, popular novels, which are documents that people *are* willing to pay to read.)

This analysis might also apply to a yellow-pages directory. Such directories typically are given to households for free, and profits are made solely from charges to advertisers. This outcome can be rationalized if advertisers obtain a greater benefit from an additional reader than vice versa. Later in the chapter I will discuss a further rationale for this policy having to do with competition. Similarly, if men on average gain more from interaction in a nightclub than women, then it could be profitable to subsidize admission by women.

In general terms, unless they act to drive the industry to monopoly, cross-group network externalities act to intensify competition and reduce platform profits. To be able to compete effectively on one side of the market, a platform needs to perform well on the other side (and vice versa). This creates a downward pressure on both sides compared to the case where no cross-group effects exist. This implies that platforms would like to find ways to mitigate network effects, as is discussed in the next section.

Finally, as in all markets with network externalities, there is the possibility that one platform will corner (both sides of) the market if the externalities are strong. (And this outcome is not necessarily bad from a social-welfare point of view when externalities are strong.) Another way to put this is that it can be very hard for an entrant in such markets to get started. (Think of trying to launch a new journal, a new real estate agency, or a new dating agency.) One way to overcome this entry barrier, which is to charge on the basis of a successful transaction, is discussed in the next section.

2.2.2 Fixed Charges or Per-Transaction Charges?

Platforms might charge for their services on a "lump-sum" basis, which is to say that an agent's tariff does not explicitly depend on how well the platform performs on the other side of the market. Alternatively, if it is technologically feasible, the tariff might be a function of the platform's performance on the other side. One example of this latter practice is where a TV channel or a newspaper makes its advertising charge an increasing function of the audience or readership it obtains. (To do this, there must be a credible third party that can accurately estimate audiences.) A related kind of tariff is when charges are levied on a "per-transaction" basis. Important examples of this are credit and debit cards (where the charge paid by retailers is levied as a percentage of the revenue transacted) or telephony (where the relevant charges are levied on a per-minute basis). The bulk of a real estate agent's fees are only levied in the event of a sale.[4]

The crucial difference between the two forms of tariffs is that cross-group externalities are less important with per-transaction charges, since a fraction of the benefit of interacting with an extra agent on the other side is eroded by the extra charge then incurred. For instance, if the charge for placing an ad in a newspaper is levied on a per-reader basis, when it decides whether to place an ad, an advertiser does not have to form a view about how many readers the newspaper will attract. (It will place an ad when its perceived benefit—which is most naturally considered to be expressed on a per-reader basis—exceeds the per-reader charge, and this calculation does not depend on the total number of readers.) Because network effects are lessened when advertisers pay charges on a per-reader basis, it is plausible that platform profits are higher when this form of charging is used.[5] Similarly, if a consumer does not pay an up-front fixed fee for using a credit card, but only pays for each transaction, then he or she will not have to consider the number of businesses that accept the card when deciding whether to start using the card.

This point implies that charging on a per-transaction or success-only basis is an excellent strategy for a new entrant in a two-sided market. If an agent has to pay a new platform only in the event of a successful interaction, then that agent does not need to worry about how well the new platform will do in its dealings with the other side. That is, to attract one side of the market, the new platform does not first have to get the other side "on board."[6]

2.2.3 Single-Homing or Multihoming?

The current jargon has it that when agents choose to use only one platform, they are "single-homing"; when they use several platforms, they are "multihoming." (Clearly, this distinction does not arise where there is a monopoly platform.) It turns out that it makes a big difference to outcomes whether groups single-home or multihome.

It is perfectly tractable to model and analyze the case where both sides of the market single-home.[7] However, it is not easy to come up with major real-world examples of such a phenomenon. (Perhaps men and women might generally visit just a single nightclub in an evening, or smokers and nonsmokers might visit a single restaurant in an evening, in which case this model would apply, but it is hard to think of other examples.)

Also, one might consider the opposite case where both sides join all platforms. Again, though, it is not easy to think of many examples of such markets. (One possible example is credit cards, where many businesses accept several cards, and many people carry several cards. However, most people with several cards tend to favor a single card, and have perhaps been sent or supplied with a second card without really applying for it. It is important to distinguish between carrying a second credit card and actually using this second card.) The reason this configuration is unlikely is that if (all of) the other side of the market multihomes, then there is little reason to do so yourself. To take a pertinent example, if everyone can speak English as a second language, there is no reason for a native English speaker to invest in learning another language. Similarly, if all businesses accept all major credit cards, there is no benefit to a consumer carrying more than one (and vice versa).

This leaves one remaining important case to consider.[8] This is where one side of the market single-homes and the other multihomes. I have sometimes called these cases "competitive bottlenecks." There are several important examples of this situation—see section 3 below—and the source of the basic market failure is that the multihoming side, if it wishes to interact with an agent on the single-homing side, has no choice except to deal with that agent's chosen platform. Thus, platforms have monopoly power over providing access to their single-homing customers for the multihoming side. This monopoly power naturally leads to high prices being charged to the multihoming side, and typically there will be too few agents on this side being served from a social point of view. This tendency toward high prices is tempered somewhat when the single-homing side benefits from having many agents from the other side on the platform, for then high prices to the multihoming side will drive away that side and thus disadvantage the platform when it tries to attract the single-homing side. However, this point is never sufficient to undermine the basic result that the price charged to the multihoming side is too high.

By contrast, platforms have to compete for the single-homing customers, and in many cases, the monopoly profits from the multihoming side are passed on to the single-homing side in the form of a low price (or even a zero price) for that group. In sum, the single-homing side makes an "either-or" decision when it comes to platform choice, which can make that side of the market very competitive. By contrast, the multihoming side decides whether to deal with one platform independently of whether it deals with other platforms, and there is no competition for their customers. If the single-homing market is very competitive, then platforms will not make excessive profits overall. There is nevertheless market failure present, and the price to the multihoming side is too high in equilibrium (and the price to the single-homing side is too low).[9] The effect of a merger between two platforms is also asymmetric across the two groups. Since they face monopoly prices regardless, the multihoming side is not affected by such a merger (they are already fully exploited). The single-homing side will be treated less favorably after the merger since their price is related to the degree of market power held by platforms. Of course, the platforms' profits will rise after the merger.

2.2.4 Exclusionary Contracts

At least two distinct types of exclusionary contracts are relevant to two-sided markets.

2.2.4.1 Agents Are Asked to Deal Exclusively with One Platform

There are several examples where platforms attempt to persuade agents on one side of the market to join one platform or the other exclusively (i.e., to single-home). For instance, a broadcaster will pay a premium to obtain attractive content (sports rights, movies, and so on) for its sole use. The incentive to do such deals can easily be understood within the framework of the "competitive-bottleneck" model. In a framework where one side of the market single-homes while the other multihomes, there is a unilateral incentive for a platform to obtain agents on the multihoming side exclusively. The reason is that such a policy makes the rival platform's service to the single-homing agents less attractive, and hence allows the platform to obtain more profits from the single-homing side. This strongly suggests that a platform will be prepared to pay more (or charge less) for exclusive access to (ordinarily) multihoming agents.

On its own, this is not enough to make multihoming agents *agree* to exclusive contracts: after all, they might obtain greater utility by dealing nonexclusively with all platforms than by dealing exclusively with one platform. However, it is easy to construct plausible models where agents who would otherwise multihome find it in their interest to deal exclusively with a single platform. In this case the multihoming side is better off when platforms choose to compete for their exclusive use. We expect that the single-homing side is made worse off with this change, as platforms switch the competitive efforts from their side to the other side. Finally, we expect that the ability to secure exclusive deals with the multihoming group will make the platforms worse off in equilibrium, since cross-group network externalities become more significant.

These predictions can be illustrated using the model of exclusive rights for content in a duopoly pay-TV industry suggested in Armstrong 1999, section 3.[10] In that model, there are two pay-TV platforms, which are initially symmetrically placed. Viewers subscribe to one platform or the other. A provider of some form of premium content (e.g., sports rights or blockbuster films) enters the industry and decides whether to accept the platforms' price offers for its content. While viewers prefer a platform's output when the platform shows the new content, for simplicity suppose that the rights holder cares only about its revenue (and not about how many people see its content). If only one platform obtains the content, that platform has a competitive advantage over its rival in the market for viewers. A specific example involves the following payoffs for the various parties under the regimes of exclusive and nonexclusive contracts:[11]

	Viewer surplus	A's profits	B's profits
Both A and B obtain premium content	50	25	25
Only A obtains premium content	36.5	36	16
Only B obtains premium content	36.5	16	36

If the rights holder deals nonexclusively with the platforms, it will agree to sell its content for no payment (assuming that it incurs no cost for selling the rights in this market). This is an instance of the competitive-bottleneck model, where the multihoming side has its entire surplus extracted. Looking at the table above, it is clear that a platform will be willing to pay a positive price if the rights holder agrees to give it the content exclusively. (If its rival makes no counteroffer, a platform would be willing to pay up to 9 = 36 – 25 for the exclusive rights.) However, if the two platforms compete to sign up the content exclusively, each will be willing to pay up to 20 = 36 – 16 for such rights, since it knows that its rival will have exclusive rights if it fails to secure the content itself. Therefore, when platforms compete to sign up the multihoming side exclusively, the ordinarily multihoming side is made better off, the single-homing side (the viewers in this case) is made worse off, and the platforms are made worse off. Thus, although a platform has a unilateral incentive to sign up the multihoming side exclusively, when both platforms try to do this they are made worse off in classic "prisoner's dilemma" fashion. In addition, total welfare is lowered when the premium content is sold exclusively. (Total welfare, defined to be the sum of viewer surplus and industry profit, is equal to 100 = 50 + 25 + 25 when the rights are obtained by both channels, while it is equal to only 88.5 = 36.5 + 16 + 36 when only one channel supplies the premium content.) One reason exclusive content lowers welfare in this model is that some consumers switch to their less preferred platform in order to view the premium content.

2.2.4.2 Agreements to Exclude Rival Agents from the Same Platform

Several of the important examples of two-sided markets involve retailers on one side and consumers on the other. In these applications, an interesting issue is the extent of competition between retailers *within* platforms. For instance, a TV channel might be able to charge more to show a car ad if it promised not to show a rival manufacturer's ad in the same slot. Or a shopping mall might charge a high rent to a bookshop with the promise that it will not let another bookshop into the same mall. We expect that greater retailing competition will mean less profit per consumer for a retailer but that consumers will obtain higher surplus per retailer (or per retailer type) due to the lower prices that prevail with competition. Thus we expect that if the platform allowed retailing competition, it would make less money from the retailing side of the market but more from the consumer side (if it charged for entry). One hypothesis that could be investigated is: platforms would allow competition within the platform if consumers were charged for entry, but if consumers had free entry, then platforms would restrict competition in order to drive up the revenues obtained from retailers. I discuss this point further at the end of the chapter in the context of shopping malls.[12]

2.3 Applications of the Competitive-Bottleneck Model

2.3.1 Call Termination in Telecommunications

Armstrong (2006, section 3.1) and Wright (2002) propose a model of competition between mobile telecommunications networks. Subscribers wish to join at most one mobile network (i.e., they single-home). People on the fixed telephony networks wish to call mobile subscribers. For a specified charge, someone can call any given mobile network, and in this sense the people who call mobile networks multihome. Subscribers will choose the network with the tariff that leaves them with the most surplus. A network's tariff has two ingredients: the charges for subscription and outbound calls that affect the subscriber's welfare directly, and the charges the network makes to others for delivering calls *to* the subscriber (the so-called termination charges). Unless the subscribers care directly about the welfare of people who might call them, the latter charges affect the subscribers' welfare only insofar as they affect the number of calls they receive. High termination charges will typically reduce the number of calls made to mobile networks, and this is detrimental to the subscribers' welfare if they obtain benefits from receiving calls.

The prediction from this model is that mobile networks will offer relatively low charges for subscription and outbound calls but high charges for call termination. In particular, the model predicts that high profits made from each platform's monopoly on call termination are passed on to subscribers, in the form of subsidized handsets and the like. More precisely, the equilibrium call-termination charge is chosen to maximize the welfare of mobile subscribers and mobile networks combined, and the interests of people who call mobile networks are ignored. This feature—that the single-homing side is treated well and the multihoming side's interests are ignored in equilibrium—is a characteristic of all the "competitive-bottleneck" models: although the market *for* subscribers might be highly competitive, so that mobile networks have low equilibrium profits, there is no competition for providing communication services *to* these subscribers.

The policy implications of this way of looking at the industry are easy to grasp. First and foremost, the unregulated termination charge will be set at too high a level from the point of view of social welfare. Whether this market failure justifies the cost of detailed regulation is a matter of judgment. Even if the market for mobile subscribers is vigorously competitive, each operator holds the same monopoly position over providing call termination to its subscribers. Thus the need to regulate call termination, if judged appropriate, is not a temporary measure until competition somehow becomes effective, but is always needed. Moreover, there is no justification for a policy that controls the termination charges of "large operators" while leaving smaller operators free to set such charges as they like. (Such a policy will give smaller operators an artificial advantage in being able to attract subscribers.) If regulation is introduced to reduce termination charges, the results will be that callers to mobile subscribers will be better off while mobile subscribers are worse off since their subsidy is reduced or eliminated. The net effect on the mobile networks themselves is hard to predict, although in some natural models (including perfect competition for subscribers) there is no net effect on their profits.

It essentially makes no sense to speak of *the* market for mobile telephony in this case: there is a market for subscribers, which is—to a greater or lesser extent—competitive, and there is a market for call termination, which is monopolistic. These markets are linked, and monopoly profits in the latter segment are competed away in the former segment. The fact that platforms do not make excessive profits overall does not mitigate the social costs of monopoly pricing for call termination.[13]

2.3.2 Advertising in Media Markets

One of the most natural applications of these ideas is to advertising in media markets. These markets have long been recognized as being "two-sided," where the media platform (newspaper, magazine, radio station, TV channel, and so on) provides content in order to attract readers (or viewers or listeners), and this audience is then "sold" to the advertisers. Some of these markets fit the competitive-bottleneck framework better than others. For instance, due to time constraints many people read just a single newspaper each day. If an advertiser wishes to reach a particular reader (at least using the newspaper medium), it must place an ad in that reader's chosen newspaper, and pay whatever that newspaper asks. Similarly, many people listen to a single radio station most of the time. Also, to the extent that there are multiple yellow-pages directories, it is plausible that many people will consult a single directory when they are looking for something, and so an advertiser has to place an ad in that directory to have a chance of obtaining business from that person.

On the other hand, television viewers switch channels frequently, especially following the introduction of the remote control. If an advertiser wishes to reach the bulk of viewers, it need not place an ad on all channels, but only on a single channel (e.g., the channel that has the lowest advertising charges) and hope that viewers will eventually switch to that channel at the right time.[14] Specialist magazines are probably in between: some readers will get one such magazine, but enthusiasts will buy two or more; some advertisers will place an ad in each magazine (which they need to do to reach the single-homing readers), and some will place an ad in a single outlet (i.e., they will single-home).[15]

Anderson and Coate (2005) and Armstrong (2006, section 5) present a model where media platforms compete for readers/viewers/listeners (say, readers from now on), and advertisers wish to gain access to these readers. Readers might view ads as a nuisance (in which case, all else being equal, they prefer to use the platform with the lower level of advertising), or they might obtain useful information from the ads. Suppose that readers use a single platform, so that the competitive-bottleneck framework is appropriate. In this case, to reach a particular potential consumer, an advertiser must place an ad in that consumer's chosen platform. It is plausible to assume that the amount that an advertiser is willing to pay a platform for an ad is proportional to the number of consumers who use that platform (at least if the advertiser's product is manufactured with a constant unit cost). Over a wide range, the more ads a platform shows, the more advertising revenue per reader it will obtain. A platform will choose its level of advertising to trade off the revenue from advertising it obtains with the extra utility (or disutility) its readers enjoy from extra advertising.

To be specific, suppose that if a platform shows n ads, it can obtain advertising revenue per reader of $R(n)$. Suppose that each reader has utility $U(n)$, which could be a decreasing function if readers dislike ads, from seeing the n ads. Then a platform will choose the number of ads n^* to maximize $U(n) + R(n)$. (I assume here that costs of operating the platform are not affected by the number of ads.) However, the total surplus of advertisers is some increasing function n, say, $V(n)$. Social welfare is maximized when the number of ads maximizes $U(n) + R(n) + V(n)$, rather than just $U(n) + R(n)$. Thus, in this model the interests of advertisers are ignored, and there is *too little* advertising. This is precisely analogous to the previous result that there were too few calls made to mobile subscribers.

One further interesting possibility to note is that the revenue from advertising, $R(n)$, might be so large that readers are offered access to the platform for free. Since a platform receives advertising revenue $R(n)$ from each additional reader it attracts, the effect of this advertising revenue is exactly as if the platform's marginal cost of supplying service to an additional reader is reduced by $R(n)$. If $R(n)$ is sufficiently large, then, if feasible, platforms would actually like to *pay* readers to use the platform, so that the platform can then benefit from the large advertising revenue. Since it is hard to see how people can be paid to read a newspaper or watch TV, the outcome is that readers are offered the service for free. This provides a rationale for why yellow-pages directories are supplied for free, why some local newspapers are free, and also why we might expect to see free-to-air television funded by advertising continuing to exist even when the technology now exists to extract payment from viewers.

The policy implications of this view of the market are again clear. The price for advertising is too high, although whether this is justification enough to intervene is a matter of judgment. The disadvantage caused to advertisers is not mitigated if the market for readers or viewers is very competitive. Similarly, however, advertisers are not disadvantaged any further if two newspapers merge.

2.3.3 Shopping Malls and Supermarkets

The final application I wish to cover is shopping malls and supermarkets, platforms that bring consumers and products physically together. There are very close connections between this and the previous application, where media outlets were used to bring consumers and products together in an informational sense via advertising.

2.3.3.1 Shopping Malls Consider first the case of shopping malls. A shopping mall is a commercial enterprise that sets the rents for stores and, potentially, sets an entry fee for consumers. I assume that stores in the mall set their own retail prices to consumers, and that rents paid to the mall are lump-sum in nature (and are not revenue-sharing agreements, for instance). Assume for now that each store is a local monopoly, and there is no competition between stores in the mall. It is natural to suppose that consumers visit a single mall over the relevant period—the mall that leaves them with the most surplus—and that people do not buy a book in one mall and then go to another to buy wine for instance. As such, this framework fits exactly into the competitive-bottleneck model discussed earlier.

Suppose first that malls charge consumers for entry. Consumers are more likely to visit a mall with many stores and/or with a low entry fee. Similarly, a store is more likely to locate in a mall if that mall is visited by many consumers and/or if it has a low rental charge. Given that the consumers single-home, if a store wishes to have the chance to sell to a particular consumer it must locate in that consumer's favored mall. Again, then, platforms hold a monopoly over providing access by stores to their consumers, and can charge rents accordingly. Malls will not charge sky-high rents, though, since one means with which to attract consumers is to offer a wide variety of stores. But the outcome is that rents are chosen to maximize the welfare of consumers and the mall, while the interests of the stores are ignored. The outcome is that rents are too high, and from a social point of view there are consequently too few stores. Stores are exploited, but this is not necessarily caused by malls having significant market power in the market for consumers (because of geographic isolation, for instance).

As in the case of media platforms, it is quite possible that a mall obtains so much additional rental revenue from stores for each additional consumer it attracts, that the mall chooses to let in consumers for free. It would then like to *pay* consumers to turn up at the mall, but that is rarely feasible, and the next best thing is to let consumers enter for free. (It is possible to introduce further degrees of subsidy, for instance by having free car parking, or even free buses to the mall, or providing extra features—cinemas and other entertainment services—in order to lure further consumers in.) Thus, with this interpretation, malls choose not to charge consumers for entry, not because they cannot do so for technological reasons, but because they do not wish to.

2.3.3.2 Degree of Competition within a Mall Besides determining the balance of its charges levied on stores and consumers, a shopping mall has to decide how much competition to allow within the mall. Most stores have rivals to some degree, and the mall must decide, for instance, whether to have a single bookshop or to have more than one. Stores facing limited intramall competition will presumably charge higher prices than they would if there was a rival in the same mall. Thus, with limited competition in the mall, a mall can charge higher rents to stores but less to consumers (who know they will face higher prices once they reach the mall). However, in many cases, the gains to consumers from competition will outweigh the losses to stores, since the deadweight loss due to prices being above marginal cost is lessened. Thus, when consumers *can* be charged for entry, a plausible outcome is that the mall will prefer to have competition: its rental income from stores will decline, but the extra amount they can extract from consumers more than makes up for this loss. If for some reason malls cannot charge consumers for entry, then the prediction would be that malls would prefer less competition, since their sole source of revenue comes from profits generated by market power within the mall.[16]

2.3.3.3 Supermarkets The main difference between supermarkets and malls is that in the former case the platform sets the retail prices directly.[17] Nevertheless, some predictions of the shopping-mall framework carry over to the supermarket case. Again, a natural assumption is that consumers prefer one-stop shopping, and visit a single supermarket for their (say) weekly grocery shopping. This means that a supplier who wishes to reach a given consumer must supply that consumer's chosen supermarket and take whatever that supermarket is willing to pay for its supplies. The more a supermarket offers to pay for supplies, the greater the number of suppliers who will be willing to supply. A consumer is more likely to visit a supermarket that has a wide variety of products and/or that has low prices. The outcome in this framework is that supermarkets will choose their supply prices (and the consequent product range) in order to maximize the welfare of consumers and the supermarket, and the interests of suppliers are ignored. The supply price is too low, and the range of products offered for sale is also too small, from the viewpoint of social welfare. To the extent that there is vibrant competition between supermarkets for consumers, however, this outcome is to the benefit of consumers. Supermarkets use their strong bargaining position over suppliers (due to the monopoly they hold over providing access to their consumers) to drive down supply prices, and these low prices are then passed on to consumers.

2.4 Conclusions

The aim of this chapter has been to clarify some of the policy implications of the recent literature on two-sided markets. I focused on the case of "competitive bottlenecks"—where agents on one side of the market choose to go to one platform or another, while agents on the other side choose to join all platforms—since this situation seems to be particularly important in practice.

The reason one side chooses to "single-home" depends on the specific context: most people wish to subscribe to a single mobile telephony network, many people have the time to read only a single newspaper per day, and many people prefer "one-stop" shopping to visiting a variety of locations for their shopping needs. The group that wishes to interact with the single-homing group does not have this preference for single-homing, at least in the applications described. To interact with an individual on the single-homing side—in the applications, to make a call to a telephone subscriber or to sell a product to a consumer—an agent on the other side must join that individual's platform. As such, a platform holds a monopoly in providing access to its single-homing customers. Platforms do not *compete* for business from the multihoming side.

The outcome is the following. Platforms exploit their monopoly position on the multihoming side by setting high charges to that group. How high these charges are depends on how much the single-homing group cares about the volume of business on the multihoming side. The profits from the multihoming side are used to fund aggressive marketing efforts toward the single-homing side: in the applications this took the form of cheap (or free) handsets for mobile subscribers, newspapers with a cover price below cost, or free entry into shopping malls. If the market for single-homing customers is fierce (this depends on how close substitutes the platforms' services are to the single-homing agents), the platforms will fully dissipate the monopoly profits from the multihoming side in their attempts to attract the other side. Even if the platforms do not make excessive profits overall, however, there remains a market failure in these markets, which is that the multihoming side faces too high a charge from the point of view of social welfare. In the applications, this implied that it cost too much to call a mobile subscriber, that it cost too much to place an ad in a newspaper, and that stores paid too much to locate in a mall. This outcome—where overall profits are not excessive but there is a suboptimal balance of prices—is reminiscent of models of switching costs, where firms compete hard to sign up new customers with low initial prices in order to reap monopoly profits from these customers once they are locked in.[18] However, in models of switching costs, it is the same agent who is first subsidized and then exploited, whereas in these competitive-bottleneck models there is often a distributional impact of the pricing policy: one group is exploited in order to subsidize another group's consumption.[19]

Notes

1. Rysman (2004) estimates the importance of cross-group network effects in the market for yellow pages. He estimates that externalities are significant on both sides of the market: consumers are more likely to use a directory containing more ads, while an advertiser will pay more to place an ad in a directory that is consulted by more consumers.

2. See Doane, McAfee, and Hendricks 2003 for more information about this market.

3. For instance, see Armstrong 2006, section 4, for a model where one group's price depends solely on the benefit it brings to the other group and not on the benefit it enjoys itself from interacting with the other group.

4. In rough terms, the pioneering paper by Rochet and Tirole (2006) focuses on the case of per-transactions charges, whereas Armstrong (2006) emphasizes fixed charges. See Rochet and Tirole 2006 for a synthesis of these approaches in a monopoly framework.

5. For a formal argument along these lines, see Armstrong 2006, section 5. This argument applies when there are positive network externalities for viewers (so that viewers like ads). If viewers dislike ads, then per-viewer charges for advertising act to make the market more competitive.

6. For analysis of this point, see Caillaud and Jullien 2001, 2003.

7. For instance, see the relevant sections in Caillaud and Jullien 2001, 2003; Armstrong 2006.

8. This is a great simplification. Of course, there are many cases where only some agents on the other side multihome, in which case it may well be sensible to multihome

yourself. For instance, if there is a danger that a store will only accept one card, then there might be a precautionary motive to carry all major cards.

9. A related situation occurs with auctioning monopoly franchises. Suppose a government decides to auction off the monopoly right to supply some service, and that the price of the monopoly service will not be regulated. Suppose that the franchise is awarded to the bidder who offers the most to the government. Then the likely outcome of this process will be (i) a monopoly price for the service (with the usual welfare losses) and (ii) almost all monopoly profits are competed away in the auction process and passed on to taxpayers.

10. See Armstrong and Wright 2006 for further analysis.

11. This example is generated using a Hotelling model of competition between two channels, as described in Armstrong 1999, section 3. In this model, if channel i offers program quality v_i at the price p_i, while its rival offers quality v_j at the price p_j, then i will attract a fraction

$$\frac{1}{2}+\frac{(v_i-p_i)-(v_j-p_j)}{2t}$$

of the population of subscribers. Here, t is the product differentiation parameter, which represents the degree of substitutability between the two channels. The numbers reported in the text are generated by supposing that $t = 50$, that without the premium content each channel supplies program quality $v = 20$, and that premium content adds a value 30. That is, if channel A has the premium context exclusively, its quality is $v_A = 50$ while its rival has quality $v_B = 20$. The numbers reported in the table are generated by calculating the equilibrium subscription prices p_A and p_B, and the resulting market shares, profits, and consumer surplus, in each of the three scenarios.

12. See also Baye and Morgan 2001 for a model of a monopoly platform that transmits price information from competing sellers to potential buyers. The platform sets charges to buyers and sellers who use its platform, and must decide how many sellers (i.e., how much competition) to allow onto the platform. See also Dukes 2003 and Dukes and Gal-Or 2003 for models of advertising when advertisers compete for consumers.

13. See Competition Commission 2003 for an investigation into the UK market that makes use of the kind of analysis described in this section.

14. However, if advertising is assumed to be "persuasive" in form, and repeated viewing of an ad by an individual is valuable to the advertiser, then the fact that viewers switch channels does not overcome the monopoly problem: a channel has a monopoly over providing advertising access to its viewers for the period of time when those viewers watch the channel.

15. See Kaiser and Wright 2006 for more on this industry. They provide evidence in the case of "DIY" magazines, for instance, that 10 percent of readers buy two magazines and 17 percent of advertisers place an ad in two magazines. It is perhaps surprising that there is so little multihoming by advertisers, given that there is essentially single-homing by readers.

16. Thus in Baye and Morgan 2001, where consumers wish to learn the prices offered by competing firms from a platform, the platforms charge consumers a positive price and in return they set a low advertising charge in order to stimulate competition. If for some reason the platforms could *not* charge consumers, then this implies they would choose to have less competition (fewer sellers) on the platform.

17. See Smith and Hay 2005 for an analysis of the differences between supermarkets and shopping malls, as well as the third institution of shopping "streets."

18. For instance, see Klemperer 1995.

19. In the case of mobile telephony, however, the distributional effect is nowadays less important. Many or most people both make calls to mobile networks and are subscribers to such networks. In this case, people are treated approximately equally, but most of them would be better off if they paid less to call mobile networks and paid more to subscribe to such networks.

References

Anderson, S., and S. Coate. 2005. "Market Provision of Broadcasting: A Welfare Analysis." *Review of Economic Studies* 72(4): 947–972.

Armstrong, M. 1999. "Competition in the Pay-TV Market." *Journal of the Japanese and International Economies* 13(4): 257–280.

Armstrong, M. 2002. "The Theory of Access Pricing and Interconnection." In M. Cave, S. Majumdar, and I. Vogelsang, eds., *Handbook of Telecommunications Economics*. Vol. 1. Amsterdam: North-Holland.

Armstrong, M. 2006. "Competition in Two-Sided Markets." *Rand Journal of Economics* 72.

Armstrong, M., and J. Wright. 2006. "Two-Sided Markets, Competitive Bottlenecks and Exclusive Contracts." *Economic Theory*, forthcoming.

Baye, M., and J. Morgan. 2001. "Information Gatekeepers on the Internet and the Competitiveness of Homogeneous Product Markets." *American Economic Review* 91(3): 454–474.

Caillaud, B., and B. Jullien. 2001. "Competing Cybermediaries." *European Economic Review* 45(4–6): 797–808.

Caillaud, B., and B. Jullien. 2003. "Chicken and Egg: Competition among Intermediation Service Providers." *Rand Journal of Economics* 34(2): 309–328.

Competition Commission. 2003. *Reports on References under Section 13 of Telecommunications Act 1984 on Charges Made by Vodafone, Orange, O2 and T-Mobile for Terminating Calls made by Fixed and Mobile Networks*. London: HMSO.

Doane, M., P. McAfee, and K. Hendricks. 2003. "Evolution of the Market for Airline Information." In M. Baye, ed, *Advances in Applied Microeconomics, Vol. 12: Organizing the New Industrial Economy*. Greenwich, CT: JAI Press.

Dukes, A. 2003. "The Advertising Market in a Product Oligopoly." *Journal of Industrial Economics* 52(3): 327–340.

Dukes, A., and E. Gal-Or. 2003. "Negotiations and Exclusivity Contracts for Advertising." *Marketing Science* 22(2): 222–245.

Evans, D. 2003a. "The Antitrust Economics of Multi-Sided Platform Markets." *Yale Journal on Regulation* 20: 325–382.

Evans, D. 2003b. "Some Empirical Aspects of Multi-Sided Platform Competition." *Review of Network Economics* 2(3): 191–209.

Kaiser, U., and J. Wright. 2006. "Price Structure in Two-Sided Markets: Evidence from the Magazine Industry." *International Journal of Industrial Organization* 24(1): 1–28.

Klemperer, P. 1995. "Competition When Consumers Have Switching Costs." *Review of Economic Studies* 62(4): 515–539.

Rochet, J.-C., and J. Tirole. 2003. "Platform Competition in Two-Sided Markets." *Journal of the European Economic Association* 1(4): 990–1029.

Rochet, J.-C., and J. Tirole. 2006. "Two-Sided Markets: A Progress Report." *Rand Journal of Economics*, 72.

Rysman, M. 2004. "Competition between Networks: A Study of the Market for Yellow Pages." *Review of Economic Studies* 71(2): 483–512.

Smith, H., and D. Hay. 2005. "Streets, Malls and Supermarkets." *Journal of Economics and Management Strategy* 14(1): 29–59.

Wright, J. 2002. "Access Pricing under Competition: An Application to Cellular Networks." *Journal of Industrial Economics* 50(3): 289–316.

3 Antitrust Analysis of Tying Arrangements

Jay Pil Choi

3.1 Introduction

Tying arrangements recently have been a major and contentious issue in many high-profile antitrust cases in the United States and Europe. Examples include the Microsoft case, the Visa and MasterCard case, and the proposed GE/Honeywell merger that was blocked by the European Commission. More specifically, the Microsoft case in the United States was concerned with bundling of the dominant Windows operating system with Internet Explorer, while the bundling of the operating system and Media Player was an issue in the European case.[1] The Visa and MasterCard case was concerned with tying of debit and credit cards. The case was settled with the two card associations agreeing to pay $2 billion and $1 billion, respectively, to a class of merchants and to lower their interchange fees. In the GE/Honeywell case, one of the main issues raised by the proposed merger concerned the possibility of "bundling" and its likely impact on competition in the markets for jet aircraft engines and avionics.[2] The aim of this chapter is to review recent developments in the antitrust analysis of tying arrangements and to discuss relevant cases concerned with tying arrangements in light of theoretical advances in this area.

It is well documented that tying arrangements can serve many purposes, and numerous theories have been proposed to explain the motives for the practice and to find the ensuing antitrust and welfare implications. The most prominent view is that they serve as a vehicle for price discrimination. Papers in this tradition start with Stigler 1963 and include Adams and Yellen 1976 and Schmalensee 1984, among others. They demonstrated that bundling can increase profit even in the absence of cost advantages to providing goods in combination or interdependency in demand for the component products.[3] A variation on this theme is the metering argument in which the purchase of an indivisible machine is accompanied by the requirement that all complementary variable inputs be purchased from the same company. By marking up the variable inputs above marginal cost, the seller can price discriminate against intense users of the machine with the sale of variable inputs as a metering or monitoring device for the intensity of the machine usage. Other explanations given in this literature include monitoring the cheating on a cartel price, evasion of price controls, protection of goodwill reputation, economies of joint sales, and so on.[4]

The anticompetitive role of tying or bundling exemplified by the so-called leverage theory is more controversial. According to the leverage theory, a multiproduct firm with monopoly power in one market can monopolize another market that otherwise would have been competitive by using the leverage provided by the market power in the first market. By foreclosing sales in the second market, tying provides the mechanism to accomplish this. However, the logic of the theory has been criticized and subsequently dismissed by a number of authors from the University of Chicago school such as Bowman, Posner, and Bork, who have argued that the use of leverage to affect the market structure of the tied good (second) market is impossible. It was not until Whinston 1990 that the leverage theory was resuscitated with its first formal treatment. Since then, the theory has been refined and extended in several directions. Recent high-profile cases of tying mentioned above also rekindled the interest in the antitrust analysis of tying and spawned a new line of research. This chapter focuses on recent developments in this area.

The rest of the chapter is organized in the following way. Section 3.2 describes the leverage theory of tying and the Chicago school criticism of its implausibility. This was largely responsible for the replacement of leverage by price discrimination in the theory of tying before the leverage theory was revived by Whinston (1990). The Chicago school's contribution lies in revealing serious logical flaws in the early analysis of leverage and helping delineate conditions under which leverage theory does not apply. Section 3.3 presents the contribution of Whinston (1990), who demonstrated that the Chicago school arguments have limitations and can break down in certain cases. In particular, he maintains that the Chicago school argument hinges crucially on the assumption that "the tied good market has a competitive, constant returns-to-scale structure."[5] If scale economies exist and the structure of the tied-good market is oligopolistic, tying can be an effective strategy for a monopolist to extend monopoly power to the tied-good market by inducing *exit* by the rival firms. I also describe subsequent work that identifies further conditions under which the Chicago school arguments may not hold. Section 3.4 describes models of tying that incorporate incentives to innovate. This literature demonstrates that even in the absence of exit by the rival firm (hence, no changes in the market structure in the tied-good market), tying can be a profitable strategy via its long-term effects on competition through innovation. Section 3.5 discusses tying in the context of merger analysis in complementary markets. Section 3.6 discusses tying in the so-called two-sided markets that are characterized by intergroup network externalities. Section 3.7 concludes by discussing antitrust policy implications.

3.2 The Leverage Theory of Tying and the Chicago School Criticism

The key intellectual rationale for the historically harsh treatment of tying arrangements by the courts in the United States has been the so-called leverage theory.[6] According to the leverage theory of tying, a multiproduct firm with monopoly power in one market can monopolize a second market using the leverage provided by its monopoly power in the first market. The theory, however, came under attack and was largely discredited as a result of criticisms originating in the Chicago school (see, e.g., Bowman 1957; Posner 1976; Bork 1978).

The Chicago school criticism can be explained by the following simple model. Consider two independent products, A and B. They are unrelated in the sense that they can be consumed independently and their values to consumers are independent of whether they are consumed separately or together.[7] Consumers, whose total measure is normalized to 1, are assumed to be identical and have a unit demand for each product valued at v_A and v_B, respectively. To focus on the strategic motive for bundling, I assume that there is no cost advantage or disadvantage associated with bundling. The market for product A is monopolized by firm 1 with unit production cost of $c_A(<v_A)$. It is assumed that entry into market A is not feasible. Firm 1 may have a patent or have an installed base that makes entry unprofitable in the presence of network externalities (Farrell and Saloner 1986). The market for product B, however, is served by two firms, firm 1 and firm

2, who engage in Bertrand competition. For simplicity, product B is assumed to be homogeneous. Unit production costs for product B are given by c_{B1} and c_{B2} for firm 1 and firm 2, respectively. Both firms are already in the market and have paid sunk costs of entry, if there are any.[8] In such a case of no exclusion of the rival firm, tying is always a weakly dominated strategy if the production cost of each firm is given and cannot be altered.[9] To see this, I consider the following two-stage game.

In the first stage, firm 1 (the monopolistic supplier of product A) decides whether or not to bundle the two products. A price game ensues in the second stage with the bundling decision in the previous stage as given. The timing assumption reflects the fact that the bundling decision through product design is a longer-term decision that cannot be easily modified as compared to the price decision. The outcomes are described below and depend on each firm's bundling decision in the first stage.

3.2.1 No Bundling

If the two products are not bundled, they can be analyzed independently. With the assumption of identical consumers and rectangular demand, firm 1 can extract the whole consumer surplus in market A and have profits of $(v_A - c_A)$. In market B, the low-cost producer serves the whole market at the price of max (c_{B1}, c_{B2}). Thus, firm 1 will have the profit of $\max[c_{B2} - c_{B1}, 0]$ in market B. The overall profit for the monopolist is therefore given by

$$\Pi_1 = (v_A - c_A) + \max[c_{B2} - c_{B1}, 0] \tag{1}$$

3.2.2 Bundling

Suppose that the monopolist bundles products A and B and charges price P for the bundled product. In this case, consumers have two choices. The first option is to buy the bundled product from the monopolist at price P, and the second is to buy only product B from firm 2. For the first option to be chosen by the consumers, P should satisfy the following condition:

$$v_A + v_B - P \geq v_B - c_{B2} \tag{2}$$

This implies that the maximum price the tying firm can charge for the bundled product is given by $P = v_A + c_{B2}$. Firm 1's profit selling at that price is given by $(v_A + c_{B2}) - (c_A + c_{B1}) = (v_A - c_A) + (c_{B2} - c_{B1})$. Thus, firm 1's profit with bundling is given by

$$\tilde{\Pi}_1 = \max[(v_A - c_A) + (c_{B2} - c_{B1}), 0] \qquad (3)$$

Thus, $\tilde{\Pi}_1 < \Pi_1$ unless firm 1 has cost advantages in market B, in which case it can be verified that bundling has no effect ($\tilde{\Pi}_1 = \Pi_1$).[10] This implies that firm 1 never has the incentive to bundle for the purpose of monopolizing the tied-good market. As a result, price discrimination, as opposed to leverage, has come to be seen as the main motivation for tying (Stigler 1963; Adams and Yellen 1976; McAfee, McMillan, and Whinston 1989).

Note that given cost levels for each firm, nonbundling promotes *static* efficiency since it leads to production of B by the most efficient supplier. With bundling, however, production can come from the tying firm even though it has a higher cost of B as long as the cost disadvantage ($c_{B1} - c_{B2}$) is less than the surplus available in market A ($s_A = v_A - c_A$). In this simple model, the social and private incentives for (un)bundling coincide.

3.3 The Revival of the Leverage Theory

However, Whinston (1990) has revived the leverage theory of tying. He shows that if the market structure in the tied-good market is oligopolistic and scale economies are present, tying can be an effective and profitable strategy to alter market structure by making continued operation unprofitable for tied-good rivals. To understand Whinston's argument, I now modify the two-stage game analyzed above such that firm 2 makes an entry decision after firm 1's bundling decision. The entry entails sunk fixed costs. More specifically, consider the following three-stage game.

In the first stage, firm 1 (the monopolistic supplier of product A) decides whether to bundle the two products. In the second stage, firm 2 makes its entry decision given firm 1's bundling decision. If it decides to enter the market, it pays a sunk cost of K.[11] If there is entry by firm 2, a price game ensues in the final stage. The bundling decision is assumed to be *irreversible*. Thus, the model applies to physical or technical tying rather than contractual tying.[12]

I apply backward induction to solve the game. The outcomes in the final stage are the same as above if there is entry. If there is no entry, firm 1 charges ($v_A + v_B$) if the products are bundled, and v_A and v_B for products A and B, respectively, if the two products are not bundled. In either case, firm 1 gets the monopoly profits of $(v_A + v_B) - (c_A + c_{B1})$ without entry by firm 2.

Now suppose that $K < c_{B2} - c_{B1} < (v_A - c_A)$. The first inequality means that firm 2 can successfully enter market B if there was no bundling since its cost advantage is more than the sunk cost of entry. However, the second inequality implies that the cost advantage for firm 2 is not sufficiently high to compete against the bundled products since firm 1 is still able to sell the bundled products with a positive profit even if firm 2 priced its product at its marginal cost c_{B2}—that is, $\tilde{\Pi}_1 = (v_A - c_A) + (c_{B2} - c_{B1}) > 0$. Thus, firm 2 is foreclosed from market B since it cannot recoup its sunk cost of entry when firm 1 engages in bundling.

Let $s_A = v_A - c_A$ (>0) denote the monopoly surplus in market A. One way to interpret the result above is that after bundling, firm 1 behaves as if its cost of B were $c_{B1} - s_A$. The reason is that after bundling firm 1 can realize the monopoly surplus of s_A only in conjunction with the sale of product B. Thus, the firm is willing to sell product B up to the loss of s_A. This implies that firm 1 will price more aggressively after bundling and capture a larger market share in market B.[13] The Chicago school criticism of the leverage theory of tying missed this "strategic effect" due to their adherence to the assumption of competitive, constant returns-to-scale structure in the tied-good market. It is important to keep in mind, however, that in Whinston's basic model, inducing the exit of the rival firm is essential for the profitability of tying arrangements.[14] Thus, if the competitor has already paid the sunk cost of entry and there is no avoidable fixed cost, tying cannot be a profitable strategy.[15]

The analysis of Whinston has been subsequently extended in several directions by various authors such as Carlton and Waldman (2002), Choi and Stefanadis (2001), and Nalebuff (2004). Whinston's model assumes that entry into the monopolized market is impossible and shows how tying can be used to extend monopoly power in one market into an otherwise competitive market. These papers, in contrast, consider an oligopolistic environment and show that bundling can be used to deter entry into a complementary market to preserve the monopolized market or strengthen market power across several markets.

The basic intuition for these results in Carlton and Waldman 2002 and in Choi and Stefanadis 2001 is that entry in one market is dependent on the success of entry in a complementary market. Carlton and Waldman develop a dynamic model where an entrant with a superior complementary product today can enter the primary product market in the future. They show that bundling can be used to deny an entrant sales when it has only the complementary product, and this reduced sales today can prevent future entry into the primary market in the presence of scale economies. In Choi and Stefanadis 2001, entry takes place through innovation. They show that bundling reduces entrants' R&D incentives and hence the probability of entry since success in both products is required to gain access to the market.

Nalebuff (2004) considers a situation in which an incumbent with two independent products faces one product entrant. He analyzes the strategy of bundling as an entry-deterrence device when the incumbent does not know in which market the entry will take place. Nalebuff shows that bundling allows the incumbent to credibly defend both products without having to lower prices in each market.

3.4 Tying and Innovation

Whinston's paper mainly focuses on the effects of tying on pricing incentives. In Choi 1996, 2004, I extend Whinston's model by introducing R&D incentives and uncover another channel through which tying can affect competition. As demonstrated by the recent Microsoft case, this extension is especially important in understanding tying incentives in innovative industries.[16]

To highlight the importance of R&D, I abstract from the issue of entry/exit by the rival firm and consider a model in which bundling is not profitable in the absence of R&D competition. Instead, I show that the profitability of tying can be established through its effect on R&D incentives. As shown in section 3.2, with price competition only, using bundling to increase market share in the tied-good market is not a profitable strategy in itself. However, bundling also affects R&D competition. The tying firm's R&D incentives in the tied-good market increase since it can spread out the costs of R&D over a larger number of units, whereas the rival firms' R&D incentives decrease. If this positive effect via R&D competition dominates the negative effect via price competition, tying can be beneficial for the tying firm even in the *absence* of exit by the rival firms

More specifically, I analyze a three-stage game identical to that in section 3.2, except that firms engage in R&D competition before the pricing game, thereby endogenizing the final production cost of each firm. That is, in the first stage, the monopolistic supplier of product *A* decides whether to bundle it with the competitively supplied product *B*. As in Whinston 1990 and Carbajo, De Meza, and Seidman 1990, I assume that this precommitment is made possible through costly investments in product design and the production process. In the second stage, the two firms engage in cost-reducing R&D activities. A price game ensues in the third and final stage, with the cost structure inherited from the realizations of R&D. As usual, I solve the game via backward induction. The analysis of the pricing-game stage is the same as in section 3.2.

To focus on the impact of tying arrangements on R&D competition in the tied-good market, I ignore the possibility of R&D in market A and focus on the incentives for R&D in market B.[17] Let m_1 and m_2 be the levels of cost-reducing R&D investments by firm 1 and firm 2, respectively. The R&D outcomes are stochastic and independent across firms: let x_1 and x_2 denote the cost realizations after R&D for firm 1 and firm 2. Then, x_1 is a random variable drawn from $[0, c_1]$ by a c.d.f. $F(.|m_1)$ with positive density $f(.|m_1)$ for all $m_1 > 0$. Similarly, x_2 is a random variable drawn from a c.d.f. $G(.|m_2)$ with positive density $g(.|m_2)$ with all $m_2 > 0$. Let $F_{m1}(.|m_1)$ and $F_{m1m1}(.|m_1)$ be the partial derivative and the second partial derivative of $F(.|m_1)$ with respect to m_1, respectively. $G_{m2}(.|m_2)$ and $G_{m2m2}(.|m_2)$ are defined analogously. I make the following assumptions.

Assumption 1 $F_{m1}(.|m_1) > 0$, $G_{m2}(.|m_2) > 0$, $F_{m1m1}(.|m_1) < 0$, and $G_{m2m2}(.|m_2) < 0$ for all m_1, m_2, $x_1 \in (0, c_1)$ and $x_2 \in (0, c_2)$.

Assumption 2 $F_{m1}(x_1|0) = \infty$, $G_{m2}(x_2|0) = \infty$, $F_{m1}(x_1|\infty) = 0$, $G_{m2}(x_2|\infty) = 0$, for all $x_1 \in (0, c_1)$ and $x_2 \in (0, c_2)$.

Assumption 1 means that raising investment in R&D reduces cost in the sense of (reverse) first-order stochastic dominance, and does so at a diminishing rate. Assumption 2 is a boundary condition that guarantees an interior Nash equilibrium in R&D investments.

3.4.1 No Bundling

In this case, consumers' purchase decisions for each product are independent of each other, which implies that each market can be analyzed separately.

Given firm 2's investment level m_2, firm 1 chooses m_1 to maximize the following expression:

$$\begin{aligned} E[x_2 - x_1|x_1 \le x_2] - m_1 &= \int_0^{c_2}\int_0^{x_2}(x_2 - x_1)dF(x_1|m_1)dG(x_2|m_2) - m_1 \\ &= \int_0^{c_2}\int_0^{x_2}F(x_1|m_1)dx_1 dG(x_2|m_2) - m_1 \end{aligned} \tag{4}$$

where the last line follows by integration by parts. The first-order condition for the optimal investment level of firm 1 is given by

$$\int_0^{c_2}\int_0^{x_2} F_{m_1}(x_1|m_1)dx_1dG(x_2|m_2)=1 \tag{5}$$

Similarly, firm 2's optimal choice of m_2 given m_1 is derived as

$$\int_0^{c_1}\int_0^{x_1} G_{m_2}(x_2|m_2)dx_2dF(x_1|m_1)=1 \tag{6}$$

Equations (5) and (6) implicitly define firm 1's and 2's reaction functions, respectively, $m_i = R_i(m_j)$, where $i = 1,2$ and $i \neq j$. Total differentiation of the first-order conditions yields the result that $R_i' < 0$. Let m_1^* and m_2^* be the Nash-equilibrium R&D investment levels under nonbundling. Then, (m_1^*, m_2^*) can be derived by finding the intersection of the two reaction functions. I further assume that $|R_i'| < 1$. This ensures the uniqueness and the stability of the Nash equilibrium.

3.4.2 Bundling

Without bundling, firm 1 sells product B only in the event of $S = \{(x_1,x_2) \in [0, c_1] \times [0, c_2] \mid x_1 \leq x_2]\}$. In other words, any marginal cost reduction from investing in R&D is useful only when event S occurs. With bundling, firm 1 behaves as if its cost of product B were $(x_1 - s_A)$, where $s_A = v_A - c_A$ (>0). Thus, firm 1 sells the bundled product in the event of $\tilde{S} = \{(x_1, x_2) \in [0, c_1] \times [0, c_2] \mid x_1 \leq x_2 + s_A]\}$, which is larger than set S. In the event of set $\tilde{S}$, the tying firm's profit (gross of R&D investment cost) is given by $x_2 + s_A - x_1$. Thus, given firm 2's investment level m_2, the tying firm's optimization problem is to maximize the following expression:

$$\begin{aligned} &E[x_2+s_A-x_1|x_1\leq x_2+s_A]-m_1\\ &\quad=\int_0^{c_2}\int_0^{x_2+S_A}(x_2+s_A-x_1)dF(x_1|m_1)dG(x_2|m_2)-m_1\\ &\quad=\int_0^{c_2}\int_0^{x_2+S_A}F(x_1|m_1)d\,x_1dG(x_2|m_2)-m_1 \end{aligned} \tag{7}$$

where the last line once again follows by integration by parts. The first-order condition for the optimal investment level of firm 1 is given by

$$\begin{aligned} &\int_0^{c_2}\int_0^{x_2+s_A}F_{m_1}(x_1|m_1)dx_1dG(x_2|m_2)\\ &\quad=\int_0^{c_2}\int_0^{x_2}F_{m_1}(x_1|m_1)dx_1dG(x_2|m_2)+\int_0^{c_2}\int_{x_2}^{x_2+s_A}F_{m_1}(x_1|m_1)dx_1dG(x_2|m_2)=1 \end{aligned} \tag{8}$$

Equation (8) implicitly defines firm 1's reaction function under bundling, $\tilde{m}_1 = \tilde{R}_1(m_2)$. The comparison of (5) and (8) immediately gives the result that for any given level of m_2, $\tilde{m}_1 = \tilde{R}_1(m_2) > m_1 = R_1(m_2)$: firm 1 has greater incentives for R&D after bundling. The reason for this result is that the marginal cost reduction through R&D translates into profits *conditional* on the firm being able to sell product *B*. With tying arrangements, the set of outcomes under which firm 1 sells is larger, ($\tilde{S}$ vs. S), and as a result firm 1's R&D incentives increase.

In contrast, firm 2's chances of selling product *B* decrease with firm 1's tying arrangements. Thus, firm 2's R&D incentives are reduced as a result of bundling. To verify this, note that the first-order condition for firm 2's optimal investment level is given by

$$\int_0^{c_1} \int_0^{x_1 - s_1} G_{m_2}(x_2|m_2)dx_2 dF(x_1|m_1) = 1 \tag{9}$$

Equation (9) defines firm 2's reaction function under bundling, $\tilde{m}_2 = \tilde{R}_2(m_1)$. The comparison of (6) and (9) gives the desired result—that is, for any given level of m_1, $\tilde{m}_2 = \tilde{R}_2(m_1) < m_2 = R_2(m_1)$. Let $\tilde{m}_1^*$ and $\tilde{m}_2^*$ denote the Nash-equilibrium R&D investment levels for the firm 1 (the tying firm) and firm 2 (the rival firm), respectively, under bundling. Then, ($\tilde{m}_1^*$, $\tilde{m}_2^*$) can be derived as the intersection of the two reaction functions $\tilde{R}_1$ and $\tilde{R}_2$.

With bundling by firm 1, both firms' reaction curves shift. To analyze the effects of bundling on R&D incentives, it is more convenient to consider the change in equilibrium as a result of sequential shifts of the two reaction curves (see figure 3.1). Let ($\hat{m}_1^*$, $\hat{m}_2^*$) be the intersection point of $\tilde{R}_1(m_2)$ and $R_2(m_1)$. Since $\tilde{R}_1(m_2)$ is an outward shift of $R_1(m_2)$, we have $\hat{m}_1^* > m_1^*$ and $\hat{m}_2^* < m_2^*$ with a stable Nash equilibrium.[18] $\tilde{R}_2(m_1)$ is an inward shift of $R_2(m_1)$, which implies that $\tilde{m}_1^* > \hat{m}_1^*$ and $\tilde{m}_2^* < \hat{m}_2^*$. Thus, we have $\tilde{m}_1^* > m_1^*$ and $\tilde{m}_2^* < m_2^*$. Therefore, we can conclude that with bundling, the tying firm's R&D investment level increases ($\tilde{m}_1^* > m_1^*$), and the rival firm's R&D investment level decreases ($\tilde{m}_2^* < m_2^*$). This result renders some credibility to the argument that tying by a dominant firm can stifle innovation incentives by competitors in the tied-good market.

In my model, market foreclosure does not necessarily lead to exclusion of the rival firm. Rather, market foreclosure in the product market translates into foreclosure in R&D markets. In the static model of price competition where the industry rent is *fixed*, bundling reduces the tying firm's overall profits since it intensifies the effective price competition

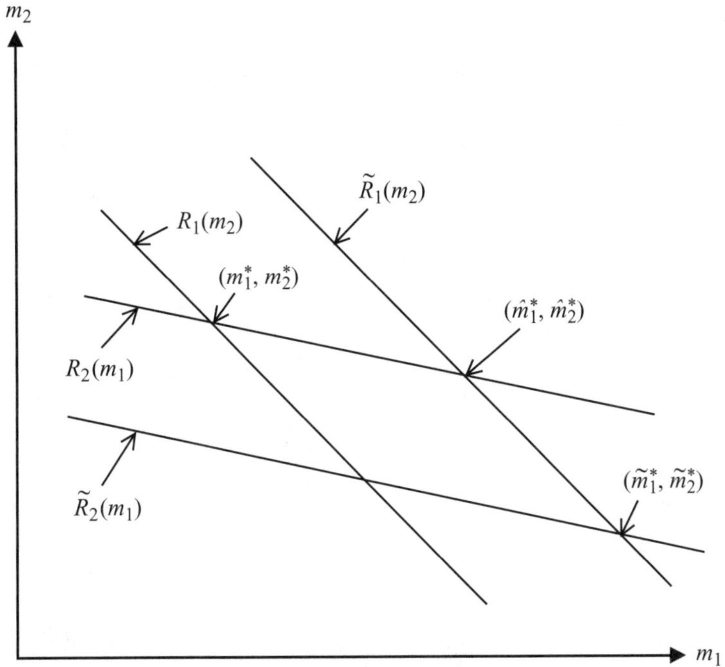

Figure 3.1
Equilibrium in R&D investment under bundling and nonbundling

in the tied-good market. However, in the presence of dynamic rents that can be created through R&D, bundling may be a profitable strategy. The change in R&D incentives through bundling enables the tying firm to capture a larger share of the dynamic rents. If this effect outweighs the negative effect of more aggressive price competition, bundling will be a privately optimal strategy even in the absence of exit by the rival firm.

An important question for antitrust policy is whether, in the presence of R&D competition, bundling is socially beneficial. In this model, the answer to this question rests on the nature of R&D competition, and there are two aspects of R&D to consider in evaluating its efficiency. R&D competition can promote a *diversity* of research lines and thus increase the aggregate probability of success (the level of cost reduction) if the outcome of the research project is uncertain. On the other hand, R&D competition can also result in the *duplication* of research efforts to the extent that their outcomes are correlated (Dasgupta and Maskin 1987). The desirability of unfettered

R&D competition hinges on the trade-off between diversity and duplication.

To explore welfare implications further, consider the following simple specification of the R&D process. Each firm has the option of engaging in *fixed*-intensity R&D activities, the cost of which is given by I. The outcome of R&D is modeled as a random draw for the firm's production cost. Let me further assume that the two firms are symmetric. They have the same initial cost, c ($c_{B1} = c_{B2} = c$), and have access to the same technology.[19] Specifically, if firm i invests in R&D at cost I, its production cost will be given by a realization of the random variable x_i, drawn from $[0, c]$ with c.d.f. $F(.)$ and with positive density $f(.)$. With this specification of R&D, let me analyze each firm's incentive to engage in R&D activities depending on whether firm 1 bundles. Note that by assuming symmetry in the initial costs I abstract away from the issue of the *static* efficiency of bundling.

Define $\mu_{11} = E[x_j - x_i \mid x_j > x_i]$ and $\mu_{10} = E[c - x_i]$, where x_i and x_j denote the post-R&D costs for firm i and firm j, respectively, $j \neq i$. In other words, μ_{11} is the expected cost advantage of a firm when it has a lower post-R&D cost compared to its rival firm, assuming that the rival firm is also engaged in R&D. In contrast, μ_{10} denotes the expected cost saving from R&D and is the expected cost advantage of a firm when it is the only firm engaged in R&D. Thus, $\mu_{10} > \mu_{11} > 0$.

To simplify the analysis, I further assume that that $s_A = v_A - c_A$ is sufficiently large that $x_1 - s_A$ is always less than x_2.[20] This implies that once the two products are bundled the tying firm always finds it optimal to sell the bundled product, regardless of the R&D outcomes, and forecloses the rival firm. It should be emphasized that the simplifying assumption is made purely for expositional simplicity and is not crucial for the analysis. Even if I consider the possibility that the tying firm cannot sell the bundled product profitably (i.e., $x_1 - s_A > x_2$), the main qualitative result will not change. The partial market foreclosure due to bundling reduces R&D incentives for the rival firm. However, with the assumption above, it is immediate that firm 2 has no incentive to invest in R&D since it knows that it will be completely foreclosed from market B. Given this fact, the tying firm will invest in R&D if and only if I is less than $\mu_{10} = E[c - x_i]$, which is the expected cost saving from R&D.

In contrast, without bundling the equilibrium in R&D is characterized in the following way:

(i) If $I \in \boldsymbol{L} = [0, \mu_{11}]$, both firms invest in R&D.

(ii) If $I \in \boldsymbol{M} = (\mu_{11}, \mu_{10})$, there are two (asymmetric) pure-strategy equilibria in which either only firm 1 or only firm 2 invests in R&D and there is one (symmetric) mixed-strategy equilibrium in which both firms invest with probability $(\mu_{10} - I)/(\mu_{10} - \mu_{11})$.

(iii) If $I \in \boldsymbol{H} = [\mu_{10}, \infty)$, neither firm invests in R&D.

Finally, the socially optimal configuration of R&D investment is given by

(i) If $I \in \boldsymbol{L} = [0, \mu_{11}]$, both firms should invest in R&D.

(ii) If $I \in \boldsymbol{M} = [\mu_{11}, \mu_{10}]$, only one firm should invest in R&D.

(iii) If $I \in \boldsymbol{H} = [\mu_{10}, \infty)$, neither firm should invest in R&D.

Combining all the results above, the effects of tying on welfare can be summarized in the following way (see figure 3.2). If $I \in L$, the benefit of R&D diversification outweighs the cost of duplication. Thus, it is better to have both firms engage in R&D. In this case, nonbundling results in both firms investing in R&D, and the private and social incentives coincide. Bundling, however, eliminates firm 2's incentives to invest in R&D by foreclosing the market for firm 2. As a result, there is dynamic-inefficiency associated with bundling.

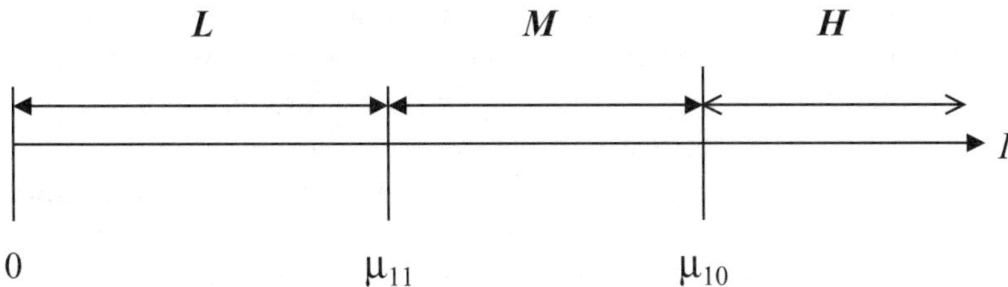

R&D equilibrium without bundling	Both firms invest in R&D	Symmetric mixed-strategy equilibrium	No firm invests
R&D equilibrium with bundling	Only one firm (the tying firm) invests	Only one firm (the tying firm) invests	No firm invests
Socially optimal outcome	Both firms invest in R&D	Only one firm invests	No firm invests

Figure 3.2
Market Equilibrium vs. socially optimal outcome

If $I \in \mathbf{M}$, in contrast, the benefit of R&D diversification is outweighed by the cost of duplication. Thus, it is better to have only one firm engage in R&D. Bundling ensures that the private and social incentives coincide. Without bundling, whether private incentives result in socially optimal outcomes depends on which of the multiple equilibria are selected. If one of the two asymmetric pure-strategy equilibria is chosen, the private incentives again coincide with the socially optimal incentives. However, if the symmetric mixed-strategy equilibrium is played, bundling improves dynamic efficiency. The reason is that with the symmetric mixed-strategy equilibrium, the dynamic rents associated with R&D are completely dissipated with competition. Thus, in this case, bundling can serve as a welfare-improving coordination mechanism.

3.5 Merger with Bundling in Complementary Markets

The possibility of bundling also has played an important role in merger analysis in complementary markets, since a merger between producers of complementary goods enables the merging firms to offer the products sold independently prior to the merger as a bundle. This possibility became a stumbling block for the proposed merger between GE and Honeywell in the aerospace industry. Choi (2003) provides a framework to analyze the effects of mergers in complementary markets when the merged firm can engage in bundling.[21]

Consider two *complementary* components, A and B, which consumers combine in fixed proportions on a one-to-one basis to form a final product. For instance, A and B can be considered as operating systems and application software, respectively, to form a computer system. In the case of the proposed GE-Honeywell merger, they correspond to engines and avionics to form an aircraft.

I assume that there are two differentiated brands of each of the two components A (A_1 and A_2) and B (B_1 and B_2). There are four ways to form a composite product, A_1B_1, A_1B_2, A_2B_1, and A_2B_2. Let me denote the price of brand A_i by p_i and the price of brand B_j by q_j, where $i = 1,2$ and $j = 1,2$. Then the composite product A_iB_j is available at the total *system* price of $s_{ij} = p_i + q_j$ (see figure 3.3).

Let D^{ij} denote demand for the composite product A_iB_j. The demand function for the components then can be derived from the demand functions for the composite goods. For instance, component A_i is sold as a part of composite goods A_iB_1 and A_iB_2. Thus, the demand for component A_i is given by

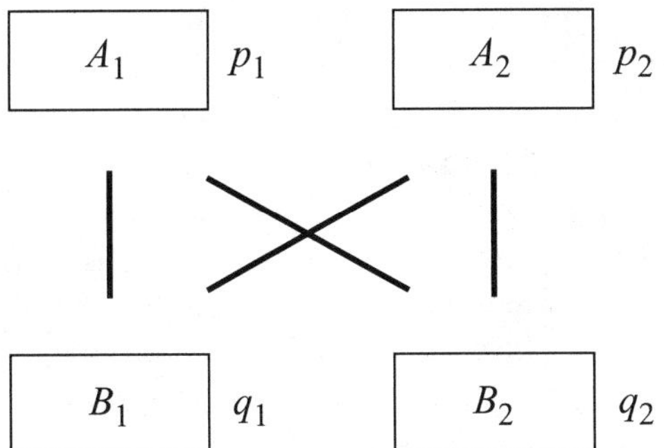

Figure 3.3
Diagrammatic representation of the premerger situation

$D^{Ai} = D^{i1} + D^{i2}$

Similarly, the demand for component B_j is given by

$\mathrm{D}^{Bj} = \mathrm{D}^{1j} + \mathrm{D}^{2j}$

For simplicity, I assume the following linear and symmetric demand system:

$$D^{11}(s_{11}, s_{12}, s_{21}, s_{22}) = a - b\, s_{11} + c\, s_{12} + d\, s_{21} + e\, s_{22}$$
$$D^{12}(s_{12}, s_{11}, s_{22}, s_{21}) = a - b\, s_{12} + c\, s_{11} + d\, s_{22} + e\, s_{21}$$
$$D^{21}(s_{21}, s_{22}, s_{11}, s_{12}) = a - b\, s_{21} + c\, s_{22} + d\, s_{11} + e\, s_{12}$$
$$D^{22}(s_{22}, s_{21}, s_{12}, s_{11}) = a - b\, s_{22} + c\, s_{21} + d\, s_{12} + e\, s_{11}, \text{ where } a, b, c, d, e > 0$$

To ensure that composite goods are gross substitutes, it is assumed that $b > c + d + e$, where the a parameter represents the market size, the b parameter represents the own-price elasticity of demand for that system, and the c, d, and e parameters represent the cross-price elasticity of demand across systems. Without loss of generality, I assume that constant-unit production costs are zero.[22]

In such a framework, Choi (2003) analyzes how the market equilibrium changes after a merger between A_1 and B_1 when the merged firms engage in mixed bundling. The main results are summarized as follows. First the merged firm will reduce the price of its bundled system and expand market share relative to the situation prior to the merger. Prior to the merger, any price cut by one of the merging firms will tend to benefit the other's sales. In the absence of the merger, neither party will take account of this benefit of a price cut on the other's sales. Following the merger, however, the merged entity can "internalize" these "pricing externalities" arising from the complementarity of their components by reducing the price of the bundle to below the level the two players would choose if acting independently.[23] This will expand the merged firm's sales and market share.

Second, the merged firm will raise the prices of its stand-alone components, relative to their levels prior to the merger. The merged firm has less to lose from raising its stand-alone prices because a proportion of those customers that switch away from the stand-alone components as a result of the price increase will simply switch to the bundle offered by the merged firm rather than to the competing system from independent firms. As such, the merged party will have an increased incentive to set high prices for its components. This raises the price of "mix-and-match" systems (i.e., systems including a component of the merged firm alongside a competitor's component) and makes them less attractive to buyers.

Third, in response to the price cut by the merged firm for their bundled system and the price increase for the "mix-and-match" systems, the independent rivals will cut prices in order to retain some market share. However, they will not cut their prices as much as the merged firm (i.e., their system will remain more expensive than the bundled system of the merged firm) since—in the absence of countermerger—they cannot internalize the externality arising from the complementarity of their components. As a result, they will fail to recapture all of their prior market shares. The merger would therefore reduce the profits of the merged firm's competitors. This reduction in profits follows directly from the combination of a loss of market share and the need to cut prices. Thus, there is a distinct possibility of exit by outside rival firms.

As an example, consider the case where $a = b = 1$ and $c = d = e = 1/4$ (see figure 3.4). Then it can be shown that with the independent ownership (premerger) structure, $p_1^I = p_2^I = q_1^I = q_2^I = 4/5$. The total price of each composite good is 8/5 and each firm gets profits of 24/25. After the merger between A_1 and B_1, the merged entity (A_1-B_1) charges $\tilde{s} = 11/8$ for the bundle and $\tilde{p}_1 = \tilde{q}_1 = 1$ for separate components. Thus, it offers discount for the bundle ($11/8 < 1 + 1 = 2$). Independent producers, A_2 and B_2, charge $\tilde{p}_2 = \tilde{q}_2 = 3/4$ for their component products. Therefore, the prices for composite products, A_1B_1, A_1B_2, A_2B_1, and A_2B_2, are given by 11/8, 7/4, 7/4, and 3/2, respectively, where $7/4 < 3/2 < 11/8$. After the merger A_1-B_1 receives the profits of 129/64 ($>24/25 + 24/25$), whereas independent producers get 27/32 ($<24/25$). This implies that

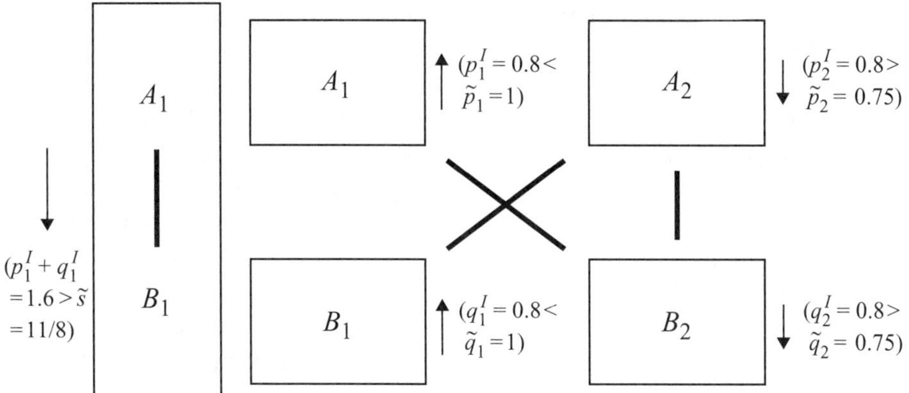

Figure 3.4
Diagrammatic representation of postmerger per-unit margins (with $a = b = 1$, $c = d = e = 1/4$)

A_1 and B_1 together increase their combined profits after merger, while independent producers' profits decrease.

The analysis suggests that a merger with bundling in complementary markets may have both anticompetitive effects and efficiency benefits. The efficiency benefits, for instance, take the form of internalizing pricing extenalities for the merged firm. The potential anticompetitive effects would take the form of market foreclosure, over either the short or the medium term. If the financial impact of the merged firm's bundling made its rivals unable to cover their fixed costs of production, their short-term exit could be expected. Alternatively, even if their postmerger profitability enabled them to remain in the market over the short term, it might not justify new R&D investment or capital expenditure. This would have serious consequences for their viability over the medium term.

Even in the absence of such foreclosure effects, mixed bundling by the merging parties could adversely affect consumer and social welfare. With heterogeneous consumer preferences, some buyers gain and others lose. For instance, those who previously purchased both products from the two merging firms would gain due to the lower bundle price. However, those who purchased a "mix-and-match" system and wished to continue doing so would suffer due to the increased standalone prices charged by the merged firm. In Choi 2003, I conduct a welfare analysis by numerical simulation under the assumption that $c = d = e < 1/3$. I find that there could be significant welfare loss when c

(cross-substitutability parameter) is sufficiently large. When c is close to zero, each system is essentially a separate product, and there is little direct competition between systems. In this case, the structure of each system market is equivalent to the one considered by Cournot and mergers are welfare enhancing. In cases with high degrees of substitutability and intense competition among systems (i.e., high c), however, the model suggests that the effects of mergers on social welfare are negative.

In Choi 2003, I also analyze the effects of a merger with pure bundling under which the firm only sells the bundle and does not make the individual components available individually. While the analysis of mixed bundling is more appropriate in the short run, the possibility of pure bundling can be important for the long-run analysis since the merged firm can practice pure bundling in the form of technical tying when it develops *new generations* of products by making its products available only as an integrated system, incompatible with the individual components offered by outside suppliers. With a simulation analysis, I show that for most parameter values pure bundling is less profitable than mixed bundling for the merged entity. It is also shown that outsiders' profits are affected more adversely with pure bundling. I can conclude that the merged firm will not practice pure bundling since mixed bundling yields higher profits as an accommodation strategy. However, as in Whinston 1990, pure bundling can still be profitable if the exclusion of rivals through predation is possible with pure bundling, but not with mixed bundling.

3.6 Tying in Two-Sided Markets

Motivated by the recent tying cases involving credit card payment systems and Microsoft, a few studies analyze the effects of tying arrangements on platform competition in so-called two-sided markets. A favorite example to illustrate the defining characteristics of two-sided markets is dating services or nightclubs, where each member of two distinct groups of people (men and women) derives value from interacting with members of the other group. In this example, members of each group obviously derive higher utility as more people from the other group patronize the same dating service or nightclub. This type of *intergroup network externality* is not limited to dating services. Other examples with more significant economic importance include auction sites such as eBay and Yahoo where buyers and sellers get together to consummate a deal, credit card payment systems such as Visa and MasterCard where both merchants and consumers need to participate in the same system, video game platforms such as PlayStation, X-box, and GameCube where game developers and consumers constitute the two distinct sides, and so on.[24] In such markets, the need to get all sides of the market to get on board creates a so-called chicken-and-egg problem (Caillaud and Jullien 2003), in that members of each group are willing to participate in the market only if they expect many members from the other side to participate. The burgeoning literature on two-sided markets is mainly concerned with the optimal pricing structure to coordinate the demands of distinct groups of customers. Formal economic analysis of tying that explicitly accounts for the peculiarities of two-sided markets, however, is scarce.[25] Two exceptions are Rochet and Tirole 2003b and Choi 2004.

More specifically, Rochet and Tirole (2003b) provide an economic analysis of the tying practice initiated by payments card associations Visa and MasterCard in which merchants who accept their credit cards were also forced to accept their debit cards. This tie-in practice, the so-called honor-all-card rule, has been challenged recently by major merchants, including Wal-Mart, in a class-action suit. In the class-action suit on behalf of thousands of retailers, the stores argued that Visa and MasterCard unfairly required merchants to accept their debit cards, which require a customer's signature to verify a transaction, to exclude PIN-based online debit cards. They show that in the absence of tying, the interchange fee between the merchant's and the cardholder's banks on debit is too low and tends to be too high on credit compared to the social optimum. Tying is shown to be a mechanism to rebalance the interchange fee structure and raise social welfare.

In Choi (in preparation), I develop a preliminary model that reflects the Microsoft case in the EC where it has been alleged that the company's tying practice of requiring Windows operating system users to accept its Windows Media Player software is predatory and hurts digital media rivals such as RealNetworks. In this streaming-media software case, content providers and consumers constitute the two sides of the market.

In my model, there are two intermediaries competing for market share within each group.[26] There is free entry in the market for content provision. Content providers are heterogeneous in their fixed costs of creating content, which need to be incurred twice if they multihome—that is, make their content available in digital form on both platforms.

The choice of consumers' platform is analyzed by adopting the Hotelling model of product differentiation in which the two platforms are located at the two extreme points of a line. Consumers are uniformly distributed along the line and each consumer's utility of participating in a platform depends on the number of content providers on the same platform.

In this model I compare the market outcomes under tying and no tying and provide a welfare analysis. There are three channels through which tying can affect social welfare due to the monopolization of both sides of the market. First, all consumers patronize the tying firm's platform. This implies that there is less variety in the market. As a result, there are less desirable matches between the consumers and platforms, leading to higher overall "transportation costs." Second, content is provided only on the tying firm's platform, whereas the same content was produced on both platforms in the absence of tying. Thus, there are savings in duplication costs under tying. Third, the number of entrants in the content side of the market that determines the availability of content can differ across regimes. The first effect is negative, while the second effect is positive. The sign of the third effect is ambiguous. The coordination of consumers on the tying firm's platform enhances the incentive to enter the content side of the market. However, the tying firm's pricing decision in that side of the market can offset this positive effect. The preliminary result thus suggests that the welfare implications of tying depend on the relative magnitude of intergroup externalities and the extent of product differentiation. If the extent of intergroup externalities is significant compared to that of product differentiation, tying can be welfare enhancing since the benefit from internalizing the intergroup network externalities outweighs the loss of product variety. Otherwise, tying reduces welfare.

Tying can be a very effective mechanism through which a dominant firm in a related market can penetrate one side of the two-sided market to gain an advantage in competition for the other side. As a result, we are expected to observe more tying cases in two-sided markets, and it is essential to understand the impacts of tying on competition in such markets and their welfare consequences. Both Rochet and Tirole 2003b and Choi (in preparation), however, are tailored to analyze specific cases of the payment card and media software industries, respectively. It would be desirable to develop a unified and more general framework that can encompass a variety of two-sided market situations, including the possibility of multihoming.[27]

3.7 Concluding Remarks on Policy Implications

I have conducted a selective review of recent developments in the theory of tying. Traditionally, tying arrangements have received a harsh treatment in the U.S. courts and had a status very close to *per se* violation for a long time with the leverage theory being the key intellectual rationale behind such treatment. The criticisms originating from the Chicago school, however, exposed the logical flaws of the theory and instead stressed the efficiency rationale for tying, which led to a more benign view of such arrangements. The subsequent literature has refined the classical leverage theory by identifying conditions under which tying can be used to preserve monopoly power or extend monopoly power in one market to another, showing that the Chicago school argument can break down in a variety of settings.

The welfare implications of tying arrangements are in general ambiguous, because tying could have efficiency effects even when it has harmful exclusionary effects. Microsoft's tying of Internet Explorer and Media Player with its operating system is a case in point. The literature suggests that such technical tying can be exclusionary under certain conditions. At the same time, however, there may be offsetting effects of tying such as enhanced performance due to a seamless integration of products and reduced costs of distribution if the tying good and the tied good are often used.

As such, there seems to be a consensus emerging among economists that tying should not be treated as *per se* violation of antitrust laws and that the rule of reason should be adopted in the assessment of tying arrangements.[28] However, beyond the general principle that any sensible antitrust policy should balance possible efficiency effects against potential anticompetitive effects, it seems to be an elusive goal to come up with a simple legal standard to apply in antitrust cases, since the appropriate antitrust policy will depend on the specifics of the case.

Finally, one serious drawback of the tying literature at this point is that it invariably assumes that multihoming is not allowed. For instance, Carlton and Waldman (2002, 199) assume that "if a consumer purchases a tied good consisting of one unit of the monopolist's primary good and one unit of its complementary good, then the consumer cannot add a unit of the alternative producer's complementary good to the system." However, multihoming is common in many industries such as software and payment card industries. For example, many users have more than one media player or messenger and many consumers carry multiple credit cards. The implications of such behavior for the effects of tying arrangements seem to be an important research agenda.

Appendix: The Analysis of Asymmetric Cost Structures in Section 3.4

In the appendix, I analyze the case where the two firms are asymmetric in their initial costs. Otherwise, I retain all the assumptions in section 3.4. Furthermore, I assume that the realization of the R&D outcome is uniformly distributed; if a firm with a current unit cost of c performs R&D, the outcome will be a random variable $\tilde{c}$ distributed uniformly over $[0,c]$. When the two firms differ in their initial costs, this specification captures the following features of the R&D process:

Diminishing returns to R&D When a firm with a current unit cost of c invests in R&D, the expected cost saving is given by $c/2$. As the original cost level c approaches the limit zero, the expected cost saving or improvement from R&D decreases.

Experience effects However, the final expected cost (*post*-R&D cost) will be smaller for a firm with a lower initial production cost (*pre*-R&D cost).

The analysis in this appendix runs parallel to that in section 3.4, which can be considered a special case of the analysis in the appendix.

3.A.1 No Bundling

To analyze how the incentives for R&D depend on the initial cost structure, suppose that the initial costs of the two firms are given by c_L and c_H, where $c_L < c_H$. The firm with the initial cost of c_L (c_H) is called the low- (high-) cost firm. Let me denote the R&D decision of firm i by $I_i \in \{0, I\}$, $i = L, H$. Let $\pi_i(I_i, I_j)$ be the expected profit for firm i when its investment level is given by I_i and the other firm's investment level is given by I_j, where $i, j = L, H$, and $j \neq i$. Then

$$\pi_H(I, I) = E[x - y \mid x > y] - I$$

where x and y denote post-R&D cost for the low-cost firm and the high-cost firm, respectively. By using the fact that x is uniformly distributed on $[0, c_L]$ and y is uniformly distributed on $[0, c_H]$,

$$\begin{aligned}\pi_H(I,I) &= E(x|x>y) - E[y|x>y] - I \\ &= \int_0^{c_L} \frac{x}{c_H}\frac{x}{c_L}dx - \int_0^{c_L}\left(1-\frac{y}{c_L}\right)\frac{y}{c_H}dy - I \\ &= \frac{c_L^2}{6c_H} - I = \frac{c_L}{6\gamma} - I, \text{ where } \gamma = \frac{c_H}{c_L} \geq 1\end{aligned}$$

By proceeding in a similar manner, I have

$$\pi_H(I,0) = \frac{c_L^2}{2c_H} - I = \frac{c_L}{2\gamma} - I$$

$$\pi_H(0,0) = \pi_H(0,I) = 0$$

$$\pi_L(I,I) = \frac{3c_H^2 - 3c_H c_L + c_L^2}{6c_H} - I = \frac{c_L}{6\gamma} + \frac{(\gamma-1)c_L}{2} - I$$

$$\pi_L(I,0) = c_H - \frac{c_L}{2} - I = \left(\gamma - \frac{1}{2}\right)c_L - I$$

$$\pi_L(0,0) = c_H - c_L = (\gamma-1)c_L$$

$$\pi_L(0,I) = \frac{(c_H - c_L)^2}{2c_H} = \frac{(\gamma-1)^2 c_L}{2\gamma}$$

Thus, I can draw the following payoff matrix as in figure 3.A.1. A straightforward calculation yields the following result.

The low-cost firm (L) \ The high-cost firm (H)	R&D investment	No investment
R&D investment	$\frac{c_L}{6\gamma} + \frac{(\gamma-1)c_L}{2} - I, \frac{c_L}{6\gamma} - I$	$(\gamma - \frac{1}{2})c_L - I, 0$
No investment	$\frac{(\gamma-1)^2 c_L}{2\gamma}, \frac{c_L}{2\gamma} - I$	$(\gamma-1)c_L, 0$

Figure 3.A.1
The payoff matrix of the R&D game with nonbundling

Proposition A1 Without bundling, the equilibrium in R&D is characterized in the following way.

The Large Efficiency-Gap Case ($\gamma = c_H/c_L > 5/3$) In this case, the equilibrium is unique and is characterized as follows:

(i) If $I \in \boldsymbol{L} = [0, \frac{c_L}{6\gamma}]$, both firms invest in R&D.

(ii) If $I \in \boldsymbol{M} = [\frac{c_L}{6\gamma}, \frac{c_L}{2}]$, only the low-cost firm invests in R&D.

(iii) If $I \in \boldsymbol{H} = [\frac{c_L}{6\gamma}, \infty)$, neither firm invests in R&D.

The Small Efficiency-Gap Case ($\gamma = c_H/c_L < 5/3$) In this case, the same behavior as in the large-gap case constitutes an equilibrium behavior. But the equilibrium is not unique for the intermediate values of I. More specifically, in this case there exists a set $m = [(3\gamma - 2)c_L/6\gamma, c_L/2\gamma]$, contained in $\boldsymbol{M}$ ($m \subset \boldsymbol{M}$). If $I \in \boldsymbol{m}$, there are two additional equilibria, one in pure strategies where only the high-cost firm invests and another in mixed strategies where the low-cost firm invests with probability $3(c_L - 2\gamma I)/2c_L$ and the high-cost firm invests with probability $3\gamma(c_L - 2I)/2c_L$.

3.A.2 Bundling

Once again, let me make the assumption that $s_A = v_A - c_A$ is sufficiently large that $x_1 - s_A$ is always less than x_2. Then, firm 2 has no incentive to invest in R&D since it knows that it will be completely foreclosed from market B. Given this fact, the tying firm will invest in R&D if and only if I is less than $c_{B1}/2$, which is the expected cost saving from R&D.

Proposition A2 With bundling, the rival firm has no incentive to engage in R&D, whereas the tying firm engages in R&D if its expected cost saving from R&D outweighs the cost of R&D investment ($I < c_{B1}/2$).

For the analysis of the first-best socially optimal configuration of R&D decisions, I first note that if only one firm is to invest in R&D, it should be the low-cost firm for efficiency. This follows from the assumption of *experience effects* in the R&D process. Thus, we can consider three possible configurations of R&D investment. If both firms invest in R&D, the expected total cost of product B is given by E [Min $(x, y)] + 2I$, where x is uniformly distributed on $[0, c_L]$ and y is uniformly distributed on $[0, c_H]$. If only the low-cost firm invests in R&D, the expected total cost is $E[x] + I$. Finally, if nobody invests in R&D, the total cost is simply c_L. This leads me to the following proposition.

Proposition A3 The socially optimal configuration of R&D investment is given by

(i) If $I \in \mathbf{L} = [0, \frac{c_L}{6\gamma}]$, both firms invest in R&D.

(ii) If $I \in \boldsymbol{M} = [\frac{c_L}{6\gamma}, \frac{c_L}{2}]$, only the low-cost firm invests in R&D.

(iii) If $I \in \boldsymbol{H} = [\frac{c_L}{6\gamma}, \infty)$, neither firm invests in R&D.

A comparison of propositions A1–A3 reveals that the private R&D incentives are more closely aligned with the socially optimal incentives under bundling when the cost asymmetry is taken into account. The social incentives and private incentives coincide without bundling in the case of the large efficiency gap, and also in the small efficiency-gap case to the extent that the equilibrium with the low-cost firm investing is chosen in the case of the multiple equilibria-parameter region. Thus, bundling will distort efficiency in the R&D decision if it changes the incentives.

With the knowledge in hand of how the R&D competition and the price competition play out under bundling and nonbundling, I can now analyze the incentive to bundle for firm 1. I consider two cases depending on whether or not the monopolistic supplier of product A is also initially the more efficient supplier of product B.

1. *Firm 1 is initially more efficient than firm 2 in market B* ($c_{B1} < c_{B2}$). In this case, it has been shown that bundling has no (harmful) effect on the tying firm's profits without R&D considerations. Since bundling eliminates the incentives to invest in R&D for the rival firm, bundling will guarantee that the tying firm maintains a cost advantage in market B. Thus, there is no adverse effect of bundling from the price competition. The only effect from bundling is to reduce the R&D incentives of the rival firm. I can conclude that firm 1 always has an incentive to bundle if it has an initial cost advantage in product B.

2. *Firm 1 is initially less efficient than firm 2 in market B* ($c_{B1} > c_{B2}$). In this case, it is still possible that the tying firm turns out to have a higher

production cost even after it invests in R&D while the rival firm did not. Thus, the monopolistic supplier of *A* has to consider the negative consequences of price competition in its bundling decision. Only when the beneficial effects of bundling in capturing dynamic rents outweigh the negative effects of price competition, will it bundle. Moreover, the portion of R&D benefits in cost reduction used to catch up with the rival firm's cost, which is $(\gamma - 1)$, does not contribute to the net profit. Thus, firm 1 will choose to bundle only when its initial cost disadvantage is not sufficiently large. A straightforward calculation of firm 1's profits under bundling and nonbundling yields the result that firm 1 chooses to bundle if and only if $\gamma = (c_{B1}/c_{B2}) < 1 + \sqrt{2/3}$.

Proposition A4 If $I \in \boldsymbol{L} \cup \boldsymbol{M}$ and $(c_{B1}/c_{B2}) < 1 + \sqrt{2/3}$, firm 1 (weakly) prefers to bundle. If $I \in \boldsymbol{L}$, bundling unambiguously reduces welfare by eliminating the R&D incentives of the rival firm. If $I \in \boldsymbol{M}$, there are two cases to consider.

Case 1 $(c_{B1} < c_{B2})$ If $\gamma = (c_{B2}/c_{B1}) < 5/3$, bundling can increase welfare by serving as a coordinating mechanism in the R&D game.

Case 2 $(c_{B1} > c_{B2})$ If $5/3 < \gamma = c_{B1}/c_{B2} < 1 + \sqrt{2/3}$, bundling reduces welfare by inducing the less efficient firm to invest in R&D at the expense of R&D investment by the more efficient firm.

If $\gamma = (c_{B1}/c_{B2}) < 5/3$, the welfare consequences of bundling depend on the selection of equilibrium under nonbundling. If the equilibrium is the one in which only the more efficient rival firm invests in R&D, bundling reduces welfare. However the mixed-strategy equilibrium is played, bundling partially solves a coordination-failure problem and improves welfare.

Notes

1. The U.S. Department of Justice and Microsoft reached a settlement in November 2001. The settlement agreement contains no provision for forced unbundling. In the European case, the European Union ruled that Microsoft is guilty of abusing the "near-monopoly" of its Windows PC operating system and fined it a record 497 million euros ($613 million). The case is being appealed by Microsoft.

2. Another major issue that proved to be a stumbling block in the remedy negotiations between the merging parties and the European Commission was the role and competitive implications of GECAS, GE's aircraft leasing and financing arm. The proposed merger was blocked by the European Commission in 2001. The case was appealed to the

European Court of First Instance (CFI). On December 14, 2005, the CFI upheld the Commission's decision in GE/Honeywell even though it found errors in the Commission's assessment of the conglomerate and vertical effects of the merger.

3. More general conditions for the optimality of bundling are provided in McAfee, McMillan, and Whinston 1989. They show that bundling is always optimal when reservation values are independently distributed in the population of consumers. Recently, the Adams-Yellen framework has been generalized to allow the goods to be substitutes and complements. For instance, Lewbel (1985) demonstrates that complementarity is neither necessary nor sufficient to make bundling optimal.

4. For a comprehensive review of reasons for tying, see Nalebuff 2003.

5. Whinston 1990, 838.

6. The leading case is *Motion Pictures Patents Co. v. Universal Film Manufacturing Co.*, 243 U.S. 502 (1917). Other cases include *International Salt v. U.S.*, 332 U.S. 392 (1947), and *Northern Pacific Railway Co. v. U.S.*, 356 U.S. 1 (1958).

7. The Chicago school criticism applies equally to the case of complementary products. See Whinston 2001 for more details.

8. Thus, entry and exit are *not* issues in this model. This turns out to be an important assumption, as explained in section 3.3.

9. This result also holds for the case of complementary products. See Choi 1996 and Farrell, Monroe, and Saloner 1998.

10. Variables corresponding to bundling are denoted by a tilde.

11 If firm 2 is already in the market, it can avoid a fixed cost of operation K by exiting from the industry.

12. One example of technical tying through product design is Microsoft's integration of Internet Explorer (web browser) and Media Player into its operating system. By designing these application programs to share the same files called dynamic linked libraries, it is difficult to remove them without jeopardizing the stability of the operating system.

13. In the terminology of Fudenberg and Tirole 1984, bundling is a "top-dog" strategy, while nonbundling softens price competition and is a "puppy-dog" strategy. (See Tirole 1988 for a discussion of the taxonomy of business strategies.)

14. Whinston (1990) points out that if heterogeneity of consumer preferences is allowed for the tying good, tying can also serve as a price-discriminating device and exclusion of the rival firm is not necessary for the profitability of tying. See Carbajo, De Meza, and Seidman 1990 as well.

15. In a related paper, Carbajo, De Meza, and Seidmann (1990) also provide a strategic incentive for bundling. However, they are not concerned with the rival's entry or exit decisions. Instead, they show that bundling may be profitable because it induces one's rival to price less aggressively. This is due to the assumption in their model that consumers are heterogeneous and can have different reservation values. However, for a given individual the reservation prices for the two goods are identical. In their model, tie-in provides a partitioning mechanism to sort consumers into groups with different reservation-price characteristics. The firm with bundled products sells to high-reservation-value consumers, while the competitor sells to low-reservation-value

consumers. As a result, the rival firm can raise its price in equilibrium. The overall effect on the market is a relaxation of competition. See also Chen 1997.

16. See also Gilbert and Riordan 2003. They show that a monopoly supplier of an essential system component may have an incentive to engage in technological tying when firms invest to improve their products. In contrast to Choi 2004, they consider tying of two *complementary* products and assume that the wholesale price of the essential component controlled by the tying firm is *fixed* and cannot be used to extract rents from more efficient rivals of the complementary product.

17. In Choi 1996, in contrast, the leverage of monopoly power occurs as a result of creating an interdependence of R&D competition between the two product markets. Thus, the model in the present chapter abstracts from this mechanism by assuming the R&D possibility in only one market.

18. See Bulow, Geanakoplos, and Klemperer 1985 for the details of the proof.

19. See the appendix to this chapter for an analysis of the asymmetric case.

20. A sufficient condition for this to hold is that $s_A = v_A - c_A > c_{B1}$. If this condition holds, the tying firm will still sell the bundled product even in the case where the rival firm reduces its production cost to zero and the tying firm maintains its initial production cost.

21. The framework in Choi 2003 is an extension of Economides and Salop 1992. The latter authors analyze a model of competition with complementary products in which they derive equilibrium prices for a variety of organizational and market structures that differ in their degree of competition and integration. However, they limit the strategy space of the merged entity and do not consider the possibility of *bundling*. See also Choi 2001 for a discussion of the GE-Honeywell merger.

22. If there are positive constant-unit production costs, the prices in the model can be interpreted as per-unit margins.

23. Cournot ([1838] 1927) was the first to note that mergers among complements reduce prices. He considered the merger of two monopolists producing complementary goods (zinc and copper) that are used as inputs for a final good (brass). My model extends his analysis to a case where both input producers face oligopolistic competition.

24. See Evans 2003 and Rochet and Tirole 2003a for more examples of multisided markets.

25. The general economics of multisided markets are provided in Armstrong 2002, Rochet and Tirole 2003a, and Caillaud and Jullien 2003.

26. The model is a modification of the framework developed by Armstrong (2002) and Rochet and Tirole (2003a).

27. For instance, many users have more than one media player or messenger and many consumers carry multiple credit cards. The possibility of multihoming and its implications for market competition have not been emphasized enough in the literature.

28. See Motta 2004; Tirole 2005.

References

Adams, William J., and Janet L. Yellen. 1976. "Commodity Bundling and the Burden of Monopoly." *Quarterly Journal of Economics* 90:475–498.

Armstrong, Mark. 2002. "Competition in Two-Sided Markets." Unpublished manuscript.

Bork, Robert H. 1978. *The Antitrust Paradox: A Policy at War with Itself.* New York: Basic Books.

Bowman, Ward. 1957. "Tying Arrangements and the Leverage Problem." *Yale Law Journal* 67:19–36.

Bulow, Jeremy I., John D. Geanakoplos, and Paul D. Klemperer. 1985. "Multimarket Oligopoly: Strategic Substitutes and Complements." *Journal of Political Economy* 93:488–511.

Caillaud, Bernard, and Bruno Jullien. 2003. "Chicken and Egg: Competition among Intermediation Service Providers." *Rand Journal of Economics* 34:309–328.

Carbajo, Jose, David De Meza, and Daniel J. Seidman. 1990. "A Strategic Motivation for Commodity Bundling." *Journal of Industrial Economics* 38:283–298.

Carlton, Dennis W., and Michael Waldman. 2002. "The Strategic Use of Tying to Preserve and Create Market Power in Evolving Industries." *Rand Journal of Economics* 33:194–220.

Chen, Yongmin. 1997. "Equilibrium Product Bundling." *Journal of Business* 70:85–103.

Choi, Jay Pil. 1996. "Preemptive R&D, Rent Dissipation, and the Leverage Theory." *Quarterly Journal of Economics* 111:1153–1181.

Choi, Jay Pil. 2001. "A Theory of Mixed Bundling Applied to the GE-Honeywell Merger." *Antitrust* 16:32–33.

Choi, Jay Pil. 2003. "Merger with Bundling in Complementary Markets." Unpublished manuscript.

Choi, Jay Pil. 2004. "Tying and Innovation: A Dynamic Analysis of Tying Arrangements." *Economic Journal* 114:83–101.

Choi, Jay Pil. 2006. "Tying in Multi-Sided Markets." Unpublished manuscript.

Choi, Jay Pil, and Chris Stefanadis. 2001. "Tying, Investment, and the Dynamic Leverage Theory." *Rand Journal of Economics* 32:52–71.

Cournot, Augustine. [1838] 1927. *Researches into the Mathematical Principles of the Theory of Wealth.* Translated from the French by Nathaniel Bacon. New York: Macmillan.

Dasgupta, Partha, and Eric Maskin. 1987. "The Simple Economics of Research Portfolios." *Economic Journal* 97:587–595.

Economides, Nicholas, and Steven C. Salop. 1992. "Competition and Integration among Complements, and Network Market Structure." *Journal of Industrial Economics* 50:105–123.

Evans, David S. 2003. "The Antitrust Economics of Multi-Sided Platform Markets." *Yale Journal on Regulation* 20:325–381.

Farrell, Joseph, Hunter Monroe, and Garth Saloner. 1998. "The Vertical Organization of Industry: Systems Competition versus Component Competition." *Journal of Economics and Management Strategy* 7:143–182.

Farrell, Joseph, and Garth Saloner. 1986. "Installed Base and Compatibility: Innovation, Product Preannouncements, and Predation." *American Economic Review* 76:940–955.

Fudenberg, Drew, and Jean Tirole. 1984. "The Fat Cat Effect, the Puppy Dog Ploy and the Lean and Hungry Look." *American Economic Review, Papers and Proceedings* 74:361–368.

Gilbert, Robert J., and Michael H. Riordan. 2003. "Product Improvement and Technological Tying in a Winner-Take-All Market." Unpublished manuscript.

Lewbel, Arthur. 1985. "Bundling of Substitutes or Complements." *International Journal of Industrial Organization* 3:101–107.

Matutes, Carmen, and Pierre Regibeau. 1988. "Mix and Match: Product Compatibility without Network Externalities." *Rand Journal of Economics* 19:221–234.

McAfee, Preston R., John McMillan, and Michael D. Whinston. 1989. "Multiproduct Monopoly, Commodity Bundling, and Correlation of Values." *Quarterly Journal of Economics* 104:371–384.

Motta, Massimo. 2004. *Competition Policy: Theory and Practice*. Cambridge: Cambridge University Press.

Nalebuff, Barry. 2003. "Bundling, Tying and Portfolio Effects, Parts 1 and 2." Department of Trade and Industry Economics Paper No. 1. London.

Nalebuff, Barry. 2004. "Bundling as an Entry Barrier." *Quarterly Journal of Economics* 119:159–188.

Posner, Richard A. 1976. *Antitrust Law: An Economic Perspective*. Chicago: University of Chicago Press.

Rochet, Jean-Charles, and Jean Tirole. 2003a. "Platform Competition in Two-Sided Markets." *Journal of the European Economic Association* 1:990–1029.

Rochet, Jean-Charles, and Jean Tirole. 2003b. "Tying in Two-Sided Markets and the Impact of the Honor All Cards Rule." Unpublished manuscript.

Schmalensee, Richard. 1984. "Gaussian Demand and Commodity Bundling." *Journal of Business* 57:S211–S230.

Stigler, George J. 1963. "*United States v. Loew's Inc.*: A Note on Block Booking." *Supreme Court Review* 152:152–157.

Tirole, Jean. 1988. *The Theory of Industrial Organization*. Cambridge, MA: MIT Press.

Tirole, Jean. 2005. "The Analysis of Tying Cases: A Primer." *Competition Policy International* 1:1–25.

Whinston, Michael D. 1990. "Tying, Foreclosure, and Exclusion." *American Economic Review* 80(4): 837–859.

Whinston, Michael D. 2001. "Exclusivity and Tying in U.S. v. Microsoft: What We Know, and Don't Know." *Journal of Economic Perspectives* 15:63–80.

4 Curing Sinus Headaches and Tying Law: An Empirical Analysis of Bundling Decongestants and Pain Relievers

David S. Evans
and Michael A. Salinger

4.1 Introduction

At virtually any pharmacy, grocery store, or convenience store, one can purchase "cold tablets" that contain more than one active ingredient. The main components of these medicines are pain relievers, decongestants, antihistamines, and cough suppressants. Tablets (or other dosage forms) containing just one of the ingredients are also available. The tablets that contain more than one active ingredient are therefore examples of bundled products.[1] This chapter reports an empirical analysis of the effects of this bundling.

Bundling and the related practice of tying have been central to several high-profile antitrust cases around the turn of the twenty-first century in both the United States and Europe.[2] The broad policy issue raised by these cases is how to distinguish anticompetitive cases of bundling and tying from the bundling and tying that occurs commonly under competition, presumably because it is efficient. Making that distinction requires a better understanding of bundling and tying under competition than the existing literature provides. This chapter is part of a project to advance our understanding of bundling and tying under competition, both theoretically and empirically.

The remainder of this chapter is organized as follows. The following two sections provide background for our analysis. In section 4.2, we discuss the antitrust treatment of bundling and tying, which is the policy issue that motivates our analysis. Section 4.3 briefly describes what we view as the principal shortcomings of the existing economics literature on bundling and tying and offers a new framework that we propose to address those shortcomings.

Sections 4.4 to 4.6 then present our analysis of the bundling of cold medicines and pain relievers. Section 4.4 describes the data and establishes three main empirical regularities. First, the discounts for buying bundled products are substantial. Second, so are the discounts for buying products in larger package sizes. Third, some products come in different dosages. For example, acetaminophen is sold as regular strength (325 milligrams), extra strength (500 milligrams), and arthritis strength (650 milligrams). Holding package size constant, the cost per unit of active ingredient is lower for higher dosages. Qualitatively, none of these results is surprising; our contribution lies in quantifying them.

Section 4.5 shows how to apply the framework described in section 4.3 to the bundle discount. Under that theory, a bundle discount can be the result of two distinct cost effects. One is marginal cost savings (that could arise, for example, from conserving on the number of packages and tablets produced). The other is a reduction in the contribution to fixed costs of each product offering (such as the cost of a shelf slot or the system cost of an additional stock-keeping unit). As we will explain,[3] whether the private savings consumers get from the bundle reflect social savings as well depends on the relative contribution of each. Thus, to estimate cost savings from bundling, we must empirically identify these two effects.

The key empirical contributions in the chapter are presented in section 4.6, which we summarize in some detail here to motivate the analysis. We exploit the regularities in the pricing of different package sizes to identify the marginal cost savings and fixed cost-increase effects. Some economists might argue that this pricing should be viewed as an optimal quantity-dependent pricing scheme. We suggest the alternative hypothesis that it reflects the same cost factors that give rise to discounts for bundled products. Suppose, for example, that a particular medicine—acetaminophen—is available in packages of 50, 100, and 200 tablets, with the price per tablet a decreasing function of tablet size. There seems to be no reason to rule out the possibility that some customers would ideally like to purchase 150 tablets. Such customers could either buy one package of 100 tablets and one of 50 tablets, thus sacrificing potential economies of package size, or one package of 200 tablets that contains 50 more tablets than they want. We estimate how high fixed costs would have to be to make it unprofitable to offer package sizes that we do not observe. As a basis for these estimates, we extend the model discussed in section 4.3 to package-size effects.

We estimate that, in this case, the marginal cost savings from bundled products exceed the fixed costs of the product offerings, so bundling lowers costs. For example, we estimate that the price of a package of 48 tablets that combines two active ingredients is $3.60 less[4] than the sum of the prices of the same ingredients sold in separate packages of 48 tablets each. We decompose this $3.60 into a marginal cost increment of $2.40 and an average fixed cost of $1.20. The net cost effect is the difference between the two, or $1.20. The gain would be substantially larger for tablets that contain three active ingredients. Moreover, these cost effects do not capture the value of the convenience consumers get from bundled products.

We can also use our framework to estimate the cost savings from having the separate products available rather than having consumers who want just one component buy the bundled product. This type of calculation is important for addressing the policy issues associated with the antitrust laws concerning tying. Tying occurs when a bundled product is offered and at least one of the separate products is not. Since tying can be an antitrust violation, the law encourages companies, at least those with market power, to offer the products that it bundles as separate goods as well. For consumers who want just one component of a bundle, buying the separate component rather than the bundle saves the marginal cost of the components they do not want. However, the separate component is itself a distinct product that generates a fixed cost of offering it. Selling the separate component only saves costs if the fixed cost is less than marginal costs avoided by not providing customers with the part of a bundle they do not want.

While in most of the cases we consider, our estimates indicate that the separate products save costs, there is one case in which we estimate that it does not. Of course, this result does not imply that the separate product should not be offered. In the example we consider, consumers who want, for example, just pain relief, would strictly prefer not to have to take a decongestant at the same time. Just as a complete welfare analysis of bundling and tying would have to account for the convenience value of the bundle for consumers who want all the components, so would it also have to account for the possibility that some consumers would pay not to have a component of a bundle.

The concluding section argues that the approach we have developed in this chapter can and should be used more generally to examine the economics of bundling specifically and possible efficiency explanations for various business practices that are often found suspect under the antitrust laws.

4.2 Policy Background

The policy issue that motivates our analysis is the antitrust treatment of bundling and tying. Bundling is the practice of selling in combination two or more goods that could be sold separately. Tying occurs when a firm sells a bundled product but does not sell one of the components individually. "Mixed bundling" arises when a firm sells all the components separately but offers a discount for the bundled product. In principle, it is tying rather than bundling that has historically raised antitrust concerns.[5] However, a sufficiently large bundle discount is sometimes interpreted as a virtual tie, and mixed bundling has emerged as an issue in its own right in Europe.[6]

Courts in the European Community and in the United States have found that tying should be treated with almost as little doubt as price fixing. In both cases the courts have decided that the offense is unlawful *per se*. That is, the courts do not need to inquire much, if at all, into the competitive effects of the practice or give much weight to procompetitive justifications. In the United States, tying is the only unilateral practice for which the courts have not incorporated microeconomic reasoning, following in the tradition established by certain economists and legal schools associated with the University of Chicago.[7]

4.2.1 European Community Tying Law

In the European Community, *Hilti* is one of the two leading cases on tying (the other being *Tetra Pak II*).[8] Hilti made nail guns used for construction work. The nail guns at the time of the case used separate cartridges and nails. Hilti had patents on the cartridges for use in its guns. It required customers buying its cartridges to also buy its nails. Cartridges and nails are obviously used in fixed proportions when only a fixed number of nails fit on a cartridge and neither nails nor cartridges are reusable. The European Court of Justice, affirming a decision by the Court of First Instance, agreed that this was an unlawful tie because Hilti was dominant in cartridges and cartridges and nails were separate products.

Economists recognize this case as a straightforward application of the Chicago single-monopoly profit theorem.[9] With fixed proportions there is only one possible monopoly profit. Hilti can earn all of its monopoly profits from the cartridges and is therefore indifferent, on this basis at least, on whether it sells the nail at a competitive price or someone else does. Price discrimination based on metering for the intensity of use of the nail gun cannot explain the practice either, since the cartridges are not reusable and therefore can account for the intensity of use—the nails provide no additional ability to meter beyond that available with the cartridges as they are used in fixed proportions. Thus, Hilti's explanation that there were safety issues seems more persuasive than a monopolization story.

4.2.2 U.S. Tying Law

In the United States, tying law is based on the Supreme Court's decision in *Jefferson Parish*.[10] A hospital had an exclusive contract with a group of anesthesiologists and required surgical patients to use one of those anesthesiologists. A competing anesthesiologist claimed this was an unlawful tie. The Supreme Court enunciated a new test for tying that was somewhat more forgiving than the earlier ones. A tie was unlawful if there were two separate products, a firm with market power in one product required customers to take the other product, and this requirement affects a not-insubstantial amount of interstate commerce. Two products were separate if there was enough consumer demand for the tied product to offer it separately.

The Supreme Court agreed with the appeals court that surgical and anesthesiology services were separate products. The record showed that many anesthesiologists were not employed by hospitals; patients, women having babies for example, sometimes hire their own anesthesiologists. The appeals court had rejected a number of arguments presented by the hospital that there were efficiencies from having an exclusive contract with a group of anesthesiologists. The Supreme Court nevertheless found that the tie was not unlawful because *Jefferson Parish* did not have market power. That leads one to question the power of the test: if the tie was not efficient, and if *Jefferson Parish* did not have market power to secure an extra monopoly profit, why did it engage in the tie in the first place?

The situation is not quite as extreme in practice as it is on paper. Tying, unlike price fixing, is common and conducted by many companies quite openly. MIT Press, for example, will not sell you this chapter without your also taking Michael Waldman's. Competition authorities ignore many cases they could prosecute. And the courts in the United States often find reasons to define tying away.[11] But companies that get caught up in tying cases find that these cases lead to significant changes in their businesses.

In March 2004, the European Commission found that Microsoft had engaged in an unlawful tie by distributing Windows with media-player technologies included without also offering Windows with media-player technologies excluded.[12] To remedy this violation the Commission required Microsoft to distribute a version of Windows with 182 media-player-related files deleted (although it has allowed Microsoft to distribute this at the same price as the complete version since media players are generally available for free).[13]

Microsoft also faced a claim brought by the U.S. Department of Justice that it tied its operating system to its browser.[14] A district court found that was illegal under the *Jefferson Parish* test. An appeals court created a "software platform" exception to the standard *per se* test and remanded the case to be considered under the "rule of reason."[15] The Justice Department decided not to retry the charge.[16]

Microsoft is not the only company to face tying claims. In April 2003, MasterCard and Visa settled a class-action case for $3 billion in cash and more in concessions after a district court judge found, on summary judgment and before a jury trial on the fact, that the card associations had passed most, and possibly all, of the tests necessary for finding an unlawful tie.[17] The card association required merchants that accepted their credit cards to also take their debit cards (as part of a general rule known as the "honor-all-card rule"). As part of the settlement, the card associations agreed to let merchants take credit cards without also taking debit cards. American Express is facing a similar class-action lawsuit because it "ties" merchants' acceptance of its corporate card to the acceptance of its noncorporate cards.[18]

4.2.3 Bundling

Although it is not the focus of the analysis below, it should be mentioned that another strand of antitrust law in the European Community and the United States finds that what we have called mixed bundling can be anticompetitive. The issue hinges on pricing. At the simplest level, a company can offer choices but set the prices in such a way that it is equivalent to tying. The more interesting case, though, involves setting prices for the various bundles in ways that arguably foreclose competitors from competing in certain product markets. The Court of First Instance found in several cases that "fidelity discounts"—discounts that in effect encouraged firms to buy multiple products from a single firm—violated Article 82 of the EC Treaty.[19]

In the United States, in a controversial decision, the Third Circuit Court of Appeals affirmed a jury verdict that found that 3M had violated the Sherman Act by providing discounts for purchasing several

3M products. It did so apparently in the absence of any evidence that any of the individual prices were below marginal cost.[20]

4.3 Economics Literature on Bundling and Tying

In this section, we briefly comment on the existing economics literature on bundling and tying and then describe the alternative framework we have developed for understanding bundling and tying under competition.

4.3.1 Existing Literature

The economics literature on bundling and tying has largely been a normative one motivated by the antitrust issues. The early legal hostility toward tying was based on informal notions that the practice could be used to leverage monopoly in one market into some other market. George Stigler (1983) presented an alternative interpretation that gave rise to the price-discrimination strand of the literature. Then, starting with Whinston 1990, the literature has revisited the foreclosure theory using game theory as an analytic tool. We now understand that one can construct a formal economic model in which tying is used to exclude competitors.

Ironically, even though the intent of the literature has been to provide insight into antitrust policy, it has simply failed to address the most important issue policymakers need to confront. Both tying and mixed bundling are common practices under competition. The challenge for antitrust policy is to distinguish anticompetitive tying and bundling from the tying and bundling that commonly occur under competition and are therefore presumed to be efficient. The literature suffers from three major shortcomings that prevent it from achieving this task. First, it is based on the assumption that firms have market power. Second, it is based on the assumption that bundling and tying do not create efficiencies of any type, which is why bundling and tying occur under competition. Even at a theoretical level, one cannot distinguish between competitive tying and anticompetitive tying by understanding anticompetitive tying alone. One needs to understand competitive tying as well to know the difference. The third shortcoming of the literature is that it is almost entirely theoretical.

The lack of empirical content is problematic for two distinct reasons. First, courts cannot be expected to distinguish perfectly between competitive and anticompetitive examples of bundling and tying. In light of the risk of error, the relative frequency of competitive and anticompetitive tying and bundling and the costs of "false convictions" and "false acquittals" are relevant considerations in formulating legal standards.[21] For the foreseeable future, notions of the relative frequencies will have to be subjective,[22] but careful observation of bundling and tying in practice would seem to be helpful and indeed essential in judging the probabilities. Second, the economics literature has not developed the analytic framework to do the cost-benefit analysis of actual cases in which tying and bundling help some customers but harm others.

4.3.2 A New Framework

In Evans and Salinger 2004, 2005, we present a new model of bundling and tying designed to address the shortcomings of the existing literature. First, we examine these practices under competition and thereby provide a basis for comparing competitive and anticompetitive theories of these practices. Second, while further development is needed, we believe that our framework has the potential to be more tractable for empirical analysis than existing models. Indeed, the empirical analysis we present in this chapter represents the first attempt to implement the model empirically.

To understand tying under competition, one must first recognize that consumers differ in their preferences for what they want. Businesses cannot necessarily customize their offerings to provide each customer exactly what he or she wants. A simple framework that captures this basic idea goes as follows. There are two goods, A and B, which can be sold separately or in combination. Some customers want just good A, some want just good B, and some want both. Those who want both might strictly prefer to buy them in bundled form. This could be because the bundling provides convenience, in which case they would be willing to pay a premium to buy the bundle rather than to buy the components separately. Alternatively, bundling might save marginal costs that, under competition, get passed on to consumers through lower prices.

Given this general setup, mixed bundling gives each group of customers the exact product its "members" want. Assuming that there are at least some people in each of the three demand groups, anything other than mixed bundling represents a limitation on the set of products offered. If the bundle is the "good" not offered, then no tying occurs. If, however, the bundle is offered and one or both components are not, then the result is tying.

As is generally recognized in the economics literature on product selection, companies cannot customize their offerings to the preferences of each customer because of scale economies associated with each product offering. To be offered, therefore, the presence of some demand for a good is not sufficient. There must be a critical mass of customers. The simplest way to capture these scale economies is to assume a fixed cost associated with each product offering, where each component and the bundled product are separate offerings.

The assumption of a fixed cost of a product offering poses a dilemma for modeling tying under competition. Under perfect competition, price equals marginal cost. With a fixed cost associated with each product offering, however, marginal cost is less than average cost, and marginal cost pricing would not allow a firm to cover its cost. Rather than assuming perfect competition, therefore, we assume that markets are perfectly contestable in the sense of Baumol, Panzer, and Willig 1982. We then model the set of products offered by looking for "sustainable prices."

To take an example, consider pure bundling, which means that the bundle is offered but neither component is. When that happens, customers who want just good A or just good B have to buy the bundle and discard the good they do not want. Under the contestability assumption, the price of the bundle equals its average cost, which is the sum of the marginal cost and the fixed cost averaged over all the customers who buy it. For pure bundling to be sustainable, it must not be possible to offer, say, just good A at a price below the price of the bundle under pure bundling. If the marginal cost of good A is less than the marginal cost of the bundle, as would typically be the case, then pure bundling would not be sustainable given sufficiently large demand for good A. If, however, demand for just good A is sufficiently limited, then the marginal cost savings from providing good A alone might be less than the fixed cost of the separate product offering. If so and if the same is true for good B, then pure bundling can be sustainable.

Simple as the framework is, it leads to powerful insights. In particular, pure bundling can occur under two distinct types of circumstances. One is that most customers want both goods, there are marginal cost savings from offering them together, and demand for the separate goods, while present, is too small to justify offering them. A commonly cited but trivial example is shoes—few people want their shoes without laces and few want only one shoe; but few does not mean none since surely some people have their favorite laces and there are at least a few amputees and people in casts who only want one shoe. Men's and women's suits are an interesting example. In the United States, tailoring is usually tied in for men, so men who have their own favorite tailor are perhaps disadvantaged; tailoring is usually not tied for women, who sometimes complain that this is discriminatory.

The other condition that gives rise to pure bundling in this model is that fixed costs are very high. In this case, pure bundling can arise even if no one wants both components. If so, everyone in effect purchases an unwanted component. Yet, the high fixed cost makes it efficient to provide a standardized product that meets the needs of a diverse group of customer wants. For example, some computer software is sold in boxes that contain both a Macintosh and PC version. It is likely that very few people want both. Many college textbooks contain more material than can be covered in a single course so that they can be useful for professors with diverse preferences about what material they want their students to read.

We now turn to our empirical application of this framework.

4.4 The Pricing of Pain-Relief, Cold, Sinus, and Allergy Medicines

The primary data collected for this chapter were the prices of all cold[23] and pain-relief medications sold at the Walgreens[24] at 757 N. Michigan Ave. in Chicago on April 3, 2003. For each package, we observe the brand, the price, dosage form,[25] quantity of each active ingredient per unit, and number of units. We have supplemented the data with some prices offered at the CVS website[26] and have generally checked prices on the web and at other outlets to confirm that the regularities we document are not specific to this particular location and time.

4.4.1 Empirical Regularities

We will ultimately use a price regression to describe the bundle discount. To guide the specification of that regression, it will be useful to explore less formally some strong regularities that are present in the data. We will also use these stylized facts to argue for a cost-based explanation for the bundle discount.

4.4.1.1 Bundle Discounts and Brand-Name Premiums Johnson & Johnson's Tylenol is the dominant brand of the pain reliever acetaminophen and Pfizer's Sudafed is the dominant brand of the decongestant pseudoephedrine hydrochloride. Each Extra Strength Tylenol contains 500 mg of acetaminophen and each Maximum Strength Sudafed contains 30 mg of pseudoephedrine hydrochoride. Johnson & Johnson does not offer a Tylenol-brand pseudoephedrine hydrochloride, nor does Pfizer offer a Sudafed-brand acetaminophen. However, both a Tylenol Sinus Caplet and a Sudafed Sinus and Headache Caplet contain 30 mg of pseudoephedrine hydrochloride and 500 mg of acetaminophen.[27] Table 4.1 lists the prices we observed for 24-tablet packages of these products and for their store-brand equivalents.[28] Table 4.1 illustrates two general phenomena in the pricing of this class of product. First, branded products command a substantial premium over the price of the CVS product—from around 30 to 50 percent. Second, within both the branded and nonbranded segments, the price of the combination product is much lower than the sum of the prices of the stand-alone products. The incremental cost to a consumer of the pseudoephedrine hydrochloride in the Tylenol Sinus Caplet over purchasing just Extra Strength Tylenol is $2.00, which is only 44 percent of the price of buying a package of 24 Sudafed tablets. The incremental price of the acetaminophen in the Sudafed Sinus and Headache Caplets is $1.40, which is 35 percent of the price of buying a package of 24 Extra Strength Tylenol tablets. The comparisons are even more striking with the CVS products. The incremental price of the acetaminophen in the combination product over pseudoephedrine hydrochloride tablets is

Table 4.1
Prices for 24 tablet/caplet packages

Brand	Combination	Pseudoephedrine HCI alone	Acetaminophen alone
Tylenol	$5.99	NA	$3.99
Sudafed	$5.99	$4.59	NA
CVS	$3.99	$3.49	$2.99

Note: Tylenol: "Tylenol Sinus Caplet" (the combination product) and "Tylenol Extra Strength Caplets." Sudafed: "Sudafed Sinus and Headache Caplet" (the combination product) and "Sudafed Sinus & Cold." CVS: "Non-Aspirin Sinus Caplets Maximum Strength" (the combination product), "Nasal Decongestant Tablets Maximum Strength," and "Non-Aspirin Caplets Extra Strength." NA denotes a combination that was not offered. Doses are 30 mg of pseudoephedrine hydrochloride and 500 mg of acetaminophen.
Source: Downloaded from CVS website, http://www.cvs.com, February 11, 2004.

only $0.50, or 17 percent of the price of buying acetaminophen tablets separately.[29]

There are also products that combine pseudoephedrine hydrochloride and ibuprofen. Here, the comparisons are not quite as clean because we observed package sizes of 20 rather than 24 for the combination product. Still, as we will document in section 4.4.2 below (and as is well known), the price per pill is generally a decreasing function of package size. Thus, comparing the price per pill of the bundled product with the sum of the prices per pill of the component products sold in somewhat larger packages understates the gains from bundling. We observed a price of $6.29 for a package of 20 Advil "Cold & Sinus" tablets, which is less than $0.32/tablet. To buy Advil and Maximum Strength Sudafed separately in 24-tablet packages, the sum of the prices per pill would be more than $0.49/tablet.[30] On a per-pill basis, the price of the bundled product was 64 percent of the price of the components. For the store-brand versions, the per-pill price of the bundled product was less than $0.21, which was 21 percent less than $0.27, the sum of the per-pill prices of the two separate products.[31]

The strong stylized fact that emerges from this set of comparisons is that the prices consumers pay for combinations of medicines—both branded and store-brand—are substantially less than the prices they would pay to buy the same active ingredients as separate medicines. Of course, consumers who want all the components of the combination medicines likely get convenience as well as the lower price.

4.4.1.2 Pricing of Different Dosages The phenomenon of lower prices for combining the same active ingredient into fewer pills and distinct packages that we observed with combination drugs applies to different doses of the same medicine.

4.4.1.2.1 Pain Relievers Tylenol comes in three dosage forms for adults:[32] Regular Strength (325 mg/tablet), Extra Strength (500 mg/tablet), and Arthritis Strength (650 mg/tablet). In a sense, each Arthritis Strength tablet is a bundle of two Regular Strength tablets. As a result, buying two packages of, say, 100 Regular Strength Tylenol rather than one package of 100 Extra Strength Tylenol is analogous to buying Tylenol and Sudafed separately rather than in "sinus-tablet" form.

Table 4.2 presents prices we observed that reveal the economies of combining products as well as the general pricing structure for Tylenol. First, note that in the two cases in which the number of tablets is held

Table 4.2
Prices for different Tylenol dosages

Number	Regular Strength (325 mg)	Extra Strength (500 mg)	Arthritis Strength (650 mg)
50		$7.19	$7.39
60		$7.89	
100	$9.39	$9.99	$10.99
150		$14.29	

Source: Prices observed at Walgreens at 757 N. Michigan Ave. in Chicago on April 3, 2003.

constant (50 and 100), the incremental price of the higher levels of extra ingredients is small. At the 50-tablet size, the Arthritis Strength contains 30 percent more active ingredient for an incremental price of only $0.20, or 2.8 percent. At the 100-tablet size, the Arthritis Strength price is 10 percent higher than the Extra Strength price. In turn, Extra Strength contains approximately 50 percent more active ingredient than Regular Strength for an incremental price of $0.60, or 6.4 percent. The comparison that most corresponds to the bundling comparison in the previous section is between purchasing one package of 100 Arthritis Strength tablets and two packages of 100 Regular Strength Tablets. The amount of active ingredient is the same, but buying two packages of Regular Strength entails two packages rather than one and twice as many tablets. As table 4.2 indicates, the price of the one Arthritis Strength package is $10.99, while the price of two Regular Strength packages is $18.78.[33]

Table 4.3 shows similar data for Walgreens' acetaminophen. Here, the evidence is more mixed. The clean comparison that is comparable to the cold medicines is the 100-tablet size. The total price of two packages of Regular Strength acetaminophen is $9.98, which is about 25 percent more than the $7.99 price of a single package of Arthritis Strength. However, it is not universally true that the per-milligram price of the Arthritis Strength is lower than the per-milligram price of the others.[34]

4.4.1.2.2 Decongestants Pseudoephedrine hydrochloride comes in three dosage forms. "Maximum Strength" contains 30 mg per tablet. The "12-hour version" contains 120 mg per tablet and the "24-hour version" contains 240 mg per tablet. Table 4.4 lists the prices that we observed for different package sizes and dosage forms of Sudafed, Contac (another brand of pseudoephedrine hydrochloride), and

Table 4.3
Prices for different Walgreens acetaminophen dosages and package sizes

Quantity	Regular Strength (325 mg)	Extra Strength (500 mg)	Arthritis Strength (650 mg)
24		$2.99	$3.99
50			$5.49
60		$3.99	
100	$4.99	$5.99	$7.99
175		$7.99	
250		$8.99	$13.99
500		$11.99	

Source: Prices observed at Walgreens at 757 N. Michigan Ave. in Chicago on April 3, 2003.

Table 4.4
Prices for different brands, dosages, and package sizes of pseudoephedrine hydrochloride

Number of tablets	30 mg/tablet Sudafed	Walgreens	120 mg/tablet Contac	Sudafed	Walgreens	240 mg/tablet Sudfed
5						$5.99
10			$6.79	$6.49	$3.99	$9.99
20			$9.49	$10.49	$6.49	
24	$6.79	$3.49				
48	$9.49	$5.99				
96		$14.99				

Source: Prices observed at Walgreens at 757 N. Michigan Ave. in Chicago on April 3, 2003.

Walgreens pseudoephedrine hydrochloride. Table 4.4 provides one clean comparison that is analogous to the bundling analysis above. The price of one package of ten 24-hour Sudafed tablets is $9.99, whereas the sum of the prices of two packages of ten 12-hour Sudafed tablets is $12.98. Note further that the price of five 24-hour Sudafed tablets is somewhat less than the price of ten 12-hour tablets and that the price of ten 24-hour Sudafed tablets is somewhat less than the price of twenty 12-hour tablets. The differences are not large. However, the obvious source of cost savings from the 24-hour version concerns placing the medicine into tablets. Since the absolute difference in the number of tablets is small, one would not expect large cost differences.[35]

4.4.1.3 Package Size Effects The third empirical regularity we document concerns package size, which is another form of bundling. A package of 200 tablets is a bundle of two packages of 100 tablets. In addition to providing evidence of another source of gains from bundling, evidence on the prices of different package sizes will yield insights into the fixed costs of product offerings.

Pain-relief medications provide better evidence about package-size effects than do decongestants or antihistamines because they come in a broader range of package sizes. Figure 4.1 presents the data on Extra Strength acetaminophen and Figure 4.2 presents the data on ibuprofen. Each graph contains two series, one for branded versions and one for the Walgreens product. All four of the series are concave and would appear to have a positive intercept.

4.4.2 Regression Results

With the above results in hand, we now seek to estimate a single regression equation to characterize the gains consumers realize from purchasing bundled products. The data set we collected had 305 observations. However, these included a variety of dosage forms, such as tablets, liquids, and liqui-gels. To avoid any misspecification from how we treat dosage forms, we restricted attention to tablets or delivery forms typically priced the same as tablets.[36] This eliminated a large

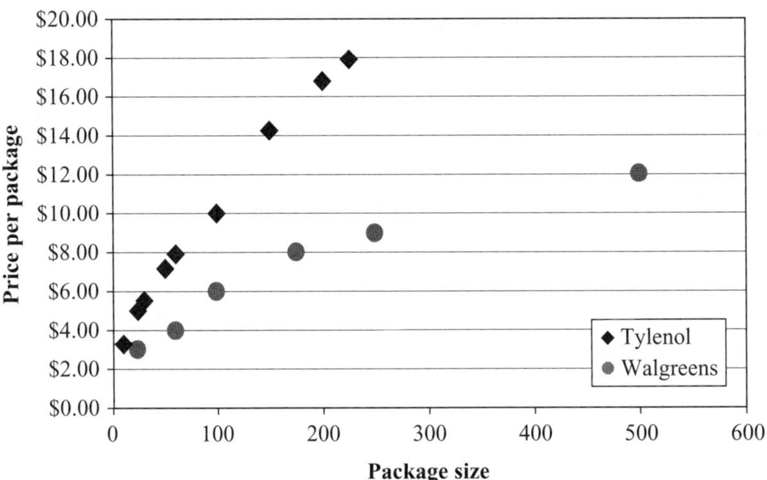

Figure 4.1
Extra Strength acetaminophen prices

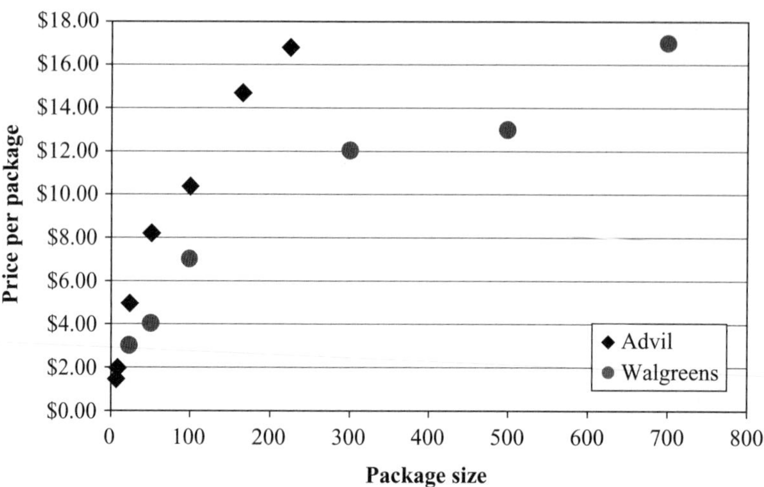

Figure 4.2
Extra Strength acetaminophen prices

fraction of the medicines containing cough suppressants. Also, the variety of active ingredients to treat coughs is substantially greater than the variety of decongestants, antihistamines, and pain relievers; we were concerned that we would be unable to get reliable estimates of how each cough suppressant is priced. As a result, we excluded cough medicines. More precisely, we restricted attention to tablets in which the active ingredients were limited to the pain relievers acetaminophen and ibuprofen, the decongestant pseudoephedrine hydrochloride, and the antihistamines chlorpheniramine maleate and diphenhydramine HCl.[37] This left us with 112 observations.

To capture brand effects and the nonlinearities in package size documented above, we chose the following specification:

$$P_i = b_0 + b_1 B_i + b_2 T_i + b_3 T_i^2 + b_4 T_i B_i + b_5 T_i^2 B_i + \sum_{j=1}^{N} c_j Z_{ij} \tag{1}$$

where:

P_i is the price of package i

T_i is the number of tablets in package i

B_i is a brand-name dummy for package i

Z_{ij} is the amount of ingredient j in package i

The presence of a brand premium raises issues about the effect of bundling in this case.[38] To see the general issue, consider table 4.1. For the branded products, the bundle discount is computed as the price of Tylenol Sinus (or Sudafed Sinus Headache) with the sum of the prices of Tylenol Extra Strength and Sudafed Maximum Strength. Both of the prices of the component products include a brand premium.[39] Unless the price of the bundled product includes a double brand premium, part of the bundle discount reflects a brand-premium effect.[40]

Our specification allows the brand premium to be a quadratic function of the number of tablets. While this functional form allows for some flexibility in estimating how companies impose a brand premium, it does not allow the brand premium to be a function of the number of active ingredients. Neither does it allow for the brand premium to depend on the volume of active ingredient per tablet.[41] We ran regressions in which the brand premium could depend on the number of active ingredients. They provided no evidence that bundled, branded products command a higher (absolute) premium than do unbundled ones.[42]

Our estimated equation is

$$\begin{aligned} R_i = {} & 2.31 + 0.029T_i - 3.3\times10^{-5}T_i^2 + 0.63B_i + 0.054T_iB_i - 1.23\times10^{-4}T_i^2B_i \\ & (7.25)^{*}\ (1.89) \quad (4.12)^{*} \qquad (1.47) \quad (5.15)^{*} \qquad (2.85)^{*} \\ & + 0.014IB_i + 0.012AC_i + 0.065PH_i + 0.035CM_i + 0.042DI_i \\ & (0.95) \qquad (0.85) \qquad (5.13)^{*} \qquad (1.90) \qquad (2.90)^{*} \\ & s = 1.24,\ R^2 = 0.91,\ F = 132.31^{*},\ N = 112 \end{aligned} \tag{2}$$

(Note: Values in parentheses are absolute values of asymptotic t-statistics based on heteroskedasticity-consistent standard errors. An asterisk (*) denotes significance at 1 percent (two-tailed) level.)

where:

IB_i = ibuprofen in package i in units of 200 mg

AC_i = acetaminophen in package i in units of 500 mg

PH_i = pseudoephedrine hydrochloride in package i in units of 30 mg

CM_i = chlorpheneramine maleate in package i in units of 2 mg

DI_i = diphenhydramine in package i in units of 25 mg

The coefficients on the active ingredients are all positive, although only the ones on the pseudoephedrine HCL and diphenhydramine variables are significant. The coefficients on the amount of acetaminophen and ibuprofen are small and imprecisely determined. That they are small makes sense. The price of both bulk acetaminophen and bulk ibuprofen is approximately \$8/kg,[43] which would contribute \$0.004 per 500 mg acetaminophen tablet and \$0.0016 per 200 mg ibuprofen tablet.

These regressions reveal three primary sources of gains to consumers from buying bundled products. The first is the intercept term of \$2.31, which is highly statistically significant. The purchaser of the bundled product pays one fixed component in the price term. Purchasers of the two separate products would pay two. The second source of gains is associated with the number of tablets. It is $0.029\ T_i - 3.3 \times 10^{-5}\ T_i^2$. Again, purchasers of the bundled product pay this component once. Purchasers of two separate products would pay it twice. This component of the savings comes to \$0.67 for 24-tablet packages and \$1.29 for 48-tablet packages. Thus, the cost-based savings without brand effects is \$2.98 for 24-tablet packages and \$3.60 for 48-tablet packages. The third source of gains applies only to purchasers of branded products. It is given by $0.63 + 0.54\ T_i - 0.00012\ T_i^2$. It amounts to \$1.84 and \$2.92 for 24-tablet and 48-tablet packages, respectively.[44]

4.5 Modeling the Bundle Discount

This case was selected because it has features that our model is designed to capture. The different medications can be (and are) sold both separately and in combination. The assumption of diverse consumer preferences seems applicable. To use the example in table 4.1, some people have a headache and want just acetaminophen. Some people have a cold and want just a decongestant. Some have a sinus headache and want both.[45] Because of savings in packaging, making tablets, and transactions expense, the marginal cost of the bundled product is less than the sum of the marginal costs of the unbundled items. Given that mixed bundling prevails,[46] fixed costs seem not to be so large as to prevent a good that people want from being offered. Yet, some fixed cost is present. Each additional stock-keeping unit (sku) imposes a cost on a retailer because it must order the product, maintain inventories, and so on. In addition, each distinct product sold by a retailer must occupy a shelf slot. The cost of these slots is an example of what accountants refer to as "semifixed" or "step" costs. They are not fixed with respect to all levels of output, but they are incurred in discrete units (or "steps"). Whether such costs should be deemed primarily fixed or primarily marginal depends on the size of the steps relative to total demand. We do not have the information one would need to determine whether shelf space should be considered a fixed or marginal expense, but it is at least plausible that it is more nearly fixed.[47]

The substantial brand premiums in the model might cast doubt on the applicability of the contestability assumption. We have two responses. First, our econometric specification allows us to estimate the size of the brand premium and thereby remove it from our estimate of costs. Second, even if, say, Tylenol is a dominant brand in acetaminophen, a monopoly model may not be the best for understanding its pricing behavior. Like any modeling assumption, the contestability assumption is meant as an approximation, not literal truth. The implication of the assumption is that prices are driven primarily by costs with the elasticity of demand playing a less important role. The rationale for the assumption is that the firm faces enough competitive constraints from both actual competition (other pain relievers like ibuprofen and generic acetaminophen) and potential competition (other pharmaceutical companies that are plainly capable of producing the product) to place strict limits on the extent to which prices can exceed costs.

The choice between a competitive model and a monopoly model is particularly crucial because the result we are most interested in explaining is the bundle discount. We interpret the bundle discount as reflecting costs. The models of bundling as price discrimination might seem to suggest an alternative, demand-based explanation. In comparing the competing explanations, one must be clear on what the model must explain. The key stylized fact we have established is not just that there is a bundle discount, but that it is so large. A cost-based model provides a simple explanation. Since the active ingredients represent a small portion of the cost of the product, the cost of producing and selling a package of tablets with, say, acetaminophen and pseudophedrine hydrochloride is only slightly greater than the cost of producing and selling a package of tablets with acetaminophen alone. Because the bundled products likely provide convenience, we question whether a monopoly price-discrimination model would imply a bundle discount (as opposed to a premium) at all, much less one as steep as the one we observe.

In any event, our primary purpose here is not to assert that the model is a complete explanation but, rather, to advance the techniques for assessing whether the set of product offerings is optimal. Even assuming that the bundle discount is cost-based, its welfare implications are more complicated than one might initially expect. To see this point, we need to present the model more formally.

In the simplest version,[48] let X_1 be the number of people who want just good 1, X_2 be the people who want just good 2, and X_B be the number of people who want both. Let F be the fixed cost of a product offering, c_1 and c_2 be the marginal cost of goods 1 and 2, respectively, and c_B be the marginal cost of the bundle with $c_B \leq c_1 + c_2$. Letting p_1, p_2, and p_B be the prices of goods 1 and 2 and of the bundle, then the contestable prices are

$$p_i = c_i + \frac{F}{X_i} \qquad i \in \{1,2,B\} \tag{3}$$

and the discount for the bundle (DB) is given by

$$DB \equiv p_1 + p_2 - p_B = c_1 + c_2 - c_B + \frac{F}{X_1} + \frac{F}{X_2} - \frac{F}{X_B} \tag{4}$$

As equation (4) makes clear, there are two possible sources of the bundle discount. One is marginal cost savings, $c_1 + c_2 - c_B$. The other concerns fixed costs. A customer who buys the two components separately contributes to two fixed costs; the purchaser of the bundled product only contributes to one.

Without knowing X_1, X_2, and X_B, we cannot be sure that the bundle discount is attributable at all to fixed costs. As a practical matter, however, it likely is. To cover its costs, a retailer must "mark up" the prices of the items it sells. Unless the retail markup on the bundled item is at least the sum of its markups on the components—and there is no reason to suppose that it is—then part of the customer savings reflects retail markups.

A key result in Evans and Salinger 2004 is that mixed bundling can occur even if it is not the set of offerings that minimizes total costs. Under mixed bundling, there has to be a bundle discount,[49] but the private savings from the bundle discount do not necessarily represent social savings. If we let SB be the cost savings from offering the bundle[50] (stated on a per-customer basis to aid comparability with the bundle discount), then

$$SB = c_1 + c_2 - c_B - \frac{F}{X_B} = DB - \frac{F}{X_1} - \frac{F}{X_2} \tag{5}$$

The first three terms of (5), which reflect marginal costs, are identical to (4). With the marginal costs, private savings reflect social savings. The last term of (5) is also the last term of (4). There is a social fixed cost of offering the bundle that must be subtracted from the marginal cost savings. In a contestable market, purchasers of the bundle bear this cost as well. The difference between (4) and (5) comes from the two terms in (4) that reflect the average fixed costs of the two component goods. If those who want both components were to buy them separately, the prices they would pay would reflect these fixed costs. When they buy the bundle instead, they get a private benefit from not contributing to those fixed costs, but there is no corresponding social benefit because the fixed costs of the components are not reduced.

The last part of equation (5) provides a simple approach to inferring the cost savings from the bundle (under mixed bundling) from the bundle discount. It says that the cost savings (per consumer of the bundle) are the bundle discount minus the average fixed cost portion of the prices of the two separate goods.

The following pair of examples illustrates the point:

Example 1: $c_1 = c_2 = 2$, $c_B = 2.9$, $F = 0$, $X_1 = X_2 = X_B = 100$
Example 2: $c_1 = c_2 = 1$, $c_B = 1.9$, $F = 100$, $X_1 = X_2 = X_B = 100$

In both cases, the unique sustainable outcome is mixed bundling with $p_1 = p_2 = 2$ and $p_B = 2.9$.[51] The bundle discount is substantial. In example 1, the bundle discount entirely reflects social savings. The total cost of meeting demand with mixed bundling is 690. The cost of meeting demand with components selling would be 800, or 110 more. In example 2, the total cost of meeting demand with mixed bundling is also 690, just as in example 1. In contrast to example 1, however, the total cost of meeting demand with components selling would be only 600.[52] Unless the bundled product provides convenience for the customers who want both items, the mixed bundling would be inefficient despite the substantial bundle discount.

A similar point applies to the individual components. Under mixed bundling, the price of each component has to be less than the price of the bundle,[53] but that does not imply that offering the separate good lowers costs. If we let DC_i and SC_i be the discount and cost savings (per customer of good i) of offering good i (given that the bundle is offered), we have

$$DC_i = p_B - p_i = c_B - c_i + \frac{F}{X_B} - \frac{F}{X_i} \tag{6}$$

$$SC_i = c_B - c_i - \frac{F}{X_i} = DC_i - \frac{F}{X_B} \tag{7}$$

Equation (7) says that to infer the cost savings from having a component available separately, one must subtract the average fixed-cost component of the price of the bundled good from the component discount.

Referring back to our pricing regression, the bundle discount has three components: the intercept, the coefficients on the tablet variables, and the coefficients on the brand-name variables. As noted above, we focus on the first two. The estimated equation distinguishes between price components that are fixed and variable with respect to package size. Within our model, however, the key distinction is whether the costs are fixed or marginal with respect to a customer. The cost of placing active ingredients into tablets and, to some extent, the cost of the package itself, are examples of costs that are marginal with respect both to package size and to the customer. To the extent that package costs rise less than proportionately with the number of tablets, however, then part of packaging cost would be reflected in our intercept term. Even though this component is fixed with respect to package size, it is variable with respect to the customer.[54] Another example of this kind of cost is the cost of the time it takes a clerk to process a transaction. Finally, some costs are fixed both with respect to the customer and to the size of the package. The costs of having an additional sku and, to a large extent, the cost of shelf space are examples.[55]

4.6 Decomposing Fixed and Marginal Cost Effects with Package-Size Pricing Regularities

We now show how to use the package-size regularities documented in section 4.4 to decompose the bundle and component discounts into marginal-cost and fixed-cost components. This decomposition will then allow us to measure the (possibly negative) cost savings (per customer) from each product.

Our interpretation of quantity discounts as being cost-based raises issues similar to whether the bundle discount reflects costs or price discrimination. The theory of quantity-dependent monopoly pricing would seem to provide an alternative explanation. As with the bundle discount, there are several responses. First, costs provide a compelling explanation. The pills themselves represent a relatively small fraction of the cost. Packaging costs appear to be significant and subject to scale economies. Many aspects of the transaction cost would seem to be independent of the size of the package. Second, all the products come in a relatively small number of package sizes, which is the phenomenon that we exploit. Even in a monopoly model, it would be hard to explain that without reference to some fixed cost of a product offering. Third, consider pseudoephedrine hydrochloride, which generally comes in packages of 24 and 48. It seems hard to rule out the possibility that some people would like to buy 72. Theories of nonlinear pricing would generally predict that they should be given a lower price per tablet than the people who wish to purchase 48. Whether they bought one package of 48 and one of 24 or two packages of 48, their price per pill that they want would be higher than for people who wish to purchase 48 tablets.

4.6.1 Theory

The key to understanding the size of the the product-specific fixed costs is to observe products that could conceivably exist but do not.[56] In the cases we have considered, product tying does not occur. Among the products sold in bundled form that we have considered, all the component medicines are available separately. Rather than looking to products that do not exist, we look to package sizes that are not offered. The price-package size relationships presented in figures 4.1 and 4.2 provide evidence of economies of package size. As a consequence, customers who want a large quantity are better off buying one large package than several smaller ones. However, not all possible package sizes are offered. For example, the Walgreens in question sold Extra Strength Tylenol in packages of 24, 100, 150, 200, and 225. It did not, however, sell packages of 175. There does not seem to be any reason to suppose that there were no customers who would most prefer to buy 175. Such a customer must choose between buying a package of 200 and wasting 25 of them or buying a package of 150 and supplementing the package of 150 with, say, another package of 24.[57] Given the economies of package size, neither of these solutions would give the customer as good a price as he or she would get if a package of 175 were available on the market.

To estimate the cost factor that prevents the package of 175 from being sold, we need to introduce some theory that extends the contestability analysis from our previous paper. The general approach is to view the set of products offered and their prices as a sustainable market outcome, which means that entry with another product (in this case, a different package size) is not profitable. Let Q_i, Y_i, and P_i be the package size, number of purchasers, and price of package i for $i = 1$ or 2 with $Q_1 < Q_2$. Let C(.) be the marginal cost of selling a package of a particular size to an extra customer. Then, the contestability result that price equals average cost implies

$$P(Q_i) = \frac{F}{Y_i} + C(Q_i) \tag{8}$$

Let $\overline{Q}$ be the average of Q_1 and Q_2, and assume that if $\overline{Q}$ were offered at a lower price, half the people who buy Q_2 would buy $\overline{Q}$ instead. The price at which it could be offered would be

$$P(\overline{Q}) = \frac{2F}{Y_2} + C(\overline{Q}) \tag{9}$$

We now need to make the simplifying assumptions that Q_1 and Q_2 are close enough to each other that a linear approximation of the marginal cost function is reasonable and that $Y_1 = Y_2$. With these additional assumptions, it is straightforward to show that the condition that makes it impossible to offer the package size halfway between Q_1 and Q_2 is[58]

$$\frac{F}{Y_2} > \frac{P_2 - P_1}{2} \tag{10}$$

4.6.2 Results

The left-hand side of (10) is the component of the price that goes to covering the fixed cost. Each successive pair of package sizes yields an estimate. Figure 4.3 shows a histogram of our estimates of the lower bounds of the fixed costs taken from the data underlying figures 4.1 and 4.2. The mean value is $1.33, the median is $1.20, and the modal range is $1.00 to $1.50. Taking the median as our estimate, we estimate that $1.20 of each package price represents a contribution to fixed costs.

In section 4.4, we estimated a cost-based savings[59] of $2.98 and $3.60 for 24-count and 48-count packages of tablets with two active ingredients. Given our estimate of $1.20 as the part that reflects a contribution to fixed costs, the implied marginal cost savings are $1.78 and

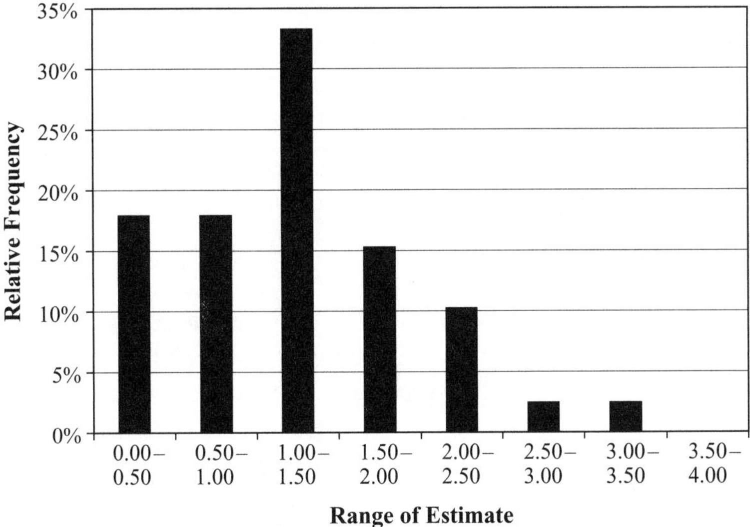

Figure 4.3
Estimated lower bounds of offering average fixed costs

$2.40. Using equation (5), we estimate that the cost savings per customer from the bundled products are $0.58 and $1.20, respectively.

Both the private and net savings would be larger for tablets that combine three active ingredients. The private savings are twice as large, so they are $5.96, which reflects $3.56 in marginal cost savings and $2.40 in average fixed cost. From the marginal cost savings of $3.56, which represents a social benefit, we must subtract the $1.20 average fixed cost of the additional offering. The net cost savings are $2.36.

The gains from bundling would also be larger for larger packages. For example, for packages of 48 tablets, our regression equation implies private gains of $3.60 and $7.20 for tablets that combine two ingredients and three ingredients, respectively. The net effect on costs would then be savings of $1.20 and $3.60 for the bundled products.[60]

We can also use equation (8) to estimate whether there are cost savings from offering the stand-alone products. Consider again the example in table 4.1. The regression results indicate that for people who want just acetaminophen, the marginal cost of buying acetaminophen bundled with pseudoephedrine hydrochloride would be $\$0.065 \cdot 24 = \$1.56$. Because this exceeds our estimate of the average fixed cost of $1.20, we estimate the cost savings from having the stand-alone acetaminophen product to be $0.36. For consumers who want just pseudoephedrine hydrochloride, the regression results imply that the marginal cost of buying it bundled with acetaminophen would be $\$0.012 \cdot 24 = \$0.29$. Because this incremental cost is less than the average fixed cost, it would lower costs not to offer the 24-tablet package of just pseudoephedrine hydrochloride. In other words, tying would lower costs.[61]

4.7 Conclusions

Any economist who looks at the state of debate on the anticompetitive use of tying should find it quite unsettling. On the one hand, there is an economics literature that assumes away all efficiencies and documents, unsurprisingly in light of modern game theory, that it is possible to locate assumptions under which tying is anticompetitive. We have no doubt that firms can sometimes engage in tying that reduces consumer welfare, but the economics literature is not much help in identifying these situations. On the other hand, there is a case law that places much of the weight of the tying analysis on whether a product is a single product or a tie of two separate products. The *Jefferson Parish* test seems to suggest that one mainly needs to look at whether there is material demand for the tied product. The D.C. Circuit Court of Appeals provided an elegant (although only weakly supportive) rationale for this test: it is supposed to be a proxy for whether the "tie" is efficient or not; if there is no demand, then the markets have revealed that a single product consisting of the tying and tied goods is efficient. Little thought is required to come up with countless examples that demonstrate that this is not a powerful test (i.e., it leads to many errors). Competitive markets provide shoes with shoelaces, cars with tires, men's suits with tailoring, newspapers with television listings, and so forth.

Economists might criticize the courts for sloppy analysis, but one looks at the economics literature in vain to see our profession providing the antitrust authorities or courts with much useful guidance. There is a vast gulf between the Chicago school view that "there's a single monopoly profit so it must be efficient" to the game-theoretic view that "without efficiencies it could be anticompetitive." In between, there is essentially no empirical evidence that would explain what product configurations emerge in reasonably competitive markets. And one sees this divide in the court cases in which defendants offer explanations for tying that are based on little empirical analysis, or theoretical reasoning, and that courts and antitrust authorities quickly dismiss as being gratuitous (see our earlier discussion of *Jefferson Parish*).

Our contribution in this chapter and our companion articles is twofold. First, we have provided a theoretical framework that, while admittedly being based on assumptions that one can question and that future work should modify, can be empirically implemented. Second, and this is the specific purpose of this chapter, we have shown how it is possible to estimate the key primitives of the model at least for the example we have chosen, namely, the extent of offering-specific fixed and variable costs of a product. Both the framework and the empirical results highlight the importance of the fixed cost of offering particular product configurations in "pretty competitive" markets. Costs play a more central role in this analysis than in the existing literature.

Of course, this trilogy of investigations provides only a first step. On the theoretical side, alternatives to the contestability assumption need to be explored, and it would be useful to embed the analysis in a model in which the degree of market power could vary. On the empirical side, we see two priorities. One is to improve the estimates of the fixed costs of product offerings.[62] The other is to estimate the convenience value from bundling and unbundling.[63] Neither will be easy. But given that the theory identifies these factors as being key to both the private decision to bundle and tie and to the welfare analysis of these practices, some effort to overcome the challenges is warranted.

The general approach we have applied to tying could be usefully applied to other business practices that are sometimes questioned as being anticompetitive. That approach involves developing a positive theory for why certain practices emerge in "pretty competitive" environments and ascertaining the extent to which efficiency helps explain those practices. The theory is designed to encourage empirical investigation.

At this stage of development this approach is subject to the same criticism as the game-theoretic work on tying. Just as that approach assumes efficiency away, our approach assumes anticompetitive explanations away. Over time, industrial-organization economists need to develop theories that can account for both pro-competitive and anticompetitive explanations and that can be tested empirically.

Notes

Evans is Managing Director, Global Competition Policy, LECG, LLC, and Visiting Professor, Faculty of Laws, University College London; Salinger is Director of the Bureau of Economics at the Federal Trade Commission while on leave from his position as an economics professor at the Boston University School of Management. The authors thank Irina Danilkina, Chris Nosko, Sannu Shrestha, and Ori Stitelman for exceptional research support, and Tim Bresnahan, Howard Chang, Georg Getz, Anne Layne-Farrar, Nick Nichols, Bernard Reddy, and Richard Schmalensee for comments and suggestions. Microsoft Corporation provided research funding, for which the authors are grateful. The authors submitted this paper for publication prior to Salinger's appointment at the FTC. The opinions expressed are those of the authors alone and we retain responsibility for all errors. They do not necessarily reflect the views of the Federal Trade Commission, any individual Commissioner, or any other organization.

1. A bundled product is one that combines more than one product that could be sold separately.

2. *U.S. v. Microsoft and New York, et al. v. Microsoft*, Civil Action Nos. 98–1232 and 98–1233 (TPJ), July 17, 1998; *In re Visa Check/MasterMoney Antitrust Litig.*, No. 96-CV-5238, 2003 U.S. Dist. LEXIS 4965, at 6 (E.D.N.Y. Apr. 1, 2003); Commission Decision of 24.03.2004 (Case COMP/C-3/37.792—Microsoft), available at http://europa.eu.int/comm/competition/antitrust/cases/decisions/37792/en.pdf. Apple is facing a host of antitrust lawsuits in Europe and the United States over its alleged tying of iPod and the iTunes music store. In November 2004, Conseil de la Concurrence, the French competition authority, dismissed a suit brought by Virgin against Apple asking the French government to compel Apple to license Fairplay, its DRM technology. See Apple Conseil de la Concurrence, Décision n° 04-D-54 relative à des pratiques mises en oeuvre par la société Apple Computer, Inc. dans les secteurs du téléchargement de musique sur Internet et des baladeurs numériques, November 9, 2004. In 2005, a French consumer group launched another lawsuit against Apple and Sony's proprietary music formats, claiming that the respective digital rights management used by both companies, which prevents songs bought from their online music stores from being played on other manufacturers' media players, is limiting consumers' choice. See Jo Best, "Apple, Sony Sued over DRM in France," *Silicon.com*, February 14, 2005, http://news.zdnet.com/2100-9588_22-5575417.html. Apple is also facing a similar antitrust lawsuit in the United States. See Peter Cohen, "iTunes User Sues Apple over FairPlay DRM," *MacCentral*, January 26, 2005, http://www.macworld.com/news/2005/01/06/slattery/index.php. Also see *Kinetic Concepts, Inc. v. Hillenbrand Indus.*, 262 F. Supp. 2d 722 (W.D. Tex. 2003).

3. See section 4.3.

4. The percentage difference would vary with the active ingredients but would generally be between 30 and 50 percent.

5. See Areeda and Hovenkamp 2000.

6. See Kallaugher and Sher 2004; Kamann and Bergmann 2005.

7. See Evans and Padilla, 2005.

8. Case C-53/92P, *Hilti AG v. Commission* [1994] ECRI-667; Case T-5/02, *Tetra Laval v. Commission*, 2002 E.C.R. II-4382.

9. Director and Levi 1956. Also see Tirole 1988.

10. *Jefferson Parish Hosp. Dist. No. 2 v. Hyde*, 104 S. Ct. 1551 (1984).

11. *Compuware Corp. v. IBM*, 259 F. Supp. 2d 597 (E.D. Mich., 2003).

12. Commission Decision of 24.03.2004 (Case COMP/C-3/37.792—Microsoft), at ¶¶ 792–993.

13. Id., at ¶¶ 1011–1023.

14. *U.S. v. Microsoft and New York, et al. v. Microsoft*, Civil Action Nos. 98–1232 and 98–1233 (TPJ), July 17, 1998.

15. *U.S. v. Microsoft*, 253 F.3d 34 (D.C. Cir. 2001), at 158.

16. The appeals court in another part of the decision found that the government had failed to prove the existence of a browser market and precluded it from retrying that portion of the case. That made it especially difficult for the Justice Department to proceed under a rule-of-reason analysis since it needed to demonstrate harm in the browser market.

17. *In re Visa Check/MasterMoney Antitrust Litig.*, No. 96-CV-5238, 2003 U.S. Dist. LEXIS 4965, at 6 (E.D.N.Y. Apr. 1, 2003); Jennifer Bayot, "Final Pact Approved in Long-Running Debit Card Litigation," *New York Times*, December 20, 2003, section C, page 4.

18. Merchant class-action suit against American Express, Citigroup, and MBNA (New York, 2003); "Stop Me if You've Heard This One: Merchants Sue Card Company," *The Green Sheet, Inc.*, February 01, 2005, http://www.greensheet.com/PriorIssues-/050201-/7.htm.

19. These included buying different types of tires (Case T-203/01, Manufacture française des pneumatiques Michelin v. Commision, September 30, 2003) and providing discounts to travel agents who used a particular airline (Case T-219/99, British Airways plc v. Commission, December 7, 2003). Coca Cola settled a related case with the European Commission by agreeing to eliminate various bundled discounts (Commission Decision of 10/19/2004 (CASE COMP/39.116/B-2—COCA-COLA)).

20. See Rubinfeld 2005.

21. See Hylton and Salinger 2001.

22. See Grimes 2002; Hylton and Salinger 2001.

23. We use the term *cold* to include medications labeled as sinus, allergy, and cough as well.

24. Walgreens is the largest pharmacy chain in the United States. It has a 20 percent share of retail pharmaceutical sales. CVS is the second-largest pharmacy chain with a 16 percent share. Source: "CVS Is Good Medicine for Investors," *Dow Jones News Service*, February 25, 2004.

25. Dosage forms include tablets, caplets, liquid, "gel tabs," and so on.

26. The website www.cvs.com is a vehicle for ordering pharmaceuticals (and other products) to be delivered by mail. The website is operated by CVS, which also operates a large chain of retail pharmacies.

27. Novartis also offers a product that contains 500 mg of acetaminophen and 30 mg of pseudoephedrine hydrochloride, Tavist Allery/Sinus/Headache.

28. These data are taken from www.cvs.com rather than from our Walgreens data set. To isolate the bundle discount, we need to hold package size constant. To do so, we need all six of the products in table 4.1 (just acetaminophen, just pseudophedrine, and the combination tablet in branded and generic form) available in a common package size. Our Walgreens data set did not generate such a comparison, but the data we obained from the CVS website did.

29. In our Walgreens data set, the comparable prices were $6.99 for 24 Tylenol Sinus tablets, $4.99 for 24 Extra Tylenol tablets, and $6.79 for 24 Sudafed tablets. Thus, the price of the branded combination product was only $0.20 higher than the stand-alone Sudafed product. For the Walgreens brands, the prices were $2.99 for 24 tablets of Extra Strength acetaminophen and $3.49 for 24 Maximum Strength pseudoephedrine hydrochloride tablets. While we did not observe a Walgreens version that combined just these two active ingredients, we did observe a package of 24 tablets with these two ingredients and 25 mg of the antihistimine, Diphenhydramine HCl. The price was $3.99.

30. The price we observed for 24 Advil tablets was $4.99. As reported in note 29, we observed a price of $6.79 at Walgreens for a package of 24 Sudafed tablets.

31. The Walgreens products are WalProfem tablets (ibuprofen), WalPhed (pseudoephedrine hydrochloride), and WalProfem Cold & Sinus. The prices we observed were $4.29 for 20 WalProfem Cold & Sinus tablets, $2.99 for 24 WalProfem tablets, and $3.49 for 24 WalPhed tablets.

32. It also comes in junior and children's doses.

33. Note further that a package of 60 Extra Strength Tylenol has about the same active ingredient as 100 Regular Strength and costs $1.50 less.

34. All but one of the prices in table 4.3 are $0.01 less than an even dollar, with the other being $0.01 less than an integral multiple of $0.50. This feature of the pricing could be part of the explanation for why the price of Arthritis Strength does not show evidence of bundling efficiencies. For example, a price of $3.49 for the package of 24 might not be sufficient to cover the incremental cost. Also, as we will discuss further below, if demand for this package size of Arthritis Strength is sufficiently low, then a higher margin might be needed to cover the fixed cost of the shelf space.

35. Note that one odd feature of the table is that the price of 96 Walgreens Maximum Strength tablets is more than double the price of a package with half the number of tablets. That price is the exception, however. In general, the price per tablet is lower for larger package sizes.

36. This filter excluded any medicines in liquid or packet form as well as "liqui-gels," which typically sell for a premium. It includes caplets.

37. Thus, we excluded medicines with cough suppressants. The products we observed contained a much greater variety of cough suppressants than of the other types of ingredients, and we were concerned that we did not have sufficient data to estimate with much accuracy the price effects of each cough suppressant.

38. A log specification might seem superior for handling the brand premium. There are two reasons, though, why a log specification is inappropriate for this application. First, interpreting the intercept term as reflecting costs (in a way that will be made precise in the next section) requires a linear specification. Second, the separate ingredients presumably affect costs additively. A log specification would presume that they do so multiplicatively.

39. The fact that Tylenol is a Johnson & Johnson brand while Sudafed is a Pfizer brand is of interest, but a similar issue would arise if the same company owned both.

40. As we will see, the brand effect accounts for a substantial piece of the bundle discount in this case. Exactly how to interpret this effect would require a better understanding of the source of brand premiums than one can currently get from the economics literature. The branding effect could easily be the subject of an entire other chapter. In this chapter, we merely document the effect and leave its explanation as a potential avenue for future research.

41. If, for example, one compares the three different strengths of Tylenol described above, it would be of interest to estimate whether the brand premium depends on the number of tablets or on the amount of acetaminophen.

42. We believe that the branding effect of bundling is potentially of great interest in understanding branding, but we do not pursue it in more detail here because we suspect that it is not a common effect of bundling.

43. See http://www.the-innovation-group.com/ChemProfiles/Acetaminophen.htm and www.tulika.com/exportprices.htm.

44. These estimates are for the savings from buying a bundled medicine with two active ingredients as compared with buying the components separately. The effect would be twice as large for products with three active ingredients as compared with buying all three separately.

45. The model assumes that consumers who want just one component are willing to buy it as part of the bundle. In economics terminology, we assume free disposal. That plainly does not apply to this case. Many people with just a headache would no doubt prefer just a pain reliever to a pain reliever–plus–decongestant combination.

46. This comment requires some qualification. To take one example, Johnson & Johnson sells acetaminophen alone and acetaminophen in combination with pseudoephedrine HCl. It does not sell pseudoephedrine HCl alone. While this is technically tying from the standpoint of the company, the market outcome does not entail tying. One can purchase pseudoephedrine HCl. Moreover, because Johnson & Johnson does sell Tylenol without any additional active ingredients, its tying is not the sort that could raise antitrust concerns.

47. One relevant piece of information is the number of shelf slots devoted to an item. In grocery stores in the United States, it is common to observe multiple slots devoted to two-liter bottles of Coca-Cola, and the number of slots increases when Coca-Cola is a sale item. In that case, the shelf space should be treated as a marginal cost. When just one shelf slot is devoted to an item, there is a stronger case for treating shelf space as a fixed cost.

48. In this version, demand by each group is treated as being perfectly inelastic within the range of prices that might prevail. See the appendix to David S. Evans and Michael A. Salinger, "The Role of Cost in Determining When Firms Offer Bundles and Ties" (2004 working paper, available at http://ssrn.com/abstract=555818), for an extension to price-sensitive demand.

49. Otherwise, consumers who want both components would not buy the bundle.

50. *SB* represents the savings from offering the bundle given that goods 1 and 2 are also offered.

51. This point should be obvious for example 1. For example 2, the prices under pure components selling would be \$1.50 (calculated as $1 + 100/200$) for each item. Customers who buy both pay a total of \$3. This outcome is not sustainable because it is susceptible to entry with the bundle at a price of \$2.90. Similarly, pure bundling is not sustainable. The price under pure bundling would be $2.9 + 100/300 \approx 3.23$. That price is not sustainable because an entrant could break even selling either component at a price of \$3.

52. In example 2, there are some marginal cost savings from bundling. If there were no marginal cost savings from bunding, then mixed bundling would still be sustainable (and inefficient), but it would not be the unique sustainable outcome. Components selling would be sustainable as well. Mixed bundling can be the unique sustainable outcome with no marginal cost savings from bundling if X_B is greater than the geometric mean of X_1 and X_2. For a more complete explanation, see David S. Evans and Michael A. Salinger, "The Role of Cost in Determining When Firms Offer Bundles and Ties" (2004 working paper, available at http://ssrn.com/abstract=555818).

53. Another simplifying assumption of our model is that consumers who want just one of the goods get no utility or disutility from the other good. As a result, they view the bundle as a perfect substitute for the good they want. That assumption does not pertain to our application, since, for example, many consumers who want just a pain reliever would prefer not to have to take a decongestant as well. Just as it would be easy to incorporate a convenience value for the bundle in the model, we could also assume that consumers who want just one component are willing to pay a premium not to have it bundled with the other.

54. Our argument that the packaging cost is reflected at least partially in the intercept term does not require that the packaging-cost equation literally has a positive intercept. If we observed packaging costs directly, our estimates of the marginal cost savings from bundling would be based on the cost of a package of a given size, such as 24 tablets or 48 tablets. Taken, literally, the intercept reflects the cost of a 0-tablet package, which is irrelevant for computing the gains from bundling. Given our choice of a quadratic functional form, however, the cost of a package of a particular size would be reflected in part in the intercept.

55. It is possible that some costs might be variable with respect to package size but fixed with respect to the customer. This could happen if, for example, larger packages require more shelf space. Our procedure for estimating the component of price that covers fixed costs ignores this possibility.

56. Other papers that use or suggest an analogous approach to estimating fixed costs are Bresnahan and Reiss 1987; Pakes and McGuire 1994; Ericson and Pakes 1995; Fershtman and Pakes 2000; Miravete 2004; Pakes, Ostrovsky, and Berry 2004.

57. This choice would, of course, leave the consumer one pill short of his or her desired quantity.

58. This condition only ensures that the existing offering is sustainable with respect to entry halfway between two package sizes that are offered. More generally, one might impose the condition that the offering be sustainable with respect to all possible intermediate package sizes. In doing so, however, one would probably not make our simplifying assumptions about marginal cost and demand.

59. By cost-based savings, we mean those not related to branding effects.

60. The calculations are $\$3.60 - 2 \cdot \$1.20 = \$1.20$ and $\$7.20 - 3 \cdot \$1.20 = \$3.60$.

61. Assuming that the groups that want just pseudoephedrine HCl and that want the bundled product are of equal size, tying would also be sustainable. By pricing the bundled product to attract the group that wants just the decongestant, the average fixed costs could be reduced from $1.20 to $0.60. This $0.60 price reduction would more than offset the $0.29 marginal cost associated with the extra active ingredient.

62. We acknowledge that the approach we use in this chapter is crude.

63. The difficulty of doing so in this case is that when customers can buy bundled goods at a discount, it is hard to observe how much more they would be willing to pay for the bundled product if they had to. In theory, one could estimate the convenience premium indirectly by combining the increased quantity demanded with the elasticity of demand, but neither of those would be easy to estimate either.

References

Areeda, Philip, and Herbert J. Hovenkamp. 2000. *Antitrust Law: An Analysis of Antitrust Principles and Their Application*. 2nd ed. New York: Aspen Law & Business.

Baumol, William J. 1982. "Contestable Markets: An Uprising in the Theory of Industry Structure." *American Economic Review* 72:1–15.

Baumol, William J., John C. Panzar, and Robert D. Willig. 1982. *Contestable Markets and the Theory of Industry Structure.* New York: Harcourt Brace Jovanovich.

Bresnahan, Timothy F., and Peter C. Reiss. 1987. "Do Entry Conditions Vary Across Markets?" Brookings Papers on Economic Activity: Special Issue on Microeconomics (3): 833–871.

Crawford, Gregory. 2004. "The Discriminatory Incentives to Bundle: The Case of Cable Television." Working paper, University of Arizona.

Director, Aaron, and Edward H. Levi. 1956. "Law and the Future: Trade Regulation." *Northwestern University Law Review* 51 (May-June): 281–296.

Ericson, Richard, and Ariel Pakes. 1995. "Markov-Perfect Industry Dynamics: A Framework for Empirical Work." *ReStud* 62 (1): 53–82.

Evans, David S., and A. Jorge Padilla. 2005. "Designing Antitrust Rules for Assessing Unilateral Practices: A Neo-Chicago Approach." *University of Chicago Law Review* 72 (winter).

Evans, David S., and Michael A. Salinger. 2004. "The Role of Cost in Determining When Firms Offer Bundles and Ties." Working paper. http://ssrn.com/abstract=555818.

Evans, David S., and Michael A. Salinger. 2005. "Why Do Firms Bundle and Tie? Evidence from Competitive Markets and Implications for Tying Law." *Yale Journal on Regulation* 22 (1): 37–89.

Fershtman, Chaim, and Ariel Pakes. 2000. "A Dynamic Oligopoly with Collusion and Price Wars." *RAND Journal of Economics* 31(2): 207–236.

Grimes, Warren S. 2002. "The Antitrust Tying Law Schism: A Critique of Microsoft III and A Response to Hylton and Salinger." *Antitrust Law Journal* 70:199–230.

Hylton, Keith N., and Michael A. Salinger. 2001. "Tying Law and Policy: A Decision Theoretic Approach." *Antitrust Law Journal* 69:469.

Kallaugher, John, and Brian Sher. 2004. "Rebates Revisited: Anti-Competitive Effects and Exclusionary Abuse under Article 82." *European Competition Law Review* 25(5): 263–285.

Kamann, Hans-Georg, and Ellen Bergmann. 2005. "The Granting of Rebates by Market Dominant Undertakings under Article 82 of the EC Treaty." *European Competition Law Review* 26(2): 83–89.

Miravete, Eugenio. 2004. "Are All Those Calling Plans Really Necessary? The Limited Gains from Complex Tariffs." CEPR Discussion Paper No. 4237. http://ssrn.com/abstract=509009.

Morrison, Steven A., and Clifford Winston. 1987. "Empirical Implications and Tests of the Contestability Hypothesis." *Journal of Law and Economics* 30(1): 53–66.

Pakes, Ariel, and Paul McGuire. 1994. "Computing Markov-Perfect Nash Equilibria: Numerical Implications of a Dynamic Differentiated Product Model." *RAND Journal of Economics* 25(4): 555–589.

Pakes, Ariel, Michael Ostrovsky, and Steven T. Berry. 2004. "Simple Estimators for the Parameters of Discrete Dynamic Games (with Entry/Exit Samples)." NBER Working Paper No. W10506. http://ssrn.com/abstract=552302.

Rubinfeld, Daniel L. 2005. "3M's Bundling Rebates: An Economic Perspective." *Chicago Law Review* 72:243–264.

Stigler, George J. 1983. "A Note on Block Booking." In George J. Stigler, *The Organization of Industry*, chap. 15. Chicago: University of Chicago Press.

Tirole, Jean. 1988. *The Theory of Industrial Organization*. Cambridge, MA: MIT Press.

Whinston, Michael. 1990. "Tying, Foreclosure, and Exclusion." *American Economic Review* 80:837–859.

5 Economics, Politics, and Merger Control

Vivek Ghosal

5.1 Introduction

In this chapter I examine the pattern of merger control by the Antitrust Division of the U.S. Department of Justice. Specifically, I look at the number of mergers challenged in court by the Division over a long time period, 1958–2002. While several previous studies (which I review in section 5.3) have focused on the total number of antitrust court cases initiated by the Division, few appear to examine merger control. Merger enforcement is one of the central tasks of the Division, and there were several changes in the enforcement climate in the late 1960s and early 1970s that warrant close scrutiny and provide an interesting opportunity for empirical examination. First, starting in that period, the contributions by Stigler (1964), Demsetz (1973, 1974), and Williamson (1968) are thought to have had a significant influence on antitrust enforcement and regulation (also see Bork 1978; Landes and Posner 1981). Their contributions led to deemphasizing the relatively naive market-concentration-based approach that prevailed in the 1950s and 1960s,[1] and placed greater emphasis on the pro-competitive and efficiency aspects of mergers and other business conduct.[2] Baker (2002, 2003), Crandall and Winston (2003), Kovacic and Shapiro (2000), Mueller (1996), and Peltzman (2001) present the main arguments in this literature.[3] One way to view this is that for a given market-power effect, more mergers were allowed under the new regime due to the emphasis on pro-competitive effects and careful evaluation of entry conditions. Second, the U.S. Supreme Court has played a special role in the evolution of antitrust law and can be viewed as the final arbitrator of merger challenges and antitrust court cases in general. The speech by Hewitt Pate (2004), the assistant attorney general for the Antitrust Division, presents an overview of the salient role of the U.S. Supreme

Court in shaping antitrust law. The Supreme Court justices are nominated by the president and confirmed by the Senate. Republican presidents are expected to appoint more conservative justices, who may be more lassiez faire and ideologically less inclined to side with the Antitrust Division in blocking mergers and more inclined to emphasize the pro-competitive and efficiency aspects of business conduct. Examining the composition of the Republican-nominated Supreme Court justices, we find that they had a simple majority between 1958 and 1962, were in the minority between 1963 and 1969, regained a simple majority in 1970–1971, and attained a two-thirds majority starting in 1972, which they have not relinquished.

The above considerations may reasonably lead us to believe that the overall intellectual and ideological climate may have changed so as to emphasize the pro-competitive and efficiency aspects of business conduct, causing a regime shift in merger enforcement toward a situation where fewer mergers are challenged. While we may have a rough idea of the time period when these effects occurred, we cannot precisely identify the date of the regime shift. Since we do not have an explicit variable that allows us to capture such a regime shift, in section 5.5 I use time-series econometric techniques to detect potential regime shifts.

Turning to the shorter-run political effects, in numerous legal, economic, and business writings spanning several decades, the perception is that Republicans are less inclined to block mergers, and to take antitrust action in general, due to their pro-business emphasis.[4] To examine the political effect, I consider a relatively conservative pro-business Republican stance versus a more liberal pro-consumer Democratic stance. Over the sample period of 1958–2002, there have been ten different presidents and six switches of the party in power. This makes it possible to measure the impact of political changes and answer the question: Do Republicans challenge fewer mergers than Democrats? Further, I argued above that the influence of pro-competitive aspects and efficiency considerations may have had an important impact on merger evaluation. Given this, it may be of interest to examine whether the Republican versus Democratic effect has changed before and after the potential regime shift. This becomes an interesting hypothesis to examine, because under a no-efficiency-considerations regime, say the older regime of the 1950s and 1960s, the Republicans may not have a clear way out of not challenging mergers. But under an efficiency-considerations regime, they may emphasize pro-competitive aspects and efficiencies to challenge fewer mergers. Finally, studying merger enforcement by the Antitrust Division is particularly interesting due to its institutional structure. The U.S. president directly appoints the assistant attorney general who heads the Antitrust Division. This setting potentially sets the stage for shifts in enforcement with switches of the party in power. I return to this discussion in section 5.3.

Apart from the above intellectual and ideological forces, and the shorter-run political changes, the same time frame saw some key administrative milestones for the evaluation of mergers. First, the Merger Guidelines were introduced in 1968; these guidelines were designed to streamline the procedures and lend greater transparency to the process. Second, a separate Economic Analysis Group of the Antitrust Division was established in 1972–1973. Some have argued that economic analysis of mergers took on greater significance from this point on. Third, the Hart-Scott-Rodino Act was passed in 1976, after which mergers above a certain valuation threshold had to be filed for clearance. The threshold was $15 million until 2001, when it was increased to $50 million.

In summary, in this chapter I take a close look at merger enforcement by the Antitrust Division over the period 1958–2002, focusing on potential regime shifts and the impact of partisan politics. In my empirical analysis I control for several other relevant factors such as the Division's level of funding, merger waves in the United States, and level of economic activity, among others. While my main focus is on merger enforcement, I also take a quick look at the bigger picture presented by the total civil enforcement by the Division—which, along with merger control, includes monopolization and restraint-of-trade cases. Overall, this chapter aims to present a clearer understanding of the underlying shorter- and longer-run forces driving merger control and uses relatively recent econometric techniques to detect potential regime shifts in enforcement.

The chapter is organized as follows. To motivate the empirical analysis, in section 5.2 I examine the patterns in the data. Section 5.3 provides a brief review of some theoretical results and summarizes previous empirical findings. The empirical model and econometric issues related to identifying regime shifts in merger enforcement are presented in sections 5.4 and 5.5. Estimation results appear in section 5.6, and the chapter concludes with some final remarks in section 5.7.

5.2 Data

To motivate the empirical analysis in the following pages, I begin by taking a look at the data. The data are annual and cover the period 1958–2002. Data on the total number of mergers challenged by the Antitrust Division, on the total number of civil cases, and on funding are from the Division's historical statistics. Data on the U.S. merger wave are from the Federal Trade Commission's merger series for the period 1958–1977 and from the Thompson's Financials M&A database for the period 1978–2002. Data on the party of the president and the composition of the House and the Senate are from U.S. historical archives. Aggregate U.S. data on GDP and corporate profits, among other things, are from the Economic Report of the president.

Figure 5.1 displays the data on the total number of mergers challenged. There is considerable temporal variation, with the data showing a marked decline in the early 1970s and a noticeable increase in the early 1990s. The absolute number of mergers challenged, however, is not a good indicator of the intensity of merger enforcement, because the total number of mergers in the United States, presented in figure 5.2, varies widely over time with a significant surge in the 1990s. Given this, it is more meaningful to look at the ratio of the total number of mergers challenged by the Division to the U.S. merger wave. These data are displayed in figure 5.3, which reveals a very distinct downward shift in enforcement starting around the early 1970s and with no meaningful increase later. To shed light on the bigger picture of

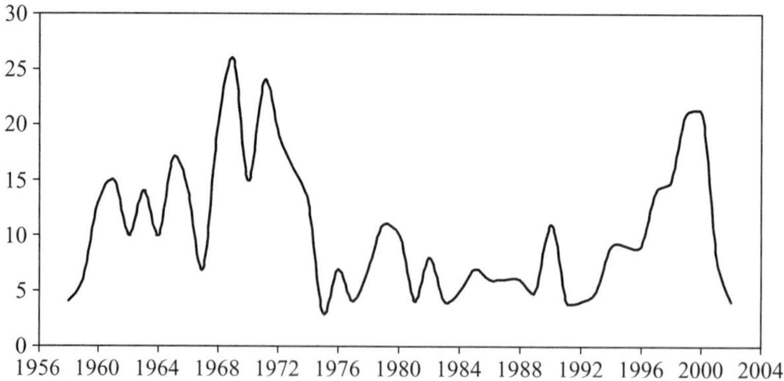

Figure 5.1
Total number of mergers challenged

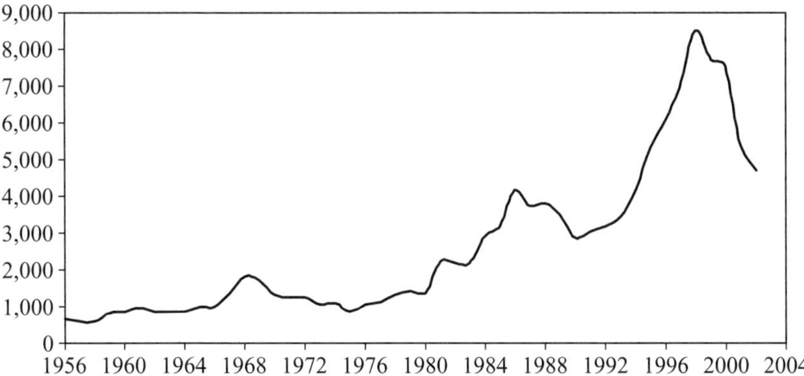

Figure 5.2
Total number of mergers in the United States

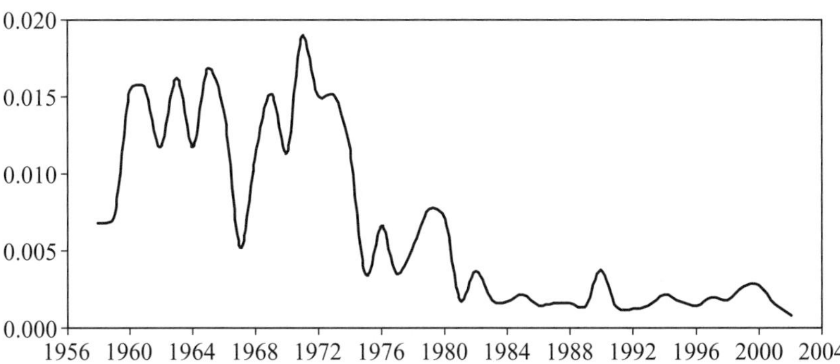

Figure 5.3
Ratio of the number of mergers challenged to the total number of mergers in the United States

antitrust enforcement, figure 5.4 displays the total number of civil court cases (monopolization and restraint-of-trade cases along with the number of mergers challenged) initiated by the Division. While there are some differences in the intertemporal path, the pattern seems roughly comparable to the merger series in figure 5.1. The Division's nominal dollar funding was converted to real values using the GDP deflator; these data are presented in figure 5.5.

Turning to the political variables, figure 5.6 presents the data on the party of the president. Over the period 1958–2002, the United States had ten different presidents, with Republicans in office for twenty-four years and Democrats for twenty years. Since the presidential term is

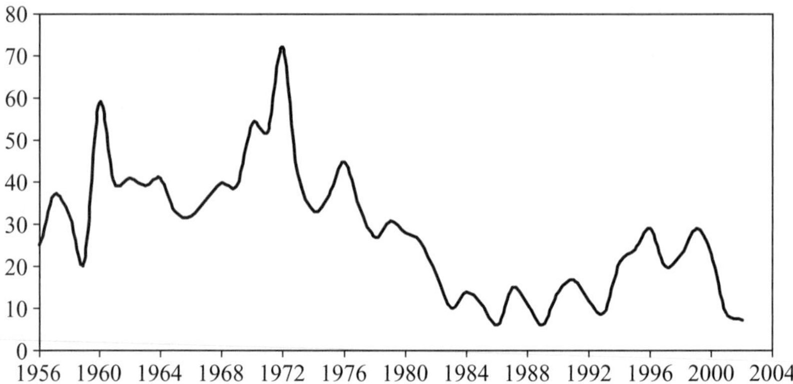

Figure 5.4
Total number of civil antitrust court cases

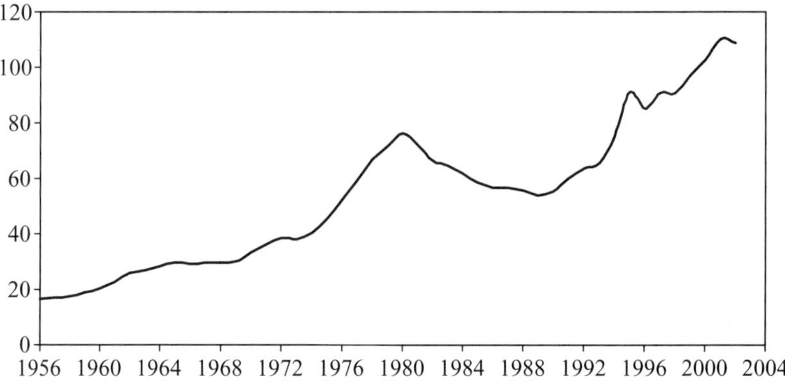

Figure 5.5
Antitrust Division's funding

for four years and several presidents won second terms, there is an obvious high degree of persistence in this variable. Apart from potential presidential effects, I also consider the Republican versus Democratic composition of the House and the Senate; these data appear in figures 5.7 and 5.8. The Democrats generally had a majority in the House. A similar picture emerges for the Senate, but here the Republicans had a majority for a few more years than in the House. Since various appointments to the House and Senate committees and subcommittees and funding decisions are dependent on which party has a majority, the political composition of the House and the Senate may

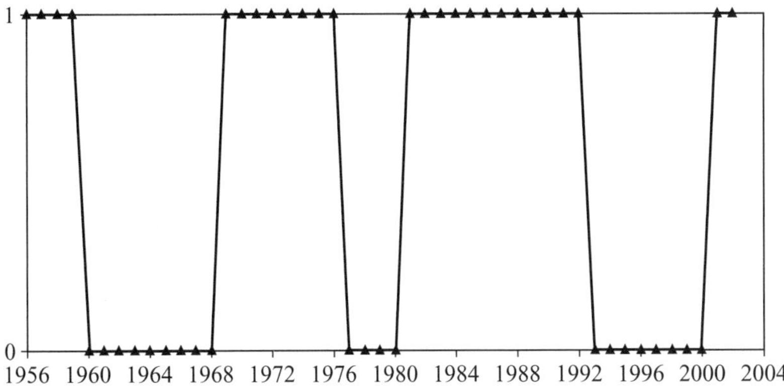

Figure 5.6
Party of The President: Republican = 1

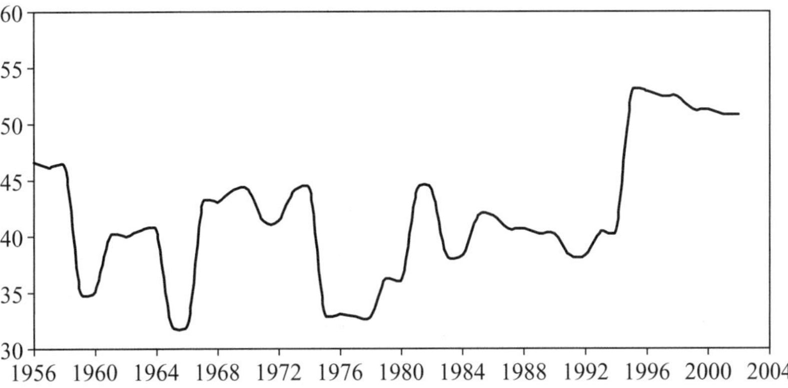

Figure 5.7
The percentage of Republicans in the House

be important political influences exerted on the Antitrust Division via the budgetary and related processes. Table 5.1 presents the summary statistics for the variables I consider in my analysis (I present a full discussion of some of the other control variables in section 5.4).

5.3 A Brief Review of the Literature

In this section I first review some insights from two theoretical papers that provide guidance for my empirical analysis. I then briefly summarize the existing empirical literature. The well-known paper by

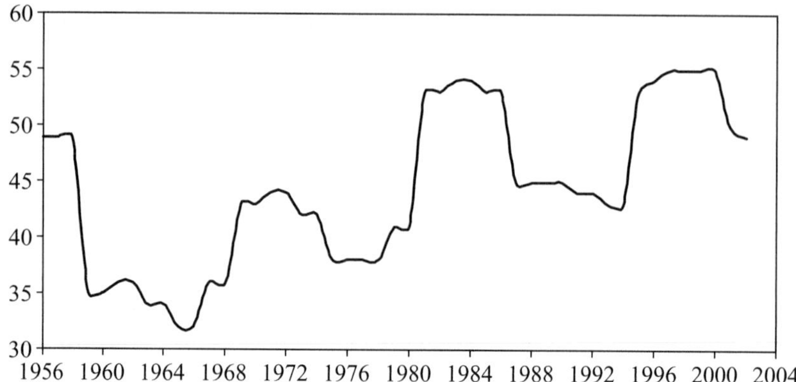

Figure 5.8
The percentage of Republicans in the Senate

Table 5.1
Summary statistics

Variable	Mean	Standard deviation	Minimum	Maximum
Total merger challenges	10.44	5.99	3.00	26.00
Ratio of total merger challenges to U.S. merger wave	0.0065	0.0057	0.0008	0.0189
Total civil cases	28.04	15.13	6.00	72.00
President	0.53	0.50	0.00	1.00
House	0.41	0.06	0.32	0.53
Senate	0.44	0.07	0.35	0.55
ΔGDP	161.24	114.13	−101.70	372.90
ΔProfit	8.94	34.04	−63.32	112.31
ΔFunds	2.04	4.15	−6.07	16.02
ΔMerge	91.64	581.17	−2187.00	1562.00

Note: A Δ indicates first-difference.

Peltzman (1976) models a regulator who faces a trade-off between the interests of two groups, say, producers and consumers. The relevant variables capturing group interests are commodity price p for consumers and profits π for producers. The regulator's objective function is written as $M = M(p, \pi)$, with $M_p < 0$, $M_{pp} < 0$, $M_\pi > 0$, $M_{\pi\pi} < 0$, and $M_{p\pi} = 0$ (Peltzman 1976, 222–223). In this model, the equilibrium will not result in protection for only one group. I highlight two useful predictions for my empirical analysis. First, one can conceptualize change in political regimes by considering different weights attached to producer and consumer interests by the Republicans and Democrats. Producer interests would be assigned a higher weight under Republican administrations, who are assumed to be more pro-business and thus less committed to vigorous merger enforcement. Second, Peltzman (1976, 225–227) considers changes in equilibrium resulting from changes in economic conditions. An important result is that, given positive marginal consumer (producer) opposition to higher (lower) prices (profits), the regulator in general will not force the entire adjustment onto one group. For example, if corporate profits (π) are depressed, the political wealth effect would imply that the regulator's incentive to let prices fall will be attenuated so prices would not fall as far as they would in an unregulated setting; consumers will buffer some of the producer losses. Other things being equal, this implies that merger enforcement in general is likely to be relatively slack (vigorous) when corporate earnings or economic conditions are weaker (stronger). Peltzman's setting results in a direct relationship between the intensity of antitrust enforcement and corporate profits or economic conditions. In our context, when corporate profits and economic conditions are depressed, the antitrust regulator may be less inclined to be vigorous in merger enforcement.

Next I review some results from Faure-Grimaud and Martimort (2003), who examine the link between the institutional structure of the regulatory agency and policy implementation across different political principals. I focus on Faure-Grimaud and Martimort's affiliated-regulator setting where the political principal delegates the task to a regulatory agent, and the agent changes with a change in the principal. The affiliated-regulator setting fits the Antitrust Division, because the president directly appoints the assistant attorney general who heads the Antitrust Division of the U.S. Department of Justice, and the Senate confirms the appointment. Over our sample period (1958–2002) there have been ten different presidents and twenty-seven different assistant attorneys general. In Faure-Grimaud and Martimort's model, all principals dislike giving up rents to firms, but the propensity to extract rents varies across the principals. This difference in propensity is referred to as the degree of polarization (Faure-Grimaud and Martimort 2003, 418). In my analysis this would be proxied by the difference in the level of merger enforcement between the Republicans and Democrats. Since the Antitrust Division's affiliated regulators are short-lived, they have relatively less scope for being captured by firms and can be dismissed by the president if there is deviation from a desired policy stance. Thus, one can expect a relatively close match between the principal's (president's) agenda and what is implemented by the affiliated regulator, setting the stage for potentially large shifts in merger enforcement.[5] I summarize two useful points for my empirical analysis: (1) given the affiliated-regulator structure of the Antitrust Division, we potentially expect a clear distinction between Republicans and Democrats in the intensity of merger enforcement, and (2) the estimated difference between Republicans and Democrats in the degree of merger enforcement provides us with a proxy for the degree of polarization between the two parties. I also consider whether the degree of polarization has changed over time.

Turning to empirical studies of antitrust enforcement, several papers have examined the determinants of the total number of antitrust court cases initiated. The precedent was set by Posner (1970), who examined the time series of the Antitrust Division's court cases. He did not find any relationship between the party of the president and case activity. Examining the link between the level of GNP and the number of cases, he concluded that enforcement appeared directly related to the level of economic activity. Siegfried (1975) concluded that economic factors do not appear to influence antitrust enforcement. Using Federal Trade Commission (FTC) data, Faith, Leavens, and Tollison (1982) examined the link between political influence and case activity and found support for the private-interest theory of FTC behavior. Amacher, Higgins, Shughart, and Tollison (1985) used FTC data and the political-party affiliation of the commissioners and found weak evidence that Democrat-dominated commissions pursue enforcement more vigorously than commissions dominated by Republicans do. They found no consistent link between economic activity and cases initiated. Coate, Higgins, and McChesney (1990) used FTC merger data to examine political influence and found evidence in support of the interest-group hypotheses. Pittman (1992) did not find evidence that political factors have systematically affected antitrust enforcement. Ghosal and Gallo (2001) found no effect of the party of the president, and that case activity appeared to be countercyclical. Collectively, the previous empirical findings show that (1) there does not appear to be systematic evidence that the party of the president matters for antitrust case activity, and (2) the relationship between economic activity and case activity is ambiguous—the typical finding appears to be either a weak positive link or no link. In contrast to the above studies, this chapter examines data over a long period (1958–2002) and is one of the more comprehensive studies in recent years. The long time series enables me to conduct rigorous econometric analysis to detect potential regime shifts and examine the role of politics. Even the above studies that were done from the late 1970s onward did not examine the issue of regime shifts, which appears important for enhancing our understanding of merger enforcement.

5.4 Empirical Model

I use a partial-adjustment model to examine the intertemporal pattern of merger enforcement. Let C_t denote the number of mergers challenged by the Antitrust Division in period t and C_t^* the desired number of challenges. The desired number C_t^* is a function of relevant driving variables that I detail below. The partial-adjustment model is given by $C_t - C_{t-1} = \lambda(C_t^* - C_{t-1})$, where the actual change in the number of mergers challenged is a fraction λ (0λ1) of the desired change. Going from one period to the next, the actual change in the number of cases is likely to be less than the desired change due to the presence of adjustment costs, which arise from the Antitrust Division facing resource constraints given by the number of attorneys, economists, support staff, and funding. I then rewrite the above expression as

$$C_t = \lambda C_t^* + (1 - \lambda)C_{t-1} \tag{1}$$

I model the desired C_t^* as a function of the relevant driving variables. Let C_t^* be specified as

$$C_t^* = a_1P_{t-1} + a_2R_{t-1} + a_3F_{t-1} + a_4W_{t-1} + a_5E_{t-1} + a_6V_{t-1} + u_t \tag{2}$$

where P_t = political party with $P = 1$ if conservative/pro-business, else $P = 0$; R_t = regime with $R = 1$ if new conservative/pro-business regime, else $R = 0$; F_t = funding allocated to the antitrust division; W_t = the total number of mergers in the United States (merger wave); E_t = aggregate economic conditions (GDP or corporate profits); and V_t = number of (unobserved by the econometrician) mergers filed that raise serious antitrust concerns. First, I assume that the relevant factors take time to affect the number of cases, hence I use lagged values. Second, the motivation for the driving forces for C_t^* are as follows. The Division's willingness to initiate new merger challenges depends on the political stance, *P*, and the regime they are operating under, *R*. A switch to a more conservative, pro-business environment may result in fewer mergers challenged; a_1 and a_2 are expected to be negative. The ability to initiate new merger cases may depend on the level of funding, *F*, and last year's funding is assumed to be a good predictor of current funding, which allows the Division to pursue cases; a_3 is expected to be positive. The U.S. merger-wave variable, *W*, potentially embeds multiple effects. For example, (1) greater number of mergers may imply an absolute increase in the number of mergers blocked, and (2) with an increase in the number of mergers in the United States, significant amounts of resources will have to be utilized to evaluate them, potentially allowing fewer mergers to be carefully screened. As a result the sign of a_4 appears ambiguous. The economic-activity variable, *E*, is motivated by the results in Peltzman 1976. Peltzman posits a positive relationship; a_5 is predicted to be positive. Finally, the desired number of mergers challenged is expected to be positively related to the (unobserved by the econometrician) number of mergers filed that raise serious antitrust concerns *V*; a_6 is expected to be positive. The error term is assumed to be iid: $u_t \sim (0,\sigma_u^2)$.

Next I specify the equation for the (unobserved) *V* as

$$V_t = b_1P_{t-1} + b_2R_{t-1} + b_3C_{t-1} + b_4W_{t-1} + b_5E_{t-1} + v_0 + e_t \tag{3}$$

Regarding the factors that influence the temporal variation in *V*, I assume that these effects take time and only use lagged values. The presence of a conservative, pro-business political party, *P*, may imply a greater number of anticompetitive mergers filed because firms may feel these mergers are more likely to be cleared; b_1 is positive. Similarly, if the regime is more favorable, such as one that places emphasis on pro-competitive effects and efficiencies, more firms may be inclined to file for mergers even if the market-power effects are large; b_2 is positive. If the Antitrust Division is vigorously pursuing merger challenges, *C*, then potentially fewer mergers would be filed that raise serious antitrust concerns due to the greater likelihood of a challenge by the Division; $b_3 < 0$. Periods characterized by greater mergers in the United

States (W) might make firms file for more mergers due to the view that the Division is resource-constrained and mergers may receive less scrutiny; $b_4 > 0$. The economic-activity variable, E, controls for the link between economic conditions and antitrust violations. Finally, I assume that every period produces some given number of (unobserved) mergers filed that raise serious antitrust concerns, v_0. The error term is assumed to be iid: $e_t \sim (0,\sigma_e^2)$.

Now I use equation (3) to replace V_{t-1} in equation (2) and then use that to replace C_t^* in equation (1). The resulting expression is of the following general form:

$$C_t = c_0 + \Sigma_f \alpha_f P_{t-f} + \Sigma_g \beta_g R_{t-g} + \Sigma_h \delta_h F_{t-h} + \Sigma_i \theta_i W_{t-i} + \Sigma_j \gamma_j E_{t-j} + \Sigma_k \rho_k C_{t-k} + \varepsilon_t \tag{4}$$

where $\varepsilon_t = (u_t + a_1 e_{t-1})$, and f, g, h, i, j, and k are the lag lengths. Given the structure of the above equations, the lags $f = g = i = j = k = 2$ and $h = 1$. The coefficients in equation (4) are typically combinations of the coefficients in equations (1) to (3). The error term ε_t is similar to a MA(1) process. Given my assumptions for the error terms u_t and e_t, and assuming zero covariance between u_t and e_t, ε_t is a linear combination of two iid errors; $\varepsilon_t \sim \text{iid}(0, \sigma_u^2 + a_1^2\sigma_e^2)$.

I close with some additional comments regarding the specification. First, as noted earlier, I do not include current-period variables in equations (2) and (3). This is because it is reasonable to assume that various effects take time. Second, if we consider a richer dynamic specification in equations (2) and (3), then equation (4) will retain the same form but will include additional lags. My experiments showed that deeper lags were not significant. The error term ε_t could be a higher-order MA(.) process; I formally test for this in section 5.6. Third, two variables in equation (4) may potentially be endogenous: the Antitrust Division's funding (F) and the United States merger wave (W). In section 5.6, I conduct econometric tests to evaluate this.

5.5 Detecting Regime Shift

In the introduction I discussed the potential reasons for expecting a regime shift in merger enforcement. Since I do not have explicit variables to control for this, I detect potential regime shifts by using econometric techniques for identifying structural breaks in merger-enforcement data. The methodology tests for a structural break at an unknown date, because while we may know the rough time period during which a break may have occurred, we cannot identify the precise break date (see Andrews 1993; Hamilton 1994, chap. 22; Stock 1994; Stock and Watson 1996, 2003). Let C_t be the number of mergers challenged in court and τ the hypothesized break date. The dummy variable $D(\tau)$ is defined as $D_t(\tau) = 0$ for $t \leq \tau$ and $D_t(\tau) = 1$ for $t > \tau$. A baseline regression including the unknown break point is given by $C_t = c_0 + \Sigma_k \rho_k C_{t-k} + \xi D_t(\tau) + \omega_t$, which includes lags of C to account for its own dynamics and allows for a change in the intercept before and after the hypothesized break point. Under the null hypothesis of no break, $\xi = 0$. It is useful to clarify what a break date means. Suppose C_t has observations over $t = 0, \ldots, T$ and the statistical tests reveal a structural break in year τ. This tells us that the mean of C_t series in the $t = 0, \ldots, \tau$ interval is different from the $t = \tau + 1, \ldots, T$ interval. So literally nothing may happen in the year τ (the detected break date), but events in the $\tau + 1$ to T period result in a sample mean that is different from the preceding period.

Since the break date τ is unknown, I consider a series of break dates between two potential dates τ_0 and τ_1. For each possible break date, I estimate the above specification and get an F-statistic from testing $\xi = 0$ against the alternative of $\xi \neq 0$. I focus on the largest of the resulting F-statistics from the sequence and use the Quandt likelihood ratio (QLR) statistic to detect the break point. As noted in Stock and Watson 1996, the distribution of the QLR statistic depends on the number of restrictions being tested q ($q = 1$ in the baseline equation), and on the width of the end points τ_0/T and τ_1/T, where T is the total sample size; τ_0 and τ_1 cannot be too close to the sample end points. Following Stock and Watson 1996, I consider 15 percent trimming—that is, $\tau_0 = 0.15T$ and $\tau_1 = 0.85T$. Given the full sample period of 1958–2002, this implies that I test for a structural break in merger enforcement during the interval 1965–1996.

The baseline specification above can be augmented to include additional explanatory variables $\Psi' X_t$ and interaction terms between $D_t(\tau)$ and explanatory variable(s) of interest, $\Phi' X_t D_t(\tau)$, where X is a vector of explanatory variables and Ψ and Φ are the coefficient vectors. For this extended specification, the null hypothesis is $\xi = \Phi = 0$. Estimating an augmented specification to test for structural breaks is important, because omission of relevant variables may falsely generate a structural-break observation. From my earlier discussion in equation (4), the components of $\mathbf{X}$ would be P, F, W, and E. The regime variable R is replaced by $D_t(\tau)$. For the interaction term, I only consider one—$D_t(\tau)\Sigma_m\zeta_m P_{t-m}$—which is the interaction between the regime-shift dummy and the party-of-the-president dummy. Following my discussion of Faure-Grimaud and Martimort 2003 in section 5.3, my goal is to examine possible changes over time in the degree of polarization between Republicans and Democrats. Finally, I note two issues. First, apart from when there is a change in the president, we have $P_t = P_{t-1}$. The presidential dummy P is highly persistent and, for numerous observations, the current and lagged values are identical. Given this, I only enter one lag of the presidential effect P_{t-1}. Second, to a greater or lesser extent, many of the explanatory variables (the Antitrust Division's funding, the total number of mergers in the United States, GDP, and corporate profits) appear nonstationary. I formally tested for nonstationarity using the Augmented Dickey-Fuller and Phillips-Perron (1988) unit root tests; these tests have a null hypothesis of difference stationary. Using conventional significance levels, these tests could not reject the null that these variables are difference stationary. Given this, I entered the Antitrust Division's funds, GDP, corporate profits, and the merger-wave variables in first differences. The final specification I estimate is given by

$$C_t = c_0 + \alpha_1 P_{t-1} + \Sigma_h \delta_h \Delta F_{t-h} + \Sigma_i \theta_i \Delta W_{t-i} + \Sigma_j \gamma_j \Delta E_{t-j} + \Sigma_k \rho_k C_{t-k} + \xi D_t(\tau) + \zeta_1 D_t(\tau) P_{t-1} + \varepsilon_t \qquad (5)$$

where, as discussed for equation (4), the error term is a moving-average process, $\varepsilon_t = (u_t + a_1 e_{t-1})$. For testing for structural breaks, the null hypothesis is $\xi = \zeta_1 = 0$. I implemented the following sequence. First, I estimated equation (5) with a parsimonious lag structure, $h = i = j = k = 2$. Given that there are only forty-five annual time-series observations, I did not experiment with higher lags to conserve degrees of freedom. Second, I dropped all statistically insignificant second lags. Insignificant first lags were not dropped. Third, I reestimated with the optimal lag lengths. Table 5.2 presents the results for testing for all potential break dates between 1965 and 1996. The estimated break date for the absolute number of mergers is 1974 and the test statistic is significant at the 5 percent level. For the ratio of mergers challenged to total U.S. merger wave, the estimated break date is also 1974 and the test statistic is significant at the 1 percent level. These imply that the sample means for the merger series are significantly different before and after 1974. For the total number of civil cases a break is detected in 1972 and the test statistic is significant at the 1 percent level.

Table 5.2
Structural break dates

Variable	Largest F-statistic	Break date: τ = year
Total merger challenges	07.45*	$\tau = 1974$
Ratio of total merger challenges to U.S. merger wave	14.77*	$\tau = 1974$
Total civil cases	31.35*	$\tau = 1972$

Note: The results are from estimating equation (5.5) with $q = 2$ restrictions. The F-statistics are compared with critical values of the QLR-statistic with 15% trimming. The critical values are 1% = 7.78, 5% = 5.86, and 10% = 5.00. An asterisk (*) indicates significance at least at the 10% level. Total civil cases is the sum of Sherman 1, Sherman 2, Clayton 7, and other civil cases.

5.6 Estimation and Results

I first examine whether the U.S. merger wave and the Antitrust Division's level of funding are potentially endogenous. Then I present the estimation results.

5.6.1 Potential Endogeneity

An increase in the number of mergers challenged by the Division may reduce merger activity. Thus the U.S. merger wave W is potentially endogenous to the number of mergers challenged C. Of course, the number of mergers challenged is not the only factor affecting mergers; shifts in technology, stock-market movements, deregulation, and other factors determine mergers; see Jovanovic and Rousseau 2001. Moreover, the Antitrust Division's funding (budget) is approved by the legislature. Requests for increases in funding may follow an increase in merger-enforcement activity, potentially making funds endogenous. However, the number of court cases is not the only factor influencing funding; the party of the president, composition of the House and the Senate, complexity of cases, and internal investigations, among other factors, are likely to determine funding. Given these considerations, we examine whether the merger wave (W) and funds (F) may potentially be endogenous in equation (5).

My first option was to pursue the Hausman-test route. However, finding instrumental variables for F and W proved challenging. I experimented with federal government spending and lagged cases as potential instruments for funding, but the explanatory power of the first-stage regressions was very low, indicating that these were poor instruments. Since using weak instruments causes serious inference

Table 5.3
Econometric causality tests

Panel A. Granger causality test.
Specification: $F_t = a + \Sigma_m b_m F_{t-m} + \Sigma_n c_n C_{t-n} + u_t$, where a, b, and c are parameters.
Null hypothesis: $c_n = 0\ \forall n$.

1. Funding
Total merger cases: $F = 0.5562$
Total civil cases: $F = 0.6917$

2. Merger wave (F is replaced by W in the above specification)
Total merger cases: $F = 0.4018$
Total civil cases: $F = 0.9238$

Panel B. Geweke-Meese-Dent causality test.
Specification: $C_t = d + \Sigma_k p_k F_{t-k} + \Sigma_w q_w F_{t+w} + \Sigma_g r_g C_{t-g} + e_t$, where d, p, q, and r are parameters. The test includes k lags and w leads of funds.
Null hypothesis: $q_w = 0\ \forall w$.

1. Funding
Total merger cases: $F = 0.6273$
Total civil cases: $F = 0.7928$

2. Merger wave (F is replaced by W in the above specification)
Total merger cases: $F = 0.7205$
Total civil cases: $F = 0.9872$

Note: The p-values are reported above. In panel A, we estimated the model with lags m and $n = 1,2$. In panel B, the lags k, w, and $g = 1,2$.

problems, I did not pursue this option. The alternate strategy I implemented was to use the Granger and Geweke-Meese-Dent procedures to test for (econometric) causality (or joint determination) by using information about the dynamic relationships between pairs of variables. The Granger test examines whether lagged values of C affect current values of W and F. The Geweke-Meese-Dent test examines whether lead values of W and F affect current C. Hamilton (1994, 307–308) provides an insightful discussion of these tests. Table 5.3 presents the equations and the test results. For the U.S. merger wave, I replaced F with W in the above equations. For funds, F, the results from testing are presented in table 5.3 (panel A), and panel B presents the results from testing for the merger wave W. Given the p-values, both F and W appear best treated as predetermined over our sample period. The data over 1958–2002 reveal little evidence that these variables are jointly determined with the number of merger challenges C. Given this, I do not pursue instrumental variable estimation. OLS estimates corrected for the MA(.) error structure will provide us with unbiased and consistent parameter estimates and standard errors using the Newey-West (1987) procedure.

5.6.2 Results

The general specification I estimate is given by equation (5). The $D_t(\tau)$ regime-shift dummies are replaced by the detected break dates noted in table 5.2. In my estimation I account for the MA(1) error structure; see the discussion of equation (4). To check whether the error term required a higher-order MA(.) specification, as would result from a richer lagged structure in equations (2) and (3), I implemented a Lagrange-multiplier test for an MA(2) error structure. The test statistics are reported at the bottom of table 5.4. For merger cases and the ratio of merger cases to total U.S. mergers, an MA(1) structure is sufficient. For total civil cases we require an MA(2) error structure. The summary statistics of the model variables are presented in table 5.1 and the main estimation results are reported in tables 5.4 and 5.5. As noted in table 5.4, except for the coefficients for the constant term, Pres_{t-1}, $D(X)$ and $D(X)\text{Pres}_{t-1}$, the reported numbers are the coefficient estimates multiplied by one standard deviation of the respective variable. Because there is considerable variation in the size of the estimated coefficients and in the means and standard deviations of the variables, the estimates multiplied by one standard deviation of the respective variable give us a quick look at the quantitative effect.

For the total number of mergers challenged (table 5.4, column A), the regime shift resulted in the intercept dropping from about ten cases to five, signaling a large quantitative effect. A better way of looking at merger challenges is to examine column B, which presents the ratio of mergers challenged to the total number of mergers in the United States. The summary statistics in table 5.1 indicate that for the sample period as a whole this ratio is 0.0067, implying that typically less than 1 percent of the mergers are challenged. The regime shift resulted in the intercept dropping from about 0.0113 to 0.0036, which is a large quantitative effect. For the merger cases (column A) and the ratio of merger cases to the merger wave (column B), neither the Pres nor the $D(\cdot)$Pres coefficients are statistically significant, indicating that after we control for the regime shift, there is no presidential, or political, effect and there has been no change in this effect before and after the regime shift. In other words, for merger challenges we do not find evidence of polarization (à la Faure-Grimaud and Martimort) between the political parties.

In contrast to merger enforcement, the bigger picture represented by the number of total civil cases (table 5.4, column C) reflects a more interesting pattern. The detected regime shift is around 1972, which is

Table 5.4
Estimation results: Economic activity measure—GDP

	A. Total merger challenges	B. Ratio of total merger challenges to U.S. merger wave	C. Total civil cases
Constant	10.019*	0.0113*	13.054*
	(0.001)	(0.001)	(0.001)
$Pres_{t-1}$	0.376	0.00029	11.422*
	(0.884)	(0.825)	(0.025)
$D(1974)$	−4.916*	−0.0077*	−8.825*
	(0.011)	(0.001)	(0.001)
$D(1974)*Pres_{t-1}$	−2.807	−0.00127	−10.670*
	(0.367)	(0.451)	(0.089)
$\Delta Funds_{t-1}$	−0.095	0.0003	2.623*
	(0.835)	(0.240)	(0.009)
$\Delta Funds_{t-2}$	—	—	—
$\Delta Wave_{t-1}$	0.465	—	2.382*
	(0.360)		(0.008)
$\Delta Wave_{t-2}$	1.859*	—	—
	(0.005)		
ΔGDP_{t-1}	0.912*	0.00007	−0.023
	(0.092)	(0.844)	(0.987)
ΔGDP_{t-2}	—	−0.00007*	—
		(0.013)	
$Cases_{t-1}$	1.531*	0.001*	5.734*
	(0.010)	(0.097)	(0.001)
$Cases_{t-2}$	—	—	3.343*
			(0.001)
Adj-R^2	0.5350	0.7924	0.7106
LM: $\chi^2(2)$	0.311	0.242	0.010

Notes:

1 The specification we estimate is given by equation (5). A Δindicates that the variable is first-differenced. $D(1974)$ is the structural break dummy (see table 5.2).

2 Except for the Constant, $Pres_{t-1}$, $D(1974)$ and $D(1974)*Pres_{t-1}$ coefficients, the reported numbers are the coefficient estimates multiplied by one standard deviation of the respective variable. This is done because there is considerable variation in the size of the means and standard deviations across the variables. Multiplying by one standard deviation gives us a reasonable glimpse at the quantitative effect.

3 The bottom-row LM: $\chi^2(2)$ presents the p-values from the LM test for a MA(2) error structure. Given the results, the specification in column C was estimated with a MA(2) structure and those in columns A and B with MA(1).

4 p-values (two-tailed), using the Newey-West (1987) heteroscedasticity and serial correlation consistent standard errors, are in parentheses. An asterisk (*) indicates statistical significance at least at the 10% level.

Table 5.5
Estimation results: Economic activity measure—corporate profits

	A. Total merger challenges	B. Ratio of total merger challenges to U.S. merger wave	C. Total civil cases
Constant	10.625*	0.0108*	13.200*
	(0.001)	(0.001)	(0.001)
$Pres_{t-1}$	0.274	0.00032	10.159*
	(0.913)	(0.805)	(0.050)
D(•)	−4.141*	−0.0085*	−7.798*
	(0.030)	(0.001)	(0.001)
D(•)*$Pres_{t-1}$	−3.135	−0.00071	−10.653*
	(0.299)	(0.625)	(0.081)
$\Delta Funds_{t-1}$	−0.083	0.0002	2.017*
	(0.863)	(0.627)	(0.087)
$\Delta Funds_{t-2}$	—	0.0004*	—
		(0.063)	
$\Delta Wave_{t-1}$	0.697	—	3.195*
	(0.147)		(0.008)
$\Delta Wave_{t-2}$	1.975*	—	—
	(0.009)		
$\Delta Profit_{t-1}$	−0.194	0.00007	0.578
	(0.756)	(0.766)	(0.545)
$\Delta Profit_{t-2}$	—	−0.0004*	−2.210*
		(0.068)	(0.094)
$Cases_{t-1}$	1.704*	0.001*	5.911*
	(0.021)	(0.100)	(0.001)
$Cases_{t-2}$	—	—	3.285*
			(0.001)
Adj-R^2	0.5161	0.7817	0.7195

Note: See table 5.4.

roughly similar to that for merger challenges. The Pres (positive) and $D(\cdot)$Pres interaction terms (negative) indicate that the pre-regime-shift number of total civil cases initiated was higher under Republican presidents. Post–regime shift, the court cases are noticeably lower under Republican presidents. Pre–regime shift, the Republicans were in power during the Nixon-Ford administrations (1969–1976), as well as for part of the Eisenhower administration (1958–1960). An examination of the data in figure 5.4 indicates that the positive pre-regime-shift Republican effect is being driven by outcomes from about two years during the Nixon administration, so this does not appear to be a pervasive Republican effect, but a more idiosyncratic one from a couple of years of data. Overall, an interpretation of the Pres and $D(\cdot)$Pres effects is that for the total civil cases there has been a significant polarization between Republican and Democratic administrations after the regime shift. In other words, post–regime shift, the Republicans have systematically initiated fewer civil cases than the Democrats.

In terms of the other variables, an increase in the Division's funding appears to have no effect on merger challenges. The effect on total civil cases is positive, but the quantitative effect is modest. The estimates of the Wave coefficient show that periods reflecting a greater number of mergers in the United States show subsequent increases in merger cases and total civil cases, and the numbers imply rather small quantitative effects. Economic conditions, as measured by change in GDP, have mixed effects across the different types of cases, and the estimated quantitative effects are rather small. In all specifications, the lagged dependent variables are significant. The impact of the economic-activity variables in general does not lend support to the Peltzman-type (see section 5.3) balancing effect for merger enforcement in particular or overall civil enforcement in general. In table 5.5 I present the results with corporate profits as an alternative measure of economic conditions. Aside from small differences, the results are largely similar to those with GDP. The overall conclusion is that funding for the Antitrust Division, merger waves, and economic conditions appear to have relatively modest quantitative effects on the Antitrust Division's merger enforcement and total civil cases.

Next I turn to table 5.6, which presents results comparable to those in table 5.4, but without the regime-shift dummy. The regression adjusted R^2s are considerably lower. For merger cases, the lagged GDP and Wave variables—which were significant earlier—are now insignificant. For total civil cases, the presidential dummy is now insignificant, as is the funding variable. Overall, controlling for regime shifts appears important in enhancing our understanding of the forces affecting merger enforcement as well as overall civil enforcement.

Finally, I reestimated the main specification after including the percentage of Republicans in the House and in the Senate as additional controls for the political effects. These results are presented in table 5.7. While there are marginal differences, the inclusion of the House and Senate variables, which turn out to be generally insignificant, do not affect my central inferences regarding the party of the president and the regime shift. This result may not be terribly unexpected since over the forty-five-year sample period (1958–2002), the Republicans have

Table 5.6
Estimation results: No regime-shift dummies

	A. Total merger challenges	B. Ratio of total merger challenges to U.S. merger wave	C. Total civil cases
Constant	5.791* (0.005)	0.0036* (0.039)	4.901 (0.410)
$Pres_{t-1}$	–2.348 (0.151)	–0.0012 (0.261)	1.261 (0.699)
$\Delta Funds_{t-1}$	–0.631 (0.235)	–0.00008 (0.804)	1.652 (0.121)
$\Delta Funds_{t-2}$	—	—	—
$\Delta Wave_{t-1}$	0.639 (0.107)	—	2.382* (0.031)
$\Delta Wave_{t-2}$	1.046 (0.262)	—	—
ΔGDP_{t-1}	0.045 (0.952)	0.00015 (0.776)	–1.642 (0.309)
ΔGDP_{t-2}	—	–0.0011* (0.027)	—
$Cases_{t-1}$	3.324* (0.001)	0.004* (0.001)	8.400* (0.001)
$Cases_{t-2}$	—	—	3.810* (0.024)
Adj-R^2	0.3772	0.6492	0.5582

Note: The above regressions are similar to those in table 5.4 but do not include the regime-shift dummy *D*(1974).

had a majority in the House for only eight years and a majority in the Senate for thirteen years.

5.7 Discussion and Concluding Remarks

I comment on my main findings in the following paragraphs. First, I find evidence of a dramatic downward regime shift in merger enforcement starting around 1974. In the introduction I noted that several factors could have contributed to this—for example, the emphasis on pro-competitive and efficiency aspects of firms' practices, the increasingly conservative composition of the U.S. Supreme Court, and some administrative changes such as the issuance of merger guidelines. While it is difficult to separate these forces, in particular since it is hard to gauge when these began to assert themselves, one may be inclined

Table 5.7
Additional results

	Total merger challenges	Ratio of total merger challenges to U.S. merger wave	Total civil cases
Constant	10.4221	0.0114	13.4921
	(0.001)	(0.001)	(0.001)
$Pres_{t-1}$	0.5663	0.0003	11.7782
	(0.826)	(0.798)	(0.022)
D(1974)	−5.330	−0.0077	−6.7260
	(0.003)	(0.001)	(0.003)
D(1974)*$Pres_{t-1}$	−2.1028	−0.0016	−12.0053
	(0.519)	(0.356)	(0.055)
$House_{t-1}$	3.3378	−0.0013	−0.5873
	(0.038)	(0.173)	(0.828)
$Senate_{t-1}$	−2.0636	−0.0001	−4.3615
	(0.197)	(0.974)	(0.157)

Notes:
[1] The specifications in table 5.4 were augmented by the percentage of Republicans in the House and in the Senate. The House and Senate are dummy variables with House (Senate) = 1 if Republicans are in majority; else zero.
[2] The funding, merger-wave, economic-activity (GDP), and lagged dependent variables are not reported above.

to believe that lesser emphasis on market concentration, increased emphasis on pro-competitive and efficiency considerations, and a more conservative Supreme Court may be the dominant driving factors behind the regime shift. One can cite two significant Supreme Court decisions that roughly coincide with our identified structural-break period. The first decision is *U.S. v. General Dynamics Co.* (1974), where the Supreme Court went against the antitrust mindset of the 1950s and 1960s and did not find a violation even thought the existing market shares were high. The government's case had defined the product market as coal. The Court disagreed with this definition and considered the market to be the more overarching energy, which included oil, gas, and nuclear and geothermal power. The Court also disagreed with the government's narrow geographic market definition and broadened it considerably, arguing that the market should be defined in terms of the transportation networks and freight charges that determine the cost of delivering coal and other energy. In addition, the Court considered issues related to actual and potential competition and entry conditions. This wide-ranging evaluation of market conditions was a radical departure from the narrow concentration-based mindset of earlier decades. The second significant Supreme Court decision is *Continental TV v. GTE Sylvania* (1977), where the Court emphasized concepts related to competition in the market and argued that vertical restrictions are likely to promote interbrand competition by allowing producers to achieve efficiencies in distribution. This is the first time that the Court explicitly looked at efficiencies to argue in favor of the procompetitive effects of the business practice.

While these landmark cases roughly correspond to our estimated structural-break date, a more detailed examination of merger cases during this transition period along with the specific rulings by the courts would shed greater light on the turning points in merger enforcement in particular and antitrust in general.

Second, and contrary to popular belief, I do not find empirical evidence that Republicans initiate fewer merger challenges than Democrats. A popular belief appears to be that "Reagan killed antitrust." At least in terms of merger enforcement, this does not appear to hold true. If we look at figure 5.1, there is a sharp drop in mergers challenged during the Ford administration. The number of mergers challenged during the Carter administration continued to remain low and there was a further drop going from the Carter to the Reagan administration. Toward the end of the graph we see an increase in the number of mergers challenged during the Clinton administration. However, as I have noted earlier, figure 5.3 is a more accurate representation of the intensity of merger enforcement, because it plots the ratio of the number of mergers challenged to the total number of mergers in the United States. We see an even clearer pattern: a sharp drop during the Ford administration, it continues to be low during the Carter administration, a further decline under Reagan, and no increase during the Clinton administration. One of the more interesting comparisons is between the Reagan (widely considered the icon of conservatism) and Clinton administrations; the ratio of the number of mergers challenged to the total number of mergers in the United States is virtually identical at 0.002 (i.e., only 0.2 percent of the mergers in the United States were challenged)! In terms of absolute numbers, the Clinton administration blocked more mergers, but this does not account for the dramatically greater number of mergers in the United States during that period. Overall, a careful look at the data does not reveal a clear Republican (or political) effect in terms of merger enforcement. It appears that pro-market winds and a conservative stance by the Supreme Court have dominated merger control since the mid-1970s, leaving little or no additional room for partisan politics to play a role.

In contrast to merger enforcement, the data on the Antitrust Division's total civil enforcement show different patterns in some respects. As with merger enforcement, the total civil-enforcement data show a regime shift in the early 1970s. However, in contrast to the merger challenges, the empirical findings on total civil enforcement show that post–regime shift the Republicans have initiated fewer cases than Democrats, implying a clear political effect in the nonmerger component of enforcement, and that the degree of polarization between Republicans and Democrats has increased post–regime shift. Given these results for the total civil cases, it will be useful to study the individual components of civil enforcement related to the Sherman 1, Sherman 2, Clayton 7, and other civil violations. I am pursing this in my ongoing research (Ghosal 2005).

Notes

I thank seminar participants at CESifo's Venice Summer Institute (2004), the Wissenschaftszentrum Berlin (WZB), Deutsches Institut für Wirtschaftsforschung (DIW, Berlin), and the International Industrial Organization Conference (Atlanta, 2005) for helpful discussions and suggestions. Part of this chapter was completed when I was a research visitor at WZB during the summer of 2003, and I am grateful for their financial support and hospitality.

1. Cases such as Von's Grocery (1966), Brown Shoe (1962), and Pabst Brewing (1966), among others, are well known for their narrow focus on market concentration; see Fisher 1987, Schmalensee 1987, and White 1987.

2. For mergers, the 1974 Supreme Court decision in the General Dynamics case is an important example of this change. For antitrust more generally, the *Continental TV v. GTE Sylvania* (1977) case is an important turning point. I return to a discussion of these cases in section 5.7.

3. Also see Gugler and Siebert 2004 for a discussion of efficiency versus market-power effects in the semiconductor industry.

4. In other areas of policy, such as corporate taxation, environmental protection, taxes on higher income brackets, welfare reform, and affirmative action, there are significant literatures that shed light on the often-marked differences between Republicans and Democrats.

5. This is in contrast to many regulatory agencies, which have a "panel" of commissioners who are longer-lived and appointed by different political principals—similar to the independent-regulator setting in Faure-Grimaud and Martimort 2003. For example, the sister antitrust agency, the Federal Trade Commission, has U.S. congressional oversight and a different institutional structure than the Antitrust Division: a panel of

commissioners for FTC versus a single presidentially appointed AAG for the Antitrust Division. In Faure-Grimaud and Martimort 2003, the independent regulator who spans many political principals and is subject to greater capture by the firms. In this setting one would get a dampening of the pure political effect with changes in political principals.

References

Amacher, Ryan, Richard Higgins, William Shughart, and Robert Tollison. 1985. "The Behavior of Regulatory Activity over the Business Cycle: An Empirical Test." *Economic Inquiry* 23:7–19.

Andrews, Donald. 1993. "Tests for Parameter Stability and Structural Change with Unknown Change Point." *Econometrica* 61:821–856.

Baker, Jonathan. 2002. "A Preface to Post-Chicago Antitrust." In R. van den Bergh, R. Pardolesi, and A. Cucinotta, eds., *Post-Chicago Developments in Antitrust Analysis*. Cheltenham: Edward Elgar.

Baker, Jonathan. 2003. "The Case for Antitrust Enforcement." *Journal of Economic Perspectives* 17:27–50.

Bork, Robert. 1978. *The Antitrust Paradox*. New York: Basic Books.

Coate, Malcom, Ryan Higgins, and Fred McChesney. 1990. "Bureaucracy and Politics in FTC Merger Challenges." *Journal of Law and Economics* 33:463–482.

Crandall, Robert, and Clifford Winston. 2003. "Does Antitrust Policy Improve Consumer Welfare? Assessing the Evidence." *Journal of Economic Perspectives* 17:3–26.

Demsetz, Harold. 1973. "Industry Structure, Market Rivalry and Public Policy." *Journal of Law and Economics* 16:1–9.

Demsetz, Harold. 1974. "Two Systems of Belief about Monopoly. " In H. Goldschmidt, H. M. Mann, and J. F. Weston, eds., *Industrial Concentration: New Learning*. Boston: Little Brown.

Faith, Roger, Donald Leavens, and Robert Tollison. 1982. "Antitrust Pork Barrel." *Journal of Law and Economics* 25:329–342.

Faure-Grimaud, Antoine, and David Martimort. 2003. "Regulatory Inertia." *RAND Journal of Economics* 34:413–437.

Fisher, Franklin. 1987. "Horizontal Mergers: Triage and Treatment." *Journal of Economic Perspectives* 1:23–40.

Ghosal, Vivek. 2005. "Regime Shift in Antitrust." Working paper, Georgia Institute of Technology.

Ghosal, Vivek, and Joseph Gallo. 2001. "The Cyclical Behavior of the Department of Justice's Antitrust Enforcement." *International Journal of Industrial Organization* 19:27–54.

Gugler, Klaus, and Ralph Siebert. 2004. "Market Power versus Efficiency Effects of Mergers and Research Joint Ventures: Evidence from the Semiconductor Industry." National Bureau of Economic Research, Working Paper No. 10323.

Hamilton, James. 1994. *Time Series Analysis*. Princeton, NJ: Princeton University Press.

Jovanovic, Boyan, and Peter Rousseau. 2001. "Mergers and Technological Change: 1885–1998." Working paper, University of Chicago.

Kovacic, William, and Carl Shapiro. 2000. "A Century of Antitrust and Legal Thinking." *Journal of Economic Perspectives* 14:43–60.

Landes, William, and Richard Posner. 1981. "Market Power in Antitrust Cases." *Harvard Law Review* 94:937–996.

Long, William, Roger Schramm, and Robert Tollison. 1973. "The Economic Determinants of Antitrust Activity." *Journal of Law and Economics* 16:351–364.

Mueller, Dennis. 1996. "Lessons from the United States's Antitrust History." *International Journal of Industrial Organization* 14:415–445.

Newey, Whitney, and Kenneth West. 1987. "A Simple Positive-Definite Heteroscedasticity and Autocorrelation Consistent Covariance Matrix." *Econometrica* 55:703–708.

Pate, Hewitt. 2004. *Antitrust Law in the U.S. Supreme Court.* Washington, DC: Antitrust Division, U.S. Department of Justice.

Peltzman, Sam. 1976. "Toward a More General Theory of Regulation." *Journal of Law and Economics* 19:211–240.

Peltzman, Sam. 2001. "The Decline of Antitrust Enforcement." *Review of Industrial Organization* 19:49–53.

Phillips, Peter, and Pierre Perron. 1988. "Testing for a Unit Root in Time-Series Regressions." *Biometrica* 335–346.

Pittman, Russell. 1992. "Antitrust and the Political Process." In D. Audretsch and J. Siegfried, eds., *Empirical Studies in Industrial Organization: Essays in Honor of Leonard Weiss.* Amsterdam: Kluwer Academic Publishers.

Posner, Richard. 1970. "A Statistical Study of Antitrust Enforcement." *Journal of Law and Economics* 13:365–419.

Schmalenesee, Richard. 1987. "Horizontal Merger Policy: Problems and Changes." *Journal of Economic Perspectives* 1:41–54.

Siegfried, John. 1975. "The Determinants of Antitrust Activity." *Journal of Law and Economics* 18:559–574.

Stigler, George. 1964. "A Theory of Oligopoly." *Journal of Political Economy* 72:44–61.

Stock, James. 1994. "Unit Roots, Structural Breaks and Trends," In R. F. Engle and D. L. McFadden, eds., *Handbook of Econometrics,* vol. 4. New York: North-Holland.

Stock, James, and Mark Watson. 1996. "Evidence on Structural Instability in Macroeconomic Time-Series Relations." *Journal of Business and Economic Statistics* 14:11–30.

Stock, James, and Mark Watson. 2003. *Econometrics.* New York: Addison Wesley.

White, Lawrence. 1987. "Antitrust and Merger Policy: A Review and Critique." *Journal of Economic Perspectives* 1:13–22.

Williamson, Oliver. 1968. "Economies as an Antitrust Defense: The Welfare Tradeoffs." *American Economic Review* 58:18–36.

6 Market Definition with Differentiated Products—Lessons from the Car Market

Randy Brenkers and
Frank Verboven

6.1 Introduction

Market definition has been a key instrument in all areas of competition policy, including investigations of agreements between firms, abuses of dominant positions, and mergers. The importance of market definition stems from the antitrust authorities' strong reliance on market shares as a measure for market power of the firms under investigation. To make market definition more consistent with economic notions of market power, current practice in both the United States and Europe requires that market definition should be based, at least in principle, on the hypothetical monopoly test (or SSNIP test). Roughly speaking, this test asks whether a hypothetical monopolist over a group of products could profitably raise its prices by about 5 to 10 percent. If this is the case, the products are concluded to constitute a relevant market, in which firms with a high market share may exercise significant market power.

The modern market-definition approach is considerably more in line with economic principles of market power. At the same time, however, the approach has been challenged in favor of other approaches, notably the "simulation approach." This approach directly specifies a model of the market, to make precise predictions about potentially anticompetitive events, such as mergers.[1] While one may expect an increased reliance on simulation approaches, it is also clear that market definition will remain important in the coming years. In most areas there are still influential legal guidelines that rely heavily on market shares as a basis for making decisions. Furthermore, there may not always be an obvious and commonly accepted model of the market that can be used for making market-power predictions based on the simulation approach. It therefore remains important to continue thinking about carefully applying the market-definition approach.

This chapter aims to draw lessons from a rigorous application of the market-definition approach when products are differentiated. We are inspired by a recent European case, the European Commission's new block exemption on vertical restraints in the car market, which heavily relies on the computation of market shares. The new framework, Regulation 1400/2002, was introduced in October 2002 and allows a set of restrictive practices to all car manufacturers with market shares below certain thresholds. Specifically, manufacturers with a market share below 30 percent can choose to form either exclusive or selective distribution agreements with their dealers (but not both), and manufacturers with market shares between 30 and 40 percent can form selective distribution agreements. Firms with market shares above these thresholds cannot rely on the block exemption regulation to form exclusive or selective agreements.

To apply the Regulation, it is necessary to appropriately define the relevant markets. While this is not an easy task in general, it appears to be even more difficult in the case of cars for several reasons. First, cars are not homogeneous products. Cars are differentiated and the degree of differentiation does not appear to be symmetric between different cars. To define the relevant markets, it is therefore essential to have a good understanding of the substitution patterns between cars. Second, the manufacturers do not sell cars directly to end-consumers, but rather indirectly through their retailers. It is thus necessary to understand the substitution patterns at the manufacturer level, but in practice we only have data at our disposal at the retail level. Third, to define the relevant markets, one has to know the manufacturers' price-cost margins, and this information is not generally available at the product level for cars. Even if margin data would be available, it is questionable that they would be reliable.

Our approach to product market definition takes into account these various issues. We essentially require the following two pieces of information: (1) the statistical information necessary to estimate a product-differentiated demand system at the retail level, and (2) a suitable oligopoly model to measure current price-cost margins and to link retail-level demand to wholesale-level demand. Based on this information, we define the relevant market based on the hypothetical monopolist or SSNIP test. On the one hand, our approach is thus consistent with common market-definition principles, and in fact it is more general than previous approaches to implementing the SSNIP test, notably critical elasticity analysis and market definition based on standard (and untested) industry classifications about market segmentation. On the other hand, our approach shares a lot of features with the simulation approach. It has similar data requirements, and it makes similar assumptions about current market power in the industry.[2]

We first apply the market-definition approach to the European car sector, and subsequently ask several questions that are relevant to practitioners implementing the block-exemption regulation. Which firms would and which firms would not satisfy the market-share thresholds to be eligible for selective or exclusive distribution? To which extent would our answers have been different if no rigorous market definition had been used, but rather a definition based on standard industry classifications? We find that our approach leads to different conclusions regarding market definition, as compared to a traditional approach based on standard industry classifications. In several cases a narrower market definition is warranted, while in other cases a wider definition is needed. As a result, our approach is able to more conclusively identify the firms that violate the market-share thresholds stipulated in the block-exemption regulation for cars. Apart from these general conclusions, we also highlight several practical issues in market definition that arise in this case, in particular issues relating to the fact that firms sell multiple products. These may play a role in other cases as well.

The outline of the chapter is as follows. In section 6.2, we provide a background discussion on the regulation of vertical restraints in the car sector and the role of market-share thresholds. In section 6.3, we present our methodology for defining the relevant product markets based on the hypothetical monopolist or SSNIP test (taking as given that markets are geographically segmented in the various countries). Section 6.4 presents our results from the relevant market definition. Section 6.5 uses these findings to identify which firms do and do not satisfy the market-share thresholds, and uses these findings to draw some policy implications for practitioners. Section 6.6 concludes the chapter.

6.2 Vertical Restraints, Safe Harbors, and Market-Share Thresholds

6.2.1 Principles of Block-Exemption Regulations

Article 81(1) of the EC Treaty prohibits agreements that may affect trade between member states, and which prevent, restrict, or distort competition. Article 81(3) allows for exemptions to this prohibition, if there are benefits that outweigh the anticompetitive effects and if consumers receive a fair share of these benefits. Such exemptions can be obtained on an individual basis, but to avoid replicating similar investigations exemptions can also be granted for whole categories of agreements. In this case they are referred to as block-exemption regulations.

Block-exemption regulations may be characterized by two main properties. First, they typically define a set of agreements and market-share thresholds for which there is a *safe harbor*—that is, a presumption that the benefits from the agreement outweigh the possible anticompetitive effects. If the firm proposing the agreement has a market share above the stipulated threshold, the agreement is not necessarily illegal, but an individual exemption needs to be obtained. Second, block-exemption regulations may also define a set of agreements, called "hardcore restrictions," for which there is a presumption that the benefits would not outweigh the possible anticompetitive effects. These may be "black clauses"—that is, agreements that are illegal regardless of the market share of the firms.

6.2.2 The Block-Exemption Regulations for Vertical Agreements and for the Car Sector

An important block-exemption regulation is Regulation 2790/1999 for vertical agreements.[3] The general principles behind this regulation were to be more consistent with economic analysis and to be less prescriptive—in other words, to provide more flexibility to the firms. The regulation provides safe harbors for several vertical agreements, such as single branding, exclusive distribution, selective distribution, tying, recommended retail prices, and so on. In particular, both exclusive distribution and selective distribution are exempted for firms with a market share of up to a 30 percent, even if these agreements are combined with each other or with other nonhardcore restrictions. The regulation on vertical agreements does not apply when there are other sector-specific block-exemption regulations. This has been the case for the car sector since 1985.

A new block-exemption regulation for the car sector was introduced in 2002, Regulation 1400/2002. On the one hand, the new regulation for cars was designed to be consistent with the general principles of the 1999 block-exemption regulation on vertical agreements. On the other hand, the Commission found that a separate, stricter regulation for the car sector was desirable. This approach stemmed mainly from a concern with the "cumulative effect"—that is, the effects on competition when all firms in a market adopt similar vertical agreements. The result was a block-exemption regulation for the car sector allowing firms to adopt either selective or exclusive distribution, but no longer the combination of both restrictions,[4] as would have been possible under the former regulation for cars or under the general block-exemption regulation for vertical agreements. The condition for allowing the possibility to adopt either selective or exclusive distribution was that the firms should satisfy certain market-share thresholds.

6.2.3 Market-Share Thresholds in the Block-Exemption Regulation for the Car Sector

The market-share thresholds stipulated under the block-exemption regulation for the car sector are different from the thresholds under the general block-exemption regulation for vertical agreements. In summary, the thresholds are more stringent and are as follows:

- 40 percent market-share threshold as a safe harbor for selective distribution
- 30 percent market-share threshold as a safe harbor for exclusive distribution[5]

In practice this means that a firm with a market share below 30 percent can freely choose between either selective or exclusive distribution. A firm with a market share between 30 and 40 percent can choose only selective distribution; to be allowed exclusive distribution it would need to obtain an individual exemption from the Commission. A firm with a market share above 40 percent does not fall under the block exemption; hence it would need to request an individual exemption for either exclusive or selective distribution.

6.3 Methodology for Market Definition

The discussion in section 6.2 has shown that the decision to provide a safe harbor for vertical restraints critically depends on the market shares of the firms. The idea behind this approach is that firms with sufficiently low market shares do not have significant market power, so that the vertical restraints are not expected to seriously damage the extent of competition. To make this approach convincing, it is necessary however to first define the relevant market based on sound economic principles.

In this section, we outline our methodology for defining the relevant markets. First, we provide a qualitative discussion of some preliminary steps. These steps motivate focusing our methodology on a SSNIP test for product market definition and the role of demand substitution. Second, we outline our specific methodology, which essentially only requires information to estimate the demand for new cars, combined with a model of current equilibrium pricing behavior. Finally, we present the demand model to be estimated as the key input for implementing the SSNIP test.

6.3.1 Preliminary Steps

6.3.1.1 SSNIP Test and Focus on Demand Substitution The principles for defining the relevant market are based on the hypothetical monopolist or SSNIP test, similar to U.S. practice; see the Commission Notice 97/C, 372/03. The test searches for the smallest set of products for which a small but significant and nontransitory increase in prices would be jointly profitable. The considered price increase is typically in the range of 5 to 10 percent. The profitability of such a price increase may depend on three sources of competitive constraints: demand substitution, supply substitution (entry by existing firms), and potential competition (new entry). We discuss these in turn. First, the Commission Notice states that demand substitution constitutes the most immediate and effective disciplinary force on the suppliers, and should therefore necessarily be taken into account in the market-definition stage. Second, supply substitution may in principle also be taken into account in the market-definition stage, but since it is a less immediate constraint it requires additional analysis on the investment possibilities. Developing and marketing new cars typically involve substantial investment costs and significant time delays. This suggests that it is not necessary to account for supply substitution in our market-definition test. Third, the Commission Notice explicitly states that new entry should not to be taken into account in the market-definition stage, but rather at the assessment stage of competition policy analysis. In sum, to define the relevant market we apply the principles of the SSNIP test, accounting solely for demand substitution as a competitive constraint.

6.3.1.2 Focus on Product Market Definition Market definition consists of both geographic and product market definition. To define the relevant geographic markets, we follow a largely qualitative approach.

There exists an extensive previous documentation of large international price dispersion in the European car market. In addition, there is detailed institutional evidence that there are still existing trade barriers, even if there has been progress toward more integration over the past years. These existing trade barriers are to a large extent due to the selective and exclusive distribution system, which makes it difficult for independent resellers and authorized dealers to engage in cross-border trade. This has been confirmed by some limited available evidence on low parallel imports between countries despite the large price differentials. See Verboven 2002 for more extensive discussion on defining the relevant geographic markets as the national markets.[6] Within the national markets, we then define the relevant product markets following a rigorous implementation of the SSNIP test. We outline our general approach in the next subsection.

6.3.2 The SSNIP Test for Product Market Definition

6.3.2.1 General Framework The above discussion allows us to focus on defining the relevant product market accounting for the role of demand substitution. Call the products for which the hypothetical price increase is considered the insider products, and the remaining products the outsider products. Consider first the joint profits earned on the insider products before the price increase, say, $\pi_I(w)$. These profits depend on the wholesale prices w, as charged by the manufacturers to the dealers. The wholesale price vector w contains both the insiders' and the outsiders' wholesale price vectors, w^I and w^O, so we sometimes use $w = (w^I, w^O)$ to explicitly distinguish between both parts of the wholesale price vector. The insider products' joint profits before the hypothetical price increase equal the sum of each insider product j:

$$\pi_I(w) = \sum_{j \in I} (w_j - c_j) s_j^W(w) L \tag{1}$$

where I denotes the set of insider products, c_j is the marginal cost of product j, L is the total number of potential consumers, and $s_j^W(w)$ is the wholesale-level market-share function of product j—that is, the manufacturer's demand for product j as a function of the wholesale price vector. For expositional convenience and without loss of generality, the marginal cost c_j is assumed to include both the manufacturers' and the retailers' marginal cost. It is thus as if the dealers do not bear their own retail cost directly, but rather indirectly through the wholesale price they pay to the manufacturers.

The SSNIP test considers an increase in the insiders' wholesale prices, w^I, by a certain percentage λ, say 5 or 10 percent. Denote the new wholesale price vector by $w^{new} = ((1 + \lambda)w^I, w^O)$. The insider products' joint profits after the price increase are equal to

$$\pi_I(w^{new}) = \sum_{i \in I} \left((1+\lambda)w_j - c_j\right) s_j^W(w^{new}) L \tag{2}$$

On the one hand, the insiders' profit margins increase from $w_j - c_j$ to $(1 + \lambda)w_j - c_j$. On the other hand, the raise in the insiders' wholesale prices reduces the manufacturers' sales. The SSNIP test simply compares the insiders' profits before and after the price increase, given by (1) and (2), and assesses whether the profit change is positive.

The above discussion implies that the SSNIP test may be carried out with the following two pieces of information: the wholesale-level demand system $s^W(w)$, and the wholesale profit margins $w - c$. In our application, we do not have data on manufacturers' wholesale prices, so we cannot directly estimate a wholesale-level demand system. We also do not have information on manufacturers' marginal costs, so we cannot directly measure the wholesale profit margins. The only information we have at our disposal is demand information at the retail level (sales, retail prices, and product characteristics), enabling us to estimate the retail-level demand system, $s^R(p)$, where p is the retail price vector. Fortunately, this information is sufficient if one adds a model of equilibrium pricing behavior of the manufacturers and the retailers.

6.3.2.2 Adding an Equilibrium Model of Pricing Following Brenkers and Verboven 2006, we specify a two-stage model of pricing behavior by manufacturers and retailers. We provide a sketch of the model here, and refer to that paper for detailed derivations.[7] Manufacturers first simultaneously choose their profit-maximizing wholesale prices, and retailers subsequently simultaneously choose their profit-maximizing retail prices. The second-stage Nash equilibrium retail price vector is a function of the wholesale price vector set in the first stage, and is written by the system of pass-through functions $p = p(w)$. Manufacturers in turn take into account these pass-through functions when setting their own wholesale prices in the first stage.

To derive the precise form of the pass-through functions we consider two possible scenarios of retail pricing in the second stage. In the first scenario there is perfect intrabrand competition. Retailers compete vigorously with other retailers selling the same brand, so that retail prices are equal to wholesale prices—that is, $p = p(w) = w$. In this scenario wholesale prices are completely passed through into the retail prices. In the second scenario there is no intrabrand competition, so that retailers only compete with retailers selling different brands. The retail prices $p = p(w)$ are now implicitly defined by the system of first-order conditions for profit maximization by the retailers, denoted by $f(p, w) = 0$. The solution to this system shows that retail prices exceed wholesale prices by a margin, which depends on the own- and cross-price elasticities of retail demand. In this scenario the wholesale prices are not passed through completely into the retail prices.

This framework enables us to obtain the two required pieces of information.

6.3.2.3 Wholesale-Level Demand System The wholesale-level demand system $s^W(w)$ can be obtained by explicitly linking it to the estimated retail-level demand system $s^R(p)$, using the pass-through function $p(w)$. Specifically, we have

$$s^W(w) = s^R(p(w)) \tag{3}$$

Intuitively, we are making use of the fact that manufacturers' wholesale-level demand is a derived demand—that is, it is the demand by the dealers as derived from their own retail demand. In the first scenario of full intrabrand competition, the wholesale and retail prices coincide—in other words, $p = w$, so that the wholesale-level demand system reduces to the simple retail-level demand system, $s^W(w) = s^R(p)$. The SSNIP test is then simply given by comparing profits (1) and (2) after replacing the wholesale-level demands $s_j^W(w)$ by the retail-level demands $s_j^R(p)$.

Things are more complicated in the second scenario of no intrabrand competition. As mentioned above, in this case the retail prices $p = p(w)$ are implicitly defined by the first-order conditions for retail profit maximization, $f(p, w) = 0$. The SSNIP test then compares profits (1) and (2) after replacing the wholesale-level demands $s_j^W(w)$ by the retail-level demands using the implicit functions $p = p(w)$. We thus compare

$$\pi_I(w) = \sum_{j \in I} (w_j - c_j) s_j^R(p(w)) L \tag{1'}$$

with

$$\pi_I(w^{new}) = \sum_{i \in I} \left((1+\lambda)w_j - c_j\right) s_j^R(p(w^{new}))L \tag{2'}$$

Intuitively, the SSNIP test considers an increase in the insiders' wholesale prices w^I by, say, 10 percent, resulting in a new wholesale price vector w^{new}. The new retail prices p are computed by numerically solving the system $f(p, w^{new}) = 0$. On the one hand, the insider products' retail prices will typically rise by less than 10 percent, because of incomplete pass-through. On the other hand, the outsider products' retail prices may respond positively. The new retail prices then determine demand according to the estimated retail-level demand functions.

6.3.2.4 Wholesale Profit Margins To measure the wholesale profit margins $w - c$, we do not make use of accounting information. First, such information is difficult to obtain at the product level. The problem is further complicated in our application since both the wholesale prices and the marginal costs are not observed. Second, as has been extensively discussed in the empirical oligopoly literature, accounting cost information does not adequately measure opportunity costs, which ultimately determine the firms' pricing decisions. In the case of cars, it is particularly noteworthy to point out that every new car sold generates a stream of future profits on repair and maintenance services.[8] These future profits may be viewed as a negative contribution to the manufacturers' opportunity cost for selling a new car. If they are large, it is even possible that the opportunity cost of selling a car is negative.

To resolve these issues, we measure the wholesale profit margins using the equilibrium first-order conditions for profit maximization at the wholesale and the retail stage. In the first scenario of full intrabrand competition, where $p = w$, the equilibrium wholesale profit margins reduce to the standard expression for multiproduct firms, as in Berry, Levinsohn, and Pakes 1995. Loosely speaking, each product's profit margin is equal to price divided by the product's perceived price elasticity of demand.[9] In the second scenario of no intrabrand competition, the equilibrium wholesale profit margins are more complicated. Each profit margin takes a form as described in Rey and Stiglitz 1995—that is, price divided by the product's perceived *adjusted* price elasticity of demand. The adjustment refers to the fact that manufacturers do not directly influence retail prices, but only indirectly through their wholesale prices, making competition between manufacturers less intense.

6.3.3 Retail Demand for New Cars

To implement the SSNIP test, it remains to specify the retail-level demand system for new cars $s^R(p)$. As mentioned in section 6.3.1.2, our starting point is that the European car market is segmented into its various national markets. Within each national market, we then specify demand using a general version of the two-level nested logit. This logit model partitions the car market into various product segments according to common marketing classifications: subcompacts, compacts, intermediates, standard/luxury, sports, and minivans. Each segment is further partitioned in two subsegments according to country of origin: domestic and foreign cars. Consumers may have correlated preferences for all cars belonging to the same segment, because these cars share certain features such as size, performance, and prestige. Furthermore, consumers may have even more closely correlated preferences for cars belonging to both the same segment and country of origin, because these cars may share additional features such as style or image. The degree of preference correlation for products in the same subsegments and segments determines the substitution patterns in the car market. If preferences for products in the same (sub)segments are strongly correlated, products from the same (sub)segment are strong substitutes (with high cross-price elasticities), while products from different (sub)segments will be weak substitutes (with low cross-price elasticities). A finding of strong preference correlation thus has potentially important implications for the product market definition.

Various versions of the nested logit model have been derived; see Berry 1994 for the basic one-level nested logit framework, and Goldberg 1995 and Verboven 1996 for applications to the car market using a two-level nested logit.[10] Specifically, the estimating demand equation takes the following simple linear form:

$$\ln(s_j/s_0) = x_j'\beta - (\alpha/y)p_j + \sigma_{hg}\ln(\bar{s}_{j/hg}) + \sigma_g \ln(\bar{s}_{h/g}) + \xi_j$$

where s_j is overall market share of product j (i.e., sales divided by the total number of potential consumers); s_0 is the overall market share of the outside good (i.e., total number of potential consumers minus total number of actual cars sold, divided by the total number of potential consumers); $\bar{s}_{j/hg}$ is the market share of product j in its subsegment h of segment g, and $\bar{s}_{h/g}$ is the market share of all products of subsegment h in segment g; p_j is the price of product j and y is income; x_j' is a vector of product characteristics (e.g., horsepower); ϕ_j is the error term capturing unobserved product characteristics (to the econometrician); and

β, α, σ_{hg}, and σ_g are parameters to be estimated. Most notably, σ_{hg} and σ_g are "segmentation parameters," with $1 \geq \sigma_{hg} \geq \sigma_g \geq 0$. They roughly measure the correlation of preferences for cars of the same subgroup h of g, and the same group g, respectively. If σ_{hg} and σ_g are close to 1, preferences are strongly correlated within subgroups and groups, so that there is strong segmentation. If $\sigma_{hg} = \sigma_g = 0$, we obtain the simple logit model without segmentation.

In principle, the model can be estimated with a cross-section of products (cars), $j = 1 \ldots J$. In our application, we have a panel of cross-sections with five different countries over thirty years. To estimate the model, the main identification assumption is that the product characteristics entering x_j are uncorrelated with the error term ξ_j. The price p_j and the market shares $\ln(\bar{s}_{j/hg})$ and $\ln(\bar{s}_{h/g})$ may, however, be correlated with the error term, so that an instrumental variable estimator should be used. We use a fixed-effects two-stage least-squares estimator, using instruments inspired by Berry, Levinsohn, and Pakes 1995. Specifically, we adopt the following list of instruments, making use of the specific structure of the nested logit model: (1) the products' own observed characteristics x_j; (2) the number of products, and the sums of characteristics of other products of the same firm belonging to the same subsegment, interacted with a subsegment dummy variable; (3) the number of products, and the sums of the characteristics of competing products belonging to the same subsegment, interacted with a subsegment dummy variable; (4) the number of products, and the sums of the characteristics of competing products belonging to the same segment, interacted with a segment dummy variable. Note that we interact the instruments in (2)–(4) with subsegment or segment dummy variables, since we allow the differentiation parameters σ_{hg} and σ_g to differ across subsegments and segments.

6.3.4 Summary and Relationship to Other Approaches

6.3.4.1 Summary Our implementation of the SSNIP test takes the following steps:

Step 1. Estimate the retail-level demand system.

Step 2. Specify a model of pricing behavior to compute:

a. Wholesale-level demand system

b. Current profit margins

Step 3. Select a small set of insider products I as the candidate-relevant market. Compute the insiders' current joint profits, and their new joint profits after a price increase by a percentage λ. If profits increase, this is a relevant market. Otherwise select a larger set of insider products and repeat step 3.

It is instructive to relate our approach to two other approaches to define the relevant markets.

6.3.4.2 Technical Specifications or Standard Industry Classifications

A common approach in market definition is to use technical specifications of products. All products with similar characteristics are then included in the same relevant market. In specific cases, standard industry classifications are available, which are based on the technical specifications of the products. Using technical specifications or industry classifications can be misleading, since it has to be shown that consumers value the specifications in such a way that products with similar attributes are sufficiently close substitutes.

While our approach also makes use of standard industry classifications, it is important to stress that we test, using our demand model, whether these classifications are actually valid. We measure the extent to which consumer preferences are actually correlated within the segments, and also whether there is even further segmentation within the segments (by considering the subsegments).

6.3.4.3 Critical Elasticity Analysis A more recent rigorous approach that has often been used to implement the SSNIP test is critical loss or critical elasticity analysis, as introduced by Harris and Simons and subsequently elaborated on by, for example, Werden (1998).[11] In its version of critical elasticity analysis, this approach typically starts from a set of homogeneous products, and then derives the threshold elasticity corresponding to that set of products, above which a price increase would be unprofitable.[12] The threshold elasticity depends on the functional form of demand and on the set of products' current profit margins. In its ideal form, an econometric analysis would be required to estimate the price elasticity of demand corresponding to each selected candidate-relevant market definition. If it turns out that the estimated elasticity is higher than the threshold, then a larger candidate market should be considered, and the price elasticity of demand at that level should be reestimated. Apart from being cumbersome, this approach also has an inconsistency. The threshold elasticity formulas are computed based on the assumption that products within the selected market are perfectly homogeneous and that no homogeneous products are excluded. Hence, when the SSNIP test is violated and additional products are added to the market definition, the assumption that products within the relevant market are homogeneous is no longer satisfied, so that the formula for the threshold price elasticity of demand is no longer valid. Our approach avoids these difficulties.

6.4 Results on Market Definition

6.4.1 The Data

The data set to estimate the nested logit model and carry out the SSNIP tests consists of prices, sales, and physical characteristics of (essentially) all cars sold during 1970–1999 in Belgium, France, Germany, Italy, and the United Kingdom. The total number of observations is about 12,000, so a bit less than 100 models are available in every market/year. The price data are pretax and posttax list prices corresponding to the base model available in the market, as available in consumer catalogs.[13] We consistently use the prices from the August catalogs.[14] Sales are new car registrations for the model range. Physical characteristics (also from consumer catalogs) include dimensions (weight, length, width, height), engine characteristics (horsepower, displacement), and performance measures (speed, acceleration, and fuel efficiency). The data set also includes variables to identify the model, the brand, the firm, the country of origin/production location, and the market segment. The data set is augmented with macroeconomic variables including population, exchange rates, GDP, and consumer price indices for the various markets over the relevant period. Finally, there is information on dealer discounts and gross dealer margins for a selected number of models/years.

To estimate the nested logit model, we need to define segments and subsegments. Following common industry and marketing classifications, we consider six different segments: subcompacts, compacts, intermediates, standards/luxuries, sports, and minivans. We closely follow the classification of the magazine *L'Argus de l'Automobile*, but check for consistency with alternative industry classifications; see Verboven 2002 for a detailed discussion of these classification issues. Each segment is further divided in two subsegments, according to country of origin: domestic or foreign. Table 6.1 provides summary statistics by market segment, for the five countries in 1999.

Table 6.1
Summary statistics, by segment

	Mean	Std. dev.	Mean	Std. dev.
	Subcompact (144 obs.)		Compact (110 obs.)	
Horsepower (in kW)	41.73	5.46	60.61	11.39
Fuel inefficiency (liters per 100 km)	7.03	0.59	8.28	0.91
Width (in cm)	160.23	6.32	169.94	2.91
Height (in cm)	143.33	6.17	141.98	4.35
Foreign (1 if foreign)	0.35	0.48	0.36	0.48
Price (euro)	7277	1435	10515	2420
	Intermediate (118 obs.)		Standard/luxury (69 obs.)	
Horsepower (in kW)	75.73	14.11	96.93	11.07
Fuel inefficiency (liters per 100 km)	9.19	0.87	10.51	1.05
Width (in cm)	172.99	3.12	176.90	3.49
Height (in cm)	141.37	1.82	141.46	3.34
Foreign (1 if foreign)	0.31	0.46	0.36	0.48
Price (euro)	13406	3669	18907	3779
	Sports (92 obs.)		Minivan (89 obs.)	
Horsepower (in kW)	99.42	24.42	80.45	19.31
Fuel inefficiency (liters per 100 km)	9.95	1.07	10.68	2.04
Width (in cm)	171.71	5.78	175.01	9.67
Height (in cm)	132.01	6.23	169.08	8.20
Foreign (1 if foreign)	0.33	0.47	0.31	0.47
Price (euro)	18643	5405	15276	4360

6.4.2 The Demand Parameter Estimates

We only provide a brief discussion of our demand parameter estimates, with a focus on the role of the segmentation parameters σ_{hg} and σ_g, since these play a central role in the subsequent SSNIP tests. For more extensive discussion of the demand results, in a richer econometric framework, see Brenkers and Verboven 2002. Table 6.2 shows the results. The first two columns refer to the simple logit specification, in which all segmentation parameters σ_{hg} and σ_g are assumed to be equal to zero. This specification a priori rules out any segmentation within the national market, since consumers have no correlated preferences across cars within the same segment or subsegment. The third and the fourth columns present the results from a restricted specification, in which σ_{hg} is equal across all twelve subsegments, and σ_g is equal across all

Table 6.2
Parameter estimates for the logit and nested logit models

	Logit		Restricted nested logit		Flexible nested logit	
	Estimate	St. error	Estimate	St. error	Estimate	St. error
Mean-valuation parameters						
Constant	–20.209	.980	–12.853	.687	–11.176	.593
Horsepower	–.007	.002	.004	.002	.001	.001
Fuel inefficiency	–.124	.013	–.066	.008	–.050	.007
Width	.074	.004	.042	.003	.034	.003
Height	.036	.005	.023	.003	.018	.003
Foreign	–1.848	.025	–1.048	.047	–.918	.038
Price	–2.320	.231	–2.225	.130	–1.755	.098
Subsegmentation parameters						
Subcompact			.525	.028	.765	.025
Compact			same		.567	.030
Intermediate			same		.538	.033
Standard/luxury			same		.697	.028
Sports			same		.445	.032
Minivan			same		.042	.041
Segmentation parameters						
Subcompact			.318	.030	.298	.035
Compact			same		.379	.041
Intermediate			same		.311	.042
Standard/luxury			same		.450	.035
Sports			same		.143	.042
Minivan			same		.151	.066
Year dummies	Yes	Yes	Yes	Yes	Yes	Yes
Market dummies	Yes	Yes	Yes	Yes	Yes	Yes
Product dummies	Yes	Yes	Yes	Yes	Yes	Yes

segments. This is the commonly estimated version of the (two-level) nested logit model. The fifth and sixth columns present the results of a more flexible nested logit specification, in which the subsegmentation and segmentation parameters are allowed to vary by segment. To reduce the number of σ's to be estimated, we constrain $\sigma_{Dg} = \sigma_{Fg}$ (where D denotes domestic and F denotes foreign)—that is, the degree of heterogeneity within a domestic subsegment is the same as that within its foreign counterpart.

The simple logit specification in table 6.2 shows that some of the characteristics parameters have the unexpected sign (e.g., the horsepower coefficient). This no longer appears to be the case for the nested logit specifications. The parameters of the included characteristics are of the expected sign and usually significant. Horsepower, width, and height positively affect the consumers' mean valuation, whereas fuel inefficiency (measured as liters per 100 km) has a negative impact. Similarly, price has a significantly negative effect. The foreign-firm effect is negative and significant, meaning that the domestic incumbents face a competitive advantage over their foreign competitors in terms of the mean consumer valuation.

The segmentation parameters σ mostly satisfy the condition that $1 \geq \sigma_{hg} \geq \sigma_g \geq 0$, as required for the model to be consistent with random utility theory. This means that consumers tend to have more strongly correlated preferences for cars of the same subsegment than for cars of a different subsegment but within the same segment. They also have more strongly correlated preferences for cars of the same segment than for cars of a different segment. These findings imply that there is indeed strong segmentation according to the subsegments, and weaker segmentation according to the segments. The only exception to our finding of strong segmentation and subsegmentation is given by the minivan cars. This suggests that consumers do not have strongly correlated preferences across minivan cars. This may seem surprising since minivans have in common an important dimension ("space"). The interpretation for this finding is simple, however. European classifications define minivans as a fairly heterogeneous group. They do not just include the larger minivans (such as the Renault Espace) but also smaller ones, which are derived from cars in the subcompact, compact, or intermediate segments (e.g., the Renault Scenic). As such, the minivan segment is currently defined as a relatively heterogeneous group, so that a finding of limited segmentation relative to other cars is natural.[15]

Table 6.3
Substitution patterns
Cross-price elasticities with respect to cars from same subsegment

	Logit		Restricted nested logit		Flexible nested logit	
	Average	St. dev.	Average	St. dev.	Average	St. dev.
Subcompact	.0021	.0029	.056	.078	.148	.212
Compact	.0033	.0044	.108	.160	.098	.144
Intermediate	.0025	.0033	.124	.188	.105	.161
Standard/luxury	.0018	.0028	.273	.395	.463	.675
Sports	.0005	.0007	.187	.205	.117	.132
Minivan	.0011	.0014	.187	.283	.010	.014

The role of the segmentation parameters is further illustrated in table 6.3, showing the cross-price elasticities for cars of the same subsegment under alternative demand specifications. In the simple logit model, these cross-price elasticities are very small. In the nested logit models, they are considerably larger and also show substantial variation across models.

To check the sensitivity of the results, we also considered various alternative specifications. We found most parameter estimates to be robust. Most interestingly, we considered a specification for two separate subperiods—that is, the periods 1970–1985 and 1986–1999. This specification is motivated by the fact that the industry has experienced various changes over the last three decades, notably a gradual progress toward integration (Goldberg and Verboven 2005) and a correspondingly increased competition from foreign firms (i.e., nondomestic European and Japanese firms). These changes may be reflected in both a change in the mean valuation for foreign cars, and in a change in the variance around that mean (i.e., the σ_{hg} parameters, referring to the domestic/foreign subsegments). We found that the mean negative valuation for foreign cars is significantly stronger during the period 1970–1985 than during the subsequent period. However, we did not find significant changes in the deviations from that mean (i.e., the subsegmentation parameters σ_{hg}). As such, the increased integration and foreign competition is only manifested in a rise in the mean valuation attached to foreign cars, but not in changes in the deviation around that mean. These findings imply that our conclusions on market definition below remain robust when based on the estimates of the most recent period.

6.4.3 Implementing the SSNIP Tests

6.4.3.1 Selecting Candidate-Relevant Markets Textbook descriptions usually describe the following procedure for selecting candidate-relevant markets; see, for example, Church and Ware 1999. As a first candidate-relevant market, select the considered product and its next-best substitute, defined as the product with the largest cross-price elasticity of demand. If the SSNIP test fails, progressively add products that are next-best substitutes until the SSNIP test is satisfied. Assuming that the next-best substitutes can be unambiguously ranked, this procedure would lead to a unique relevant market for every product that is considered. In principle, we could follow this mechanical procedure since we can rank all products according to their estimated cross-price elasticities. In practice, several considerations lead us to conclude that this procedure would be rather impractical.

The first consideration is that the number of products for which a relevant market needs to be defined is quite large; there are about 100 different car models in each country. Since the ranking of next-best substitutes may be different for each product, this implies that a large number of candidate-relevant markets and corresponding SSNIP tests would need to be considered. Furthermore, this would result in a set of market definitions specific to every single product. For example the relevant market for product *A* may consist of product *A* and *B*, whereas the relevant market for product *B* would consist of products *A*, *B*, and *C*. While there is nothing wrong with this in principle, it prohibits a simple and transparent presentation of the relevant markets.

The second consideration is that all firms sell multiple products. Once the relevant markets have been defined for every product of the firms, it will be necessary to assess each firm's market share within each of these relevant markets corresponding to the firm's different products. This procedure will inevitably be quite cumbersome.

To resolve these practical difficulties, we follow a simplified procedure. Instead of starting with a candidate-relevant market that only includes the considered product and its closest substitute, and then progressively adding next-best substitutes, we immediately start by including all products belonging to the considered product's subsegment. If the SSNIP test fails for this subsegment, we include all products belonging to the same segment as the candidate-relevant market. And if the SSNIP test also fails here, we take the products of all segments excluding the outside good. This procedure is in the same spirit as the textbook-selection procedure, but has the advantages of limiting both the number of considered candidate-relevant markets and the number of actual relevant markets defined.

6.4.3.2 Are the Subsegments Relevant Markets? Table 6.4 presents the results from applying the SSNIP tests in all five countries for all twelve subsegments—that is, the six domestic and the six foreign subsegments. For example, the domestic subcompact subsegment in France in 1999 consists of all French subcompact cars: Citroën AX and Saxo; Peugeot 106, 205, and 206; and Renault Clio and Twingo. Each cell considers the percentage profit change from a joint price increase by 10 percent in the subsegment. Each cell contains two numbers: the first number assumes no intrabrand competition and the second number assumes full intrabrand competition. To demonstrate the importance of the demand specification, we present both the results based on the parameters of the simple logit model (top part of table), and the results based on the parameters of the flexible nested logit (bottom part).[16]

Consider first the results based on the simple logit estimates, as shown in the top part of table 6.4. All profit changes are negative, implying that the subsegments do not constitute relevant markets in any of the countries if the simple logit demand specification would be correct. This is true under both full and no intrabrand competition, although the profit changes are closer to zero under no intrabrand competition. The largest percentage profit decreases occur in the standard/luxury and sports subsegments (both domestic or foreign); they occur especially in Italy and the United Kingdom. The reason subsegments do not constitute relevant markets is that the logit model assumes that all cars are symmetric substitutes. Hence, when the prices of all products in a certain subsegment increase, this may lead to a substantial amount of substitution toward other subsegments.

The picture looks different when the SSNIP tests are based on the demand parameters of the nested logit model, which we showed to be empirically superior to the simple logit model in our application. The bottom part of table 6.4 shows that profits increase in most subsegments, both under full or no intrabrand competition. The main exceptions are (1) the minivan subsegments in all countries, whether domestic or foreign, and (2) all domestic subsegments in Italy. We conclude that most subsegments may be defined as relevant markets, with the exception of the minivan subsegments and the domestic

Table 6.4
Profit changes when subsegments are candidate-relevant markets

Results based on logit estimates

	Belgium		France		Germany		Italy		UK	
	Domestic subsegments									
Subcompact	0.0	–0.2	0.0	–0.4	0.0	–0.5	0.0	–0.6	–0.1	–0.7
Compact	0.0	–0.3	–0.2	–1.1	–0.1	–0.8	–0.6	–1.8	–0.4	–1.4
Intermediate	–0.2	–1.0	–0.3	–1.3	–0.7	–1.9	–0.9	–2.3	–1.0	–2.4
Standard/luxury	–1.1	–2.6	–1.9	–3.4	–1.1	–2.5	–2.2	–4.3	–2.0	–3.8
Sports	–1.3	–2.8	.	.	–1.4	–3.0	–2.0	–3.6	–1.5	–3.0
Minivan	–0.6	–1.7	–1.7	–3.2	–1.2	–2.6	–2.0	–3.6	–1.7	–3.2
	Foreign subsegments									
Subcompact	.	.	0.0	–0.3	0.0	–0.4	0.0	–0.2	0.0	–0.5
Compact	.	.	–0.1	–0.8	0.0	–0.7	–0.2	–1.1	–0.3	–1.2
Intermediate	.	.	–0.3	–1.4	–0.2	–1.1	–0.7	–2.0	–0.6	–1.9
Standard/luxury	.	.	–1.3	–2.9	–0.9	–2.3	–2.7	–4.8	–1.8	–3.6
Sports	.	.	–0.9	–2.3	–0.6	–1.9	–1.4	–2.9	–2.2	–4.1
Minivan	.	.	–0.5	–1.7	–0.3	–1.3	–0.8	–2.2	–0.9	–2.3

Results based on flexible nested logit estimates

	Belgium		France		Germany		Italy		UK	
	Domestic subsegments									
Subcompact	9.3	16.8	2.4	9.9	4.7	12.8	–0.3	–0.6	1.9	10.3
Compact	4.5	9.7	0.6	3.0	2.5	6.5	–0.8	–2.2	2.1	5.4
Intermediate	5.6	9.8	1.0	2.7	1.8	3.9	–0.9	–2.3	0.6	3.5
Standard/luxury	17.3	26.3	–1.7	2.4	8.7	19.2	–3.8	–5.8	–2.3	2.7
Sports	4.3	7.1	.	.	2.1	4.3	–1.5	–2.8	0.9	3.5
Minivan	0.2	0.2	–0.6	–1.6	–0.4	–1.2	–1.1	–2.6	–0.7	–1.8
	Foreign subsegments									
Subcompact	.	.	7.3	14.3	8.8	16.1	12.6	19.8	12.7	19.9
Compact	.	.	3.4	6.6	2.5	4.8	5.5	9.7	5.3	8.2
Intermediate	.	.	3.4	5.5	4.0	6.5	6.5	9.5	6.4	9.2
Standard/luxury	.	.	12.9	20.7	7.0	10.8	10.6	17.9	15.9	25.2
Sports	.	.	3.6	6.6	2.7	5.0	4.2	7.3	5.1	7.5
Minivan	.	.	0.0	–0.6	0.0	–0.4	0.0	–0.3	–0.1	–0.8

Note: Each cell contains two percentage price increases. The first cell is the percentage profit increase under no intrabrand competition; the second cell is the corresponding number under full intrabrand competition.

subsegments in Italy. This conclusion holds regardless of whether there would be full or no intrabrand competition: under both cases the signs of the profit changes are usually the same, and only the magnitudes differ.[17] It is interesting to observe that the magnitudes of the profit effects are usually smaller (in absolute value) under no intrabrand competition than under full intrabrand competition. The interpretation is as follows. Under full intrabrand competition, a 10 percent wholesale price increase is fully passed on to the consumers, whereas under no intrabrand competition, it is only passed on incompletely. Hence, under no intrabrand competition the retail price increase is typically lower than 10 percent, making the magnitude of the profit effects (whether positive or negative) closer to zero.

We now discuss why the minivan subsegments and the domestic subsegments in Italy do not constitute relevant markets. The explanation for the minivans clearly has to do with our obtained demand parameter estimates. Recall that most of the segmentation parameters were estimated to be substantially larger than zero, implying that consumers are not inclined to substitute out of a subsegment or segment when prices increase in that segment. We only found the segmentation parameters of the minivan subsegments and segments to be close to zero. As a result, consumers are comparatively more likely to substitute out of the minivan subsegments after a price increase. The amount of substitution out of the minivan subsegments thus apparently turns out to be sufficiently large to render a 10 percent price increase unprofitable.

Our finding that the domestic subsegments in Italy are not the relevant markets may seem more surprising at first, since we estimated a relatively strong degree of segmentation in all nonminivan subsegments. The explanation is that a single firm, Fiat, owns all the products in the domestic subsegments in Italy, and that this firm is already setting its prices to maximize the profits. These two elements imply that Fiat would have no incentives to further raise prices in the domestic subsegments in Italy. This of course resembles the issues in the notorious Cellophane case (*U.S. v. E.I. du Pont*, 1956). The SSNIP test only shows that there are no profit incentives for additional price increases above the current levels in the domestic subsegments in Italy. But this does not mean that current market power is not already high. To resolve these issues, practitioners have often advocated a SSNIP test that considers price increases above a competitive benchmark, rather than price increases above the current level. But this leads to the question what exactly should be that competitive benchmark. As an alternative solution, we simply turn next to consider wider candidate-relevant markets—that is, the various segments. We then come back to the issues later and will discuss whether they are of practical relevance in our specific application.

6.4.3.3 Are The Segments Relevant Markets? Table 6.5 considers the larger market definitions—that is, the segments, which include the domestic and the foreign subsegments. As before, the top part of the table shows the results using the parameters of the simple logit model, while the bottom part shows the results using the parameters of the nested logit model. The results based on the simple logit parameter estimates confirm our earlier findings: even enlarging the market definition to include both domestic and foreign products of the same segment leads to negative profit effects. Hence, using a simple logit model would still be misleading and show that segments do not constitute relevant markets.

The results based on the nested logit model show that almost all segments can now profitably raise their prices by 10 percent, under both the scenarios of no and full intrabrand competition. In particular, this is also true for the segments in Italy. Hence, to obtain a relevant market

Table 6.5
Profit changes when segments are candidate-relevant markets

Results based on logit estimates

	Belgium		France		Germany		Italy		UK	
Subcompact	0.0	–0.2	0.0	–0.1	0.0	–0.3	0.0	0.0	0.0	–0.4
Compact	0.0	–0.3	–0.1	–0.8	0.0	–0.5	–0.2	–1.1	–0.2	–1.0
Intermediate	–0.2	–1.0	–0.3	–1.2	–0.4	–1.3	–0.7	–2.0	–0.6	–1.9
Standard/Luxury	–1.1	–2.6	–1.4	–2.9	–1.0	–2.4	–2.4	–4.4	–1.8	–3.6
Sports	–1.3	–2.8	–0.9	–2.3	–1.2	–2.7	–1.5	–3.0	–1.8	–3.5
Minivan	–0.6	–1.7	–1.1	–2.4	–0.7	–1.8	–0.9	–2.3	–1.1	–2.5

Results based on flexible nested logit estimates

	Belgium		France		Germany		Italy		UK	
Subcompact	9.3	16.8	4.4	12.9	7.4	16.2	4.9	7.7	8.4	18.1
Compact	4.5	9.7	3.6	8.6	3.4	8.4	5.4	9.8	6.3	11.7
Intermediate	5.6	9.8	2.9	6.0	4.4	8.2	5.8	9.0	6.4	11.2
Standard/Luxury	17.3	26.3	13.8	23.1	10.8	21.9	10.3	16.4	17.1	27.4
Sports	4.3	7.1	3.6	6.6	2.7	5.4	3.7	6.2	3.8	7.2
Minivan	0.2	0.2	0.0	–0.2	0.1	0.1	0.1	–0.2	0.0	–0.2

Note: Each cell contains two percentage price increases. The first cell is the percentage profit increase under no intrabrand competition; the second cell is the corresponding number under full intrabrand competition.

definition for the domestic products in Italy it is sufficient to enlarge the market definition from the subsegment to the segment level.

The only segments for which price increases by 10 percent sometimes remain unprofitable are the minivan segments. This is the case in France, Italy, and the United Kingdom under the scenario of full intrabrand competition. In the other minivan cases the profit effects are positive, but they are typically very small. These findings again follow from our demand parameter estimates, which showed that the minivan segments are not clearly segmented from the other products. Note however that we found positive profit effects for the minivan segments when we considered 5 percent price increases instead of 10 percent price increases. Hence, the question of whether to consider minivan segments as separate relevant markets appears to be a borderline decision for practitioners. In the discussion below, we take a prudent approach and will assume that the minivan segments are not relevant markets. This implies that for these products the relevant market definition is at the aggregate country level—that is, all new cars.[18]

6.5 Policy Implications

Our results from applying the market-definition tests at various levels may be summarized as follows:

- The relevant market for minivan cars is defined at the highest level—that is, at the aggregate country level.
- In Italy, the relevant markets for domestic cars are defined at an intermediate level—that is, at the segment level.
- In all other cases, the relevant markets for cars are defined at the lowest level—that is, at the subsegment level.

Given these relevant market definitions, we can now analyze which firms satisfy the market-share thresholds required to be eligible for selective or exclusive distribution under the block-exemption regulation. Since a firm sells multiple products, it will typically be present in several relevant markets—that is, in both the subcompact market and the intermediate markets. It is therefore necessary to verify whether the firms satisfy or violate the 30 or 40 percent market-share thresholds in each of the defined markets in which they are active.[19]

We begin with an overview of the firms violating the 30 and/or 40 percent market-share thresholds. Next, we discuss several general lessons that may be drawn from our approach.

6.5.1 Firms Violating the Market-Share Thresholds

We begin by identifying the firms that violate the 40 percent market-share threshold. These are the firms that cannot rely on the block-exemption regulation to be eligible for either selective or exclusive distribution. We proceed in three steps. First, we compute the firms' market shares under three possible levels for market definition: the subsegment level, the segment level, and the aggregate country level. Second, we identify all firms violating the 40 percent market-share threshold in each of these market definitions. Third, we identify the *critical* violations—that is, we add an asterisk to those cases for which our earlier results imply that it is actually appropriate to define the market at that level (or at a narrower level). The firms appearing without an asterisk are thus firms that would violate the thresholds based on standard industry classifications, but without solid econometric support from our SSNIP-test methodology. The results from this procedure are shown in table 6.6.

To explain table 6.6, consider Germany as an example. First, no firm in Germany exceeds the 40 percent threshold at the aggregate country level. Hence, if practitioners would apply a country-level market definition for all new cars, this would make all car manufacturers in Germany eligible to form selective distribution agreements. However, we found earlier that the relevant markets may be defined at narrower levels (with the exception of minivans). Consider first the segment level. There is one firm in Germany that exceeds the 40 percent market-share threshold at the segment level: VW in the compact, intermediate, and sports segments. These violations are also critical, since we previously found that markets may be defined at the segment level (with the exception of minivans). Consider now the even narrower subsegment level. Several additional firms in Germany exceed the 40 percent thresholds at this level: Mercedes in the domestic standard/luxury subsegment, VW in nearly all of the domestic subsegments, and Renault in the foreign minivan subsegment (due to the Renault Espace). But the 40 percent threshold violations are only critical for VW and Mercedes, and not for Renault, since we could not define a separate market for the foreign minivan subsegment where Renault's violation occurs.

More generally, table 6.6 reveals the follow patterns regarding the identity of firms that critically violate the 40 percent thresholds. First, the main critical violations of the 40 percent thresholds turn out to come from the European m.ass manufacturers: Renault, PSA, VW, Fiat, Ford, and GM. The European producers active in the niche segments (BMW,

Table 6.6
Firms with market shares above 40% within alternative-product markets

	Belgium	France	Germany	Italy	UK
	Country-level market definition				
	—	—	—	—	—
	Segment-level market definition				
Subcompact	—	—	—	Fiat*	—
Compact	—	—	VW*	—	—
Intermediate	—	PSA*	VW*	—	—
Standard/luxury	—		—	—	—
Sport	VW*	VW*	VW*	—	—
Minivan	—	Renault	—	Renault	—
	Subsegment-level market definition, domestic subsegments				
Subcompact	—	PSA* Renault*	VW*	Fiat	Ford*
Compact	—	PSA* Renault*	VW*	Fiat	Ford*
Intermediate	—	PSA*	VW*	Fiat	Ford* GM*
Standard/luxury	—	Renault*	Mercedes*	Fiat	GM*
Sport	—	—	VW*	Fiat	Ford*
Minivan	—	Renault	—	Fiat	Ford
	Subsegment-level market definition, foreign subsegments				
Subcompact	—	—	—	—	—
Compact	—	—	—	—	—
Intermediate	—	—	—	—	—
Standard/Luxury	—	—	—	—	—
Sport	VW*	VW*	—	—	—
Minivan	—	—	Renault	Renault	Renault

Note: All firms with a market share above 40% in the considered market are listed. If the considered market was also found to be a relevant market, the firm is denoted with an asterisk.

Mercedes) and the Asian producers (e.g., Toyota, Nissan, Mazda) do not violate the 40 percent thresholds. Second, the critical violations by the European mass producers are mainly due to a strong presence in their home countries: Renault and PSA in France, VW and Mercedes in Germany, Fiat in Italy, and Ford and GM in the United Kingdom. The only critical violations by European firms in foreign markets are by VW, which has a market share exceeding the 40 percent threshold in the foreign sports subsegment in Belgium and in France.

We now identify the firms violating the 30 percent but not the 40 percent threshold. Those firms could still not rely on the block exemption to be eligible for exclusive distribution, but they could rely on it for selective distribution. The results are presented in table 6.7. Several points are worth noting. First, the critical violations again mainly come from the European manufacturers. Second, the violations now no longer necessarily come from the European mass manufacturers in their respective home countries. They also come from the European niche players and/or European manufacturers in foreign markets: BMW in Belgium; VW, BMW, and Mercedes in France; Mazda and Ford in Germany; VW, BMW, and Mercedes in Italy; BMW and PSA in the United Kingdom.[20] Finally, there is one non-European-based firm that critically violates the 30 percent threshold—that is, Mazda in Germany (due to its strength in the sports segment).

6.5.2 Discussion

We now turn to a discussion of several specific points. First, we come back to the issues in Italy, where we could not define relevant markets at the domestic subsegment level, due to the strong market power of Fiat (resembling the issues in the Cellophane case). Table 6.6 shows that Fiat violates the market-share thresholds in all domestic subsegments (with a market share of virtually 100 percent) but that these violations are noncritical since the markets are not defined at the subsegment level in Italy. In our application, however, the end result for Fiat is not seriously affected. In two cases Fiat turns out to critically violate the market-share thresholds at the larger segment level, for which we could define a relevant market. It violates the 40 percent market-share threshold in the subcompact segment, and the 30 percent threshold in the intermediate segment.

Second, we discuss how the conclusions from our market-definition methodology may differ from those based on more traditional "intuitive" approaches. One approach would be to define the markets at the

Table 6.7
Firms with market share between 30% and 40% in alternative-product markets

	Belgium	France	Germany	Italy	UK
	Country-level market definition				
	—	—	VW*	—	—
	Segment-level market definition				
Subcompact	—	PSA* Renault*	—	—	—
Compact	—	—	—	—	—
Intermediate	—	—	—	VW*	—
Standard/luxury	BMW*	—	BMW* Mercedes*	Fiat*	BMW*
Sport	—	—	—	—	Ford*
Minivan	—	—	—	—	Renault
	Subsegment-level market definition, domestic subsegments				
Subcompact	—	—	—	—	GM*
Compact	—	—	—	—	GM*
Intermediate	—	—	—	—	—
Standard/luxury	—	—	BMW*	—	BMW*
Sport	—	—	Mercedes*	—	—
Minivan	—	—	GM VW	—	GM
	Subsegment-level market definition, foreign subsegments				
Subcompact	—	VW*	—	—	PSA*
Compact	—	VW*	—	VW*	—
Intermediate	—	VW*	—	VW*	—
Standard/luxury	BMW*	BMW* Mercedes*	Ford*	BMW* Mercedes*	BMW*
Sport	—	—	Mazda*	VW*	—
Minivan	—	GM	—	—	—

Note: All firms with a market share between 30% and 40% in the considered market are listed. If the considered market was also found to be a relevant market, the firm is denoted with an asterisk.

aggregate country level. In this case, only one firm would be detected to violate the 30 percent threshold (VW) and no firm would be found to violate the 40 percent threshold. Another approach would be to simply define the markets at the segment level following standard industry classifications. We can distinguish between two types of possible mistakes here. On the one hand, the segments may define the markets too narrowly, so that firms are mistakenly concluded to violate the thresholds. This turns out to be the case for Renault. In the minivan segment, it has a market share of over 40 percent in France and Italy, and one of over 30 percent in the United Kingdom (due to the strong position of the Renault Espace). Our analysis implies that it would be unwarranted to conclude that Renault violates the thresholds here, since we found that the market for minivan cars is wider than the segment level. On the other hand, the segments may also define the markets too widely, so that firms may be mistakenly concluded to satisfy the thresholds. We find several examples of this. For example, Ford and GM in the United Kingdom and Mercedes in Germany satisfy the 40 percent threshold at the segment level, but not at the subsegment level, which our analysis showed to be a narrower relevant market. Similarly, BMW and Mercedes in France and Italy, Ford and Mazda in Germany, and GM and PSA in the United Kingdom all satisfy the 30 percent threshold at the segment level, but again not at the narrower and more relevant subsegment level. In sum, compared to the market-definition approach based on standard industry classifications, our methodology may result in detecting either more or fewer firms violating the market-share thresholds.

Finally, we discuss an issue that relates to the fact that firms sell multiple products. What should practitioners decide if firms violated the market-share thresholds in only one or a few of the subsegments in which they are active? Strictly speaking, this would imply that such firms are eligible for selective or exclusive distribution only for products that belong to the subsegments with sufficiently low market shares. For example, table 6.6 implies that Mercedes in Germany could not form either selective or exclusive distribution for its products in the standard/luxury segment, but it can form selective distribution in the other subsegments. If Mercedes finds it technologically impractical to set up a separate distribution network for its cars in the standard/luxury segments, it may be forced to refrain from both selective and exclusive distribution for all its products. Hence, because firms sell multiple products and may not be able to set up product-specific distribution systems, there is a risk that a mechanical application of the market-share criteria may be overly, and presumably unintentionally, restrictive. For this reason, practitioners may find it desirable to interpret their rules less strictly—for example, by allowing at most one violation in the various relevant markets if technical constraints prevent separate distribution systems for the different products.

6.6 Conclusions

Against the background of the new block-exemption regulation for cars, this chapter has studied the relevant product markets in five countries of the European passenger-car sector. We suggest an econometric approach that is directly consistent with the SSNIP test and that is more satisfactory than previous econometric approaches, such as critical elasticity analysis or the use of standard industry classifications to define markets. We account for the following factors: products are differentiated; there is only information to estimate a retail-level demand system and not to estimate a wholesale-level demand system; and price-cost margins are not directly observed at the product level.

Regarding market definition, we find that the relevant market for minivan cars is defined at the highest level—that is, at the aggregate country level. Furthermore, in Italy the relevant markets for domestic cars are defined at an intermediate level: the segment level. In all other cases, the relevant markets for cars may be defined at the lowest level: the subsegment level. Based on these results, we identify the firms that violate the market-share thresholds stipulated in the block-exemption regulation. We find that mainly some European domestic mass producers violate the 40 percent thresholds and are therefore not immediately eligible for either selective or exclusive distribution. Some European mass producers violate the 30 percent but not the 40 percent threshold in their foreign markets and are therefore only immediately eligible for selective distribution. Finally, some European niche players and one non-European firm violate the 30 percent but not the 40 percent market-share thresholds.

If we had defined the markets based on standard industry classifications instead of our empirical methodology, our conclusions would have been different and, in fact, inconclusive. On the one hand, assuming that the market definition is at the country level would not identify any firm violating the 40 percent threshold and only one firm in one country violating the 30 percent threshold (VW in Germany). On the other hand, using standard industry classifications to define the markets at the segment level for all products (and thus not at the subsegment level as we found) would not detect some firms violating the 40 percent thresholds in Germany (Mercedes) and in the United Kingdom (Ford and GM), and it would also not detect some firms violating the 30 percent thresholds. These examples illustrate that it is important to take the market-definition methodology seriously, and where possible apply a more rigorous approach than has often been used in the past. Apart from these general conclusions, our analysis also highlights several practical issues in market definition that arise in this case and that may play a role in other cases as well—in particular, issues relating to the fact that firms sell multiple products.

Notes

1. This approach has originally been developed to predict the effects of horizontal mergers. For an application that predicts the effects of vertical agreements, see Brenkers and Verboven 2006.

2. Its main difference relates to the "thought experiment" about market power ex post. The market-definition approach is vague about this, simply asking whether a group of firms could profitably raise prices by some percentage. The simulation approach is very explicit about it, and formulates a precise model of how market power would change in response to a merger, a vertical agreement, and so on.

3. See the Communication from the European Commission 2002a for a helpful discussion on the competition rules for vertical restraints.

4. For a detailed description of the meaning of selective and exclusive distribution, as well as other restrictions covered by the regulation, see Brenkers and Verboven 2006. Briefly stated, throughout the text *selective distribution* refers to the manufacturer's practice of imposing qualitative and quantitative criteria on its dealers. *Exclusive distribution* refers to the practice of assigning an exclusive geographic territory to the dealers. Useful policy documents describing the perceived problems with selective and exclusive distribution are by the UK Competition Commission 2000 and the European Commission 2000. A useful policy document providing an explanation of the block-exemption regulation, including discussion on market-definition and market-share thresholds, is the explanatory brochure of the European Commission 2002b, available on its website.

5. The 30 percent market-share threshold also applies to other nonhardcore restrictions. The hardcore restrictions listed in Article 4 of the block-exemption regulation are, most notably, resale price maintenance, the combination of selective and exclusive distribution, and the restriction of passive selling outside an exclusive dealer's own territory.

6. Detailed work documenting the presence of large price differentials, and the evolving role of trade barriers in the car market, can be found in BEUC 1992; Competition Commission 2000; Degryse and Verboven 2000; Goldberg and Verboven 2005.

7. In the context of horizontal mergers, Hosken et al. (2002) discuss related problems in evaluating mergers at the wholesale level, when the demand system is only known (i.e., estimated) at the retail level.

8. These profits are generated with a high degree of certainty during the first two years when the car is still under the warranty period. But after these two years, repair and maintenance are also often taken care of by the manufacturers.

9. The term *perceived* is added to mean that both the own-price elasticity and the cross-price elasticities with respect to other products of the same firms enter the expression.

10. Following Brenkers and Verboven 2006, we estimate a further generalization of the nested logit model by allowing the segmentation parameters to differ across nests. At the same time, we are more restrictive than Brenkers and Verboven 2006 since we do not allow for heterogeneity in income levels across consumers; this considerably complicates estimation.

11. Katz and Shapiro (2003) provide a very interesting discussion of some common misinterpretations of the critical elasticity formulas. One way to avoid the misinterpretations they identify is by "substituting out" the price-cost margins in the critical elasticity formulas, by using equilibrium price-cost margins from a theory of price-setting behavior. Our approach is consistent with this, since we also use equilibrium price-cost margins.

12. See Van Reenen 2004 for an example of critical elasticity analysis after having estimated a product-differentiated system instead of assuming homogeneous goods.

13. It is well known that transaction prices may differ from list prices because of discounts and other financial benefits offered by the dealers to the consumers. In the econometric literature on passenger-car demand, a consensus has emerged that list prices are nevertheless informative in obtaining price elasticities if the model is specified in a sufficiently flexible way. The reason is that while deviations from list prices may be country-specific and brand- or even product-specific, they show relatively little variation over time. One can then account for deviations by including market and product effects. Additional measurement error on the price variable is absorbed by instrumenting for price.

14. Manufacturers change list prices about three times per year. Rather than collecting price information on a weekly basis and computing the average over the year, we decided to measure the list price at a specific point in time. We chose the month of August since this falls in the middle of the year, during a period in which list prices show a long stability. For one or two markets/years (in the 1970s) we were not able to obtain an August catalog. We then used the closest available month instead. Any systematic biases will be absorbed in the market/year fixed effects.

15. As an alternative approach, one might classify each segment (say the compact segment) in two groups—that is, minivan compact segment, and nonminivan compact segment. Or one might follow a nonnested GEV model, in which "minivan" forms a separate principle of differentiation, as in Bresnahan, Stern, and Trajtenberg 1997.

16. We also considered the results from the restricted nested logit model, but in our application this gave no substantial new insights compared to the flexible nested logit, so we omitted it from the tables.

17. There are two exceptions. For the French and UK luxury/standard subsegments, we find positive profit effects under full intrabrand competition, but negative profit effects under no intrabrand competition.

18. We implemented SSNIP tests at the country level and found that profit effects are positive for all countries.

19. Our calculations should be seen mainly as illustrations to make general points, not as concrete policy recommendations. The actual computation of market shares may depend to some extent on choices of where to classify some cars. This could be relevant when the violations of thresholds are borderline.

20. Note that there are some subtleties in interpretation due to the fact that some firms own brands from a different country of origin. First, Ford owns the German/UK Ford brand, but also the Swedish Volvo brand and the UK Jaguar brand. The mentioning of Ford among foreign brands in Germany follows from the strong market share of Volvo among the foreign standard/luxury products. Second, BMW owns both the German BMW brands and the UK Rover brands. This is why BMW can appear under both the domestic and the foreign subsegment in the United Kingdom.

References

BEUC. 1992. "Parallel Imports for Cars in the EC." BEUC/222/92. Brussels: BEUC.

Berry, S. 1994. "Estimating Discrete Choice Models with Product Differentiation." *RAND Journal of Economics* 25:242–262.

Berry, S., J. Levinsohn, and A. Pakes. 1995. "Automobile Prices in Market Equilibrium." *Econometrica* 63: 841–890.

Brenkers, R., and F. Verboven. 2006."Liberalizing a Distribution System: The European Car Market." *Journal of the European Economic Association*, 4(1):216–251.

Bresnahan, T., S. Sterm, and M. Trajtenberg. 1997. Market Segmentation and the Sources of Rents from Innovation: Personal Computers in the Late 1980s. *Prand Journal of Economics* 28:517–544.

Church, J., and R. Ware. 1999. Industrial Organization: A Strategic Approach. Boston, MA: Irwin McGraw-Hill.

Competition Commission. 2000. *New Cars: A Report on the Supply of New Motor Cars within the U.K.* London: Competition Commission.

Degryse, H., and F. Verboven. 2000. *Car Price Differentials in the European Union: An Economic Analysis*. Report prepared for the European Commission. Brussels: European Commission.

European Commission. 2000. *Report on the Evaluation of Regulation (EC) No 1475/95 on the Application of Article 85(3) of the Treaty to Certain Categories of Motor Vehicle Distribution and Servicing Agreements*. Photocopy. Brussels: European Commission.

European Commission. 2002a. "Communication on the Application of the Community Competition Rules to Vertical Restraints—Follow-Up to the Green Paper on Vertical Restraints." Photocopy. Brussels: European Commission.

European Commission. 2002b. *Explanatory Brochure on the Distribution and Servicing of Motor Vehicles in the European Union*. Photocopy. Brussels: European Commission.

Goldberg, P. K. 1995. "Product Differentiation and Oligopoly in International Markets: The Case of the U.S. Automobile Industry." *Econometrica* 63:891–951.

Goldberg, P. K., and F. Verboven. 2005. "Market Integration and Convergence to the Law of One Price: Evidence from the European Car Market." *Journal of International Economics* 65(1):49–73.

Harris, B., and J. Simons. 1989. "Focusing Market Definition: How Much Substitution Is Necessary?" *Research in Law and Economics* 12:207–26.

Hosken, D., D. O'Brien, D. Scheffman, and M. Vita. 2002. "Demand System Estimation and Its Application to Horizontal Merger Analysis." Working paper.

Katz, M., and C. Shapiro. 1993. "Critical Loss: Let's Tell the Whole Story." *Antitrust Magazine*, spring, 49–56.

Rey, P., and J. Stiglitz. 1995. "The Role of Exclusive Territories in Producers' Competition." *RAND Journal of Economics* 26(3): 431–451.

Van Reenen, J. 2004. Is There a Market for Workgroup Sources? Evaluating Market-Level Demand Elasticities Using Micro and Macro Models. CEP Discussion Paper No 650.

Verboven, F. 1996. "International Price Discrimination in the European Car Market." *RAND Journal of Economics* 27(2): 240–268.

Verboven, F. 2002. *Quantitative Study of the Demand for New Cars to Define the Relevant Market in the Passenger Car sector*. Report prepared for the European Commission. Brussels: European Commission.

Werden, G. 1998. "Demand Elasticities in Antitrust Analysis." *Antitrust Law Journal* 66: 363–414.

7 Merger Control in Differentiated-Product Industries

Franco Mariuzzo, Patrick Paul Walsh, and Ciara Whelan

7.1 Introduction

The EU Merger Control Regulation No. 139/2004 has, with few notable exceptions, adopted an analytic framework similar to the U.S. Horizontal Merger Guidelines. Under Article 2 of the EU legislation, any merger that will "*significantly impede effective competition in the Common Market or in a substantial part of it*" should be blocked.[1] This moves the EU criteria closer to the U.S. practice, where mergers are prohibited if they would result in a "*substantial lessening of competition.*" While this move away from "*dominance*" may be apparent during the investigation of mergers, an analysis of market concentration is still at the center of the selection stage of all notified mergers in the European Union and United States.

In both the EU and U.S. Merger Guidelines, thresholds have been defined based on the level and changes in the Herfindahl-Hirschmann Index (HHI) to provide a screening rule on whether proposed mergers justify investigation (outlined in table 7.1).[2] Even though the thresholds are not ex ante the sole criteria to select notified mergers for further investigation, an ex post examination of concentration data and mergers challenged reveals that levels and changes in the HHI are at the center of the selection process. This evidence is documented in section 7.2.

Rather than screening on the basis of market share, we propose the use of a structural approach in differentiated-product industries to estimate and assess changes in market power that arise from mergers of undertakings. This approach only requires company product data on prices, market shares, and product characteristics. Using an industry study, which we describe in section 7.3, we outline a structural methodology to estimate company markups consistent within a structural

Table 7.1
EC and U.S. screening thresholds

	HHI	Δ HHI
EC screening thresholds		
Competitive concern	1,000–2,000	>250
Competitive concern	>2,000	>150
U.S. screening thresholds		
Competitive concern	1,000–1,800	>100
Competitive concern	>1,800	>50
No competitive concerns for HHI <1,000 for any Δ HHI		

model of equilibrium using Berry 1994. Demand primitives are estimated using a nested logit model of demand and used to back out price-cost markups from a model of company multiproduct Nash pricing. We also outline a comparable, though more sophisticated, model to estimate company markups using Berry, Levinsohn, and Pakes 1995 (henceforth BLP). In this case demand primitives are estimated using a random coefficient model of demand incorporating data on consumer demographics, and price-cost markups are estimated jointly with demand consistent with a structural model of multiproduct Nash pricing. Our theoretical framework is outlined in section 7.4.

We compare our estimates of demand primitives and price-cost markups from both of these procedures in section 7.5. The policy recommendation we propose is that thresholds based on the level and changes in the HHI that select notified mergers for further investigation should be applied to profit shares in differentiated-product industries (rather than market shares).[3] Using our results, we provide an example of a hypothetical merger in undertakings with limited combined market share that can result in a substantial increase in market power. In addition, we provide an example whereby a hypothetical merger in undertakings with very large combined market share can result in a small increase in market power. We argue that existing selection rules based on dominance may not only overlook damaging mergers but may select mergers for investigation that have little competitive concern. Over the period 1990–2004, of the 2,400 EU mergers notified, only 144 cases were selected for investigation. Most cases were allowed to proceed subject to undertakings and some withdrew. Only 18 cases were blocked (see European Commission 2004).[4] Given the low selection rates in the European Union and United States, the success of merger control depends heavily on the selection criteria. We feel structural models should be used to estimate profit shares during screening to ensure that selected mergers are more likely to be damaging and hence blocked. We conclude in section 7.6.

7.2 Merger Regulations and the Role of Concentration in Merger Screening

Under Article 2 of EU Merger Control Regulation No. 139/2004, merger control moves the EU criteria closer to the U.S. practice.[5] Thus, mergers are assessed as to whether they enhance the market power of companies and, subsequently, are likely to have adverse effects for consumers in the form of higher prices, poorer-quality products, or reduced choice.[6] The EU Merger Guidelines (2004/C 31/03) outline two ways that horizontal mergers may impede effective competition: (1) by eliminating important competitive constraints on one or more firms, which consequently would have increased market power, without resorting to coordinated behavior (noncoordinated or unilateral effects),[7] and (2) by changing the nature of competition that raises prospects for coordination (coordination effects)—that is, the merger results in collective dominance.[8] This is similar to the U.S. Horizontal Merger Guidelines. A full assessment of a merger would also examine the existence of any possible countervailing forces to market power, such as countervailing buyer power, possibility of entry that would maintain effective competition, efficiencies arising from the proposed merger, or conditions for the failing firm defense.

Yet, before these considerations are implemented during investigation, a preliminary screening of all notified mergers takes place in order to decide which mergers justify a full investigation. Both EU and U.S. guidelines still use market shares and concentration levels as first indications of the competitive importance of both the merging parties.[9] Section III of the EU Merger Guidelines outlines specific market-share and concentration levels where the Commission is likely to have, or not have, competitive concerns.[10] EU guidelines apply a HHI and change in the HHI, resulting from a proposed merger, to provide a first indication of the change in competitive pressure following a merger. "Noninterventionist" thresholds are documented in table 7.1. Except in special circumstances, detailed below, the Commission is unlikely to identify horizontal-competitive concerns in a market with a postmerger HHI below 1,000; in a market with a postmerger HHI between 1,000 and 2,000 with an increase in the HHI of less than 250; or in a market with a postmerger HHI greater than 2,000 with an increase in the

HHI of less than 150. Proposed mergers in these categories, it is said, do not normally require extensive analysis. The screening thresholds outlined in the U.S. Horizontal Merger Guidelines are slightly different and stricter than those of the EU and are outlined in table 7.1. Again, ordinarily no further analysis is required for proposed mergers yielding a postmerger HHI of less than 1,000; a postmerger HHI between 1,000 and 1,800 with an increase in the HHI of less than 100; or a postmerger HHI greater than 1,800 with an increase in the HHI of less than 50. For mergers that break the thresholds, a full investigation is justified.

The HHI and change in the HHI on market shares are not supposed to be the only criteria that selection is based on. Special circumstances can lead to selection: if a merger involves a potential entrant or a recent entrant with a small market share; if one or more parties are important innovators and this is not reflected in market share; if there are significant cross-shareholdings among the market participants; if one of the merging firms is a maverick firm with a high likelihood of disrupting coordinated conduct; if indications of past or ongoing coordination, or facilitating practices, are present; or if one of the merging parties has a premerger market share of 50 percent or more. According to well-established case law, very large market shares (50 percent or more) may in themselves be evidence of the existence of a dominant market position.[11] However, other factors—like the strength and number of competitors, presence of capacity constraints, or the extent to which the products of the merging firms are close substitutes—may be important.[12] Verouden (2004) refers to a Commission analysis relating HHI and change in the HHI (delta) to large number of past decisions.[13] Although at first glance there appeared to be little evidence of a relationship between levels and changes in HHI and those cases in which the Commission is not likely to have competitive concerns, "a further analysis, of those cases where the Commission identified competition concerns, but where either the HHI or the delta were not particularly high, revealed that typically one or several special circumstances could be identified that made the particular estimate for the market share, and consequently, the HHI and the delta not very informative" (Verouden 2004, 6).[14] Allowing for these *"special circumstances,"* thresholds are clearly reflected in past cases.

The U.S. Federal Trade Commission and Department of Justice (2003) examined concentration data and the numbers of mergers challenged for fiscal years 1999–2003. Table 7.2 relates postmerger HHI and

Table 7.2
U.S. data for fiscal years 1999–2003 on individual relevant markets in cases in which the agencies challenged mergers

Ex ante merger	Change in the HHI								
HHI	0–99	100–199	200–299	300–499	500–799	800–1,199	1,200–2,499	2,500+	Total
0–1,799	0	17	18	19	3	0	0	0	57
1,799–1,999	0	7	5	14	14	0	0	0	40
2,000–2,399	1	1	7	32	35	2	0	0	78
2,400–2,999	1	5	6	18	132	34	1	0	197
3,000–3,999	0	3	4	16	37	63	53	0	176
4,000–4,999	0	1	3	16	34	30	79	0	163
5,000–6,999	0	2	4	16	9	14	173	52	270
7,000+	0	0	0	2	3	10	44	223	282
Total cases	2	36	47	133	267	153	350	275	1,263

change in the HHI associated with decisions to challenge mergers (either in court or administratively) over this period.[15] The data relate to 173 mergers covering 1,263 relevant markets. The lowest HHI recorded just slightly exceeded 1,400. Thus, no proposed merger with a postmerger HHI of <1,000 was challenged over the period examined. The lowest value for the change in HHI is approximately 85. Thus, no merger resulting in a delta of <85 (irrespective of postmerger concentration levels) was challenged. From the table we see that there does not appear to be a violation of the "noninterventionist" thresholds set out in the U.S. Horizontal Merger Guidelines. Moreover, we observe that the number of mergers challenged tends to be higher the more (postmerger) concentrated the industry, and/or the higher the change in concentration that results from the merger. It therefore appears that market-share and concentration analysis play an important role in the initial screening stage of mergers. In what follows, we question the relevance of this for differentiated-product industries. Rather than screening on the basis of market share, we propose the use of a structural approach in differentiated-product industries to assess changes in profit shares that arise from mergers of undertakings. This will result in a set of mergers being investigated that could be very different from that selected under market-share assessment.

7.3 Industry and Data

AC Nielsen, an international marketing research company, has collated a panel database of all brands of carbonated soft drinks distributed throughout all 12,000 Irish retail stores for use in empirical analysis. The database provides bimonthly population data spanning October 1992 to May 1997 for 178 brands, identified for 13 firms and 40 product characteristics within carbonated soft drinks. The data record the retail activities of both Irish- and foreign-owned brands/firms selling throughout stores of the Irish retail sector. The evolution of the Irish grocery market from the early 1970s to its present-day structure is described in Walsh and Whelan 1999, and the data used in this chapter is outlined further in Mariuzzo, Walsh, and Whelan 2003. We have brand-level information on the per-liter brand price (weighted average of brand unit prices across all the stores selling the brand, weighted by brand sales share within the store), quantity (thousand liters), sales value (thousand pounds), store coverage (based on pure counts of stores, and size weighted by store size in terms of carbonated drinks in which the brand retails to measure effective coverage), inventories (number of days to stock out on day of audit given the current rate of purchases), firm ownership, and product (flavor, packaging, diet) characteristics.

An interesting feature of the AC Nielsen data is their identification of various product characteristics within the market for carbonated soft drinks, which group clusters of brands by forty characteristics: four flavors (cola, orange, lemonade, and mixed-fruit), five different packaging types (cans, standard bottle, 1.5-liter, 2-liter, and multipack of cans), and two different sweeteners (diet and regular). The number and size of the product characteristics were very stable throughout the period of this study. Allowing for flavor segments is standard in the analysis of carbonated soft drinks (see Sutton 1991). Packaging format is also a crucial feature of this market. First, packaging format controls for different seasonal cycles: cans peak in the summer months of June and July and 2-liter bottles peak over the winter months of December and January. Second, 90 percent of cans and standard bottles are distributed through small stores rather than chain stores. In contrast, the majority of 2-liter and multipack cans are distributed through chain stores. Packaging also controls for the nature of the buy: impulse versus one-stop shopping; small versus large store.

Another feature of the data is that companies' coverage of the forty product segments of the market with brands is very different (see Mariuzzo, Walsh, and Whelan 2003). In addition, brand coverage of stores within segments based on effective coverage of stores, where the store is weighted by its share of retail carbonated soft drinks turnover, is also very brand-specific. The top two companies, Coca-Cola Bottlers and C&C (Pepsico franchise), have broad coverage of the product segments. Yet, brand coverage of stores is not company- but product-specific. For example, Coca-Cola Bottlers has wide distribution with Regular Cola Cans, while the distribution is less aggressive in regular orange and mixed-fruit characteristics. This is where competition from the small companies (Irish/British) is greater. The important point for our econometric analysis is that (effective) store coverage is product-(brand-) and not segment- or company-specific.

7.4 Estimating Market Power

There is a long history of mapping market-share structure into market power.[16] In the case of a Cournot oligopoly homogeneous-good industry, one can show with N firms that the average price-cost margin in the industry is written as

$$\sum_j s_j \left(\frac{p - c_j}{p} \right) = \frac{\sum_j s_j^2}{\eta} = \frac{HHI}{\eta} \tag{1}$$

where s_j is the firm j market share, η denotes the industry demand elasticity, p is the industry price, and c_j is the marginal cost firm j faces. Market power in an industry with homogeneous goods is directly and positively linearly related to the HHI. While the HHI may be a good rule of thumb to use in deciding whether to investigate mergers in homogeneous industries, once one introduces differentiated goods, mapping HHI to market power becomes more problematic.

In differentiated-product industries, market share is no longer a good approximation of the ability to mark up price over cost. The market is now made up of a number of products that are differentiated, either by location or some product attributes. Some products are more similar than others in terms of these attributes. The competitive constraint on a firm's pricing is now determined by the degree of substitutability between the various goods in the market. Things become even more complex in the case in which firms produce multiple products in the market. Firms may specialize in producing goods with very similar attributes, or have a portfolio of goods with very different attributes, and may or may not locate alongside other multiproduct firms producing similar or different goods. The HHI for the market tells us little about the underlying structure of such markets or the market power of firms. Firms with small market share may well be able to extract high price-cost markups by being specialized in their product characteristics and location. The question now arises as to how we can map this complexity of multiproduct firms operating over product characteristics and locations into market power.

To evaluate market power where products are differentiated, it is necessary to estimate the degree of substitutability between the various goods in the market. However, estimating demand for differentiated products has a dimensionality problem. A linear demand system for J brands has J^2 price parameters to estimate. One must therefore place some structure on the estimation. A number of alternative demand specifications have been developed to deal with this dimensionality problem by reducing the dimensionality space into a product space.

We focus our attention on discrete-choice models used in estimating demand for differentiated products.[17] The next section outlines how we estimate demand primitives for differentiated products. In addition, given demand primitives we see how to back out price-cost margins that are consistent with a structural model of multiproduct companies pricing in a Nash equilibrium.

7.4.1 Structural Models

The discrete-choice literature has gained a level of reliability that represents the best option to estimate primitives of demand in a differentiated-product industry. Logit, nested logit, and random coefficient models are at the center of this literature. In this chapter we drop the logit model due to issues surrounding the independence of irrelevant alternatives. We embed both the nested logit and random coefficient models into a general indirect utility.[18]

This section outlines the nested logit model in Mariuzzo, Walsh, and Whelan 2003. In addition, we outline details of our random coefficient model, which extends BLP and Nevo 2001, in Mariuzzo, Walsh, and Whelan 2005. An important feature that characterizes both our models is that, unlike previous papers using market level data, we control for the effect of the traditional form of product differentiation coming from product locations across stores of the market. In particular, Mariuzzo, Walsh, and Whelan (2005) show how to construct a distribution of consumers' closeness to each product from information on product-effective coverage of stores. We write the random utility of consumer i for brand j as the sum of a mean utility (δ_j), an individual deviation from that mean (μ_{ij}), and an error component (ε_{ij}), which is assumed to be an identical and independently distributed extreme-value function. The time subscript t is omitted to avoid cumbersome notation but is present in our estimates. The utility can therefore be written as

$$
\begin{aligned}
u_{ij} &= \delta_j + \mu_{ij} + (1-\rho)\varepsilon_{ij} \\
\delta_j &= \mathbf{x}_j'^1\boldsymbol{\beta} - \left[\alpha_1 * \ln\left(D_j\right) + \alpha_0\right]p_j + \beta_{K+1} ln\left(D_j\right) + \xi_j \qquad (2) \\
\mu_{ij} &= \zeta_{ig} + \mathbf{v}_i'^A \mathbf{X}_j^2 \sigma_A + \mathbf{v}_{ij}'^C \mathbf{X}_j^2 \sigma_C + \mathbf{v}_i'^N \mathbf{X}_j^2 \sigma_N
\end{aligned}
$$

where p_j is price of product j and $\mathbf{x}_j^1$ is a column vector of K observed product characteristics (including the constant) that enter linearly in our estimates, whereas $\mathbf{X}^2$ is a matrix in which the diagonal includes a subset of the previous characteristics that enter nonlinearly in a second stage of the estimation procedure (in our model, the constant and prices). Some of the product characteristics (ξ_j) are unobserved to us but are observed by our consumers in their choices.

For the more general random coefficient model, let $\alpha_1 = \beta_{K+1} = \rho = \zeta_{ig} = 0$. This ensures that an individual deviation from mean utility (μ_{ij}) is driven by distributions in consumer demographics or random coefficients on the constant and prices. Subscripts (and superscripts) A, C, N stand for *age*, *closeness to stores*, and a *(log) normal distribution*, respectively, which individualize our (*ns*) simulated (observed and unobserved) consumer characteristics. Consumer taste for location (the probability that the product will be in the nearest store) is captured in our utility function at an individual level, by the closeness variable v_{ij}^C (which is consumer i and brand j specific). The idea is that distance has a direct effect on utility by way of an interaction with the constant, but also enters as an interaction with prices. The reason for this interaction is that one should expect price sensitivity to increase with store coverage. Our simulations are drawn from different distributions assumed to be independent and characterized by different variability. The *age* distribution only varies over time and is the same for all variables entering $\mathbf{X}_j^2$ ($v_i^A = [v_i^A, v_i^A]'$); the *normal* distribution varies itself only over time but its distributions are different for each component of $\mathbf{X}_j^2$ ($v_i^N = [v_i^N, v_i^{LN}]'$), where the normal distribution is linked to the constant and the lognormal distribution is associated to the price variable; the *closeness to stores* distribution varies both over time and over brands but is the same for each component (constant and price) of $\mathbf{X}_j^2$ ($v_{ij}^C = [v_{ij}^C, v_{ij}^C]'$).[19]

The augmented nested logit model is obtained by setting $\boldsymbol{\sigma}_A = \boldsymbol{\sigma}_c = \boldsymbol{\sigma}_N = \mathbf{0}$, and allowing α_1, β_{K+1}, ρ, ζ_{ig} to be nonzero. This will still incorporate product-specific locations into our model as part of the mean utility. This latter effect is the result of an average over individuals $D_j = \frac{100}{N}\Sigma_{i=1}^N d_{ij}$, where d_{ij} is a dummy equal to 1 when brand j is available in individual i's nearest shop. We allow D_j to have a direct effect on mean utility and an indirect effect through an interaction with prices. For consumers, ζ_{ig} is utility common to all brands within a group g and has a distribution function that depends on ρ, with $0 \le \rho < 1$. As the parameter ρ approaches 1, the within-group correlation of utility levels across products goes to 1 (products within groups are perfect substitutes). As ρ tends to zero, so too does the within-group correlation.[20] Finally, since we are dealing with discrete-choice models, we need to define a utility for the outside good,

$$u_{i0} = \underbrace{\xi_0}_{\delta_0} + \underbrace{\sigma_0 v_{i0}}_{\mu_{io}} + \varepsilon_{i0} \tag{3}$$

and following the literature, we normalize $\xi_o = \sigma_0 = 0$. The parameters to be estimated are $\{\boldsymbol{\alpha}, \boldsymbol{\beta}, \boldsymbol{\sigma}, \rho\}$. Given the above utility function, one can derive a demand function. The procedure requires integrating the utility over the error structure and normalizing it over the outside option. This leads to a probability (ø_{ij}) that individual i buys brand j over the J available brands and averaging over ns simulated individuals (and knowing the number of individuals in the economy),

$$s_j(\cdot) = \left(\frac{1}{ns} \sum_{i=1}^{ns} \underbrace{\left(\frac{e^{\delta_j(\cdot)+\mu_{ij}(\cdot)}}{1+\sum_{j=1}^{J} e^{\delta_j(\cdot)+\mu_{ij}(\cdot)}} \right)}_{\phi_{ij}} \right), \text{ for } j \in J \tag{4}$$

$$q_j(\cdot) = N s_j(\cdot)$$

The demand derived in (4) represents a general structure. If one wants to recover the demand for the nested logit model or from the random coefficient model, the following simplifications are to be added:

• Impose $\boldsymbol{\sigma}_A = \boldsymbol{\sigma}_C = \boldsymbol{\sigma}_N = \mathbf{0}$ in (2), then the nested logit model has the closed-form solution (see Berry 1994),

$$ln(s_j) - ln(s_0) = \mathbf{x}_j'\boldsymbol{\beta} - \alpha_0 p_j - \alpha_1[p_j * ln(D_j)] + \beta_{K+1} ln(D_j) + \rho ln(s_{jg}) + \xi_j \tag{5}$$

where s_j , s_0, s_{jg} are the market shares of brand j, the market share of the outside good 0, and the market share of brand j in segment g, respectively.

• Impose $\alpha_1 = \beta_{K+1} = \rho = \zeta_{jg} = 0$, then the more general random coefficient model has a structure similar to (4). The BLP specification of demand allows different individuals to have different tastes for different product characteristics. In addition, the model can allow for consumer heterogeneity in terms of their response to prices. The random coefficients are designed to capture variations in the substitution patterns. This generalization of the model comes, however, at the price of increasing computational complexity, requiring nonlinear estimators and numerical solutions based on contraction mapping and simulations together with a nonlinear two-step GMM estimator. The first stage of the econometric procedure simultaneously estimates the demand and cost function parameters (see description of cost at the end of this section)

$$\begin{aligned} ln(s_j) - ln(s_0) &= x_j'\boldsymbol{\beta} - \alpha_0 p_j + \xi_j \\ ln(c_j) &= w_j'\gamma + \omega_j \end{aligned} \tag{6}$$

given some starting value of the nonlinear parameters, α_0 and those associated with deviations from the mean ($\boldsymbol{\sigma}_A$, $\boldsymbol{\sigma}_C$, $\boldsymbol{\sigma}_N$,); the estimation of the $\boldsymbol{\beta}$ and γ parameters allows us to back out the demand unobservable (using simulations and contraction mapping techniques) and, via a structural model of equilibrium, the cost function unobservable, where w are the observed cost characteristics, by product, ($\hat{\xi}_j$, $\hat{\omega}_j$). Imposing an assumption of conditional independence $E(\xi_j|z) = E(\omega_j|z) = 0$ (where z are our instruments), one applies a second-step procedure that searches for the nonlinear parameters that minimize the distance of ξ_j and ω_j from zero.

The main reason for estimating reliable demand parameters is to compute own and cross-price elasticities that reveal the underlying substitution effects. The general formula for own and cross-price elasticities is

$$\begin{aligned} \frac{\partial s_j(\cdot)}{\partial p_j}\frac{p_j}{s_j} &\equiv \varepsilon_{jj} = \left(\frac{1}{ns}\sum_{i=1}^{ns}\phi_{ij}(1-\phi_{ij})\frac{\partial u_{ij}}{\partial p_j}\right)\frac{p_j}{s_j} \\ \frac{\partial s_j(\cdot)}{\partial p_k}\frac{p_k}{s_j} &\equiv \varepsilon_{jk} = -\left(\frac{1}{ns}\sum_{i=1}^{ns}\phi_{ij}\phi_{ik}\frac{\partial u_{ik}}{\partial p_k}\right)\frac{p_k}{s_j} \end{aligned} \tag{7}$$

which in the case of the nested logit can be simplified to the closed form,

$$\begin{aligned} \varepsilon_{jk} &= [\alpha_0 + \alpha_1 \ln(D_j)]\left[s_k + \frac{\rho}{1-\rho}s_{jg}\right]p_k \text{ } if \text{ } k \neq j \text{ and } j,k \in g \\ \varepsilon_{jk} &= [\alpha_0 + \alpha_1 \ln(D_k)]p_k s_k \text{ } if \text{ } k \neq j \text{ and } k \notin g \\ \varepsilon_{jj} &= [\alpha_0 + \alpha_1 \ln(D_j)]\left[s_j - \frac{1}{1-\rho} + \frac{\rho}{1-\rho}s_{jg}\right]p_j \text{ if } k = j \end{aligned} \tag{8}$$

It is important to note that the elasticities here refer to the percentage change in market share in response to a 1 percent change in price. We estimate the demand-side primitives and, via an equilibrium pricing system of equations, to be defined, we can back out the price-cost markup (Lerner index) for each brand. Firms maximize the sum of profits accruing from firm brands. In brand price setting, p_j, a firm takes the price of all other firms' brands as given. The firm f internalizes the cross-price effect on market share of the brands it owns (J_f) in the price setting of an individual brand,

$$\prod_f = \sum_{j \in J_f} \left(p_j q_j(\cdot) - c_j q_j(\cdot) \right) \tag{9}$$

the maximization of which leads to the first-order conditions from which we get our price equilibria,

$$\mathbf{p} = \mathbf{c} + \underbrace{\Delta^{-1}\mathbf{s}}_{markup} \tag{10}$$

where Δ is defined as

$$\Delta_{jk} = \begin{cases} \dfrac{-\partial s_k(\cdot)}{\partial p_j}, & \text{if brands } k, j \text{ are produced by the same firm} \\ 0, & \text{otherwise} \end{cases} \tag{11}$$

Two alternative approaches are available to back out the markup. A first approach is a simplified version where the markup is backed out directly from the demand side via the augmented Lerner index (Mariuzzo, Walsh, and Whelan 2003). An alternative (more complex) approach requires a simultaneous estimation of demand and marginal cost (see Mariuzzo, Walsh, and Whelan 2005). A simultaneous estimation of demand and cost not only increases efficiency in the estimates, but also gives us good instruments to better identify the (price and interactions) parameters.[21]

7.5 Comparing Results of Nested Logit and BLP Models

We estimate the nested logit demand system in equation (5). Estimates are obtained from a GMM estimation procedure. The variables p_j, $\ln(D_j) * p_j$, and $ln(s_{jg})$ are endogenous variables and must be instrumented. Our results are presented in table 7.3. In column I we present a nested logit model using no data on product locations across stores in the regression or in the instrument set. In column II we estimate the full model in equation (5). In both specifications, the chi-squared test rejects the null that the moments (instruments) are invalid. We estimate

Table 7.3
Estimation of demand: Nested logit model of demand

	Regression I		Regression II	
Dependent variable: $\ln(S_j) - \ln(S_0)$	Coefficient	(t-stat)	Coefficient	(t-stat)
Constant	−0.8	(1.0)	−3.7	(10.1)*
Default cola				
Orange	1.1	(12.5)*	0.59	(9.6)*
Lemonade	0.14	(1.6)	−0.01	(0.2)
Mixed fruit	0.45	(5.3)*	0.04	(0.6)
Default cans				
Standard	2.7	(7.9)*	1.2	(6.7)*
1.5 liter	3.4	(9.7)*	1.7	(8.9)*
2 liter	−0.3	(1.1)	−0.11	(0.7)
Multipack cans	0.2	(0.5)	0.8	(3.8)*
Default diet				
Regular	2.2	(3.5)*	1.6	(4.2)*
$+\beta_{k+1} \ln(D_{jt})$			1.2	(9.6)*
$\rho \ln(s_{gjt})^{a}$	0.91	(13.1)*	0.65	(9.6)*
$-\alpha_1 \ln(D_{jt})\, p_{jt}^{a}$			0.63	(7.5)*
$-\alpha_0 p_{jt}^{a}$	5.9	(9.1)*	2.9	(7.4)*
Company Dummies	Yes		Yes	
Packaging × *Month* Dummies	Yes		Yes	
R^2	0.61		0.81	
Numbers of observations	4,645		4,645	
Overidentification IV test	χ^2 (5) = 0.99		χ^2 (5) = 0.99	

[a] Instruments for Regression I include all the regressors, with the exception of p_{jt} and $\ln(s_{gjt})$. Inventories$_{jt}$; Hausman-Taylor instrumental variables (brands of the same firm in other segments) with respect to p_{jt}, and Inventories$_{jt}$; and BLP instruments (brands of the other firms in the same segment) with respect to mean and standard deviation of Inventories$_j$.
Instruments for Regression II include all the regressors, with the exception of p_{jt}, $\ln(s_{gjt})$ and $\ln(D_{jt})p_{jt}$. Inventories$_{jt}$; Hausman-Taylor instrumental variables (brands of the same firm in other segments) with respect to p_{jt}, $\ln(D_{jt})$, and Inventories$_{jt}$; and BLP instruments (brands of the other firms in the same segment) with respect to mean and standard deviation of $\ln(D_{jt})$ and Inventories$_j$.
* Significantly different from zero at the 5% level in a two-tailed test.

$\alpha_j = (-2.9 - .63*\ln(D_j))$. This implies from equation (8) that corresponding nested logit own-price and cross-price elasticities will be augmented by the product-specific share of consumers that can find the product in their nearest store.[22] In addition, we estimate $\rho = 0.65$; for our corresponding nested logit own-price and cross-price elasticities, this will imply that within-segment market shares will get a higher weight than the overall market share. These estimates provide a matrix of nested logit own-price and cross-price elasticities, of which there are J^2 in each bimonthly period.

The results of the BLP procedure, jointly estimating the demand and cost equations, are presented in table 7.4. The standard errors have been corrected for potential correlation between demand and supply unobservables. With reference to utility, we estimate the mean effect of our product characteristics, the coefficient on price, the parameters that define individual variability in taste for a benchmark quality and price, and the interaction terms. Our specification of the utility and cost function, choices of demand and supply-side instruments, and our structural model of equilibrium predict 80 percent of the variation in the actual market share of each product in each time period. The coefficient on price and interaction of price with consumer-taste distributions will be the focal point. Yet, it will be the quality of the other controls and the instrument set that will give us efficient estimates of our coefficients on price and consumer taste-distribution interactions with price. These determine our estimates of the own and cross-price elasticities set out in equation (7). The coefficient on price and the interaction of price with our consumer-taste distributions that reflect consumer taste for closeness are highly significant. The market-level consumer-taste distribution interactions with price are not significant. This will imply that own and cross-price elasticities will be more responsive when the distribution of consumers' distance to stores that carry the product reflects closeness to consumers. We clearly see a trade-off between covering the market and the nature of price competition that a brand faces, a typical trade-off in the theoretical literature on product differentiation. Less coverage is not a good attribute in terms of market share but can potentially lead to higher price-cost markups by making own- and cross-price elasticities less responsive to the prices of other brands. Even though the market-level interactions do not come in, we see that our product-level consumer-taste distribution for geography induces rich demand primitives. In table 7.5 we compare the demand primitives that result from the nested logit demand system and the BLP

Table 7.4
Estimation of demand and MC equation: BLP specification

		Demand	Cost
	Variables	**Coefficient (*t*-stat)**	**Coefficient (*t*-stat)**
Means			
	Constant	–6.2 (6.1)*	0.13 (.70)
	Inventories		–.20 (2.7)*
	Store coverage		.11 (2.8)*
	Price	–7.3 (6.8)*	
Default cola	**Orange**	1.3 (15.6)*	.02 (.40)
	Lemonade	.69 (6.4)*	.16 (2.7)*
	Mixed fruit	1.7 (6.5)*	–.22 (2.9)*
Default cans	**Standard**	4.5 (3.6)*	.33 (3.2)*
	1.5 liter	4.8 (3.5)*	.39 (5.1)*
	2 liter	.78 (3.4)*	–1.1 (4.3)*
	Multipack cans	–3.4 (12.2)*	–1.2 (6.2)*
Default diet	**Regular**	.71 (11.8)*	.08 (1.3)
Distribution interactions			
Parametric	**Constant**	3.4 (3.4)*	
	Price	–0.7 (.61)	
Age	**Constant**	–11.6 (2.8)*	
	Price	–2.1 (0.3)	
"Closeness to stores"	**Constant**	29.1 (18.6)*	
	Price	–11.2 (7.8)*	
R^2		.82	
GMM objective		.0073	
# Negative predicted mark-ups		0	
# of simulations		100	

Note: Demand and cost side include firm and packaging × month dummies. Observations 4,645. Instruments for demand: flavor, packaging, and diet characteristics and inventories; Hausman-Taylor instrumental variables (brands of the same firm in other segments) with respect to price, store coverage, and inventories; and BLP instruments (brands of the other firms in the same segment) with respect the mean and standard deviation of store coverage and inventories. Instruments for supply: same as demand except the Hausman-Taylor instrumental variables.

Table 7.5
Segment (weighted averages over brands) 1992–1997

Segment	Own price elasticity*	Sum of cross-price elasticity*	Own price elasticity**	Sum of cross-price elasticity**
Cola cans	–13.408	2.9194	–13.296	6.63
Cola standard	–11.384	2.4329	–8.3307	3.5272
Cola 1.5 liter	–5.8557	1.3155	–6.3414	5.6982
Cola 2 liter	–4.1667	0.82662	–5.4398	7.1344
Cola cans multipacks	–7.9963	1.7595	–9.8501	6.8057
Orange cans	–11.621	2.5775	–13.45	6.9458
Orange standard	–11.315	2.4595	–14.791	7.2123
Orange 1.5 liter	–5.8679	1.2974	–8.2648	7.9649
Orange 2 liter	–4.4812	0.93835	–6.0833	7.4632
Orange cans multipacks	–8.8926	2.0043	–12.798	8.3505
Lemonade cans	–8.9282	2.0273	–7.2687	4.5024
Lemonade standard	–11.926	2.6369	–15.899	8.1024
Lemonade 1.5 liter	–5.6547	1.2635	–5.7796	5.7165
Lemonade 2 liter	–3.9762	0.81921	–5.2258	7.1708
Lemonade cans multipacks	–8.1858	1.8823	–6.8013	4.7672
Mixed fruit cans	–12.276	2.7094	–16.43	8.2662
Mixed fruit standard	–14.400	2.9623	–12.723	6.2424
Mixed fruit 1.5 liter	–6.3776	1.4034	–8.2566	6.6438
Mixed fruit 2 liter	–4.0611	0.73015	–5.4653	6.9214
Mixed fruit cans multipacks	–5.3052	1.2756	–9.4387	6.0243
Diet segments				
Cola cans	–11.817	2.6649	–11.757	6.4163
Cola standard	–12.303	2.8268	–15.268	8.3488
Cola 1.5 liter	–5.7972	1.3042	–5.023	3.5868
Cola 2 liter	–4.2643	0.93494	–6.3843	7.6129
Cola cans multipacks	–8.7069	1.9573	–12.888	8.173
Orange cans	–10.997	2.6402	–14.889	8.5435
Orange standard	–9.9561	2.3916	–14.792	8.0678
Orange 1.5 liter	–5.4339	1.3054	–8.4619	8.2154
Orange 2 liter	–4.6477	1.0488	–6.9119	7.4193
Lemonade cans	–13.181	3.0485	–9.5058	4.6999
Lemonade standard	–12.029	2.883	–15.778	8.3728
Lemonade 1.5 liter	–6.9400	1.6513	–8.5238	8.0661
Lemonade 2 liter	–4.7671	1.0658	–3.9351	4.2408
Lemonade cans multipacks	–7.5778	1.8211	–11.733	7.9479
Mixed fruit cans	–9.0504	2.0883	–14.292	8.1215
Mixed fruit standard	–9.2219	2.1273	–14.234	8.4596
Mixed fruit 1.5 liter	–4.8644	1.4551	–6.8668	7.4791
Mixed fruit 2 liter	–4.1952	1.0073	–11.757	6.4163

* Nested logit demand model.
** BLP demand-and-supply model.

demand model, estimated jointly with supply. We average over the brands within each of our flavor, packaging, and diet segments. This in turn is averaged over our twenty-eight bimonthly periods. The elasticity of market share with respect to the own-price elasticities is similar in trends for both models, though the BLP estimates tend to be more elastic. In addition, both models estimate that the own-price elasticity is greater for cans relative to other packaging types, while 2-liter packaging is the most inelastic. We also report the sum of the cross-price elasticities for each brand, averaged by segment. The BLP model clearly estimates these to be larger.

Given these primitives, assuming multiproduct price-setting firms without symmetry in the market, a multiproduct Nash equilibrium is given by the system of J first-order conditions. Using the first-order conditions in equation (10), one can get estimates of a Lerner index per brand/product j. Aggregating these estimates over different sets of brands gives an indicator of firm or segment market power. In table 7.6 we compare estimates of bimonthly markups and profits, averaged over the period, by segment. The key characteristic is packaging type. Packaging with 1.5- and 2-liter bottles earns greater markups than cans and standard bottles. Diet drinks seem to also get a premium and the markups are very similar when one compares both frameworks.

In table 7.7 we compare estimates of bimonthly markups and profits, averaged over the period, by company. We document the price-cost markups and market shares by company for the retail carbonated soft drink market using estimates of demand primitives from our nested logit and BLP frameworks. Clearly a monotonic relationship between market power and market share does not exist in this industry. Companies with a smaller share of the carbonated soft drink market extract rents, within the product segments and stores of the market they operate in, comparable to that of multinationals who operate across most stores and product segments. It seems that inferring market power from the distribution of market shares is ill-advised in multiproduct firms in differentiated-goods industries.

7.5.1 Implications for EU Merger Control

In table 7.7 we document the HHI measures of concentration in terms of market shares and in terms of profit shares for each company. This is done for both the nested logit and BLP model. We take a hypothetical merger in our data, companies ranked 4 and 5, to illustrate that merger screening based on dominance of market shares may fail to identify, in terms of market power, a damaging merger. In addition, we take a hypothetical merger in our data, companies ranked 1 and 7, to illustrate that merger screening based on a dominance test may select a merger for investigation that has insignificant market-power implications.

Using the rules outlined in table 7.1, we observe that both models suggest that the proposed merger between the companies ranked 4 and 5 should be investigated on the basis of the HHI on profit shares. This is not the case if one only used information on market share. Companies small in output can have significant market power by being specialized into geographic and/or product segments. In addition, using the thresholds, a proposed merger between the companies ranked 1 and 7 should not be investigated on the basis of the HHI on profit shares. This would not be the case using the market share of companies' output.

Our policy recommendation is to use a structural model to estimate company markups (aggregated over products) in differentiated-goods industries. Mergers should be assessed on the basis of market-power, and not market-share, considerations as part of selection or screening of notified mergers. Merger screening may fail to identify damaging mergers using the market share of companies' output without any market-power considerations. In most industries we see waves of mergers among small companies that go unchecked, which may have significant market-power considerations. In addition, merger screening using the market share of companies may select mergers for investigation that have few market-power implications. In the European Union and United States we see very few of the selected mergers actually blocked. This must be a sign that selection based on output shares is an imperfect indicator of competitive concerns.

7.6 Conclusions and Recommendations

Recent EU Merger Control Regulation No. 139/2004 moves the EU criteria closer to the U.S. practice, where mergers are prohibited if they would result in a "substantial lessening of competition." While this move away from a dominance test may be apparent during the investigation of mergers, we highlight the fact that an analysis of market concentration is still at the center of the preliminary selection stage of all notified mergers in the European Union and United States. This chapter illustrates that the HHI measure of output concentration is not

Table 7.6
Segment (weighted averages over brands) 1992–1997

Segment	Segment share of output	Price per liter	Estimated markup*	Estimated bimonthly profit in £IR(000)*	Estimated markup**	Estimated bimonthly profit in £IR(000)**
Cola cans	4.22	1.43	0.05	99.82	0.09	185.31
Cola standard	3.78	1.26	0.08	123.69	0.10	167.56
Cola 1.5 liter	2.53	0.75	0.13	86.14	0.16	103.19
Cola 2 liter	11.1	0.50	0.22	411.28	0.22	435.13
Cola cans multipacks	1.92	0.96	0.16	103.56	0.14	83.62
Orange cans	1.85	1.38	0.08	67.66	0.08	67.11
Orange standard	2.10	1.27	0.08	78.13	0.08	72.22
Orange 1.5 liter	2.22	0.68	0.17	86.64	0.13	69.35
Orange 2 liter	8.51	0.46	0.25	327.23	0.20	270.2
Orange cans multipacks	0.49	0.97	0.14	23.85	0.11	19.12
Lemonade cans	1.41	1.41	0.06	36.41	0.09	61.4
Lemonade standard	1.38	1.16	0.13	65.57	0.09	52.43
Lemonade 1.5 liter	3.75	0.71	0.14	126.49	0.17	151.19
Lemonade 2 liter	11.8	0.47	0.29	503.17	0.23	429.55
Lemonade cans multipacks	0.36	0.97	0.13	16.43	0.13	15.36
Mixed fruit cans	2.13	1.39	0.07	72.67	0.07	71.1
Mixed fruit standard	6.29	1.37	0.08	198.65	0.07	208.64
Mixed fruit 1.5 liter	1.80	0.74	0.18	73.51	0.12	56.62
Mixed fruit 2 liter	18.8	0.41	0.0	786.74	0.22	565.8
Mixed fruit cans multipacks	0.02	0.83	0.17	1.06	0.28	1.05

Diet segments						
Cola cans 1.11	1.39	0.09	48.14	0.09	47.23	
Cola standard	0.93	1.30	0.08	34.05	0.11	43.84
Cola 1.5 liter	0.83	0.75	0.15	31.93	0.16	35.33
Cola 2 liter	2.85	0.55	0.28	149.57	0.22	118.13
Cola cans multipacks	0.63	0.6	0.17	37.21	0.14	27.56
Orange cans	0.23	1.27	0.10	10.91	0.07	7.64
Orange standard	0.05	1.19	0.12	2.08	0.26	1.68
Orange 1.5 liter	0.21	0.71	0.18	9.71	0.13	6.56
Orange 2 liter 0.72	0.56	0.22	31.74	0.18	23.89	
Lemonade cans	0.53	1.44	0.07	18.10	0.08	22.5
Lemonade standard	0.21	1.29	0.10	9.07	0.10	9.91
Lemonade 1.5 liter	1.62	0.73	0.14	58.18	0.18	66
Lemonade 2 liter	3.40	0.59	0.20	139.92	0.22	141.25
Lemonade cans multipacks	0.21	0.96	0.14	9.60	0.13	8.71
Mixed fruit cans	0.04	1.27	0.10	1.73	0.09	1.59
Mixed fruit standard	0.04	1.17	0.11	1.86	0.08	1.31
Mixed fruit 1.5 liter	0.01	0.83	0.17	0.09	0.54	0.22
Mixed fruit 2 liter	0.11	0.55	0.24	5.20	0.22	4.78

* Nested logit demand model.
** BLP demand-and-supply model.

Table 7.7
Company markups, output share, and profit share, in the last period

Companies	Brands	Output share	Markup (NL*)	Profit share (NL*)	Markup (BLP**)	Profit share (BLP**)
Rank 1	51	0.4792	0.15	0.3693	0.14	0.4600
Rank 2	36	0.2337	0.22	0.2655	013	0.2000
Rank 3	20	0.0928	0.28	0.1326	0.18	0.1100
Rank 4	4	0.0589	0.30	0.0911	0.25	0.1500
Rank 5	3	0.0553	0.32	0.0907	0.29	0.0500
Rank 6	7	0.0343	0.16	0.0285	0.10	0.0100
Rank 7	3	0.0229	0.05	0.0054	0.05	0.0100
Rank 8	5	0.0196	0.14	0.0144	0.10	0.0010
Rank 9	6	0.0028	0.15	0.0022	0.13	0.0002
Rank 10	1	0.0001	0.10	0.0001	0.10	0.0002
Rank 11	2	0.0002	0.10	0.0001	0.25	0.0000
Rank 12	1	0.0002	0.09	0.0001	0.06	0.0001
Rank 13	1	0.0001	0.07	0.0000	0.29	0.0084
HHI		3014		2420		2890
Merge 4 &5						
New HHI		3080		2585		3040
Change HHI		65		165*		150**
Merge 1 & 7						
New HHI		3234		2460		2982
Change HHI		220		40*		92**

* Nested logit demand model.
** BLP demand-and-supply model.

a good indicator of market power in differentiated-product industries. The complex operation of multiproduct firms over different product and geographic segments in these industries means that there is no theoretical foundation for the mapping of market concentration into market power. This clearly has implications for the use of the HHI and changes in HHI based on market shares as a screening device for proposed mergers. We analyze a proposed merger between two firms that has little impact on the overall HHI measure of output concentration for an industry, and thus would not be likely to undergo an investigation by antitrust authorities using the current thresholds. Yet, we show a big increase in market power as the companies, small in output, are specialized into geographic and/or product segments. In the event that a merger results from the aggregation over companies with high markups, irrespective of their overall share in the market, our profit-share indicator of market power using the HHI is clearly desirable in the screening stage of mergers in differentiated-product industries. In addition, we demonstrate the other scenario where a merger without market-power concerns is selected for investigation by antitrust authorities using the current thresholds. Given the low selection rate, it seems very costly to select mergers that will clearly not be blocked during investigation.

This chapter compares a simple and a more advanced structural approach in the estimation of market power. Our simple model is straightforward to implement, not requiring cumbersome estimation procedures or a heavy data burden.[23] More importantly, the results are similar to those estimated in the BLP model. Using estimates of market power to construct HHI in profit shares allows more accurate and informed decisions in the screening stage as to which mergers should undergo investigation. This will ensure a simple screening technique that can identify a threat to competition among notified mergers.

Notes

This chapter was written for CESifo's Venice Summer Institute 2004, "Recent Developments in Antitrust Analysis," July 21–22, 2004. We thank our discussant, Vivek Ghosal, for useful comments. We also acknowledge comments from the Competition and Regulation Group, Dublin. Finally, we thank Peter Davis, Gautam Gowrisankaran, Julie Mortimer, Ariel Pakes, and John Sutton for comments on work that this chapter is based on.

1. The European Commission has exclusive jurisdiction for mergers between firms with a combined worldwide turnover of at least 5 billion euros and a turnover within the European Economic Area of more than 250 million euros for each of them. Failure to meet these turnover thresholds, or other criteria, may result in a merger being assessed in an individual EU country.

2. The HHI is the sum of the squares of firm percentage output market share, which gives proportionately greater weight to larger players in the market. It ranges from close to zero (in an atomistic market) to 10,000 (in the case of monopoly). The postmerger HHI assumes the market share of the merging parties is the sum of the market share of the two undertakings. This does not allow for strategic responses to the merger in terms of price or quantity changes or industry dynamics in terms of entry or exit. The change in the HHI just reflects summing the market shares of the merging firms.

3. The HHI would now be the sum of the squares of the firm's profit shares, ranging from close to zero (no rents in the market) to 10,000 (monopolistic rents). The postmerger HHI assumes the profit share of the merging parties is the sum of the two undertakings. This does not allow for economies of scale or any other strategic reason for the merger. Hence, the change in the HHI just reflects summing the coming together two companies ex ante profit shares.

4. In the United States, 17,404 transactions were notified between 1998 and 2002, and only 2 percent were selected for enforcement actions.

5. This replaces Article 2 of Regulation No. 4064/1989—the "dominance" test—indicating that any merger that "creates or strengthens a dominant position as a result of which effective competition would be significantly impeded" is to be blocked.

6. By "increased market power" is meant "the ability of one or more firms to profitably increase prices, reduce output, choice or quality of goods and services, diminish innovation, or otherwise influence parameters of competition" (EU Merger Guidelines 2004/C 31/03, No. 8).

7. This may arise, for example, when merging firms have a large market share, when merging firms are close competitors, or when customers have a limited means of switching suppliers (see EU Merger Guidelines, Nos. 26–38).

8. The EU Merger Guidelines outline three necessary conditions for sustainable coordination: (1) the ability to monitor coordinating firms to determine whether they are keeping an agreement, (2) a credible punishment-deterrence mechanism if a deviation is detected, and (3) the ability to prevent the reactions of outsiders (current/future competitors) from jeopardizing expected gains from coordination.

9. As with the U.S. Horizontal Merger Guidelines, the EU Merger Guidelines acknowledge the importance of considering the relevant market for analysis. For definition of relevant market for the purpose of community competition law, see OJ C 372, 9.12.1997, p. 3, paragraphs 54–55. Once the relevant geographic and product market have been defined, a preliminary screening of all notified mergers takes place.

10. Normally current market shares are used in the analysis. However, these may be adjusted to reflect reasonably certain future changes—for example, in light of entry, exit, or expansion. (See, e.g., Case COMP/M.1806—Astra Zeneca/Novartis points 150 and 415.)

11. Case T-221/95, *Endemol v. Commission* (1999), ECR II-1299, paragraph 134; Case T-102/96, *Gencor v. Commission* (1999), ECR II-753, paragraph 205. It is a distinct question whether a dominant position is created or strengthened as a result of the merger.

12. The Commission has found cases where mergers resulting in firms holding market shares between 40 and 50 percent (COMP/M.2337—Nestle/Ralston Purina, points 48–50) and even <40 percent (Commission decision 1999/674/EC in CaseIV/M.1221—Rewe/Meinl, OJ L 274, 23.10.1999, p1, points 98–114; Case COMP/M.2337—Nestle/Ralston Purina, points 44–47) lead to the creation or strengthening of a dominant position.

13. This was done for (1) all cases where the Commission established dominance, (2) all cases where the Commission accepted remedies in phase I on the basis of serious doubts (note that "serious doubts" is the substantive standard for opening a phase II investigation), and (3) all phase I clearance cases in 2002. In total, the analysis was based on data from 1,231 markets from 207 cases (377 markets from 60 "dominance" cases, 273 remedies markets, and 356 clearance markets).

14. The most common examples of "special circumstances" were cases where one of the merging parties was a recent entrant, or where a large firm acquired a relatively small firm.

15. Since the postmerger HHI and change in HHI are most significant in evaluating mergers with straightforward horizontal effects, the table omits mergers challenged on basis of other competitive theories—for example, those based on vertical control, monopsony power, elimination of potential competition, or where competitive concerns stemmed from influence through partial ownership and aspects of corporate governance.

16. This idea is evident with the structure-conduct-performance paradigm of Bain in the 1950s, positing a one-way mapping from structure (concentration of market share) to conduct (treated as a black box) to performance (average price-cost markup across companies in an industry).

17. As an alternative one could use representative consumer choice. These models include the Distance Metric model (Pinkse, Slade, and Brett 2002; Pinkse and Slade 2002), or the Multi-Stage Budgeting model (Hausman, Leonard, and Zona 1994).

18. Anderson and de Palma 1992 is a good textbook for a detailed analysis of these models.

19. Unfortunately, as noticed by Berry, Levinsohn, and Pakes (2004) and Petrin (2002), reliance on the market-level distributions of consumer characteristics does not give us the degrees of freedom associated with microlevel data on individual choices. Moreover, the distribution of consumer characteristics relevant to products inside the market may well be different for those purchasing the outside option (see Mariuzzo 2004). Likewise, the distribution of relevant consumer characteristics may vary dramatically across products inside the market. In our example we improve our estimates of demand primitives by randomizing over data on store coverage to create a distribution of consumer disutility reflecting distance to each brand (product). We have a distribution of consumer preferences that reflects the likely convenience of the location of retail stores that carry the product in question. The interaction of this product (j) specific distribution with prices can be estimated with far greater degrees of freedom when compared to interactions using market-level distributions of consumer characteristics. This will result in a very rich set of demand primitives.

20. When $\rho = 0$, this reduces to the ordinary logit model, where substitution possibilities are completely symmetric—for example, as when all products belong to the same group.

21. Nevo's (2000) practitioners' guide is a good reference for understanding the estimation procedure. We extend his Matlab program to undertake a BLP estimate on our specific functional forms.

22. These estimates are slightly different from those in Mariuzzo, Walsh, and Whelan 2003, because we use packaging $\times$ month dummies instead of packaging $\times$ season dummies. In addition, we use a different set of instruments. This makes our nested logit model, including the interaction term for distance to a product, comparable to the demand model of BLP.

23. For the use of the structural models employing a model of supply and demand (nested logit) in the investigation stage of a merger, see Ivaldi and Verboven (2005) on the Volvo/Scania case.

References

Anderson, S. P., and A. de Palma. 1992. "Multiproduct Firms: A Nested Logit Approach." *Journal of Industrial Economics* 60:261–276.

Berry, S. 1994. "Estimating Discrete-Choice Models of Product Differentiation." *RAND Journal of Economics* 25:242–262.

Berry, S., J. Levinsohn, and A. Pakes. 1995. "Automobile Prices in Market Equilibrium." *Econometrica* 63:841–890.

Berry, S., J. Levinsohn, and A. Pakes. 2004. "Estimating Differentiated Product Demand Systems from a Combination of Micro and Macro Data: The New Car Market." *Journal of Political Economy* 112:68–105.

European Commission. 2004. *A Pro-Active Competition Policy for a Competitive Europe: Communication from the Commission*. COM (2004), 293 final, April 20. European Commission.

Hausman, J., G. Leonard, and J. D. Zona. 1994. "Competitive Analysis with Differentiated Products." *Annales D'Économie et de Statistique* 34:159–80.

Ivaldi, M., and F. Verboven. 2005. Quantifying the Effects from Horizontal Mergers in European Competition Policy. *International Journal of Industrial Organization* 23(9–10):669–691.

Mariuzzo F. 2004. "Automobile Equilibrium Prices: An Empirical Study on the Italian Market Price Elasticities." Doctoral dissertation, Department of Economics, University of Venice.

Mariuzzo, F., P. P. Walsh, and C. Whelan. 2003. "Firm Size and Market Power in Carbonated Soft Drinks." *Review of Industrial Organization* 23(3–4):283–299.

Mariuzzo, F., P. P. Walsh, and C. Whelan. 2005. "Embedding Consumer Taste for Location Convenience into a Structural Model of Equilibrium." Trinity Economic Papers 2005/3. Trinity College, Dublin.

Nevo, A. 2000. "A Practitioners Guide to Estimation of Random Coefficients Logit Models of Demand." *Journal of Economics & Management Strategy* 9(4):513–548.

Nevo, A. 2001. "Measuring Market Power in the Ready-to-Eat Cereal Industry." *Econometrica* 69:307–342.

Petrin, A. 2002. "Quantifying the Benefits of New Products: The Case of the Minivan." *Journal of Political Economy* 110:705–729.

Pinkse, J., and M. E. Slade. 2002. "Mergers, Brand Competition, and the Price of a Pint." Unpublished manuscript, Department of Economics, University of British Columbia.

Pinkse, J., M. E. Slade, and C. Brett. 2002. "Spatial Price Competition: A Semiparametric Approach." *Econometrica* 70:1111–1155.

Sutton, J. 1991. *Sunk Costs and Market Structure: Price Competition, Advertising and the Evolution of Concentration*. Cambridge, MA: MIT Press.

U.S. Federal Trade Commission and Department of Justice. 2003. "Merger Challenges Data, Fiscal Years 1999–2003." Report, December 18. www.usdoj.gov/atr/public/201898.htm.

Verouden, V. 2004. "The Role of Market Shares and Market Concentration Indices in the European Commission's Guidelines on the Assessment of Horizontal Mergers under the EC Merger Regulation." Comments prepared for the FTC and U.S. DOJ Merger Enforcement Workshop, Washington, DC, February 17–19. http://www.ftc.gov/bc/mergerrnforce/presentations/040217verouden.pdf.

Walsh, P. P., and C. Whelan. 1999. "Modelling Price Dispersion as an Outcome of Competition in the Irish Grocery Market." *Journal of Industrial Economics* 47:1–19.

8 Comparative Advertising and Competition Policy

Francesca Barigozzi and
Martin Peitz

8.1 Introduction

Until very recently several continental European countries had completely banned any form of comparative advertising, whereas in the United States, the use of comparative advertising has actually been encouraged by the Federal Trade Commission since the 1970s. While in the past the European and American approaches to this type of advertising were markedly different, today competition authorities agree in considering comparative advertising an important tool in promoting competition, such that firms and retailers are encouraged to use comparative ads. The reason is that comparative advertising, if fair and not misleading, is claimed to increase consumer information about alternative brands, products, and services and to positively affect competition among (domestic and cross-border) firms. In particular, the argument goes that direct-comparison ads would encourage consumers to make more informed purchasing decisions—moreover, comparison ads would ease the consumer's task of evaluating the performance of particular brands against other brands.

A particular understanding of this idea is the following (we elaborate on this in section 8.4). Compared to generic advertising, comparative claims provide information that is easily converted into operational knowledge by consumers. Often, content-based advertising that does not make comparisons has little meaning for consumers. Their ability to process comparative claims should be higher, on the other hand, because these claims allow consumers to make inferences from experiences involving past consumption of other products. More generally, the named competing brand serves as a reference point.[1]

For information transmission to work, consumers must not be deceived. Here, laws and legal practice are essential in ensuring that comparative advertising claims are truthful. In particular, competition policy must be designed such that the consumers' and the competitors' interest in truthful information transmission can be guaranteed.

Our main point is that comparative advertising has two possible effects on competition: in the case of experience and credence-goods characteristics, it can intensify competition by signaling the sponsoring brand's quality, whereas in the case of search-goods characteristics, it can relax price competition by differentiating products.

This chapter analyzes comparative advertising seen from a competition policy perspective. In particular, it focuses on how such policy affects the signaling role of comparative advertising. We address the following set of questions:

1. What is the legal history of comparative advertising?
2. What is the current legislation with respect to comparative advertising in the United States and Europe?
3. How have the courts interpreted the laws?
4. How does comparative advertising affect market outcomes?
5. In particular, what is the scope of information transmission by comparative advertising and how is it affected by competition policy?
6. And, more generally, what should be kept in mind when designing competition policy?

Before answering these questions, we provide definitions of comparative advertising, document the spread of comparative advertising as a marketing practice, and elaborate on the potential drawbacks of comparative advertising from a business perspective.

8.1.1 Definition of Comparative Advertising

According to the U.S. Federal Trade Commission (FTC), "Comparative advertising is defined as advertising that compares alternative brands on objectively measurable attributes or price, and identifies the alternative brand by name, illustration or other distinctive information" (Statement of Policy Regarding Comparative Advertising, Federal Trade Commission, Washington, D.C., August 13, 1979).

In the European Union, Directive 97/55/EC concerning misleading and comparative advertising reads: "Comparative advertising means any advertising which explicitly or by implication identifies a competitor or goods or services offered by a competitor."[2]

Comparative advertising can be classified according to whether it is *direct* or *indirect*.[3] In direct comparative ads the competing products either are explicitly named or can be precisely identified (by photos, images, or trademarks). We give two examples. In 1991 MasterCard launched a "campaign that used funny 30-second commercials to depict frenzied American Express Card holders rushing madly around unsuccessfully trying to find an ATM that would take their card" (Leighton 2004, 621). A 1999 General Motors Corp. ad claimed that the Cadillac Seville STS outperforms BMW 540 in a slalom race.

By contrast, indirect comparative ads do not explicitly mention competing brand names. The Avis "We try harder" campaign launched in the United States in 1962 is perhaps the most famous example.[4]

8.1.2 History and Diffusion of Comparative Advertising

In 1930 Sears compared its own line of tires to eight national brands in the United States. The ad increased Sears' tire sales. Firestone launched a counteroffensive ad that created a debate about "business ethics" and "good taste," to the effect that many newspapers, including those in New York and Chicago, refused to run the ad. The ensuing controversy about comparative advertising drew attention to the potential role of comparison in advertising and its eventual consequences. The controversy at that time ended in favor of comparative advertising in 1932, when "Plymouth was able to run an ad entitled 'Look at all three' that effectively depicted Plymouth's superiority over Chevrolet and Ford. Plymouth's sales more than doubled over the ensuing six months and comparative advertising was born" (Suasion Resources 2003).

Comparative advertising has become common in the United States since the 1970s. Different studies suggest varying figures on the relative use of comparative advertising in the United States. Muehling, Stoltman, and Grossbart (1990) find that around 40 percent of all advertising is comparative. Pechmann and Stewart (1990) find on a different data set that 60 percent of all ads are indirectly comparative and 20 percent contain direct comparative claims; the rest are noncomparative. Sectors most affected by rules on comparative advertising include food, retail, motoring, airlines, and, more recently, financial and telecommunications services. Famous examples of direct comparative ads that have delivered significant gains in market share for the sponsoring brand are Pepsi (over Coca-Cola), Burger King (over McDonald's), Tylenol (over Aspirin), Unilever (over Procter and Gamble), Visa (over

American Express), Hewlett-Packard (over IBM), and AT&T (over MCI) (see, e.g., Teather 2000).

In most EU countries comparative advertising is a relatively young phenomenon, as we will see in the next section. The rationale for the ban essentially built on the defense of trademark owners (intellectual property rights or business of competitors). In particular, both the use of a trademark without the permission of the trademark owner and the fact of taking advantage of the reputation of famous brands were considered illegal. Even where the domestic legal framework did not contain a specific ban on comparative advertising, the use of comparison in advertising was avoided because of the high risk of a court ruling that a deceptive representation of the target brand occurred.

We are not aware of any systematic study on the current diffusion of comparative ads in Europe. Casual observation and court cases suggest that they are frequently used for retailing, electronics, airlines, telephone, and other services provision; the comparison is often based on price or price levels. Probably the lack of harmonization of comparative-advertising rules among the European countries, despite Directive 97/55/EC, and the subsequent legal risks faced by the advertising firms still represent obstacles.[5] Also, since European consumers have been less exposed to comparative advertising, advertisers there may be more skeptical about its effectiveness.

8.1.3 Effectiveness of Comparative Ads

Apart from the previously mentioned legal risks, in the past, a number of advertisers have been reluctant to use comparative ads because some long-term consequences of comparison advertising may be seriously detrimental to the advertising firm. A first potentially negative effect mentioned in the marketing literature is the misidentification of sponsoring brands: comparison ads might increase the salience of the competing brand without improving consumer awareness of the brand sponsoring the message. A second important possible negative effect concerns credibility: an ad for one brand might not be viewed by consumers as a highly credible source of information about competing brands because of a likelihood of manipulative intent (see Wilkie and Farris 1975). However, this argument can be questioned. Indeed, as some practitioners have observed, the opposite might be the case. The potential challenge by the target brand (which can go to court against the sponsoring brand if the comparative claim is unfair and/or misleading) represents the strength of comparative advertising; consumers anticipate that only in the case of really motivated claims would sponsoring brands risk legal action. In section 8.4 we propose an economic model that formalizes such an argument for the use of comparative advertising.[6]

The European Association of Communication Agencies (2000, 4) lists additional features of comparative ads that have been unsuccessful for the sponsoring brand or have been challenged in court:

> Failure or legal problems with comparative advertising have frequently been linked to: (a) Denigration of competitive products or trade marks (e.g. by using sound effects, differences in lighting, positioning/size of compared products). (b) Comparing products to top-of-the-line trade marks (e.g. Nissan versus Mercedes in the US), causing lack of consumer acceptance; (c) Comparisons based upon less relevant product features. (d) Excessive techniques or claims overdramatising the claimed differences in performance/quality. (e) Using suggestive techniques, such as illustrations of consumer reactions to various products/services, without these reactions being representative for the population (e.g. on-camera "taste-tests").

In the marketing literature on comparison ads the general effectiveness of comparative advertising is still controversial (see Prasad 1976; Pechmann and Ratneshwar 1991; Jain, Buchanan, and Maheswaran 1998; Barone and Miniard 1999). Nevertheless, general agreement exists concerning the fact that a low-share or unfamiliar brand (the underdog) can enhance the relevance of an ad by naming a leading brand that consumers regularly purchase. In other words, comparison ads should be more effective in directing initial attention toward small firms wishing to take on established brands (e.g., Muehling, Stoltman, and Grossbart 1990; Pechmann and Stewart 1990). For example, according to the dealer marketing manager at Mitsubishi, the company used comparative advertising when entering the European market "to guide the consumer by making associations with top brand names" (Coleman 2000). This is the so-called underdog hypothesis; for an exposition from a marketing perspective, see Gnepa 1993.

8.1.4 Plan of the Chapter

In section 8.2 we explore the legal background. We provide answers to questions 1 and 2 posed above—that is, we elaborate on the legal history of comparative advertising and the current legislation with respect to comparative ads in the United States and Europe. In section 8.3 we present a number of legal cases, providing an answer to question 3. These cases suggest additional considerations with respect to the above questions. They also provide insights that are helpful in answering questions 4 to 6. In section 8.4 we explore some economic perspectives on comparative advertising. This material sheds further light on questions 4 to 6, by showing how comparative advertising may affect market outcomes. In particular, we elaborate on the scope of information transmission of comparative advertising and on how it is influenced by competition policy. Section 8.5 concludes the chapter.

8.2 Legislation and Legal Practice

In this section we briefly discuss comparative advertising's legal background. In particular, we focus on past and current legislation in the United States and Europe.

8.2.1 Comparative Advertising in the United States

We first describe the role of both the Federal Trade Commission and the courts in protecting competitors and consumers against false and misleading comparative advertising. Then we discuss two interesting issues in disputes arising from comparative advertising: standards of substantiation and damages.

8.2.1.1 Legislation in the United States In the United States, federal advertising legislation is reflected in two major acts: the Federal Trade Commission Act and the Trademark (Lanham) Act (the federal trademark statute prohibiting false designations of origin and false or misleading descriptions of facts). The Federal Trade Commission, when it was founded in 1914, had as its mission to protect businesses against unfair practices. In 1922 the Supreme Court ruled that the FTC had the right to regulate advertising. Specifically, this ruling allowed the FTC to regulate all aspects of false labeling and unfair methods of competition in advertising. Comparative advertising became an important issue in the 1960s and 1970s. Early on the FTC had emphasized that comparative advertising is a means of transmitting information to consumers. In 1963 it narrowed an order with respect to comparative advertising so as to allow firms to make

> truthful and non-deceptive statements that a product has certain desirable properties or qualities which a competing product or products do not possess. Such a comparison may have the effect of disparaging the competing product, but we know of no rule of law which prevents a seller from honestly informing the public of the advantages of its products as opposed to those of competing products. (60 F.T.C. at 796)

The relatively sudden increase, during the 1970s and 1980s, in the use of explicit comparisons in advertising in the United States, was in part a result of an FTC appraisal of such practices as a means of improving competition. The FTC statement reads as follows:

> The Commission has supported the use of brand comparisons where the bases of comparison are clearly identified. Comparative advertising, when truthful and non-deceptive, is a source of important information to consumers and assists them in making rational purchase decisions. Comparative advertising encourages product improvement and innovation, and can lead to lower prices in the marketplace. (Statement of Policy Regarding Comparative Advertising, Federal Trade Commission, Washington, D.C., August 13, 1979)

Both competitors and consumers can turn to the FTC regarding disputes arising from comparative advertising. Nevertheless, most complaints about comparative-advertising actions have not come from consumers, but instead from the firms that were the target of the comparison. Since 1974, instead of addressing the FTC, plaintiffs have been taking ordinary court actions based on the 1946 Lanham Act.[7] These firms have found that section 43(a) of the Lanham Act (although it does not mention advertising) holds "the key to getting more expedient and decisive action taken on their complaints. . . . Section 43(a) of Lanham Act was largely intended to clarify trademark, 'palming off', and other trade law issues. However, it has been used as a basis for private litigation against companies promulgating allegedly false comparative advertising" (Bixby and Lincoln 1989, 145). Since section 43(a) of the Lanham Act is aimed at protecting trademarks, while the main objective of the FTC is to promote competition for the consumers' benefit (also) by the use of (fair) comparative advertising, it is not surprising that target brands found trademark law a better tool to react against aggressive comparative advertising practice.

The amended section 43(a) of the Lanham Act says that

> any person who, on or in connection with any goods or services . . . uses in commerce any word, term, name, symbol, or device, or any combination thereof, or any false designation of origin, false or misleading description of fact, or false or misleading representation of fact, which . . . in commercial advertising or promotion, misrepresents the nature, characteristics, qualities, or geographic origin of his or her or another person's goods, services, or commercial activities, shall be liable in a civil action by any person who believes that he or she is or is likely to be damaged by such act.

Plaintiffs typically have used section 43(a) of the Lanham Act rather than the FTC Act "because (1) it may give them immediate relief from competitive advertising by means of an injunction, (2) it may oblige the competitor to run corrective advertising, and (3) it may allow the plaintiff to collect damages from the defendant." (Bixby and Lincoln 1989, 145).

8.2.1.2 Legal Practice: Standards of Substantiation An important issue is whether the standards of substantiation are to be higher using comparative advertising compared to other forms of advertising that makes claims about product characteristics. The position of the FTC, as stated in 1979, reads:

> On occasion, a higher standard of substantiation by advertisers using comparative advertising has been required by self-regulation entities. The Commission evaluates comparative advertising in the same manner as it evaluates all other advertising techniques. The ultimate question is whether or not the advertising has a tendency or capacity to be false or deceptive. This is a factual issue to be determined on a case-by-case basis. However, industry codes and interpretations that impose a higher standard of substantiation for comparative claims than for unilateral claims are inappropriate and should be revised. (Statement of Policy Regarding Comparative Advertising, Federal Trade Commission, Washington, D.C., August 13, 1979)

We would like to include two important caveats here. First, since target brands can take action against comparative claims and much less so against claims that are not comparative, the FTC statement of nondiscrimination may not correspond to legal practice. Second, the FTC statement becomes empty, if comparative advertising is the only means to communicate content about a product to consumers. This is the case if a target brand's product serves as a reference point for consumers because consumers do not have an understanding of absolute content statements (an example would be nutrition information for food). As one author puts it:

> To state a cause of action for misleading advertisement under the Lanham Act, *a plaintiff* must establish the following: 1) the defendant has made false or misleading statements of fact concerning his own product or another's; 2) the statement actually tends to deceive a substantial portion of the intended audience; 3) the statement is material in that it will likely influence the deceived consumer's purchasing decisions; 4) the advertisements were introduced into interstate commerce; and 5) there is some causal link between the challenged statements and harm to the plaintiff. (Leighton 2004, 586)

Further, "when materiality has to be proven under the Lanham Act, it usually must be shown that the claim at issue likely would affect purchase decisions of a significant percentage of the intended audience"

(Leighton 2004, 586). The plaintiff must provide clear results from consumers' surveys about how consumers interpret the claim and subsequently exert purchasing choices. Notice that even if the claim is not literally false it is actionable if it provides consumers with a wrong perception of reality. In other words, the content of an ad is important (it must be true), but the general impression given to consumers also matters. In particular, what matters is the way consumers *interpret* the ad.

To summarize, two situations are possible. An ad may have a literally false statement but may not be deceptive or misleading in its net impression. Or every claim in an ad may be literally true, but the net impression given by the ad can be misleading. As Wood (2003) reports, "most cases involve advertising that contains literally true statements when viewed out of context but, as presented, leaves a false or deceptive net impression."

More specifically, courts place false or misleading advertising into three categories: *implied falsity*, *literal falsity*, and *mere puffery*. Only the first two categories are actionable. With respect to the second category, "most plaintiffs prefer the court to categorize the challenged advertising as literally false because the element of deception is presumed and no costly consumer survey is required" (McKenna and Manning 2002, 2).[8]

The third category is not actionable. Puffery consists of promotional claims that no one takes literally (e.g., polar bears that enjoy sipping Coca-Cola). They are considered harmless hyperbole, obviously absurd advertising exaggerations: we all know that movie stars do not actually cook hamburgers in fast-food restaurants or that toy rabbits powered by a single battery will not keep going forever. In other words, puffery involves claims that sensible people do not take seriously.

Puffery can be used as a defense in false-advertising cases brought under the Lanham Act. When such a defense succeeds, the court finding is that the claim in the ad is merely the seller's opinion and therefore nonactionable puffery. The courts and regulatory agencies find an advertising claim to be mere puffery when it obviously is not of material importance to reasonable potential customers. We can distinguish between "puffery by exaggeration, bluster, boast, or humor," as in the case of the MasterCard advertising mentioned in the introduction, and "puffery by vagueness and/or seller's opinion," such as the ad "the most beautiful car on the market" (see Leighton 2004). However, the world of puffery is quite small for comparative ads, as the *Pizza Hut v. Papa John's* case exemplifies (although the federal court's decision was overturned). This case is discussed in section 8.3.

Also, comparative ads that may be defended as puffery may be ruled to violate trademark antidilution law. Section 43(c) of the Lanham Act contains the important norm concerning trademark dilution—that is, disparagement, blurring, or alteration of a competitor's "famous" trademark. It aims at preventing the reduction of a trademark's selling power. If a firm is the target of a comparison ad, it can base its lawsuit on section 43(c) whenever the advertising campaign alters or distorts its trademark in any way that could be regarded as spoofing the mark. More than twenty U.S. states have antidilution laws, which are sometimes stricter than the corresponding federal law (as with New York's trademark antidilution statute). In the case *Deere & Company v. MTD Products, Inc.*, the court dismissed the allegation based on the section 42(a) of the Lanham Act and found that the comparative statements were true. The Court of Appeals for the Second Circuit of New York affirmed a lower court's injunction barring the comparative advertising because it violated New York's trademark antidilution statute.[9] One law firm has argued that other states would now look to New York's Court of Appeals as persuasive authority and follow its interpretation of what constitutes "dilution" (see Wood 2003).

8.2.1.3 Legal Practice: Damages Section 35 of the Lanham Act allows plaintiffs to claim a number of damages: lost profits, corrective advertising expenses to help regain loss business, attorneys' fees, and punitive damages. Standards of proof for recovering damages for false advertising are high. In fact, to be entitled to damages, a plaintiff must show that consumers were actually deceived by the defendant's false advertising and that there was a direct cause or connection between the alleged false advertising and the injury of the plaintiff. But "in several cases, the courts have dispensed with the requirement that actual deception be proven where the defendant's conduct was found to be willful" (Raymond 2004). Thus, when misrepresentations in the ad are willful and egregious, actual deception is presumed and punitive damages can even be awarded. However, damage awards have not been common in Lanham Act cases. On the contrary, only a dozen court decisions have allowed damages in false-advertising cases and fewer still have involved comparative advertising. The most important case, with a $40 million judgment, is *U-Haul International Inc. v. Jartran, Inc.*, 793 F.2d 1034 (9th Cir. 1986). We will discuss this case in section 8.3.

The law firm Arnold and Porter suggests that damages are rare because of the perceived difficulty of proof.[10] Other authors argue that the courts are skeptical toward comparative claims in litigations concerning trademark infringement or malicious falsehood. In particular, Swan (2000, 4) says that "judges take the view that the public is neither gullible nor particularly trustful of advertising. Even if a cause of action is established, judges take some convincing that a comparative advertisement has caused any damage."

8.2.2 Comparative Advertising in the European Union

We first describe the recent harmonization of the law on comparative advertising in the European Union, then we consider legal practice focusing on the United Kingdom. Differences between the United Kingdom and the U.S. approach to comparison ads are briefly discussed. Finally the case of professional services is presented.

8.2.2.1 Legislation in the European Union Until very recently, comparative advertising was essentially not allowed in European countries. In countries where it was not explicitly banned, comparative advertising had never been very popular and frequently was regarded by courts with open suspicion, as a sort of unfair trade practice. The explicit identification of competitors had been banned in Belgium, Italy, and Luxembourg. It was generally prohibited as unfair competition in Germany and France, unless advance notification was given to the competitor. Limited comparative advertising was permitted in Spain and the Netherlands.[11] The use was restricted by the criteria of strict truthfulness and relevance in Scandinavia. (See, e.g., J. Dickerson and P. Jordan from the DLA Group in the United Kingdom, www.dla.com.) In particular, "the explicit identification of a rival or its product constituted unauthorized use of the rival's trademark or unfair denigration" (Petty and Spink 1995). Recently, the United Kingdom had, compared with other member states, a reputation of taking a rather relaxed approach (see below).

The European Union first addressed the issue of comparative advertising in the late 1970s. The position was that comparative advertising should be legal if it provides verifiable details and is neither misleading nor unfair. However, laws on comparative advertising were harmonized only in April 2000 (almost twenty years after they were first proposed): "The preamble of the directive indicates that for goods to flow freely throughout the EC, the rules governing the form and content of advertising must be uniform and notes that this currently is not the case with comparative advertising. The preamble emphasizes comparative advertising's importance as a consumer decision-making tool and a stimulus of competition" (Petty and Spink 1995).

According to current European legislation, comparative advertising is allowed only if it is not misleading, compares like with like, does not create confusion, discredit, or take unfair advantage of a rival's trademark or present goods as imitations of those bearing a protected trade name. To be more precise, Article 3a of Directive 97/55/EC of the European Parliament and of the Council of October 6, 1997, states:

> Comparative advertising shall, as far as the comparison is concerned, be permitted when the following conditions are met:
>
> (a) it is not misleading . . . ;
> (b) it compares goods or services meeting the same needs or intended for the same purpose;
> (c) it objectively compares one or more material, relevant, verifiable and representative features of those goods and services, which may include price;
> (d) it does not create confusion in the market place between the advertiser and a competitor or between the advertiser's trade marks, trade names, other distinguishing marks, goods or services and those of a competitor;
> (e) it does not discredit or denigrate the trade marks, trade names, other distinguishing marks, goods, services, activities, or circumstances of a competitor;
> (f) for products with designation of origin, it relates in each case to products with the same designation;
> (g) it does not take unfair advantage of the reputation of a trade mark, trade name or other distinguishing marks of a competitor or of the designation of origin of competing products[12];
> (h) it does not present goods or services as imitations or replicas of goods or services bearing a protected trade mark or trade name.

Several of the restrictions on comparative advertising can be defended by common sense, although they are open to interpretation, as we illustrate in section 8.3. However, a defense of condition (f) is less clear, because it requires comparisons to products with the same designation. In particular, this effectively reduces the ability of imports to establish themselves against certain homegrown products.

The authority that responds to controversies arising from comparative advertising is the competition authority in every member state. However, the directive provides for the possibility of ordinary Court actions when comparative advertising consists of acts amounting to unfair competition, or infringes on the laws on copyright, trademarks, or other distinguishing signs. Those who can take legal action include not only the competitor, but also consumers and their organizations and associations.

Section 8.7 (administrative and judicial remedies) of Directive 97/55/EC states that (i) the ad deemed to be unlawful can be provisionally suspended by the Authority; (ii) the advertiser can be asked to furnish evidence as to the accuracy of factual claims in the ad, and if evidence is not given or is deemed inadequate, the factual data shall be considered false; (iii) when the Court rules in favor of the plaintiff, the misleading ad must be withdrawn and eventually the Court's judgment published; moreover, the advertiser can be asked to publish a corrective ad.

As Petty and Spink (1995, 317) observe, "the tenor and language of the European (proposal) directive contrast sharply with the permissiveness of U.S. policy toward comparative advertising. Although legal violations, such as trademark infringement, disparagement, and passing off, are recognized in both the United States and Europe, they are more broadly construed in Europe." Moreover, they claim that "in many cases, comparisons allowed in the United States will be prohibited in Europe."

8.2.2.2 Legal Practice In spite of a common legal framework in the European Union, we are still far from a true harmonization of the various ways Directive 97/55/EC has been interpreted in the different member states.[13] The courts in different countries appear to have a different understanding of the legality of certain comparative ads (as illustrated by the comparative advertising campaigns by Ryanair; see section 8.3). Given the different histories with respect to the legality of comparative advertising and different attitudes among member states, this is hardly surprising.

As mentioned above, the lack of harmonization increases the risks for firms using comparative advertising and may therefore partly explain the more cautious use of this form of advertising in the European Union. This lack of harmonization within Europe and across different countries more generally becomes more relevant because of the increasing importance of commerce on the Internet. With online product searching and distance selling, comparative advertising has received renewed attention. The explosive growth of Internet advertising forces practitioners to verify whether their ads comply with comparative-advertising standards and social norms in various countries. In the words of Freeman and Nemiroff (2001), "if you decide to use comparative advertisements as a marketing tool in a foreign country, or even if your online ad results in sales to foreign consumers, it is important to first obtain a complete legal assessment of that country's advertising laws."[14]

As we have mentioned, within the European Union the United Kingdom today has a rather relaxed attitude toward comparative advertising. Nevertheless, to compare the legal approaches to comparative advertising characterizing European countries and the United States, it is useful to consider the United Kingdom as an EU example. In both countries the interpretation by the courts is of particular importance, because both the United Kingdom and the United States have a common-law legal system, where court cases provide precedent—that is, these cases are used by other courts within the same jurisdiction when making decisions in comparable cases.

8.2.2.3 Country Study: United Kingdom Before 1994 comparative advertising was prohibited in the United Kingdom because it amounted to trademark infringement. Then section 10(6) of the Trade Mark Act (TMA) permitted the use of another trademark for the purpose of making a comparison within certain guidelines. As Berns Wright and Morgan (2002, 14) put it,

> the TMA provides that trademarks must not be used other than in accordance with honest practice. The courts' test for honesty is an objective one. They ask: would a reasonable reader, accustomed to advertisings' use of hyperbole and even "knocking copy,"[15] find the advertisement so biased or misleading to be dishonest? The comparison must be between products intended to meet the same needs or intended for the same purpose. The comparison must be material, relevant, representative, and verifiable.

Moreover, comparative advertising must not create confusion or create the impression of a link between different trademarks. In cases of alleged trademark infringement, the plaintiff—that is, the target brand—has to prove that the use of the trademark is not honest.[16]

Some years after the TMA approval, the European directive on comparative advertising was implemented in the United Kingdom with the Control of Misleading Advertising (Amendment) Regulations 2000. As Dickerson and Jordan (2003) observe, the harmonization initiative did not lead to a relaxation of the law regulating comparative advertising in the United Kingdom, in contrast to what happened in the other member states.

Given that the use of comparative advertising has been introduced so recently, UK courts are still determining the way comparative-advertising laws are being put into practice. Several cases in the recent past suggest general encouragement of the use of comparative advertising, as we will discuss in section 8.3.

Berns Wright and Morgan (2002) compare the European directive and the UK Trademark Law on the one hand with the FTC's statements and the Lanham Act on the other. Some interesting points arise. In the FTC's approach, the *focus of protection* is only on competitors and consumers of the product, while in the directive it includes the general public as well. The *comparative claim* must compare "like with like" in the United Kingdom, while the comparison of dissimilar products is permitted in the United States. Moreover, objective claims are required in the United Kingdom, while subjective claims are permitted in the United States. *Testing* in a lawsuit must be run by an independent third party in the United Kingdom, whereas standards are not set in the United States. The *burden of the proof* as to the accuracy of factual claims in the ad is assigned to the advertisers in the United Kingdom, while it is given to the target brand in the United States.[17] In line with the previously mentioned rule for alleged trademark infringement in TMA, in the United Kingdom the plaintiff must prove the advertiser's malicious intent.

Differences between the UK and the U.S. approach to comparison ads suggests that since "the American approach of aggressive, vague, opinionated comparisons is not likely to meet the standards under the European Directive, US advertisers should begin to utilize a more benign approach to comparative communications if they desire to present the same campaigns in EU Member States" (Berns Wright and Morgan 2002, 22).[18]

8.2.2.4 Industry Study: Professional Services in the European Union

It is interesting to note that the use of advertising in the market for professional services has traditionally been illegal in all industrialized countries. Today, where it is allowed, usually advertising is legal as long as it is not comparative (see, for example, advertising regulations for lawyers in Sweden and in the United States or for accountants in Italy).[19] However, it can be argued that such advertising regulations for professional services seriously affect competition and are detrimental for consumers. In European Commission 2004, regulatory authorities in the member states and professional bodies are explicitly asked to review the rules governing professional services because these rules are not necessary for the public interest and thus are unjustified. Moreover, the Commission suggests putting in place pro-competitive and transparency-enhancing mechanisms to strengthen consumer empowerment.[20]

Analyzing the markets in which lawyers, notaries, accountants, architects, engineers, and pharmacists operate in the European Union, the Commission has identified five main categories of national legislation or self-regulation that restrict competition: fixed prices, recommended prices, advertising restrictions, entry restrictions, and tasks and regulations governing business structure and multidisciplinary practices. The Commission believes that advertising, and in particular comparative advertising, can be a crucial competitive tool for new firms entering the market and for existing firms launching new products.

It is interesting to note that advertising restrictions are justified by professional bodies on the grounds of the asymmetry of information between experts and consumers of professional services. According to this argument, consumers find it difficult to assess information about professional services and therefore need particular protection from misleading or manipulative claims. Against such a rationale for advertising bans, the Commission mentions the increasing body of empirical evidence that highlights the potentially negative effects of some advertising restrictions (see Stephen and Love 2000). This suggests that advertising restrictions may under certain circumstances increase the fees for professional services without having a positive effect on the quality of those services. As the Commission argues, the implication of these findings is that advertising restrictions do not necessarily provide an appropriate response to the asymmetry of information in professional services. Conversely, truthful and objective advertising may actually help consumers overcome the asymmetry and to make more informed purchasing decisions (we elaborate on this point in section 8.4).

The Commission reports that during the last two decades a number of member states have started to relax advertising restrictions in the professions.[21] This general practice, together with the market outcomes it has led to, suggests that sector-specific advertising restrictions in these professions may not be essential for protecting consumers from misleading claims. As a result, today the legal, notary, and pharmacy professions are able to conduct most forms of advertising in a number of member states. Obviously all professions remain subject to general legislation that prevents untruthful or deceptive advertising.

8.3 Analysis of Selected Antitrust Cases

The cases analyzed below attest to the problem of high legal risks faced by both the sponsoring and the target firm, due to ambiguities in the interpretation of the law. As we will analyze in section 8.4, comparative advertising can transmit useful information to consumers only if misleading claims are punished. In particular, the target brand challenges a false or misleading claim only if the court can protect its interest with a sufficient degree of certainty. Similarly, the (honest) sponsoring brand can credibly signal its product quality at a low cost only if sanctions are imposed on those engaging in false advertising. Thus, ex post, once a false-advertising campaign is underway, it is in the interest of consumers and the target firm for the law on misleading advertising to be enforced. From an ex ante point of view, it is in the interest of the sponsoring firm and consumers that it be enforced.

Our reading of the court cases suggests that parties involved in a court case may disagree about the meaning of misleading advertising. Judges have provided their views on the issue—see Judges Laddie and Jacob's attitude toward advertising below. Another complicating factor is that the real message transmitted in a claim is a matter of nuances (e.g., the target firm Pizza Hut was not able to prove *implied falsity* of Papa John's ad; see below). Moreover, countries' heterogeneity in culture and history increases the uncertainty faced by market participants (see the cases against Ryanair below).

8.3.1 Allegedly Misleading Comparative Advertising

Several European and U.S. cases have as a critical issue whether the comparison ad is indeed misleading. In the United Kingdom as well as in the United States, case law has evolved that provides interpretations of the law and thus additional guidance. As we mentioned in section 8.2, in the United Kingdom section 10(6) of the 1994 Trademark Act is relevant for the case analysis of comparative advertising. According to section 10(6) the use of a registered mark does not constitute copyright infringement if it is in accordance with "honest practices in industrial and commercial matters." The phrase "honest practices in industrial and commercial matters" can be criticized as vague. It may be interpreted by bodies that regulate advertising. However, in *Barclays*

Bank Plc v. RBS Advanta (1996), RPC 307, the court did not consider the suggestion that it follow statutory or agreed-on codes of conduct.

Barclays Bank Plc v. RBS Advanta concerned advertising by RBS Advanta.[22] It compared the terms of the advertiser's own credit cards with those of competing credit cards, including the Barclaycard Standard Visa. A leaflet listed fifteen dimensions, summarized by the statement that the RBS Advanta card was said to be "a better credit card all round." In addition, a brochure included a comparative table showing the main financial terms of competitive credit cards.

The plaintiff Barclay's Bank argued that the leaflet was not honest because it did not compare like with like. In particular, it was selective because it did not mention other ancillary benefits that Barclay's Bank offered to its cardholders and that RBS Advanta did not. Examples are a twenty-four-hour emergency service and an overseas emergency service. Furthermore, six or seven out of the fifteen points listed in the RBS Advanta leaflet were common to Barclaycard as well.

Judge Laddie J was not convinced and concluded that the defendant really believed it offered customers a better deal, summarized by the advertisements with the list of fifteen items. He argued that honesty had to be judged by what can be reasonably expected by the relevant public exposed to the advertisements.

Subsequent decisions have made it clear that the use of a competitive trademark is acceptable if it is honest. In the words of Laddie J, an advertisement may be dishonest if it is "significantly misleading."

The general principles have been summarized by Judge Jacob J in *Cable & Wireless PLC v. British Telecommunications PLC* (1998), FSR 383:[23]

> The primary objective of s. 10(6) of the 1994 Act is to permit comparative advertising:
>
> 1. As long as the use of a competitor's mark is honest, there is nothing wrong in telling the public of the relative merits of competing goods or services and using registered trade marks to identify them.
> 2. The onus is on the registered proprietor to show that the factors indicated in the proviso to s. 10(6) exist.
> 3. There will be no trade mark infringement unless the use of the registered mark is not in accordance with honest practices.
> 4. The test is objective: would a reasonable reader be likely to say, upon being given the full facts, that the advertisement is not honest?
> 5. Statutory or industry agreed codes of conduct are not a helpful guide as to whether an advertisement is honest for the purposes of s. 10(6). Honesty has to be gauged against what is reasonably to be expected by the relevant public of advertisements for the goods or services in issue.

6. It should be borne in mind that the general public is used to the ways of advertisers and expects hyperbole.
7. The 1994 Act does not impose on the courts an obligation to try and enforce through the back door of trade mark legislation a more puritanical standard than the general public would expect from advertising copy.
8. An advertisement which is significantly misleading is not honest for the purposes of s. 10(6).
9. The advertisement must be considered as a whole.
10. As a purpose of the 1994 Act is positively to permit comparative advertising, the court should not hold words used in the advertisement to be seriously misleading for interlocutory purposes unless on a fair reading of them in their context and against the background of the advertisement as a whole they can really be said to justify that description.
11. A minute textual examination is not something upon which the reasonable reader of an advertisement would embark.
12. The court should therefore not encourage a microscopic approach to the construction of a comparative advertisement on a motion for interlocutory relief.

This view has been restated in *British Airways plc v. Ryanair Limited* (2000), which contrasts nicely with a court's view of an advertising campaign by Ryanair in Belgium. We first consider the case in Britain before turning to the case in Belgium.

In 1999 Ryanair ran a comparative-advertising campaign in various newspapers in the United Kingdom. It first placed the so-called Bastard advertisement (with the headline "EXPENSIVE BA . . . DS!"), then later the so-called Expensive advertisement (with the headline "EXPENSIVE BA"). The Bastard advertisement appeared in February and March in several national newspapers; the Expensive advertisement appeared just once in November, in the newspaper *Evening Standard*. Before the latter, the Advertising Standards Authority had upheld a complaint by members of the public (not made by BA) against the Bastard advertisement. It considered that the headline "was likely to cause serious or widespread offence." Ryanair responded that it would not use the headline again. The court then only had to decide how legal costs of the two sides were to be allocated; both sides made the case on a matter of high principle.

In *British Airways plc v. Ryanair Limited*, the judge gave a general analysis of what constitutes misleading advertising. He commented on the testimoniy as follows:

For Ryanair the principal witness was Mr Jeans, its Sales and Marketing Director. . . . He wanted dramatically to convey the message that Ryanair was a lot cheaper than BA for what was broadly the same journey. In part the effect of

> that would be to take sales from BA, in part it would generate new sales from those who could not afford BA prices. In relation to the Bastards advertisement Mr Hobbs [for the plaintiff] sought to demonstrate that Ryanair selected the headline first and put in the price comparisons later as some sort of spurious justification for the headline. Actually the facts were that the advertising agency had been asked to produce a number of headlines (which they did somewhat sequentially). All of these were intended to go with a price comparison table—of the same sort as Ryanair had used previously. The fact that the detailed BA prices were only obtained at the last minute has no sinister significance—that would have happened whatever the headline chosen. The point of the last minute obtaining of detailed prices was to avoid the risk of any change happening before publication. It was done to ensure accuracy. (*British Airways plc v. Ryanair Limited*, December 8, 2000)

The judge continued: "Before passing from the witnesses, it is particularly pertinent to observe that no witness testified to anyone actually being misled by either advertisement. There have been no complaints about deceptiveness in respect of any of the matters alleged made by members of the public (to whom the advertisements were directed) or even by anyone independent in the trade. Complaints might have been made to either party, to the ASA or to any Trading Standards Officer in any Local Authority."

BA had three complaints: (1) it found the Bastard headline offensive; (2) it said that the individual price comparisons were unfair; and (3) and it said that in the case of Frankfurt and Dinard the destination comparisons were unfair. With respect to the headline, Ryanair promised not to repeat it. Ryanair considered both the price comparison and the destination comparison to be fair and the judge agreed.

In the advertisements Ryanair mentions only one price for BA and one for Ryanair for certain city pairs. At that point BA operated like other "flag" or "conventional" airlines under the so-called Saturday night rule. According to this rule, flying out on a weekday and flying back before the weekend costs a lot more then taking a return trip that includes a Saturday night. For example, BA's return-same-week fare from London to Frankfurt was, as quoted in the Bastard advertisement, £374; including Saturday night, the return fare would be £192. In its price comparison Ryanair noted that prices refer to "Midweek return fees," where Ryanair required a minimum of two nights' stay on its flights. Although this term is to some extent ambiguous, the judge argued that "what matters is the phrase read in the context of the advertisement—by people familiar with the Saturday night rule. My conclusion is that most people would have appreciated that what was being got at was the resented rule." Furthermore, the judge reasoned as follows: "I think people would take the advertisement to be making the most favorable comparison Ryanair could reasonably make—that is what advertisers are most apt to do. The average consumer would know BA was cheaper if one stayed over Saturday. So, he would realize that it was same week returns that were being compared." This is in line with earlier cases, according to which the consumers have an understanding of the way advertisers make their messages. In the words of Jacob J, "I do not think that the average consumer would find the price comparison misleading. He would expect there to be some sort of conditions (and indeed the small print makes that clear). In substance the advertisements were true."

With respect to destinations, there were two points. The first relates to Frankfurt. Ryanair flies to the "secondary" airport Frankfurt-Hahn, which is designated by IATA as a city airport of Frankfurt but is about sixty eight miles from the city center, whereas Frankfurt International is only around six miles from the city center. BA said that the advertisement did not make this clear. However, Judge Jacob J did not consider this to be an unfair comparison.[24] The second point relates to Dinard (a resort town in Bretagne, France) and was rather bizarre since a flight with BA would require a traveler to change planes. Hence, the ad compares the fares but does not point out that the BA fare is for a journey that suffers the additional disadvantage of having to change planes. This clearly does not make the advertisement by Ryanair dishonest, as argued by Jacob J.

Ryanair also ran advertising campaigns in continental Europe comparing its flights with those of flag carriers. Perhaps the most illuminating case is the one in Belgium, a country that traditionally has been hostile to comparative advertising. On April 24, 2001, advertisements with the text "Welcome Ryanair and its lowest fares. Goodbye Sabena and its outrageously expensive flights" appeared in six national Belgian newspapers and on publicity vehicles in Brussels. On the same day Sabena asked Ryanair to withdraw the ads. Ryanair ignored this request and on the following day released an ad with a picture of the Brussels landmark the "Mannequin Pis," a statue of a boy urinating, with the line "Pissed off with Sabena's high fares? Low fares have arrived in Belgium." Ryanair also published price comparisons indicating the vast difference between the two airlines' one-way fares. Sabena's president and CEO reacted by calling the ads "clearly defamatory." Ryanair's CEO faxed back that the ads were "valid criticisms of

Sabena's outrageously high air fares" and, hoping for free publicity, distributed the fax to every major Belgian newspaper.

Sabena then took the case to court and claimed that the ads violated Belgian comparative-advertising legislation and were unlawful because (1) the ads were misleading, (2) the text was denigrating and damaging to Sabena's reputation, and (3) Ryanair obtained an unfair advantage through the use of Sabena's logo and trademark. The claim that the ads were misleading was based on the fact that Sabena offered services to many destinations, whereas Ryanair offered flights to only four countries in Europe at the time the ads were placed. Also, no comparisons of "relevant characteristics" were made. In particular, Sabena claimed that consumers could not objectively judge the services of Sabena and Ryanair based on the terms *lowest* or *outrageously expensive*.

Ryanair defended its campaign as in the case against British Airways. It argued that the ads were not misleading. By launching its service to Brussels-Charleroi, Ryanair claimed that it had shown that lower air fares were possible. It also claimed that consumers had benefited overall, because Sabena reduced its fares on routes where it was in competition with Ryanair.

Judge J. M. Lahaye (in a judgment of the Brussels Commercial Court published on July 10, 2001) upheld Sabena's complaint. He found that Ryanair's advertising campaign was misleading and offensive and damaged Sabena's reputation. He ruled that any future comparative ads by Ryanair should include details of prices and comparisons of the quality of service. Ryanair was ordered to discontinue the ads immediately and to run corrective ads: the judge ordered Ryanair to publish an extract of the decision in Belgian newspapers and post it on its website for a period of three weeks. The court further imposed a penalty of 99,000 euros for every future breach of the order.[25]

Both of these campaigns tried to establish Ryanair as a low-cost alternative to national "flag" carriers, BA in the United Kingdom and Sabena in Belgium. They show different attitudes on the part of European courts. As mentioned in section 8.2, Belgium has in the past (before the EU directive became effective) taken a hostile stand toward comparative advertising, whereas comparative advertising has more often been tolerated in the United Kingdom since the TMA of 1994. Even after the EU directive was passed, the Belgian and UK court rulings suggest a difference in approaches.[26]

The fact that Belgium did not allow comparative advertising until recently and that its court appeared to be tougher on Ryanair than those of the United Kingdom allows for a number of interpretations. Belgian courts may still be more hostile to comparative advertising because of their legal history. Alternatively, in Belgium lawmakers and judges alike may have a more paternalistic vision, according to which there are consumers who suffer from severe misperceptions and therefore have to be protected. In such a world, comparative advertising would need to adhere to the strictest standards. Perhaps the most favorable view is that at least initially the Belgian court feels it has to protect consumers from ads like the one by Ryanair because consumers lack the experience to see the ad in the same context as, for example, British consumers would.

While the Belgian case highlights the high hurdle for comparative advertising in parts of continental Europe, standards for "honest" comparative advertising appear to be lower in other places.

This can be illustrated by a recent U.S. Lanham Act case. In *Avon Products v. S.C. Johnson & Son* (1994),[27] the court refused to prohibit the comparative-advertising campaign for the insect repellent Off by Johnson. Johnson's television commercial claimed that according to a study, four out of five Avon product users prefer S.C. Johnson's insect repellent to Avon's Skin-So-Soft bath oil, with the qualification that the preference is only for skin feel.[28] Avon called Johnson's ads "illegal efforts to confuse consumers, tarnish Avon's reputation, and gain sales at Avon's expense." In particular, Avon claimed that the ads would confuse consumers because Avon had a new insect repellent. With the suit Avon tried to make Johnson stop the advertisements, issue corrective advertising, and provide monetary damages. The court did not take measures against Johnson's advertising campaign; it argued that Avon failed to prove that consumers were actually misled or confused.[29]

In this case (as in several others) the comparison is rather ambiguous. Under the Lanham Act the plaintiff faces a high burden of proof. It has to show that consumers were likely to be misled by the ad. To do so, the plaintiff has to determine the actual messages that the ad communicates to consumers. Apparently this may seem a more "objective" criterion than the previously considered "honest practice": here the plaintiff must in fact provide evidence on the real effect that the advertising had on consumers. Notice however that, apart the fact that consumer surveys are very expensive to carry out, they can easily be manipulated.

The courts in the United States distinguish between establishment (or tests prove) claims and nonestablishment claims. In cases of nonestablishment claims, the plaintiff has to prove either that the advertising is literally false or that it communicates false information to consumers. This is clearly a higher burden of proof than for a case with establishment claims, where the plaintiff must only prove that the supporting tests are inadequate.

8.3.2 Superiority or Puffery

As noted in section 8.2, challenging a comparative ad in court is not successful when it is interpreted as puffery. However, whether a comparative ad only contains puffery is subject to interpretation. In the following cases we focus on this issue. That is, we raise the question of whether an ad merely contains puffery or whether it can transmit some information to consumers.

In 2000 a federal judge ruled that Papa John's must pay over $468,000 in damages to Pizza Hut and cease and desist from using its tag line "Better ingredients. Better pizza." The judge ruled in favor of Pizza Hut, because the ingredient comparison was misleading. In fact the claim cannot be scientifically substantiated, nor do taste tests exist that prove a statistically significant preference for Papa John's product. Note that a claim would be a generalized statement of opinion, hence puffery, notwithstanding the clear implication that the advertiser's pizzas were better than others because of the better ingredients. However, in the context of two commercials that focused on the advertiser's ingredients, the court agreed that the slogan was an implied, unsubstantiated superiority claim with the characteristics of a statement of fact. Nevertheless, the 5th Circuit Court of Appeals overturned the verdict. The court argued that Pizza Hut failed to present evidence that reasonable consumers were influenced in their purchasing decision—that is, the plaintiff failed to show *implied falsity*. (In 2001, the U.S. Supreme Court refused to review the decision.)

A case in a Dutch court suggests that comparative advertising with questionable superiority claims may survive European courts. In April 2004 a civil court in Utrecht, Netherlands, ruled on a case concerning razor manufacturers Gillette and Wilkinson. The court decided that both can claim that their most recent bladed razors are the best. Gillette launched a complaint before the court because Wilkinson had advertised its new four-bladed razor by saying that it produces the smoothest result and that it had carried out comparative tests, showing that it was even better than Gillette's three-bladed one. Gillette sued Wilkinson, claiming that this was misleading advertising. Wilkinson filed a countersuit, saying that Gillette also made superiority claims in its advertising, without being able to substantiate these claims. The court rejected Gillette's case, arguing that the advertising was not misleading. It also rejected Wilkinson's case because Gillette simply used classic advertising exaggerations, which could not be seen as misleading. The court argued that consumers would not believe the ads anyway. Hence both firms can continue to claim that they are better than their competitor (for more information see BBC news, April 23, 2004, available at http://news.bbc.co.uk/2/hi/business/3652599.stm).

For the advertising not to be misleading, consumers must either be rather sophisticated or, since advertisers can exaggerate and use hyperbole, consumers must ignore advertising content because they do not believe it contains any valuable information. In the latter case there is little possibility of more efficient information transmission with comparative claims than with generic advertising. If consumers are not able to distinguish ads that exaggerate from those that do not, firms have an incentive to exaggerate whenever they can get away with it, provided that some consumers can be fooled. Although consumers can be expected to learn about the courts' stand on comparative advertising, by allowing exaggerations and hyperbole the courts may have made it more difficult to convey information for those advertisers who otherwise would have provided truthful content statements. This may lead to socially wasteful advertising and ultimately less information in the market. Therefore, the courts must distinguish very carefully between those cases in which the ad contains puffery that is easily recognized as such by the average consumer and other cases in which claims are potentially informative but the content is exaggerated. In the latter case, we would argue that the courts should apply strict tests so as to make truthful nonexaggerated claims possible.

A case in point is *S.C. Johnson v. The Clorox Co.*, 241 F.3d 232 (2nd Cir. 2001). In this case, Clorox, the maker of Glad-Lock storage bags, ran television commercials that featured a comparative ad of Glad storage bags versus Ziploc storage bags. Both of them were filled with water and turned upside down. In the advertisement the Glad-Lock bags stayed watertight, while the Ziploc bags leaked profusely. An animated goldfish in the Ziploc bag was shown in a state of distress. To prove that the ads were misleading, S. C. Johnson simply demonstrated that their bags leaked at a slower speed than the rate represented by the advertisement. The court concluded that the content of the ads was literally false and the ads were found in violations of section 43(a) of the Lanham Act.[30]

8.3.3 Damages

In our last case we consider damages. The most famous case of punitive damages in the United States is the *U-Haul International Inc. v. Jartran, Inc.*, 793 F.2d 1034 (9th Cir. 1986). The court found Jartran guilty of willful and malicious false advertising after running a comparative-advertising campaign for more than a year. As the basis of the $40 million award, $6.4 million served to cover the cost of the false-advertising campaign and $13.6 million to air corrective advertising. Under section 35 of the Lanham Act, the court doubled the award to a total of $40 million. (see, e.g., Bixby and Lincoln 1989; Steinberg and Naidech 2003). In this case, the reason for sanctioning the defendant's *profit* was to avoid the defendant's unjust enrichment, as first established by the 2nd Circuit in 1984 for a case of false advertising (see Raymond 2004).[31]

Damages in form of corrective advertising may be needed to reestablish the lost or damaged reputation of a firm. Furthermore, damages in the form of attorney's fees are appropriate to give the target firm a sufficiently strong incentive to bring suit against comparative advertising supposed to be misleading. However, often incentives to sue are sufficiently strong even in absence of such awarded damages (see section 8.4 and Barigozzi, Garella, and Peitz 2003). Also, for a campaign that has already generated revenues, lost profits may have to be awarded to the target firm in a case of false or misleading advertising. The corresponding incentives are amplified under punitive damages. In all cases of damages it seems important to distinguish between erroneous and malicious false claims. This allows firms that believe in their product to go ahead with their campaign even if, to their surprise, the claims prove erroneous (see the discussion in section 8.4).

8.4 Economic Perspectives on Comparative Advertising

8.4.1 Views on Comparative Advertising

It is useful to distinguish between different types of advertising: persuasive advertising, advertising as a complement, directly informative advertising, and indirectly informative advertising (see also Bagwell 2006). Comparative advertising may be of any of these types.

According to the classic view of advertising, advertising is *persuasive*—that is, by modifying tastes and creating brand loyalty, advertising changes the preferences of consumers. Since consumers' willingness to pay for the goods increases, the demand for the sponsoring brand increases as well and becomes less elastic. According to this approach, advertising is an anticompetitive phenomenon. Dixit and Norman (1978) offer a formal investigation of the welfare effects of persuasive advertising. The interpretation of advertising as persuasive has been criticized because it assumes that demand is positively affected by advertising, while consumers' utility is not. In the case of *advertising as a complement* this problem is solved since it is assumed that consumers hold a stable set of preferences into which advertising enters as one argument. Becker and Murphy (1993) propose this alternative view of advertising: advertising affects demand by increasing the consumer's utility deriving from the consumption of the advertised product (advertised good and advertising are complements).[32] Since the advertising firm does not internalize the full increase in consumer surplus that its advertising engenders, with this approach there is generally a social underprovision of advertising.

When comparative advertising is persuasive it may increase the willingness to pay for the sponsoring brand and/or it may reduce the willingness to pay for the compared brand. Comparative advertising may also be seen as a complement if consumers derive benefits from consuming the advertising together with the product of the sponsoring brand. Also, when the comparative advertising is consumed together with the negatively compared good, it may decrease the utility that consumers of the competitor's product get from such a product. As shown in the case of noncomparative advertising, it is a matter of interpretation whether advertising is to be seen as persuasive or as a complement because market outcomes are the same (see Bagwell 2006). However, welfare results may differ.

Under *informative advertising*, advertising provides useful information to consumers directly or indirectly. In the real world we observe both advertising messages that are content-based credibly transmitting information to consumers about the sponsoring product, and ads that, on the contrary, are content-free (or contain questionable content claims). We consider content-based ads to potentially be *directly informative*, whereas, in the case of content-free ads, the "words" of the advertising claim (if any) provide no information to consumers. Nevertheless such ads can be *indirectly informative*. In fact, when consumers are able to infer the cost of the advertising campaign, content-free ads can works as signals. In particular, the term *dissipative advertising* indicates that it is just the cost of the ad, instead of its content, which is able to transmit information to consumers. The firm burns money in the advertising campaign and this is publicly observable; the consequence is that advertising expenses can indirectly communicate information to consumers (Nelson 1974).[33] Under such indirectly informative advertising, the sponsoring firm does not necessarily give truthful information. By the amount of the advertising expenditure the firm may be able to convince consumers that its claims are truthful.

Comparative advertising can be considered content-based because it makes a comparison or a "superiority claim." In fact, implicitly or explicitly, in every comparative ad either the message "my product is better than . . ." or "my product is as good as . . ." is contained. Thus, a comparison ad is always potentially directly informative. The comparisons often serve as benchmarking to help consumers place the product in the right category and focus on its salient aspects. In fact, in the case of food advertising for example, absolute statements on nutrition often are of little information to consumers. As another example, comparative advertising offers to new firms entering the market of telecommunications services an easy tool to explain the advantages that their contracts provide to consumers.

As we will see in this section, comparative advertising can also transmit some information indirectly. First, the cost of the advertising campaign, as in the case of generic content-free ads, can indirectly provide information to consumers. Further, what seems to be really relevant in the case of comparative ads is a second channel to indirectly convey information that operates through the reaction that a comparative ad potentially induces in the competitor. Note that in general all advertising claims can be challenged. However, as outlined above for puffery, certain comparative ads are more likely to be challenged than corresponding noncomparative ads. With the same reasoning, direct comparative ads (i.e., ads in which competitors are explicitly named) are riskier than indirect comparative ones for the sponsoring brand. In fact, when the target brand is explicitly mentioned, its incentives to react to a false claim are obviously higher.

Practitioners have recognized that the potential reaction by competitors is a distinguishing feature of comparative advertising. Several advertising agencies publish statements on their websites such as "Comparative advertising can be a very effective tool, but with it comes the risk of challenges by competitors, state attorneys general, and even the FTC." Or "Comparative advertising campaigns present greater risks—and can lead to greater rewards in the form of customer response—than traditional monadic campaigns. You should assume that any campaign you run will be seen by your competitors' upper management, who will decide whether or not to challenge the ad" (Freeman and Nemiroff 2001). We will focus on this aspect later in this section when considering how comparative advertising can intensify competition by signaling the sponsoring brand's quality.

The superiority claim always contained in the comparative ad can accompany other direct information. This is the case with pricing comparative advertising where information is given about a verifiable characteristic of the product (and of the competitor's product) such as the price. A comparative ad is usually directly informative when *easily verifiable and credible* characteristics of the sponsoring and rival brands, like the price or other search attributes, are mentioned. Later we will argue that, under certain conditions, when comparative advertising is directly informative, it relaxes price competition. This can happen because comparative advertising helps differentiate competing products.

Even when the information contained in the comparative ad is verifiable, legal disputes are frequent. Litigation often concerns the way facts are presented in the claim and/or are perceived by consumers, and sometimes concerns the facts themselves. The high number of legal issues shows that the second channel of indirect information—that is, the competitor's reaction to the comparison ad—is also important in a comparative ad with verifiable information. Nevertheless, much comparative advertising, at least in the United States, apart from the (implicit) superiority claim, does not provide other direct information. Or, in other words, the statement in the ad is so vague, general, and unverifiable that the message conveyed by the ad depends on the way consumers interpret it (an example is the Avis "We try harder" campaign). Here, if the target brand goes to court, uncertainty concerning the court's judgment is very high. The litigation outcome depends substantially on the attitude toward comparative advertising in the court and the country where the dispute occurs. (See the case of Papa John's "Better ingredients. Better pizza." in the previous section.)

It is useful to summarize, at this stage, our point about how comparative advertising can disclose information on the sponsoring brand. First, comparative advertising is always content-based because of the superiority claim. Second, comparative advertising can also transmit hard (direct or credible) information on verifiable attributes of the sponsoring product (prices or physical characteristics). This is the case for search goods (products or services with features and characteristics easily observable before purchase). Third, concerning indirect information, the amount of money burned in the advertising campaign can convey information about nonverifiable characteristics of the good as quality in experience and also credence goods (An *experience good* is a product or service where product characteristics such as quality are difficult to observe in advance, but these characteristics can be ascertained upon consumption. A *credence good*, on the contrary is a good whose utility impact is difficult or impossible for the consumer to ascertain after consumption as well.) Moreover, the superiority claim opens another channel of indirect information transmission: the potential reaction of the target brand. This indirect channel of information transmission is a peculiarity of comparative advertising and increases the signaling power of dissipative advertising.

Below we first discuss persuasive comparative advertising, then we treat informative comparative advertising in more detail. With respect to informative advertising, two subcases are analyzed: directly informative and indirectly informative comparative advertising. The subsection on directly informative advertising, in turn, includes discussions of comparative price advertising and comparative advertising of product characteristics.

8.4.2 Persuasive Advertising

In many industries with branded consumer goods, the branded good is sold in a vertically integrated structure or the manufacturer essentially controls the downstream pricing. In these cases it is appropriate not to model any retailers or intermediaries and to postulate that manufacturers sell directly to consumers. In such a setting, Aluf and Shy (2001) present a duopoly model of persuasive advertising in which advertising by one firm reduces the willingness to pay for the competitor's product; this may correspond to negative comparative advertising.[34] Advertising is assumed to increase the heterogeneity among consumers and thus product differentiation. Consequently, firms use "comparative" advertising as a product-differentiation strategy, which reduces price competition. In a simple model with inelastic demand, welfare consequences are captured by the socially wasteful advertising expenditures.[35]

In several industries retailers or intermediaries play an essential role in selling a manufacturer's product to consumers. Shaffer and Zettelmeyer (2002) analyze the effects of a manufacturer's advertising campaign on the retailer under the assumption that comparative advertising leads to an increase of consumer valuations of the advertised product and a decrease of the consumer valuations for the compared product, where the advertising campaign can be tailored to mainly affect the valuations of the core or noncore consumers of one product. However, a retailer may not necessarily like comparative advertising if it also carries the product that would lose market share as a consequence of the comparative-advertising campaign. If the retailer has market power it may refuse to participate in the campaign for the product for which the comparative-advertising campaign is launched. It is not obvious whether, or under what conditions, a manufacturer will be able to induce its retailers to participate in its campaign, even though the success of the campaign will often depend on enlisting their support. Shaffer and Zettelmeyer explore the retailer's incentives not to participate in the advertising campaign. They find that participation is more likely the larger the increase in consumers' valuations of the praised product is relative to the decrease in their valuations for the product of comparison. They also find that the type of targeting of the advertising campaign is crucial in determining whether a retailer benefits from the manufacturer's campaign. In particular, a retailer always loses from ads that are targeted at the manufacturer's core consumers and always gains from ads that are targeted at the manufacturer's noncore consumers. The intuition is that after a campaign targeted at core consumers, both manufacturers enjoy more market power, whereas the reverse holds if the campaign is targeted at noncore consumers.

In these papers with persuasive advertising, it is implicitly assumed that comparative advertising affects consumers' valuation differently than noncomparative advertising. This reflects the view that consumers can make relative judgments but that they often find it hard to interpret information without a reference point. These analyses apply to products that are well established so that their qualities are known. Nevertheless, advertising changes consumers' preferences. An alternative view is to see advertising as a complement to other product characteristics. Also in this case comparative advertising increases the consumers' valuations of the advertised product and possibly decreases the consumers' valuations of the compared product. As mentioned above, the positive analysis under both views coincides. However, welfare consequences are different. For a welfare analysis of persuasive advertising, see Dixit and Norman 1978.

8.4.3 Directly Informative Advertising

8.4.3.1 Comparative Price Advertising Perhaps the most obvious case of comparative advertising is comparative price advertising. Competition authorities had this type of advertising in mind when they started encouraging the use of comparative advertising. In fact, claims about price can easily be verified, perhaps because they represent the simplest type of direct information, as applies more generally to search good attributes. For this reason, in the case of comparative price advertising, competitors named in an ad are not the only ones who file complaints against it; many consumers who feel misled also react. Thus, "complaints from competitors refer to comparative advertising considered misleading and/or unfair. The complaints relate to comparisons based on price or price-levels. Complaints regarding comparisons in terms of quality are rarer, however" (European Commission 2000).

Note that in its pure form comparative price advertising means that consumers are aware before the advertising is placed that products are the same (or comparable) and that they only lack price information. In this case, a comparison ad allows consumers to avoid a costly search, or if they were not going to search, it makes it possible for them to purchase the good at a lower price in expected terms. Additional price information is generally thought to intensify competition, which further reduces the expected price consumers pay. However, price comparison seldom exists in pure form. For example, Ryanair not only compares prices but also transmits the message that its product is comparable to those offered by flagship carriers. That is, often the price comparison comes together with the description and comparison of other product attributes (performance, availability, nutrition, and warranties). We will consider such comparisons below.

Sometimes the price comparison comes together with a low-price guarantee (seller x announces that if the buyer finds the identical product by seller y for a lower price, it will match the competitor's price or refund the difference). As is well known in the literature on price-matching policies, such policies can lead to collusive outcomes, which is clearly detrimental to consumer welfare and, typically, also total welfare (e.g., Doyle 1988; Logan and Lutter 1989). Thus it is important to separate the issue of comparative price advertising from commitments to offer low prices. In the former case, the use of comparative advertising is likely to result in lower prices and less market power by firms. This increases welfare. In the latter case, there is the risk that firms will effectively collude in prices, resulting in a welfare loss. Considering market entry, if a firm acquires a reputation for using comparative price advertising together with undercutting against new rivals, any potential rival may want to stay outside the market.

Notice, however, that pure price-matching policies (without a specific price comparison) work very differently from comparative price advertising. In particular, they are a *less risky* strategy for the selling brand (and thus a less credible strategy from the consumer's point of view). Essentially, a misleading low-price guarantee gives consumers an opportunity to react, whereas with misleading comparative price advertising the competitor (the target brand) can react by going to court. Moreover, with a low-price guarantee consumers typically incur an opportunity cost to exert the option, and very often the price difference is so low that the costs of reaction are higher than the benefits. On the contrary, with comparative price advertising, the target brand typically has strong incentives to react to a misleading claim.

When comparative price advertising is performed on the Internet, the comparative claims should be more easily verifiable by consumers who search a product at the lowest cost on the web.[36] Thus, as a consequence of Bertrand competition, we should expect pricing at the marginal cost to be frequently reached for homogeneous products. Recent empirical literature on e-commerce and Internet price strategies shows that this is not necessarily true. In fact, firms frequently adopt obfuscation strategies and, as a result, price heterogeneity for homogeneous goods is the general outcome. It is argued that a crucial role is exerted by shop boots (search engines that online shoppers use for price comparison) which have an interest in maintaining such a price dispersion on the web (see, e.g., Baye and Morgan 2001).

8.4.3.2 Comparative Advertising of Product Characteristics In new-product markets, consumers often do not know the product characteristics of entering firms. In such cases, comparative advertising may be a useful strategy to transmit information to consumers. Advertising in general may be a tool to make consumers aware of a certain product (e.g., as modeled in Grossman and Shapiro 1984).

Comparative advertising can, in addition, establish a product in a certain segment of the market. For instance, to compete against up-market cars such as BMWs, a car manufacturer has to position its own car as being comparable in certain product characteristics to cars in the targeted segment. In this case comparative advertising is simply directly informative advertising about availability and potentially product characteristics.

When the claim in a comparative ad is easily (ex post) verifiable and deviations from the truth are severely punished, a firm never misleads consumers. As a consequence, we can assume that comparative claims are truthful and thus directly informative.[37] Similar to the case with persuasive advertising (as in Aluf and Shy 2001), it is conceivable that directly informative comparative advertising also relaxes price competition. Suppose that consumers do not observe the product characteristics and that firms may highlight the superiority of their product along certain dimensions via truthful comparative advertising. To illustrate this point, we consider a simple symmetric setting in which the firms' products can be positioned either at 0 or 1 and consumers have different evaluations for products at these two points. That is, consider a simple Hotelling specification of the market. In the linear Hotelling version with disutility parameter t, a consumer has an expected disutility of $t/2$ for each product if the probability for each configuration 0 or 1 is $1/2$. Products of the two firms are ex ante identical, so that price competition between the two firms is intense.

Now consider the possibility of comparative advertising in which firms can communicate the relative position of their products. Suppose that the realization of each product is 0 or 1 with probability of $1/2$ each and that draws are independent. Then there is a 50 percent chance that products are differentiated. In this case it is profitable for firms to communicate their difference to consumers, because this allows them to relax price competition. Hence comparative advertising may be a successful product-differentiation strategy. The general idea promoted by competition authorities that more information increases competition is violated here. The reason is that the relevant information released makes products distinguishable from each other, which increases the market power of the firms involved. The argument can also be made in a market in which firms have different qualities (for a formal analysis of this point see Barigozzi and Peitz 2006).

One lesson of this chapter is that more information in the market can lead to less competition. In its 1979 statement the FTC emphasized the opposite possibility, namely, that more information can lead to more competition. This depends on whether information reduces or increases the market power of firms. In Barigozzi and Peitz 2006 comparative advertising can be seen as a differentiation strategy. The resulting higher prices necessarily reduce consumer welfare; they also reduce social welfare—that is, total surplus—if total demand is not perfectly price inelastic. There is, however, a countervailing welfare effect: the additional information in the market that is transmitted through comparative advertising improves the matching between product and buyers. The overall effect of social welfare depends on the degree of price elasticity of demand.

8.4.4 Indirectly Informative Comparative Advertising

When comparative claims are directly informative, firms spend the minimum amount needed to transmit the desired information to consumers in the advertising campaign. However, when the claim in the ad is difficult to verify—in particular, when it contains a quality comparison—it seems important to consider how a manufacturer endogenously decides whether to use a *truthful* comparative claim or not, and how to spend for it, given the antitrust law and the way such a law is implemented.

For this consider a simple setup in which manufacturing firms sell directly to consumers. Here comparative advertising has two characteristics: it is interpreted as a *comparison quality claim* and it is dissipative. The quality claim is verifiable only by a court and the ad transmits information *indirectly*, both through its cost and through the competitor's reaction that it eventually induces.

Suppose an established and a new firm compete in a market. Consumers do not know the product quality of the new firm, whereas both firms do. The entrant's quality is either high (H) or low (L). Producing high quality leads to fixed costs F, producing low quality leads to zero fixed costs, while variable costs are zero for both qualities. It is commonly known which quality the established firm offers. Without loss of generality, it is assumed that this quality is high. Profits of the established firm depend on its own quality (always H) and consumer beliefs about the product quality of the new firm q^e. Given high quality of the established firm, its reduced profits are written as $\Pi_I(q^e)$. Given the quality of the established firm, profits of the new firm depend on its true quality q and its perceived quality q^e. Reduced profits are written as $\Pi_E(q^e,q)$. Note in particular that $\Pi_E(q^e,H) = \Pi_E(q^e,L) - F$. The established firm's profits are decreasing in the competitor's perceived quality. In particular, $\Pi_I(L) > \Pi_I(H)$. The new firm makes higher profits the higher its perceived quality. In particular, $\Pi_E(H,q) > \Pi_E(L,q)$. This gives incentives to the entrant to cheat on quality.

The two firms interact as follows. At the first stage, the product quality of the new firm is exogenously determined (for illustration: the quality is H with probability 1/2, and L with probability 1/2). Both firms observe the quality of the new firm; consumers do not. At the second stage, the entrant decides among the set of advertising types $\{c,g,n\}$, namely comparative, generic, or no advertising, respectively. Associated costs are A_c, A_g, and 0, respectively. We assume, for simplicity, that after choosing g or c the advertising cost is unavoidable and can only take a given value $A_c = A_g = A$; this emphasizes that technically the two types of advertising differ only in the "wording" of the message but that the same advertising space has to be bought. At stage 3, provided that the new firm has used comparative advertising, the established firm decides whether to go to court, paying legal costs C. The court verifies the quality of the new firm and thus whether its claim was justified. If it was not justified the new firm has to pay damages D. At the last stage, consumers observe the decisions in stages 2 and 3 (including the court verdict) but not the realization of quality at stage 1, and update their beliefs concerning the product quality of the new firm based on the observed actions in stages 2 and 3. Then they make their purchasing decisions.

To have a meaningful analysis, suppose that the new firm gains from generic advertising if this makes consumers believe in high quality, $\Pi_E(H,q) - A > \Pi_E(L,q)$. While this may make generic ads attractive, it also implies that there does not exist an equilibrium (to be precise, a perfect Bayesian equilibrium) in which the new firm uses generic advertising. This can be seen as follows. At a potential separating equilibrium with generic advertising, an entrant firm with low quality type does not use advertising—that is, the decision at stage 2 is n—whereas an entrant firm with high quality type chooses generic advertising g and forcibly pays A. The separation constraint for the low type is not to have an incentive to deceive consumers by advertising its product, $\Pi_E(L,L) \geq \Pi_E(H,L) - A$. On the other hand, the high type must have an incentive to advertise, $\Pi_E(L,H) \leq \Pi_E(H,H) - A$. Therefore, a separating equilibrium could exist only if the interior of the interval for A given by $\Pi_E(H,L) - \Pi_E(L,L) \leq A \leq \Pi_E(H,H) - \Pi_E(L,H)$ was not empty, which is impossible because the assumption on the cost of quality implies $\Pi_E(q^e,H) = \Pi_E(q^e,L) - F$.

Does comparative advertising suffer the same fate? Not necessarily. Suppose that using comparative advertising (choosing c at stage 2) makes consumers believe in high quality unless the court verdict contradicts the advertising claims. The separating constraint for a high-type entrant is again $\Pi_E(H,H) - A > \Pi_E(L,H)$. Suppose furthermore that the established firm makes higher profits, unmasking its competitor to be of low quality and receiving damages than it would make under high-quality beliefs, namely, $\Pi_I(L) - C + D > \Pi_I(H)$. When the incumbent reacts to a false claim, comparative advertising is followed by a lawsuit. The entrant's quality is uncovered and the entrant has to pay damages D. Hence, the separating constraint for an entrant of type L is $\Pi_E(L,L) - A - D \leq \Pi_E(L,L)$, which is trivially satisfied. Since $\Pi_I(L) > \Pi_I(H)$ holds by assumption, a separating equilibrium with comparative advertising necessarily exists if $D > C$ and for a sufficiently low cost of advertising, namely, for $\Pi_E(H,H) - \Pi_E(L,H) > A$. This is the only possible separating perfect Bayesian equilibrium. Note that the damages may even be zero, $D = 0$, and the argument may still hold provided that the legal costs C are sufficiently low.

Alternatively, suppose that consumers do not observe the court action but only the choice of the advertising type at the second stage. It can easily be shown that comparative advertising solves the adverse selection problem verifying the self-selection constraints if and only if $D > C$.[38]

From the analysis above, a number of observations follow. First, comparative advertising may also be an effective way to transmit information to consumers when generic advertising cannot serve as a signal of product quality. Second, the amount of damages needed to punish deceptive advertising depends on the speed of information acquisition by consumers. In the extreme case, where the court's verdict is observed before any purchases have occurred, no damages may need to be awarded. In the other extreme case, where neither the incumbent's reaction nor the court's verdict is observed by consumers, at least the direct and indirect legal costs of the incumbent have to be paid back by the entrant to provide the right incentives to the incumbent to sue for deceptive advertising.

The previous consideration also shows that the more consumers are aware of the legal dispute, the more powerful comparative advertising is as a signal. An important policy implication is that to be effective, information has to spread widely and fast. Timely corrective advertising is such a measure frequently ordered by the courts. Needless to say, promptness of the verdict is a prerequisite.

The general idea behind the example is that comparative advertising triggers strategic interaction between informed parties. This interaction allows the uniformed party (consumers) to infer about the realization of an unobservable variable (product quality).

Barigozzi, Garella, and Peitz (2003) provide a detailed analysis of a much richer model. Here firms receive a noisy signal about the entrant's product quality. In their model it depends on the parameter constellation whether comparative or generic advertising is the preferred signal. In particular, comparative advertising is likely to be used in markets in which firms receive precise information about product quality, whereas in markets with imprecise information an entrant firm may be discouraged from making comparative claims because with some positive probability, they will turn out to be false provided the incumbent goes to court. Then, if damages are sufficiently high, the incumbent indeed has an incentive to challenge any comparative claim. In effect the entrant may opt for generic advertising that avoids the challenge.

Considering, on the contrary, the interesting (separating) equilibrium where the incumbent *does not react* to a comparative claim that sometimes turns out to be false,[39] we note that our earlier observations carry over. First, the observation that the informed incumbent does not react to comparative claims is interpreted by consumers as good news about the entrant's quality, whereas if the court finds the comparative ad misleading, consumers respond differently. Second, the misleading comparative ad leads to the payment of damages. The first channel may also operate without the second, as mentioned earlier. This extends our simple example above, where no uncertainty about the entrant's quality and the court's verdict exists and the incumbent always reacts to a false claim. However, with positive probability the comparative claim turns out to be wrong with no legal action taken.

This extended model allows us to distinguish between erroneous claims according to which the entrant acted in good faith and malicious falsehood. In the latter case, the entrant is perfectly aware that its quality claim lacks any substance. In equilibrium, the entrant makes erroneous claims but malicious falsehood can be wiped out. Note that in practice, U.S. courts award higher damages in the case of malicious falsehood. This suggests that judges are aware of the importance of distinguishing between erroneous claims and malicious falsehood. To do so they have to consider the intent of a firm. Harsh sanctions against erroneous claims would lead to a higher risk of using comparative advertising. This may result in turn in less information being available in the market or in information transmission at a higher social cost, as in the case of generic advertising. In the present context, this is often undesirable from a social point of view (see below). If on the other hand malicious falsehood can be proved, the courts should punish such behavior.

In a more general setting, the issue of price signaling also arises. The classic treatment of advertising as a signal is within a monopoly setup (e.g., Milgrom and Roberts 1986; for an overview see Bagwell 2006). Barigozzi, Garella, and Peitz (2005) show that a new firm will use advertising (together with price) as a signal of quality when competing against an established firm. Since comparative advertising reduces the amount of advertising expenses needed to separate, there remains a role for comparative advertising when prices are viable signals as well.

Since dissipative advertising expenditures are wasteful, lower expenditures are, all else being equal, welfare-enhancing. The signaling cost of comparative advertising is lower than for generic advertising. Hence, welfare is improved. If in equilibrium the threat to sue the sponsoring firm is never carried out (as in the simple model above), then the possibility of going to court is merely used as a disciplining device—that is, it deters misleading claims. However, if the precision of the information available to the sponsoring brand is imperfect, the sponsoring firm may run a comparative-advertising campaign in the belief that its claims are truthful, whereas effectively they are not. Then the court system may indeed be used. Two such situations can arise depending on the information of the competitor. First, if both firms have access to the same information, the competitor may sue regardless of the information it possesses, given that there is always some chance that the court will rule the advertising claim to be wrong. If this is sufficiently likely and the competitor's benefits associated with going to court are sufficiently high (through damages and the indirect effect of information revelation to consumers), it is clearly in the interest of the competitor to take this action. Second, if the competitor has access to different sources of information than the sponsoring firm and if this information tells the target firm that the claim is false, it will go to court.

In these cases, litigation takes place. Litigation is not only costly for the parties involved but often adds a social cost if the cost inflicted on the court system is not fully covered by the two involved parties, the sponsoring firm and its competitor. This negative effect on social welfare has to be taken into account. On the positive side, the court could generate new information that consumers may use when making their purchase decision.

Note that the signaling role of dissipative advertising is of particular importance in the case of experience and credence goods. For such goods, quality claims are not verifiable by the consumer. Consider the case of experience goods. Here, consumers must consume these goods before knowing if the product characteristics suit their taste. Dissipative advertising has a positive effect in that it may allow high-quality firms to quickly transmit information to consumers about their product characteristics. Comparative advertising can have the same positive effect, but at a lower cost to the advertising firm. In the case of repeat purchases, information received after consumption allows consumers to condition their future purchases on experience. Then consumer experience can serve as a (partial) substitute for the competitor's reaction. However, even in this case comparative advertising reduces the signaling cost, in particular because of damages to be paid by the sponsoring firm of a misleading comparative ad.

The information asymmetry between firms and consumers is more severe when the former are experts who sell credence goods. As mentioned before, for such goods consumers cannot learn quality after consumption. As we pointed out in section 8.2, representatives of professions argue that (comparative) advertising must be forbidden in the consumers' interest. In fact, in their opinion consumers find it difficult to assess information about professional services and therefore need particular protection from misleading or manipulative claims. It is true that, in this case, it is more difficult for generic dissipative advertising to transmit information to consumers because the information is not verifiable ex post (after consumption) and, therefore, repeat purchases cannot be conditioned on experience. In any case, with comparative advertising information transmission still works for credence goods because the sponsoring firm is exposed to the competitor's reaction. Here the competitors (the other experts) can monitor the claim of the sponsoring firm and eventually go to court; we could call this "peer monitoring." This may enable an expert to transmit information to consumers. Therefore, we have provided a theoretical argument in support of the use of comparative advertising for professional services.[40]

Note that social costs may be high when a product is sold with a misleading claim. Then ex post control of claims may need to be supplemented by regulation of access to the market, as in the case of drugs. Applied to professional service, entry requirements can be justified. However, this does not contradict the argument in favor of the use of comparative advertising within the professions.

8.5 Conclusion

Antitrust authorities encourage the use of comparative advertising because, if fair and not misleading, it conveys useful information to consumers and can increase competition in the marketplace. The way advertising affects consumer behavior is an ongoing topic in the economics and marketing literature. In this chapter we have concentrated on the interpretations of advertising proposed by economists and their application to comparative advertising.

The aspect of comparative advertising most relevant for antitrust authorities is its role in transmitting information to consumers. This is related to the important issue of how information can be transmitted by an "interested party" to another economic agent and raises the problem of *credibility*. There is an important difference between content-free generic advertising and comparative advertising: the latter contains a "superiority claim" that potentially provokes a reaction from competing firms. Competitors (implicitly or explicitly) mentioned in the ad have to decide whether to challenge the superiority claim by engaging in a lawsuit.

When a claim in a comparative ad is easily verifiable and deviations from the truth are severely punished, an advertising firm never misleads consumers. In this case we can argue that comparative claims are truthful and comparative advertising is directly informative. With respect to directly informative advertising, Barigozzi and Peitz (2006) show that comparative claims can become a differentiation strategy. In fact, they can be used by competing firms to credibly highlight the superiority of their product along certain dimensions in order to relax price competition. Hence, contrary to what competition authorities seem to believe, it is possible that more information, as provided by comparative advertising, increases the market power of firms, instead of reducing it.

When the claim in the ad is difficult to verify, advertising firms decide whether to use truthful or false statements. In this case and as shown in Barigozzi, Garella, and Peitz 2003, together with the *cost* of the advertising campaign, the *potential reaction* of the competitor can provide an efficient channel for indirectly transmitting information to consumers. In fact, when running a false-advertising campaign, a firm will be prosecuted and condemned. This represents a cost for the mimicking firm and slacks the incentive constraint for the advertising firm. Thus, by using (dissipative) comparative advertising, signaling can be obtained at a lower cost. The signaling role of comparative advertising is particularly important when the advertising claim is based on quality characteristics that consumers cannot verify before they purchase the good. Thus, comparative quality claims can be indirectly informative for consumers if penalties are imposed for false ads—that is, if the legal system works properly.

From Barigozzi, Garella, and Peitz 2003, a second interesting lesson can be drawn: competition policies, antitrust laws, and their implementation are essential in making a comparative-advertising campaign credible. This is important because only if claims are credible can comparative advertising convey useful information to consumers. In other words, comparative ads can increase competition among firms and retailers only if claims are credible; claims are credible only if the legal system is efficient in processing false claims. If sanctions are not imposed on firms responsible for misleading ads, all claims become empty. This also applies to comparative claims defined as nonactionable "mere puffery"; they become equivalent to generic ads and are not informative.

The way consumers interpret advertising is important for the courts, as "implying falsity" claims prove. But, at the same time, consumers' perceptions are influenced by legal practices—that is, consumers learn to interpret comparative claims after observing the outcome of litigation. In this sense, legal practice deeply affects the way comparative advertising is used by firms and understood by consumers. Thus, a more restrictive legal attitude toward comparative claims, as we find in Europe, can perhaps better improve competition than the prevailing legal attitudes in the United States because a restrictive attitude is more likely to contribute to the credibility of comparative advertising. However, if consumers are sophisticated enough to distinguish between comparative advertising containing puffery, for which firms cannot be penalized, and other comparative-advertising claims, which can lead to sanctions, the U.S. legal approach would also not interfere with the flow of information from firms to consumers.

Notes

We received helpful comments from an anonymous referee.

1. Examples are telecommunication or financial intermediation services where often the terms of proposed contracts are compared with those previously offered by competitors.

2. In the real world we can observe both advertising campaigns where the sponsoring brand simply declares the merits of its product with respect to the competitors' products, and others that explicitly degrade the competing brands.

3. In the economic analysis (in section 8.4) such a distinction between *direct* and *indirect* comparative advertising is meaningless because, for the sake of simplicity, we consider only duopolistic markets such that the target brand is always the sponsoring brand's unique competitor.

4. "In 1962 Hertz was the clear leader in the car rental business, with Avis as one of the brands in the following pack. The Avis 'We try harder' campaign repositioned Hertz, creating a relative, believable, and compelling strength for Avis. The market dominance of Hertz became a weakness and Avis became the 'right choice' in the mind of consumers" ("BuildingBrands," http://www.buildingbrands.com). The campaign can be seen as the first "modern" use of comparative ads in advertising history (see Bixby and Lincoln 1989 and the references there).

5. Such harmonization is defended on the grounds that the differences in the treatment of comparative advertising among member states are an impediment to the free flow of goods and communications within the European Union (see Petty and Spink 1995; also see section 8.2.2).

6. Note that the target brand can choose between two different strategies: it can go to court against the sponsoring brand, or it can run a counteradvertising campaign. In the economic analysis proposed in section 8.4, we focus on the first strategy because it is the most frequently observed in reality. (For a theoretical analysis that investigates the role of counteradvertising, see Matthews and Fertig 1990.) In fact, practitioners believe that counteradvertising campaigns must be carefully developed and implemented to avoid a negative response, as illustrated by the following statement: "Defensive, unconvincing or ill-conceived counteradvertising can actually increase the credibility of the original comparative ad by calling attention to the comparison and failing to counter the points of concern" (Suasion Resources 2003). Hence, the superiority of the lawsuit strategy is due to the presence of a neutral third party (the court), which intervenes to monitor the content of the ad. More generally, it has been pointed out that counteradvertising creates animosity in the markets and very rarely is an effective marketing strategy.

7. Leighton (2004, 585) says: "It took Congress over 30 years to catch up with the courts. The Trademark Law Revision Act of 1988 amended Section 43(a) of the Lanham Act to ratify the robust false advertising cause of action that has been developed judicially."

8. See also *Pizza Hut v. Papa John's*, as discussed in section 8.3.

9. The comparative-advertising commercial for Yardman, MTD's lawn tractor, used an altered animation of Deere's well-known trademark logo: a "leaping deer." In the

comparative television commercials, a smaller, blurred version of this deer was depicted running across the screen in fear of an MTD tractor. However, if MTD had used the image correctly, Deere Co. would have had no basis for a lawsuit.

10. They also suggest that this may be due to out-of-court settlements after the grant or denial of a preliminary injunction. See Arnold and Porter (2002).

11. For example, the Netherlands Supreme Court condemned a comparative advertisement that promoted one brand of fertilizer and claimed that lower amounts are needed than with a competing brand. The Court admitted the general possibility of individual brand comparisons. However, it condemned the particular advertisement on the grounds that it did not disclose the difference in composition between the two products (see Petty and Spink 1995 and references).

12. Notice that point (g) is particularly relevant for the "underdog case."

13. "It appears clear that, even if some useful general principles and criteria on comparative advertising have been achieved, many aspects are still assigned to the competence of national courts for case-by-case evaluation. No doubt in the near future significant differences and contrasting solutions are likely to be found in the handling of similar cases by the courts. The harmonizing process, which inspired the EU Directive on comparative advertising, will therefore require a substantial amount of case law—and for sure, additional interpretation by the European Court of Justice—before a satisfying level of uniformed criteria will result" (Hofer 2003).

14. A legal issue related to Internet comparative advertising is that of jurisdiction. Since the Internet is accessible from most countries, a comparative ad that is legal in the country where the ad originates may be viewed by consumers in a country that restricts such advertising practices (see also Berns Wright and Morgan 2002).

15. The practice of favorably comparing one's product while denigrating its competitor.

16. Notice that, under the TMA, the plaintiff must prove that the use of its trademark by the advertiser is not honest, while, under the directive, the advertiser must furnish evidence as to the accuracy of *factual claims* in the ad.

17. The fact that the burden of the proof as to the accuracy of factual claims is given to the advertiser makes European advertising firms more cautious than their U.S. counterparts about using comparative advertising.

18. Quite different regulatory regimes have also been adopted with respect to Internet advertising. In the United States a comprehensive regulatory program is missing. Hence, the control is essentially left to the industries' self-regulation. In Europe competition policy sees the need to protect consumers from "aggressive business practice, while building trust and confidence in Internet information sources" (Berns Wright and Morgan 2002, 23).

19. "A large number of the EU professions are subject to sector-specific advertising regulation. In some cases (e.g. in France for notaries), advertising of any kind is prohibited. In others, specific media or advertising methods such as radio advertising, television advertising, 'cold calling' or specific types of advertising content are prohibited. In certain cases, there is a lack of clarity in existing advertising regulations which, in itself, may deter professionals from employing certain advertising methods" (European Commission 2004, 14).

20. From an enforcement perspective, since May 2004 the national competition authorities and the national courts have had a more prominent role in assessing the legality of rules and regulations in the professions.

21. "In the 1970s, for example, advertising restrictions were removed for the legal and accountancy professions in the United Kingdom. In the 1990s, restrictive advertising rules were removed for the legal, accountancy and architectural professions in Denmark. In the last few years, strict advertising bans have also been relaxed for the professions in Germany. The accountancy and technical professions now function effectively without the need for any significant sector-specific advertising restrictions in a large number of Member States" (European Commission 2004, 14).

22. Our presentation of this case follows Swan 2000.

23. These were established in *Barclays Bank v. RBS Advanta* and the subsequent case of *Vodafone Group plc v. Orange Personal Communications Services Ltd* (1997), FSR 34. Jacob J built on M. Crystal QC in *British Telecommunications Plc v. AT & T Communications (UK) Ltd (unreported)*, December 18, 1996.

24. Interestingly, a German court required Ryanair to state that its airport is Frankfurt-Hahn, not Frankfurt, in its ads comparing its prices to those of Lufthansa. The naive observer might conclude that British consumers must be better informed about the airlines' use of German airports than German consumers.

25. Ryanair placed an ad with an apology in Belgian newspapers. "We're Sooooo Sorry Sabena!" said the ad, which went on to list seven one-way price comparisons, maintaining that Ryanair is up to 89 percent cheaper. The ad concluded: "Ryanair is really, really sorry and promises to include this information in our future advertising." At the end of 2001 Sabena ceased to exist.

26. Ryanair had more success against Alitalia in Italy than against Sabena in Belgium. In 2002 a ruling by Italy's Competition Authority rejected a complaint by Alitalia about Ryanair's comparative campaign. Ryanair's chief executive Michael O'Leary commented: "Alitalia attacked Ryanair's comparative advertising precisely because it is true—and the Authority now confirmed it. The decision guarantees that Ryanair can continue to demonstrate the extent to which Alitalia is overcharging Italian consumers" (*Daily Mirror*, London, September 13, 2002).

27. *Avon Products, Inc. v. S.C. Johnson & Son, Inc.* (1994), 1994 U.S. Dist. LEXIS 7950, 94 Civ. 3958 (AGS) (S.D.N.Y. June 15).

28. In other commercials Johnson claimed that Off is 100 times more effective as an insect repellent than Avon's Skin-So-Soft bath oil, a product that Avon says is not meant to be used as an insect repellent. However, the court judged that this is mere puffery. For more on puffery see below.

29. The only exception is that the court prohibited a footnote in the print ad that contained the false claim that the competitor's product Skin-So-Soft was not registered with the Environmental Protection Agency as an insect repellent.

30. Compared to the Pizza Hut case, this illustrates that *literal falsity* can be a more successful strategy for the plaintiff (see also section 8.2).

31. *Burndy Corp. v. Teledyne Industries Inc.*, 748 F.2d Cir. 1984.

32. A standard example is the following: if a consumer values "social prestige," advertising may serve as an input that enables him or her to derive more social prestige when consuming the advertised product.

33. Nelson's well-known explanation of advertising as a rational phenomenon is based on the idea that its explicitly high cost works as a device to signal high quality of a brand. The signaling motive filled a gap in the understanding of a controversial economic phenomenon, namely, the apparently wasteful advertising campaigns. The argument, intended to apply to generic advertising, implies that the cost, and not the content, of an ad is what really matters.

34. To be more precise, the authors consider a Hotelling model of product differentiation, in which a comparative ad by the sponsoring brand increases the transportation cost for consumers buying the target brand's product. In the absence of comparative advertising, the two products would be perceived as homogeneous by consumers.

35. Quite differently, Shy (1992; 1995, chap. 11) focuses on the matching of heterogeneous consumers with differentiated brands, where the firms sell the branded goods over time and compete on market shares. In his model the two firms can use either noncomparative or comparative advertising. In Shy's terms, noncomparative advertising is persuasive since it tries to attract new users. In contrast, comparative advertising is informative and is targeted to experienced users: it is used to inform consumers who have already purchased the product before. By assumption, informative advertising cannot be misleading.

36. Notice that Internet price comparison performed by independent agents or by shop boots as well as over-the-counter comparisons do not represent comparative advertising since the comparison is undertaken here by a third (and neutral) party.

37. Notice that, in principle, the credibility of *all* the advertising messages should be ensured by legal sanctions on misleading advertising. In reality, as sections 8.2 and 8.3 show, the fewer verifiable statements the claims contain, the less the legal system is able to ensure that misleading advertising is punished. Thus, quality claims for experience goods pose a serious credibility issue.

38. In this case, since they do not observe the court judgment, consumers will discover that the entrant's quality was low after making their purchasing decision. Thus, the incumbent goes to court only if $\Pi_I(L) - C + D > \Pi_I(L)$, which holds for $D > C$.

39. This happens, for example, when the incumbent perceives the probability of winning the lawsuit as too low.

40. Note however that with credence goods, the court may have particular difficulties in establishing whether a claim is misleading.

References

Aluf, Y., and O. Shy. 2001. "Comparison-Advertising and Competition." Photocopy, University of Haifa.

Arnold and Porter. 2002. "Court Decisions: Antacid Wars—Plaintiff May Enjoin 'Unsubstantiated' Claim." *Consumer Products Marketing*, available at http://www.arnoldporter.com/

Bagwell, K. 2006. "The Economic Analysis of Advertising." In M. Armstrong and R. Porter, eds., *The Handbook of Industrial Organization*, vol. 3. Amsterdam: North Holland.

Barigozzi, F., P. Garella, and M. Peitz. 2003. "With a Little Help from My Enemy: Comparative versus Generic Advertising." Photocopy.

Barigozzi, F., P. Garella, and M. Peitz. 2005. "Prices and Advertising as Signals of Quality: Competing against a Renown Brand." Photocopy.

Barigozzi, F., and M. Peitz. 2006. "Informative Comparative Advertising and the Competitiveness of Markets." Photocopy.

Barone, M. J., and P. W. Miniard. 1999. "How and When Factual Ad Claims Mislead Consumers: Examining the Deceptive Consequences of Copy X Copy Interactions for Partial Comparative Advertisements." *Journal of Marketing Research* 36:58–74.

Baye, M. R., and J. Morgan. 2001. "Information Gatekeepers on the Internet and the Competitiveness of Homogeneous Product Markets." *American Economic Review* 91:454–474.

Becker, G. S., and K. M. Murphy. 1993. "A Simple Theory of Advertising as a Good or Bad." *Quarterly Journal of Economics* 108:941–964.

Berns Wright L., and F. W. Morgan. 2002. "Comparative Advertising in the European Union and the United States: Legal and Managerial Issues." *Journal of Euromarketing* 11:7–31.

Bixby, M. B., and D. Lincoln. 1989. "Legal Issues Surrounding the Use of Comparative Advertising: What the Non-Prescriptive Drug Industry Has Taught Us." *Journal of Public Policy and Marketing* 8:134–160.

Coleman, A. 2000. "Showing up rivals." *Director, London* 53(11):26.

Dickerson, J., and P. Jordan. 2003. "Comparative Advertising—A Battle in the Skies." Available at www.dea.com.

Dixit, A., and V. Norman. 1978. "Advertising and Welfare." *Bell Journal of Economics* 9:1–17.

Doyle, C. 1988. "Different Selling Strategies in Bertrand Oligopoly." *Economics Letters* 28:387–390.

European Association of Communication Agencies. 2000. "Comparative Advertising in the European Union." Position paper on comparative advertising. http://www.eaca.be/_upload/documents/briefing/Comparative%20Advertising%20in%20the%20European%20Union.doc.

European Commission. 2000. *Report from the Commission to the Council and the European Parliament on Consumer Complaints in Respect of Distance Selling and Comparative Advertising* (Article 17 of Directive 97/7/EC on distance contracts and Article 2 of Directive 97/55/EC on comparative advertising) [COM(2000)127final]. Brussels: European Commission.

European Commission. 2004. *Report on Competition in Professional Services, Commission Communication of 9 February 2004* [COM(2004) 83final]. Brussels: European Commission.

Freeman, D. R. Jr., and E. A. Nemiroff. 2001. "We're Number 1: A Guide to Comparative Advertising." http://www.advertisinglawplaybook.com/documents/We_are_Number_1.pdf.

Gnepa, T. 1993. "Observations: Comparative Advertising in Magazines: Nature, Frequency and a Test of the Underdog Hypothesis." *Journal of Advertising Research* 33:70–75.

Grossman, G. M., and C. Shapiro. 1984. "Informative Advertising with Differentiated Products." *Review of Economic Studies* 51:63–81.

Hofer, F. 2003. "Comparative Advertising in Europe: Recent Developments." http://www.htllaw.it.

Jain, S. P., B. Buchanan, and D. Maheswaran. 1998. "Comparative versus Noncomparative Messages: The Moderating Impact of Pre-purchase Attribute Verifiability." Marketing Science Working Paper Series. Rochester, NY: William E. Simon School of Business, University of Rochester.

Kihlstrom, R. E., and M. H. Riordan. 1984. "Advertising as a Signal." *Journal of Political Economy* 92:427–450.

Leighton, R. J. 2004. "Materiality and Puffing in Lanham Act False Advertising Cases: The Proofs, Presumptions, and Pretexts." *Trademark Reporter* 94(3):585–633.

Logan, J., and R. Lutter. 1989. "Guaranteed Lowest Price: Do they Facilitate Collusion?" *Economics Letters* 31:189–192.

Matthews, S. A., and D. Fertig. 1990. "Advertising Signals of Product Quality." CMSEMS Discussion Paper No. 881. Evanston, IL: Northwestern University.

McKenna, J., and W. Manning. 2002. "Lanham Act Also Applies to False Advertising Claims." *National Law Review*, May 13. Available at http://www.rkmc.com.

Milgrom, P., and J. Roberts. 1986. "Price and Advertising Signals of Product Quality." *Journal of Political Economy* 94:796–821.

Muehling, D., J. Stoltman, and S. Grossbart. 1990. "The Impact of Comparative Advertising on Levels of Message Involvement." *Journal of Advertising* 19:41–50.

Nelson, P. 1974. "Advertising as Information." *Journal of Political Economy* 84:729–754.

Pechmann, C., and S. Ratneshwar. 1991. "The Use of Comparative Advertising for Brand Positioning: Association versus Differentiation." *Journal of Consumer Research* 18:145–160.

Pechmann, C., and D. W. Stewart. 1990. "The Effect of Comparative Advertising on Attention, Memory, and Purchase Intentions." *Journal of Consumer Research* 17:180–191.

Petty, R., and P. Spink. 1995. "Comparative Advertising Law in the European Community: Will the Proposed Directive Harmonize across the Atlantic?" *Journal of Public Policy and Marketing* 14:310–318.

Prasad, V. K. 1976. "Communications-Effectiveness of Comparative Advertising: A Laboratory Analysis." *Journal of Marketing Research* 13:128–142.

Raymond, P. D. 2004. "Damage Control: What to Do If You Get Sued over Advertising." http://www.adlaw.com/rc/handbk/rf_damage.html.

Shaffer, G., and F. Zettelmeyer. 2002. "Comparative Advertising and Retailer Participation." Photocopy.

Shimp, T. 1990. *Promotion Management and Marketing Communications*. 2nd ed. Chicago: Dryden Press.

Shimp, T., and D. Dyer. 1978. "The Effects of Comparative Advertising Mediated by Market Position of Sponsoring Brand." *Journal of Advertising* 7:13–19.

Shy, O. 1992. "A Welfare Evaluation of Comparison Advertising." Working Paper 10/92. Tel Aviv: Foerder Institute for Economic Research.

Shy, O. 1995. *Industrial Organization: Theory and Applications*. Cambridge, MA: MIT Press.

Steinberg, L. B., and A. G. Naidech. 2003. "Remedies Available for False Advertising under California Business & Professions Code §17500 and section 43(A) of the Lanham Act." http://www.adlawbyrequest.com/industry/LANHAM.shtml.

Stephen, F. H., and J. H. Love. 2000. "Regulation of the Legal Profession." In B. Bouckaert and G. De Geest, eds., *Encyclopedia of Law and Economics, Volume 3: The Regulation of Contracts*, 987–1017. Cheltenham: Edward Elgar.

Suasion Resources. 2003. "Us vs. Them." *Suasion Newsletter*, May, http://www.suasionnewsletter.com/03may1.htm.

Swan, C. 2000. "Comparative Advertising Part 1: It's Only Advertising." *Intellectual Property Lawyer*, August. Available at: http://www.simkins.co.uk/articles/article167.aspx.

Teather, D. 2000. "Best of enemies." *Marketing*, London (May 11):30.

Wilkie, W. L., and P. W. Farris. 1975. "Comparison Advertising: Problems and Potential." *Journal of Marketing* 39:7–15.

Wood, D. 2003. "Strategies for In-House Legal Counsel in Bringing or Resisting a Comparative Advertising Lawsuit." Available at: http://www.adlawbyrequest.com/industry/CompAd.shtml.

9 The Effects of Disclosure Regulation of an Innovative Firm

Jos Jansen

9.1 Introduction

In many industries firms make announcements about their innovations. Preannouncements are made in, for example, the information technology, biotechnology, pharmaceutical, and car industries. Communication between firms has potential negative and positive effects on welfare.

Among the potential negative effects of preannouncements is the possibility of predation. For example, it is often claimed that Microsoft is using preannouncements of its products (e.g., operating system upgrades, game consoles) to drive competition out of its market.[1] Disclosing good news about one's own new product or production process while hiding bad news may discourage rivals from supplying a competing product. The potential anticompetitive effects of Microsoft's product preannouncements were discussed during the 1994–1995 licensing court case against Microsoft (e.g., see *United States v. Microsoft*, Civil Action No. 94-1564). Although the judge recognized that preannouncements may have anticompetitive effects, no restrictions were placed on Microsoft's announcements.[2]

Moreover, firms can use communication to facilitate collusion. Detection of deviations from collusive agreements is easier when firms frequently share information related to their strategies. Kühn and Vives (1995) and Kühn (2001) carefully analyze the conditions under which communication between firms is correlated with collusion and is unlikely to have efficiency benefits. From these conditions, which are based on economic theory, experiments, and case studies, the papers derive simple policy rules to fight collusion by restricting communication between firms.

My chapter studies the effects of imposing a simple restriction on communication between firms: the prohibition of precommitment to information-sharing rules. Firms may attempt to precommit to disclose or conceal their information through the establishment of a trade association, or the organization of frequent trade fairs. If precommitment is prohibited, then a firm can only make strategic, unilateral disclosure choices—for example, through publication in scientific journals.

More drastic restrictions on communication between innovative firms may yield welfare losses, since the following two potential efficiency gains would be foregone. First, communication between competing firms may enhance allocative efficiency, since it facilitates more efficient decision making in the product market. Kühn and Vives 1995 gives an overview of the potential positive profit and welfare effects. The assumptions of my model are such that positive profit and welfare effects emerge from communication.

Second, a firm's preannouncement can also reveal some valuable information about the innovation's contents to the competitor. When knowledge about the contents of an innovation is revealed to a rival firm after disclosure, this enables the rival firm to imitate and become more efficient itself. The improvement of productive efficiency resulting from this expropriation effect may be yet another reason for an antitrust authority not to prohibit communication between innovative firms.

A preannouncing firm faces the following trade-off. On the one hand, the firm creates a strategic advantage by revealing it is an efficient, "aggressive" Cournot competitor. On the other hand, the disadvantage of disclosure is that some of the contents of the innovation spills over to the competitor, which enables it to catch up. This expropriation effect, which is central in most patent-design literature (e.g., see Scotchmer 1991), reduces a firm's incentive to disclose its innovation. While the strategic effect gives firms an incentive to disclose innovations, the expropriation effect encourages concealment of information. Gertner (1998, 608) makes a related observation: "Firm 1 may wish to convince Firm 2 that it has low costs to induce Firm 2 to exit or produce less. If the only way to certify this information is to reveal technological secrets that Firm 2 may be able to appropriate, disclosure is unlikely." This chapter illustrates the effect of this trade-off on the innovative firm's disclosure strategy, and on the firm's production incentives.

In particular, I compare the expected profit of Cournot duopolists under precommitment with the expected profit under strategic disclosure. Under precommitment the disclosure rule of a firm is fixed before the firm learns the size of its innovation. Under strategic disclosure an innovative firm learns the size of its process innovation, and chooses strategically whether to disclose this information to its rival.

The chapter, together with a companion paper (Jansen 2006), attempts to contribute to the literature on spillovers in oligopoly, and to the literature on strategic information disclosure. Whereas the current chapter gives a simple graphic analysis of a model with one-sided asymmetric information about discrete types, the companion paper (Jansen 2006) studies the problem of information disclosure among innovative firms with two-sided asymmetric information about a continuum of types.

The literature on the effects of spillovers in oligopoly is extensive (see, for example, d'Aspremont and Jacquemin 1988; Kamien, Muller, and Zang 1992; Katsoulacos and Ulph 1998). My contribution to this literature is to investigate the effects of spillovers in a setting with asymmetric information. Anton and Yao 2003, 2004, explore information-disclosure incentives of competing, innovative firms. These papers focus on separating equilibria where, although firms do not disclose all information, the disclosed information is a perfect signal of the firm's efficiency.[3] The amount of knowledge that is expected to spill over to the rival determines a firm's disclosure strategy. The size of the knowledge spillover plays an important role in my analysis, too. But in contrast to Anton and Yao's important results, I obtain equilibria that need not be fully revealing to firms. A key difference between this chapter and Anton and Yao's work is that I study disclosure incentives of a firm with an indivisible innovation. Therefore, the only choice of an innovative firm in this chapter is between disclosure and concealment of all information. A firm in Anton and Yao's investigations chooses how much information to disclose. Furthermore, I perform profit and welfare analyses, which are absent in Anton and Yao's contributions.

Gill 2004 analyzes a related model, where an innovative firm strategically discloses information related to its innovative efficiency and the size of the innovation. This paper differs in several respects from mine. Most importantly, Gill studies R&D incentives, while I examine product market incentives. On a technical level Gill analyzes a model with discrete actions and a continuous-type space, while the present chapter explores the reverse—that is, a continuous-action space and a discrete-type space. In other words, whereas Gill studies entry-deterrence strategies, I focus on entry-accommodation strategies. Jansen 2005 also examines a related problem. But, in contrast to the present chapter, that paper focuses on R&D incentives and analyzes a model with perfectly correlated types. This yields different disclosure incentives. Both Gill and Jansen obtain concealment of information for some parameter values.

Strategic preannouncements of innovations have been analyzed in the fields of law, marketing, and economics. One of the first papers to point to the potential strategic implications of preannouncements is Ordover and Willig 1981. Among the contributions in economics are, for example, Farrell and Saloner 1986; Lopatka and Page 1995; Levy 1997; Haan 2003; Dranove and Gandal 2003; Gerlach 2004; Choi, Kristiansen, and Nahm 2004. These papers typically study the effects of preannouncements on consumer beliefs and demand. The present chapter focuses on the direct, strategic effects of information disclosure on a firm's competitor, and the potential expropriation of technological knowledge by a competitor.

In this way the chapter is intended to contribute to the literature on information sharing in oligopolistic markets. Most economics literature has focused on nonstrategic information sharing.[4] My contribution to papers such as Fried 1984, Gal-Or 1986, and Shapiro 1986 is to examine the effects of knowledge spillover on information-sharing incentives. I also provide graphic illustrations of the main results. Moreover, I study strategic disclosure incentives, and compare them with the incentives to precommit to disclosure rules.

Strategic information disclosure is extensively studied in the accounting literature.[5] But in this literature precommitment to disclosure rules is not often analyzed. An important result in strategic disclosure analysis is the so-called unraveling result. When it is known that the sender of information is informed, and there are no costs of verification or disclosure, then the sender can often do no better than to disclose his or her information, given skeptical equilibrium beliefs of the receiver. Papers that investigate this result include Grossman 1981, Milgrom 1981, Milgrom and Roberts 1986, and Okuno-Fujiwara, Postlewaite, and Suzumura 1990. Okuno-Fujiwara and colleagues give sufficient conditions under which the unraveling result applies. The sufficient condition that is violated in my model is "positive monotonicity of best response functions." This violation, which emerges in industries with positive knowledge spillovers, may cause a breakdown of the unraveling result, as I demonstrate below.

The chapter is organized as follows. In section 9.2 I describe the model. Section 9.3 discusses the equilibrium outputs and profits when the innovative firm precommits to either disclose all cost information or none. Section 9.4 gives the equilibrium outputs and disclosure choices when the innovative firm strategically discloses information, and compares expected profits under precommitment with those under strategic disclosure. Section 9.5 briefly discusses some economic policy implications of the analysis. Finally, section 9.6 concludes the chapter. The proofs of the chapter's main propositions are relegated to the appendix.

9.2 The Model

Two firms, firms i and n, produce homogeneous goods. Firm i, the innovative firm, has private information about its unit production cost, θ_i, which is either low, $\theta_i = \underline{\theta}$, with probability p, or high, $\theta_i = \overline{\theta}$, with probability $1 - p$, where $0 \le \underline{\theta} < \overline{\theta}$ and $0 < p < 1$. Firm n is not innovative, and has a high unit production cost $\theta_n = \overline{\theta}$. Firm n's marginal cost is common knowledge.

After firm i learns its cost, it makes a disclosure choice. Firm i with cost θ_i chooses the probability of disclosure $\delta(\theta_i)$—that is, with probability $\delta(\theta_i)$ the firm reveals its cost truthfully, while with probability $1 - \delta(\theta_i)$ the firm conceals and sends an uninformative message, $\varnothing$. In other words, firm i's information is verifiable. Denote firm i's realized disclosure D, where $D \in \{\theta_i, \varnothing\}$.

Finally, firms choose output levels of a homogeneous good (Cournot competition). Firm i chooses output level $x_i \ge 0$ at cost $\theta_i x_i$. Firm n's unit cost, $C(D, \kappa)$, depends as follows on the technology disclosed by firm i. If firm i discloses a low cost, then part of this knowledge, κ, spills over to firm n. In all other cases—that is, firm i discloses a high cost or nothing—no useful knowledge spills over:

$$C(D,\kappa) = \begin{cases} \kappa\underline{\theta} + (1-\kappa)\overline{\theta}, \text{ if } D = \underline{\theta}, \\ \overline{\theta}, \text{otherwise} \end{cases} \tag{1}$$

The inverse demand for the good is linear: $P(X) = A - X$, with $X \equiv x_1 + x_2$. Given cost θ_j, firm j's expected profit is

$$\pi_j(\mathbf{x}; \theta_j) = (A - \theta_j - X)\, x_j \tag{2}$$

with $\mathbf{x} \equiv (x_i, x_n)$ and $j \in \{i, n\}$. Firms are risk-neutral. I solve the game backwards—that is, I consider Bayes perfect equilibria.

9.3 Precommitment Regimes

In this section I consider two standard disclosure regimes. In the first regime firm i precommits to disclose its information θ_i. In the second regime the innovative firm precommits to conceal its information. Such ex ante precommitment could be obtained through the establishment of a trade association or the organization of frequent trade fairs.

9.3.1 Full Disclosure

When firm i precommits to disclose its marginal cost—that is, $(\delta(\underline{\theta}), \delta(\overline{\theta})) = (1, 1)$—firms base their supply decision on their relative costs. The first-order conditions of each firm's profit maximization give the following best response functions of firm i and n, respectively:

$$x_i(x_n;\theta_i) = \frac{1}{2}(A - \theta_i - x_n), \text{ and} \tag{3}$$

$$x_n(x_i;C(\theta_i,\kappa)) = \frac{1}{2}(A - C(\theta_i,\kappa) - x_i). \tag{4}$$

Derivation of the equilibrium outputs under full disclosure gives the following:

$$x_i^d(\theta_i;\kappa) = \frac{1}{3}(A - 2\theta_i + C(\theta_i,\kappa)), \text{ and} \tag{5}$$

$$x_n^d(\theta_i;\kappa) = \frac{1}{3}(A - 2C(\theta_i,\kappa) + \theta_i), \tag{6}$$

and equilibrium profit $\pi_j^d(\theta_i;\kappa) = x_j^d(\theta_i;\kappa)^2$, with $\theta_i \in \{\underline{\theta}, \overline{\theta}\}$ and $j \in \{i, n\}$.

First, if no knowledge spills over, $\kappa = 0$, then $C(\theta_i; 0) = \overline{\theta}$ for any θ_i. The extreme case of zero knowledge spillover would be relevant in industries where firm n is not allowed (e.g., through perfect and infinitely strong intellectual property rights) or not able (e.g., due to a lack of technological expertise) to imitate the efficient technology $\underline{\theta}$. The equilibrium outputs are illustrated in figure 9.1. Curve $x_n(x_i; \overline{\theta})$ is firm n's best response curve, as in (4). The curve $x_i(x_n; \theta_i)$ is the best response curve of firm i with cost θ_i for $\theta_i \in \{\underline{\theta}, \overline{\theta}\}$, as in (3). A reduction of firm i's cost shifts firm i's best response curve outward. That is, for any given

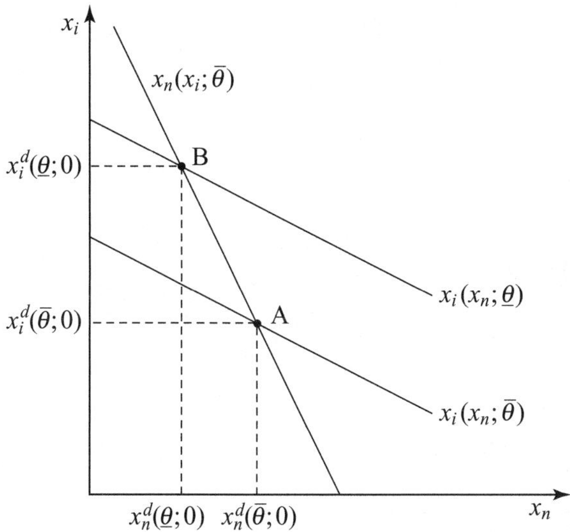

Figure 9.1
Full-disclosure output ($\kappa = 0$)

output x_n firm i supplies relatively more of the good if it is efficient. Hence, firm i's equilibrium outputs decrease in its cost, θ_i, while firm n's output increases in θ_i. In other words, outputs can be ranked as follows: $x_n^d(\underline{\theta};\ 0) < x_n^d(\overline{\theta};\ 0) = x_i^d(\overline{\theta};\ 0) < x_i^d(\underline{\theta};\ 0)$. The output changes after a reduction of θ_i are illustrated in figure 9.1 by moving from point A to B.

Second, if all knowledge spills over from the innovative firm to its competitor, $\kappa = 1$, firm n's cost reduces to $C(\theta_i, 1) = \theta_i$. This extreme case would emerge if no intellectual property rights exist and firm n can imitate the efficient technology at zero cost. I illustrate this case in figure 9.2. As in figure 9.1, the curve $x_i(x_n;\ \theta_i)$ is the best response curve of firm i with cost θ_i. A cost reduction for firm i now shifts out the best response curves of *both* firms. Firm n's best response curve shifts out from $x_n(x_i;\ \overline{\theta})$ to $x_n(x_i;\ \underline{\theta})$ after disclosure of $\theta_i = \underline{\theta}$ through the knowledge spillover. Notice that this case is identical to a model where firms have a common cost parameter. The equilibrium outputs are symmetric, since firms have identical costs, and firms supply more output when they are efficient—that is, $x_j^d(\underline{\theta};\ 1) > x_j^d(\overline{\theta};\ 1)$ for $j \in \{i, n\}$. This output expansion is illustrated by moving from point A to point B′ in figure 9.2.

Finally, in the intermediate cases, with spillover $0 < \kappa < 1$, I obtain the following comparative statics results. An increase of the knowledge

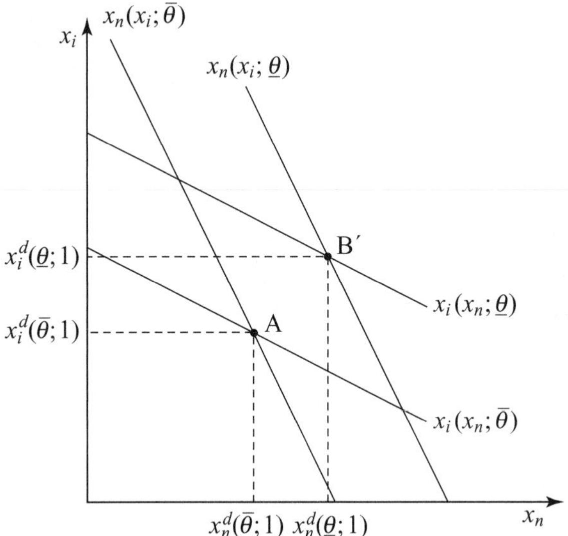

Figure 9.2
Full-disclosure output ($\kappa = 1$)

spillover shifts firm n's best response curve outward (to the right) after firm i discloses $\underline{\theta}$. Hence, an increase of the knowledge spillover increases firm n's equilibrium output, $\partial x_n^d(\underline{\theta};\ \kappa)/\partial\kappa > 0$, and decreases firm i's output, $\partial x_i^d(\underline{\theta};\ \kappa)/\partial\kappa < 0$. These comparative statics results have consequences for later analyses.

9.3.2 Full Concealment

When firm i precommits to conceal all its information—that is, $(\delta(\underline{\theta}), \delta(\bar{\theta})) = (0, 0)$—then no information spills over to firm n, and $C(\varnothing, \kappa) = \bar{\theta}$ for any κ. Firms choose their output levels such that firm i's best response is as in (3) for $\theta_i \in \{\underline{\theta}, \bar{\theta}\}$, and firm n's best response is

$$x_n(x_i) = \frac{1}{2}(A - \bar{\theta} - E\{x_i(\theta_i)\}) \tag{7}$$

Solving for the equilibrium gives the following outputs:

$$x_i^o(\theta_i) = \frac{1}{3}(A - 2\theta_i + \bar{\theta}) + \frac{1}{6}(\theta_i - E\{\theta_i\}) \tag{8}$$

$$x_n^o = \frac{1}{3}(A - 2\bar{\theta} + E\{\theta_i\}) \tag{9}$$

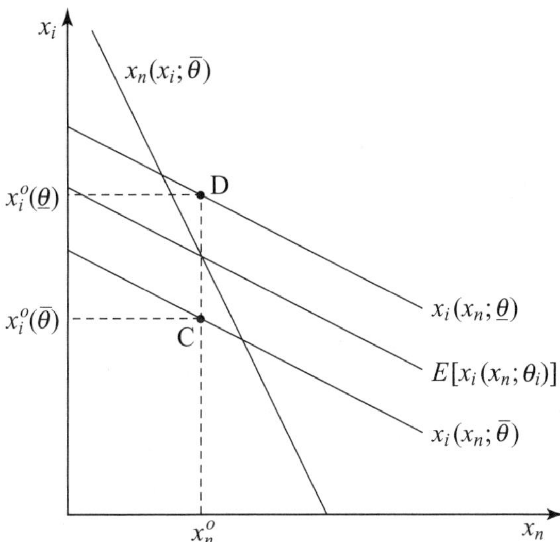

Figure 9.3
Full-concealment output

with $\theta_i \in \{\underline{\theta}, \bar{\theta}\}$. The equilibrium outputs are illustrated in figure 9.3. As in the previous subsection, $x_n(x_i; \bar{\theta})$ and $x_i(x_n; \theta_i)$ are the best response curves of firm n and firm i with cost θ_i, respectively. The curve $E[x_i(x_n; \theta_i)]$ gives the expected best response of firm i to any output chosen by firm n. The intersection of firm n's best response curve with firm i's expected best response gives firm n's equilibrium output x_n^o. The best response of firm i with cost θ_i to output x_n^o is firm i's equilibrium output $x_i^o(\theta_i)$ for $\theta_i \in \{\underline{\theta}, \bar{\theta}\}$. Again, the expected profits are $\pi_i^o(\theta_i) = x_i^o(\theta_i)^2$ and $\pi_n^o = (x_n^o)^2$.

The comparison between the firms' equilibrium outputs under full concealment gives $x_n^o < x_i^o(\bar{\theta}) < x_i^o(\underline{\theta})$. Firm n expects a relatively more efficient competitor, and therefore sets the lowest output. The equilibrium outputs are such that point D in figure 9.3 is reached if firm i is efficient, and point C is reached if the firm is inefficient.

If no knowledge spills over from the innovative firm to the competitor, then the ex ante expected outputs under full disclosure and full concealment are identical—that is, $E\{x_i^d(\theta_i; 0)\} = E\{x_i^o(\theta_i)\} = \frac{1}{3}(A - 2E\{\theta_i\} + \bar{\theta})$, and $E\{x_n^d(\theta_i; 0)\} = x_n^o$. For a positive spillover firm i's expected output under full disclosure is smaller than under full concealment, and the reverse holds for firm n. These observations are useful for the profit analysis in the next subsection.

9.3.3 Profit Comparison

The firms' equilibrium output levels determine the firms' expected equilibrium profits. Firm j's ex ante expected profits under full disclosure and full concealment are

$$\Pi_j^d(\kappa) = px_j^d(\underline{\theta};\kappa)^2 + (1-p)x_j^d(\overline{\theta};\kappa)^2 \tag{10}$$

$$\Pi_i^o = px_i^o(\underline{\theta})^2 + (1-p)x_i^o(\overline{\theta})^2 \text{ and } \Pi_n^o = (x_n^o)^2 \tag{11}$$

respectively, with $j \in \{i, n\}$. The expected profit under full disclosure is an increasing function of the output levels under full disclosure, and outputs are monotonic in the spillover. Consequently, the expected equilibrium profits are monotonic functions of the knowledge spillover—that is, $d\Pi_j^d(\kappa)/d\kappa = 2p \cdot x_j^d(\underline{\theta};\ \kappa) \cdot \partial x_j^d(\underline{\theta};\ \kappa)/\partial\kappa$ where $\partial x_j^d(\underline{\theta};\ \kappa)/\partial\kappa$ does not change sign for $j \in \{i, n\}$. In particular, firm i's expected profit is decreasing in the knowledge spillover, while firm n's expected profit is increasing in the spillover.

If no knowledge spills over from firm i to n ($\kappa = 0$), the expected equilibrium outputs under full disclosure and full concealment are identical. Consequently, the comparison of expected profits is similar to the comparison of the variances of the firms' outputs. Figure 9.4 combines figures 9.1 and 9.3. As illustrated in this figure, the variance of firm n's output is clearly greatest under full disclosure. Whereas the variance of firm n's output under full concealment is zero, the variance of firm n's output under full disclosure is greater than zero. Similarly, firm i's output variance is greatest under full disclosure, as suggested by figure 9.4. Consequently, both firms expect the highest profits under full disclosure. That is, if firm i can precommit to full disclosure, it will do so. This result is a special case of results by Fried (1984), Gal-Or (1986), and Shapiro (1986). My contribution here is to illustrate the result graphically in a simple model. Furthermore, I show below how this result changes by the introduction of a knowledge spillover.

If all knowledge spills over ($\kappa = 1$) after disclosure, then the ex ante profit comparison is determined by the comparison of equilibrium outputs. Figure 9.5 combines figures 9.2 and 9.3. Disclosure has the following effects on firm i's output. If firm i is inefficient, then firm i is perceived as less "aggressive" after disclosure of $\theta_i = \overline{\theta}$. Disclosure results in a higher output by firm n, and consequently a lower output by firm i, than after concealment. For efficient firm i the following trade-off emerges. On the one hand, firm i's expected best response curve after disclosure is above firm i's expected curve after

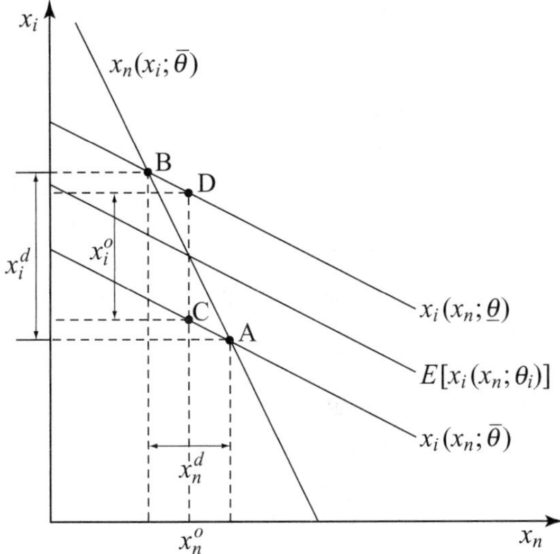

Figure 9.4
Precommitment profits ($\kappa = 0$)

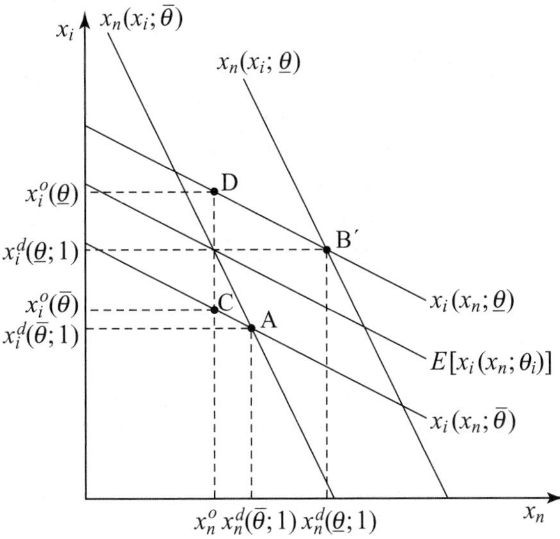

Figure 9.5
Precommitment profits ($\kappa = 1$)

concealment. Hence, after disclosure firm n expects a more "aggressive" competitor, which gives it an incentive for output reduction. On the other hand, disclosure of $\theta_i = \underline{\theta}$ makes firm n a more "aggressive" competitor since all knowledge spills over—that is, firm n's best response function shifts outward after disclosure. The former effect gives firm i an incentive to expand its output, but the latter effect gives an incentive to reduce firm i's output. The latter effect outweighs the former effect, as illustrated in figure 9.5. Hence, firm i supplies more, while firm n supplies less, under full concealment than under full disclosure, so that $x_i^o(\theta_i) > x_i^d(\theta_i; 1)$ while $x_n^o < x_n^d(\theta_i; 1)$ for any θ_i. Consequently, firm i has a higher expected profit under full concealment, whereas firm n has higher profits under full disclosure.[6]

Finally, for intermediate knowledge spillovers, the profit comparison is determined by a trade-off between the effects above. Using monotonicity and continuity of the expected profit functions, the proof of the following proposition is straightforward.

Proposition 1 A critical knowledge spillover, κ^* with $0 < \kappa^* < 1$, exists such that firm i's expected profit is greatest under full disclosure iff $\kappa < \kappa^*$—that is, $\Pi_i^d(\kappa) \gtreqless \Pi_i^o$ *iff* $\kappa \lesseqgtr \kappa^*$. Moreover, firm n always expects greater profits under full disclosure: $\Pi_n^d(\kappa) > \Pi_n^o$ for any κ.

This result qualifies previous results in the literature on information sharing in oligopoly (see, e.g., Fried 1984; Gal-Or 1986; Shapiro 1986). The innovative firm's incentive to precommit to share its information is robust to the introduction of a sufficiently small knowledge spillover. But if the knowledge spillover grows beyond a critical value κ^*, the innovative firm no longer has an incentive to precommit to share its information.

9.4 Strategic Disclosure

In the previous section firm i was able to precommit to disclosure rules. In this section I characterize the innovative firm's incentives to disclose its production cost strategically. Subsequently, I study the effects of strategic disclosure on the firms' expected profits.

9.4.1 Equilibrium Outputs

I derive the outputs given any disclosure rule $(\delta(\underline{\theta}), \delta(\overline{\theta})) \in [0, 1] \times [0, 1]$, and any feasible, disclosed message, $D \in \{\underline{\theta}, \overline{\theta}, \varnothing\}$. After firm i discloses information θ_i each firm supplies the full-disclosure equilibrium output $x_j^d(\theta_i;\ \kappa)$ for $j \in \{i, n\}$. If firm i conceals its information ($D = \varnothing$), then firm j has beliefs consistent with the disclosure rule, and assigns probability q to facing an efficient competitor, where

$$q \equiv \frac{p(1-\delta(\underline{\theta}))}{p(1-\delta(\underline{\theta}))+(1-p)(1-\delta(\overline{\theta}))} \tag{12}$$

Hence, firm j's posterior beliefs are such that its expectation of firm i's marginal cost is $E\{\theta_i|\varnothing\} \equiv q\underline{\theta} + (1 - q)\overline{\theta}$.

The derivation of the equilibrium outputs under information concealment is similar to the derivation under full concealment, where $E\{x_i(\theta_i)\}$ is replaced by $E\{x_i(\theta_i)|\varnothing\}$. That is, if firm i chooses a disclosure rule where $\delta(\underline{\theta}) \neq \delta(\overline{\theta})$, then information concealment is informative to firm n. Firm n therefore updates its beliefs about its competitor's marginal cost after concealment, which yields expected cost $E\{\theta_i|\varnothing\}$. After an increase in $\delta(\underline{\theta})$ it is more likely that a concealing firm has a high marginal cost, and therefore posterior belief q decreases—that is, $\partial q/\partial\delta(\underline{\theta}) < 0$ and $\partial E\{\theta_i|\varnothing\}/\partial\delta(\underline{\theta}) > 0$. A decrease in the probability of disclosing a high marginal cost parameter, $\delta(\overline{\theta})$, has a similar effect. The firms' equilibrium output levels are (similar to expressions (8) and (9), respectively):

$$x_i^s(\theta_i) = \frac{1}{3}(A - 2\theta_i + \overline{\theta}) + \frac{1}{6}(\theta_i - E\{\theta_i|\varnothing\}), \tag{13}$$

$$x_n^s = \frac{1}{3}(A - 2\overline{\theta} + E\{\theta_i|\varnothing\}). \tag{14}$$

An increase of disclosure probability $\delta(\underline{\theta})$ increases the expected cost of firm i after concealment, and consequently increases firm n's output x_n^s while it lowers firm i's output $x_i^s(\theta_i)$.

9.4.2 Equilibrium Disclosure

In the previous subsection I characterized equilibrium outputs for any feasible disclosure rule. This subsection derives the disclosure rules that firm i chooses in equilibrium.

First, I show that firm i never has an incentive to disclose a high marginal cost $\overline{\theta}$—in other words, in equilibrium $\delta(\overline{\theta}) = 0$ for any spillover κ. After concealment firm n expects firm i to have a marginal cost lower than or equal to $\overline{\theta}$, which makes firm n less or equally "aggressive" as under disclosure of $\overline{\theta}$. Since outputs are strategic substitutes, firm i therefore (weakly) prefers to conceal $\theta_i = \overline{\theta}$.

In the remainder of this subsection I study the equilibrium disclosure strategy of firm i with a low marginal cost, given that firm n anticipates disclosure rule $(\delta(\underline{\theta}), \delta(\overline{\theta})) = (\delta, 0)$, with $0 \leq \delta \leq 1$. Clearly, firm i's equilibrium disclosure strategy is determined by the comparison of the profit from disclosure and profit from concealment.

First, suppose that firm n has beliefs consistent with disclosure of $\underline{\theta}$—that is, $q = 0$ and $E\{\theta_i|\varnothing\} = \overline{\theta}$. If firm i conceals a low cost, then firm n expects that firm i is inefficient, and firm n chooses output $x_n^d(\overline{\theta}, \kappa)$. Efficient firm i's best response to this output is to set output $x_i^* \equiv x_i(x_n^d(\overline{\theta}, \kappa); \underline{\theta})$, as illustrated in figure 9.6. The firms' outputs are such that point E in the figure is reached. If firm i discloses a low cost with probability one, then both firms supply their full-disclosure outputs. Now, as illustrated in figure 9.6, a critical spillover, $\overline{\kappa} \in (0, 1)$, exists such that for this spillover firm n's best response curve after disclosure of $\underline{\theta}$—that is, $x_n(x_i; C(\underline{\theta}, \overline{\kappa}))$—runs through point E. For any spillover smaller than or equal to $\overline{\kappa}$ the equilibrium after disclosure of $\underline{\theta}$ is on the line B–E, and disclosure yields an equilibrium output for firm i greater than or equal to x_i^*. Since firm i's equilibrium profit is increasing in its equilibrium output level, disclosure of $\underline{\theta}$ is more profitable than or equally profitable to concealment for any knowledge spillover

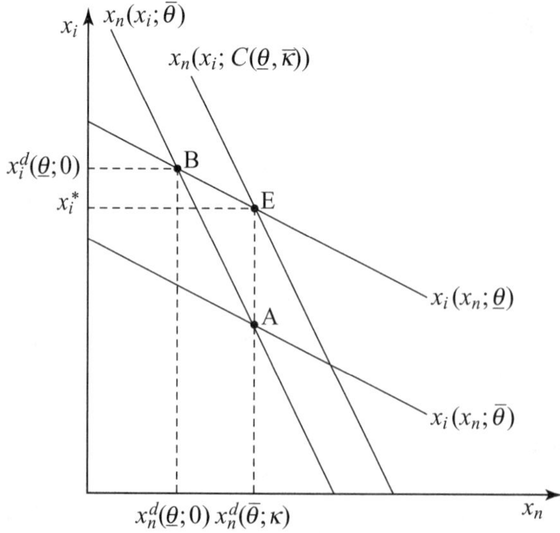

Figure 9.6
Incentive to disclose

below or equal to $\bar{\kappa}$. For these spillover values disclosure of a low cost is an equilibrium strategy. That is, for $\kappa < \bar{\kappa}$ the strategic effect of disclosure outweighs the technology expropriation effect, given beliefs consistent with full disclosure.

Second, suppose that firm n has beliefs consistent with full concealment—that is, $q = p$ and $E\{\theta_i|\varnothing\} = E\{\theta_i\}$. Now, if firm i conceals a low cost, both firms supply their full-concealment output levels. In other words, point D in figure 9.7 is reached. On the other hand, point D will be reached after disclosure of a low cost, if the knowledge spillover is such that firm n's best response curve after disclosure, $x_n(x_i; C(\underline{\theta}, \kappa))$, runs through point D. We define $\underline{\kappa}$ as the critical spillover value for which this happens, where $0 < \underline{\kappa} < 1$. For all spillovers greater than or equal to $\underline{\kappa}$, the equilibrium outputs after disclosure are on the line D–B′. These equilibrium output levels are below or equal to $x_i^o(\underline{\theta})$ for firm i, and therefore yield profits below or equal to the profit from concealment. In other words, for all spillovers greater than or equal to $\underline{\kappa}$, concealment is an equilibrium strategy for firm i.

Finally, it is clear from comparing figures 9.6 and 9.7 that critical spillovers $\underline{\kappa}$ and $\bar{\kappa}$ are such that $\underline{\kappa} < \bar{\kappa}$, since point D is clearly to the left of E, as is illustrated in figure 9.8. If $\underline{\kappa} < \kappa < \bar{\kappa}$, firm i may choose a

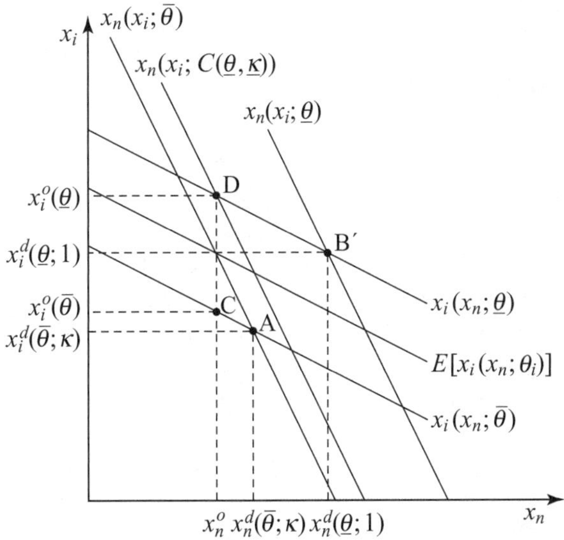

Figure 9.7
Incentive to conceal

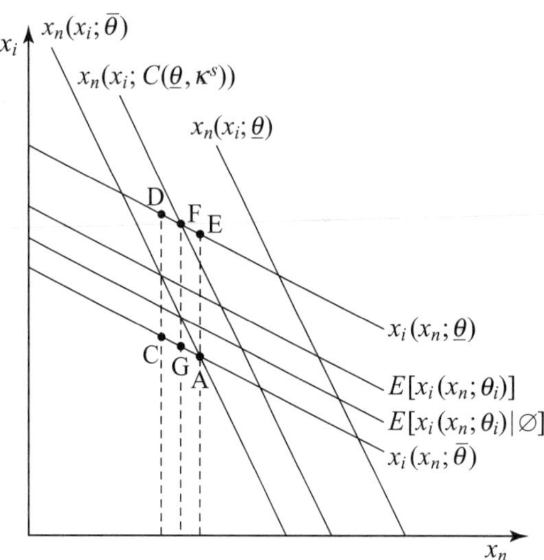

Figure 9.8
Incentive for partial disclosure

partial-disclosure rule in equilibrium—that is, $(\delta(\underline{\theta}), \delta(\overline{\theta})) = (\delta^*, 0)$ with $0 < \delta^* < 1$. If firm n has beliefs consistent with partial disclosure (i.e., $0 < q < p$ and $E\{\theta_i\} < E\{\theta_i|\varnothing\} < \overline{\theta}$), and firm i conceals its cost, then firm n chooses output level x_n^s. Output x_n^s is the output level where firm n's best response curve $x_n(x_i; \overline{\theta})$ crosses firm i's expected best response curve, given beliefs consistent with disclosure rule $(\delta^*, 0)$ (i.e., $E[x_i(x_n; \theta_i)|\varnothing]$). This output lies between the output levels under full concealment and full disclosure (i.e., x_n^o and $x_n^d(\overline{\theta}, \kappa)$ respectively), since the expected best response curve $E[x_i(x_n; \theta_i)|\varnothing]$ lies between the expected best response curve given prior beliefs, $E[x_i(x_n; \theta_i)]$, and the best response curve of inefficient firm i, $x_i(x_n; \overline{\theta})$. Efficient firm i's best response to x_n^s is to supply $x_i^s(\underline{\theta})$. This equilibrium is illustrated by point F in figure 9.8. Notice that point F lies between points D and E. Clearly, there exists one spillover value κ^s between $\underline{\kappa}$ and $\overline{\kappa}$ such that firm n's best response curve runs through point F, and firm i is indifferent between disclosure and concealment. Such a posterior belief and spillover value support the partial-disclosure rule $(\delta(\underline{\theta}), \delta(\overline{\theta})) = (\delta^*, 0)$ as an equilibrium strategy.

An increase of δ^* implies that firm n expects a less efficient competitor after concealment—that is, firm i's expected best response curve

$E[x_i(x_n;\ \theta_i)|\varnothing]$ shifts downward. Firm n's equilibrium output does therefore increase, and efficient firm i's output decreases. In other words, the equilibrium shifts to the right along line D–E in figure 9.8. Only an equal shift to the right of firm n's best response curve can maintain firm i's indifference between disclosure and concealment of $\underline{\theta}$. Hence, knowledge spillover κ^s needs to increase after δ^* increases. In summary, the equilibrium partial-disclosure probability δ^* is increasing in the spillover κ.

Analytically, the critical values $\underline{\kappa}$ and $\bar{\kappa}$ are defined as

$$\underline{\kappa} \equiv \frac{1}{2}(1-p) \text{ and } \bar{\kappa} \equiv \frac{1}{2} \tag{15}$$

respectively, and the equilibrium partial-disclosure probability is as follows:

$$\delta^*(\kappa) \equiv 1 - \frac{(1-p)(1-2\kappa)}{2p\kappa} \tag{16}$$

This completes the characterization of the strategic disclosure incentives, and yields the following proposition:

Proposition 2 The critical spillover values $\underline{\kappa}$ and $\bar{\kappa}$ exist, as defined in (15)—that is, $0 < \underline{\kappa} < \bar{\kappa} < 1$—such that firm i chooses the following disclosure rules in equilibrium:

• If $\kappa < \underline{\kappa}$, firm i's equilibrium disclosure rule is unique, and yields full disclosure.

• If $\underline{\kappa} \le \kappa \le \bar{\kappa}$, three equilibrium disclosure rules exist, yielding either full disclosure, full concealment, or partial disclosure $(\delta(\underline{\theta}),\ \delta(\bar{\theta})) = (\delta^*(\kappa),\ 0)$ with $\delta^*(\kappa)$ as in (16)—that is, $d\delta^*/d\kappa > 0$, $\delta^*(\underline{\kappa}) = 0$, and $\delta^*(\bar{\kappa}) = 1$.

• If $\kappa > \bar{\kappa}$, firm i's equilibrium disclosure rule is unique, and yields full concealment.

This result illustrates that the unraveling result in Okuno-Fujiwara, Postlewaite, and Suzumura 1990 is robust to the introduction of small knowledge spillovers. For sufficiently high knowledge spillovers (in particular, for $\kappa > \bar{\kappa}$), however, the nonmonotonicity of best response functions creates sufficiently strong incentives to conceal information, and consequently the unraveling result fails.

9.4.3 Profit Comparison

In this subsection I compare expected profits under the equilibrium disclosure rules. The expected profits under full disclosure and no disclosure are already given in expressions (10) and (11), respectively. If the spillover is κ^s from figure 9.8, the expected profit of firm i under partial disclosure $(\delta(\underline{\theta}), \delta(\overline{\theta})) = (\delta^*, 0)$ equals

$$\begin{aligned}\Pi_i^s(\kappa^s) &= p\delta^* x_i^d(\underline{\theta};\kappa^s)^2 + p(1-\delta^*)x_i^s(\underline{\theta})^2 + (1-p)x_i^s(\overline{\theta})^2 \\ &= px_i^d(\underline{\theta};\kappa^s)^2 + (1-p)x_i^s(\overline{\theta})^2\end{aligned} \tag{17}$$

since, by construction, $x_i^d(\underline{\theta}; \kappa^s) = x_i^s(\underline{\theta})$ for equilibrium disclosure rule $(\delta^*, 0)$.

The comparison of firm i's expected profit under full and partial disclosure reduces to the comparison between $x_i^d(\overline{\theta}; \kappa^s)$ and $x_i^s(\overline{\theta})$. In figure 9.8 this comparison is between points A and G, respectively. Clearly, point A yields a lower output for firm i than point G—that is, $x_i^d(\overline{\theta}; \kappa^s) < x_i^s(\overline{\theta})$, and consequently $\Pi_i^d(\kappa^s) < \Pi_i^s(\kappa^s)$. The comparison of firm i's expected profit under partial disclosure and full concealment is illustrated by the comparison between points F and D, and points G and C in figure 9.8. Both comparisons yield the highest output levels for firm i under full concealment—that is, (D, C). Hence, firm i earns the greatest expected profit under full concealment, and so $\Pi_i^s(\kappa^s) < \Pi_i^o$. Clearly, a similar comparison emerges for any other spillover between $\underline{\kappa}$ and $\overline{\kappa}$. Therefore, firm i's expected equilibrium profits are such that $\Pi_i^d(\kappa) < \Pi_i^s(\kappa) < \Pi_i^o$ for all $\underline{\kappa} < \kappa < \overline{\kappa}$.

Finally, the expected profit of firm n given partial disclosure by firm i and spillover κ^s from figure 9.8 equals

$$\Pi_n^s(\kappa^s) = p\delta^* x_n^d(\underline{\theta};\kappa^s)^2 + [p(1-\delta^*)+1-p](x_n^s)^2 = x_n^d(\underline{\theta};\kappa^s)^2, \tag{18}$$

since $x_n^d(\underline{\theta}; \kappa^s) = x_n^s$, as illustrated in figure 9.8 (point F). The comparison of expected profits under full disclosure and partial disclosure is essentially a comparison between $x_n^d(\overline{\theta}; \kappa^s)$ and $x_n^d(\underline{\theta}; \kappa^s)$, or points A and G, respectively. Under full disclosure firm n has a higher expected profit (i.e., point A is to the right of G in figure 9.8). Firm n's output level under full concealment is below its output level under partial disclosure (e.g., point C is to the left of point G in figure 9.8), and therefore firm n earns the lowest expected profit under full concealment. Hence, I have illustrated that $\Pi_n^o < \Pi_n^s(\kappa) < \Pi_n^d(\kappa)$ for all $\underline{\kappa} < \kappa < \overline{\kappa}$. I state this formally in the following proposition:

Proposition 3 For knowledge spillover $\kappa \in (\underline{\kappa}, \bar{\kappa})$, with $\underline{\kappa}$ and $\bar{\kappa}$ as in (15), the firms' expected equilibrium profits under partial disclosure $(\delta(\underline{\theta}), \delta(\bar{\theta})) = (\delta^*, 0)$, with δ^* as in (9.16), are between the expected profits under precommitment—that is, $\Pi_i^d(\kappa) < \Pi_i^s(\kappa) < \Pi_i^o$ and $\Pi_n^o < \Pi_n^s(\kappa) < \Pi_n^d(\kappa)$.

An immediate implication of the analysis of firm i's expected profits above, and monotonicity and continuity of the expected profit functions, is that the critical value κ^* from proposition 1 is below $\underline{\kappa}$. This result is illustrated in figure 9.7. For spillover $\kappa = \underline{\kappa}$ firm i's ex ante expected profit from concealment is greater than the expected profit from disclosure. By construction, an efficient firm i is indifferent between disclosure and concealment. But an inefficient firm i makes a greater profit after concealment, since its output after concealment is greatest (i.e., $x_i^o(\bar{\theta}) > x_i^d(\bar{\theta}; \kappa)$ as illustrated in, e.g., figure 9.7). Since $\pi_i^d(\kappa)$ is decreasing in κ, and $\Pi_i^o > \Pi_i^d(\underline{\kappa})$, critical value κ^* must be below $\underline{\kappa}$, as is stated below.

Corollary 1 Critical values κ^*, $\underline{\kappa}$ and $\bar{\kappa}$, from propositions 1 and 2 are such that $\kappa^* < \underline{\kappa} < \bar{\kappa}$.

Intuitively, this result is due to the fact that under strategic disclosure an efficient firm ignores the negative externality that its disclosure choice inflicts on its inefficient counterpart. Under precommitment the innovative firm internalizes this externality, which reduces the firm's incentive to disclose a low cost.

An implication of propositions 1 and 2, and the corollary is that if firm i precommits, it conceals its information for more knowledge spillover values than if it discloses strategically. In particular, for spillovers $\kappa^* < \kappa < \underline{\kappa}$ the firm prefers to precommit to full concealment (see proposition 1), while it strategically discloses its information in the unique disclosure equilibrium (see proposition 2). In the next section I discuss some economic policy implications of this observation.

9.5 Antitrust Analysis

Should an antitrust authority prohibit an innovative firm to precommit to disclose its process innovation, or should precommitment be encouraged? I address this question here.

First, I discuss the effects of information disclosure on the expected consumers' surplus. If the innovative firm's technology cannot be expropriated—that is, $\kappa = 0$—then the consumers' surplus is greatest under full disclosure. For example, Shapiro 1986 shows this formally, and Kühn and Vives 1995 gives a graphic illustration. An increase of the knowledge spillover reduces the expected equilibrium price under full disclosure, since imitation reduces the expected cost of firm n. The expected price reduction increases the expected consumers' surplus under full disclosure—that is, the expected consumers' surplus under full disclosure is increasing in spillover κ. Clearly, the consumers' surplus under full concealment does not depend on the spillover. If the spillover equals $\underline{\kappa}$ as in (15), then the consumers' surplus under full disclosure is greater than the consumers' surplus under full concealment. Consequently, due to continuity and monotonicity of the consumers' surplus, there exists a critical value κ^c with $0 < \kappa^c < \underline{\kappa}$ such that for all spillovers greater than κ^c the consumers' surplus is highest under full disclosure. Hence, if the antitrust authority maximizes exclusively the consumers' surplus, she should prohibit precommitment for all $\kappa \geq \kappa^c$. In particular, if $\kappa^c \leq \kappa^*$, then precommitment should always be prohibited.

Second, if an antitrust authority maximizes social welfare—that is, the sum of the consumers' surplus and the industry profits—then the following trade-offs emerge for extreme spillover values. If $\kappa = 0$, expected industry profits are greatest but expected consumers' surplus is smallest under full disclosure. As Shapiro 1986 for example shows, expected welfare is highest under full disclosure—in other words, the profit effect outweighs the consumers' surplus effect. Conversely, if $\kappa = 1$, then full disclosure yields a higher expected consumers' surplus and expected profit of firm n, but a lower expected profit for firm i. Although the trade-off differs from the one I had before, expected welfare remains greatest under full disclosure. For intermediate knowledge spillovers an increase of spillover κ creates the following trade-off for antitrust authority under full disclosure. On the one hand, firm i's expected profit decreases, but, on the other hand, both the expected consumers' surplus and firm n's expected profit increase. Finally, it is easy to show that if demand is sufficiently strong (i.e., the intercept A is sufficiently great), then the expected welfare is increasing in κ. Consequently, if demand is sufficiently strong, then expected welfare is greatest under full disclosure, and a welfare-maximizing antitrust authority should prohibit precommitment to communication between firms.

I state and prove these results formally in the following proposition:

Proposition 4 The critical value κ^c exists, with $0 < \kappa^c < \underline{\kappa}$, and $\underline{\kappa}$ as in (15), such that for all $\kappa \geq \kappa^c$ the expected consumers' surplus is highest under prohibition of precommitment. If $A > \frac{1}{4}(11\overline{\theta} - 7\underline{\theta})$, then expected social welfare is highest under prohibition of precommitment.

The previous discussion suggests that an antitrust authority should prohibit the firms from precommitting to information-sharing rules in many relevant cases. The prohibition of precommitment may have an additional advantage, since it may also help the antitrust authority fight collusion.

9.6 Conclusion

In this chapter I analyzed the effects of disclosure regulation and knowledge spillovers on disclosure incentives and product market competition. The analysis was conducted for industries where firms are Cournot competitors, and where the innovative firm makes announcements about a process innovation.

I have shown that disclosure regulation substantially affects firms' outputs and profits for intermediate values of the knowledge spillover. For these knowledge spillover values a strategic innovative firm discloses its technology in more cases than a precommitted firm does. The precommitted firm has less incentive to disclose its technology since the firm internalizes a negative externality that the disclosure of an efficient technology inflicts on the profit of the firm with an inefficient technology. An antitrust authority can use disclosure regulation to exploit the effect of this externality on the firms' product market conduct. Prohibiting the innovative firm from precommitting to information-sharing rules yields more (strategic) technology disclosure, and thereby potentially higher consumer surplus and social welfare.

For extreme spillover values—that is, when only very little or most of the disclosed technology can be expropriated—disclosure regulation does not affect the firms' conduct. In both cases, however, the prohibition of precommitment can have the additional advantage of helping to fight collusion between firms.

Appendix

This appendix contains proofs of propositions 2 to 4 of this chapter.

Proof of Proposition 2 Define critical spillover values $\underline{\kappa}$ and $\overline{\kappa}$ as in (15). Firm i's profit from disclosure equals

$$\begin{aligned}\pi_i^s(\underline{\theta}|\underline{\theta}) &= x_i^d(\underline{\theta};\kappa)^2 = \frac{1}{9}(A-2\underline{\theta}+C(\underline{\theta},\kappa))^2 \\ &= \frac{1}{9}[(A-2\underline{\theta}+\overline{\theta})-\kappa(\overline{\theta}-\underline{\theta})]^2\end{aligned} \tag{19}$$

The firm's profit from concealment is

$$\begin{aligned}\pi_i^s(\varnothing|\underline{\theta}) &= x_i^s(\underline{\theta};\varnothing)^2 = \frac{1}{9}\left(A-2\underline{\theta}+\overline{\theta}+\frac{1}{2}(\underline{\theta}-E\{\theta_i|\varnothing\})\right)^2 \\ &= \frac{1}{9}\left((A-2\underline{\theta}+\overline{\theta})-\frac{1}{2}(1-q)(\overline{\theta}-\underline{\theta})\right)^2\end{aligned} \tag{20}$$

The comparison of profits $\pi_i^s(\underline{\theta}|\underline{\theta})$ and $\pi_i^s(\varnothing|\underline{\theta})$ yields the following immediate observations.

Full disclosure, $(\delta(\underline{\theta}), \delta(\overline{\theta})) = (1, 0)$, is optimal if $\pi_i^s(\underline{\theta}|\underline{\theta}) > \pi_i^s(\varnothing|\underline{\theta})$ or $\kappa < \frac{1}{2}(1-q)$. Firm n's posterior belief is consistent with full disclosure if $q = 0$. Hence, full disclosure is an equilibrium strategy for all $\kappa < \overline{\kappa}$. On the other hand, full concealment, $(\delta(\underline{\theta}), \delta(\overline{\theta})) = (0, 0)$, is optimal if $\pi_i^s(\underline{\theta}|\underline{\theta}) < \pi_i^s(\varnothing|\underline{\theta})$ or $\kappa > \frac{1}{2}(1-q)$. The posterior belief consistent with full concealment is $q = p$. Therefore, full concealment is an equilibrium disclosure rule for all $\kappa > \underline{\kappa}$. Finally, a partial disclosure rule exists in equilibrium, namely, $(\delta(\underline{\theta}), \delta(\overline{\theta})) = (\delta^*, 0)$ with $0 < \delta^* < 1$, if firm i is indifferent between disclosure and concealment, given posterior beliefs consistent with partial disclosure. Indifference emerges if $\kappa = \frac{1}{2}(1-q)$. Using definition (12), it is straightforward to obtain the following expression:

$$\kappa = \frac{1}{2}\cdot\frac{1-p}{p(1-\delta^*)+1-p} \tag{21}$$

which yields equilibrium probability $\delta^*(\kappa)$ in (16). Clearly, this partial disclosure equilibrium exists for spillovers such that $\underline{\kappa} < \kappa < \overline{\kappa}$, and the partial disclosure probability δ^* is increasing in κ. This completes the proof.

Proof of Proposition 3 Firm i's expected profit under partial disclosure is decreasing in the knowledge spillover, since all terms of the following expression are negative:

$$\frac{d\Pi_i^s(\kappa)}{d\kappa} = p\delta^* \frac{\partial \pi_i^d(\underline{\theta};\kappa)}{\partial \kappa} + [p(1-\delta^*)+1-p]\left(q\frac{\partial \pi_i^s(\underline{\theta};\varnothing)}{\partial \delta(\underline{\theta})} + (1-q)\frac{\partial \pi_i^s(\overline{\theta};\varnothing)}{\partial \delta(\underline{\theta})}\right)\frac{d\delta^*}{d\kappa} \tag{22}$$

Furthermore, if $\kappa = \underline{\kappa}$, as defined in proposition 2, then $\delta^* = 0$, and $\Pi_i^o = \Pi_i^s(\underline{\kappa})$. Since Π_i^o is constant while $\Pi_i^s(\kappa)$ is decreasing in κ, it follows immediately that $\Pi_i^o > \Pi_i^s(\kappa)$ for all $\underline{\kappa} < \kappa \leq \overline{\kappa}$, with $\underline{\kappa}$ and $\overline{\kappa}$ as defined in proposition 2. The comparison of the expected profits under full and partial disclosure gives the following. If $\kappa = \overline{\kappa}$, then $\delta^* = 1$ and $\Pi_i^s(\overline{\kappa}) > \Pi_i^d(\overline{\kappa})$. For lower spillover values the comparison between firm i's expected profit under full disclosure (10) with $j = i$, and the expected profit under partial disclosure (17) reduces to the comparison of $x_i^d(\overline{\theta};\kappa)$ and $x_i^s(\overline{\theta})$, respectively. Since expressions (5) and (13) yield

$$x_i^s(\overline{\theta}) = \frac{1}{3}\left(A - 2\overline{\theta} + \overline{\theta} + \frac{1}{2}(\overline{\theta} - E\{\theta_i|\varnothing\})\right) > \frac{1}{3}(A - 2\overline{\theta} + \overline{\theta}) = x_i^d(\overline{\theta};\kappa) \tag{23}$$

I obtain $\Pi_i^s(\kappa) > \Pi_i^d(\kappa)$ for all $\underline{\kappa} \leq \kappa < \overline{\kappa}$. Hence, the innovative firm's expected profits under partial disclosure is between its expected profits under the two precommitment regimes—that is, $\Pi_i^d(\kappa) < \Pi_i^s(\kappa) < \Pi_i^o$ for all $\underline{\kappa} < \kappa < \overline{\kappa}$.

Finally, firm n's expected profit under partial disclosure $(\delta(\underline{\theta}), \delta(\overline{\theta})) = (\delta^*, 0)$ is increasing in the spillover, since

$$\frac{d\Pi_n^s(\kappa)}{d\kappa} = p\delta^* \frac{\partial \pi_n^d(\underline{\theta};\kappa)}{\partial \kappa} + [p(1-\delta^*)+1-p]\frac{\partial \pi_n^s(\varnothing)}{\partial \delta(\underline{\theta})} \cdot \frac{d\delta^*}{d\kappa} > 0 \tag{24}$$

Moreover, if $\kappa = \underline{\kappa}$, then $\delta^* = 0$, and $\Pi_n^o = \Pi_n^s(\kappa)$. Since Π_n^o is constant while $\Pi_n^s(\kappa)$ is increasing in κ, it follows immediately that $\Pi_n^o(\kappa) < \Pi_n^s(\kappa)$ for all $\underline{\kappa} < \kappa \leq \overline{\kappa}$. On the other hand, if $\kappa = \overline{\kappa}$, then $\delta^* = 1$ and $\Pi_n^s(\overline{\kappa}) = \Pi_n^d(\overline{\kappa})$. For $\kappa < \overline{\kappa}$ the comparison between firm n's expected profit under full disclosure (10) with $j = n$, and partial disclosure (18) is essentially a comparison between outputs $x_n^d(\overline{\theta};\kappa)$ and $x_n^d(\underline{\theta};\kappa)$, respectively. Clearly, the comparison of (6) for $\theta_i = \overline{\theta}$ and $\theta_i = \underline{\theta}$ yields:

$$x_n^d(\overline{\theta};\kappa) - x_n^d(\underline{\theta};\kappa) = \frac{1}{3}(1-2\kappa)(\overline{\theta} - \underline{\theta}) > 0 \tag{25}$$

for all $\kappa < \overline{\kappa}$. Hence, $\Pi_n^s(\kappa) < \Pi_n^d(\kappa)$ for all $\underline{\kappa} \leq \kappa < \overline{\kappa}$. Combining the two profit comparisons gives: $\Pi_n^o < \Pi_n^s(\kappa) < \Pi_n^d(\kappa)$ for all $\underline{\kappa} < \kappa < \overline{\kappa}$. This completes the proof.

Proof of Proposition 4 For a given industry output X the consumers' surplus equals $\frac{1}{2}X^2$. Social welfare is the sum of the consumers' surplus and the total profits—that is, $W \equiv \frac{1}{2}X^2 + \pi_i + \pi_n$. From (5) and (6) I derive the industry output under full disclosure:

$$X^d(\theta_i;\kappa) = \frac{1}{3}(2A - \theta_i - C(\theta_i,\kappa)) \tag{26}$$

Adding up (8) and (9) gives the industry output under full concealment:

$$X^o(\theta_i) = \frac{1}{3}\left(2A - \theta_i - \bar{\theta} + \frac{1}{2}(E\{\theta_i\} - \theta_i)\right) \tag{27}$$

• First, notice that the consumers' surplus under full disclosure is increasing in spillover κ:

$$\partial E\left\{\frac{1}{2}X^d(\theta_i;\kappa)^2\right\}\Big/\partial\kappa = pX^d(\underline{\theta};\kappa)\cdot\partial X^d(\underline{\theta};\kappa)/\partial\kappa > 0, \text{ since}$$
$$\partial X^d(\underline{\theta};\kappa)/\partial\kappa > 0$$

as follows from (26). For $\kappa = \underline{\kappa}(=\frac{1}{2}(1-p))$, the following holds:

$$\begin{aligned} X^d(\underline{\theta};\underline{\kappa}) &= \frac{1}{3}(2A - \underline{\theta} - \bar{\theta} + \underline{\kappa}(\bar{\theta} - \underline{\theta})) \\ &= \frac{1}{3}\left(2A - \underline{\theta} - \bar{\theta} + \frac{1}{2}(1-p)(\bar{\theta} - \underline{\theta})\right) = X^o(\underline{\theta}) \end{aligned} \tag{28}$$

while $X^d(\bar{\theta};\underline{\kappa}) > X^o(\bar{\theta})$. Hence, $E\{X^d(\theta_i;\underline{\kappa})^2\} > E\{X^o(\theta_i)^2\}$. Continuity and monotonicity of the consumers' surplus immediately yield the existence of a critical value κ^c with $0 < \kappa^c < \underline{\kappa}$ such that for all $\kappa \geq \kappa^c$ the consumers' surplus is highest under full disclosure.

• As shown for example in Shapiro 1986, $E\{W^d(\theta_i;\kappa)\} > E\{W^o(\theta_i)\}$ for $\kappa = 0$. The expected welfare under full disclosure depends as follows on the spillover κ:

$$\begin{aligned} \frac{\partial E\{W^d(\theta_i;\kappa)\}}{\partial\kappa} &= pX^d(\underline{\theta};\kappa)\frac{\partial X^d(\underline{\theta};\kappa)}{\partial\kappa} + 2p\sum_{j\in\{i,n\}} x_j^d(\underline{\theta};\kappa)\frac{\partial x_j^d(\underline{\theta};\kappa)}{\partial\kappa} \\ &= \frac{p}{9}(\bar{\theta} - \underline{\theta})[(2A - \underline{\theta} - C(\underline{\theta},\kappa)) + 2(A + 4\underline{\theta} - 5C(\underline{\theta},\kappa))] \quad (29) \\ &= \frac{p}{9}(\bar{\theta} - \underline{\theta})[4A + 7\underline{\theta} - 11C(\underline{\theta},\kappa)] \end{aligned}$$

which is positive for all κ if $A > \frac{1}{4}(11\overline{\theta} - 7\underline{\theta})$. Consequently, if $A > \frac{1}{4}(11\overline{\theta} - 7\underline{\theta})$, $E\{W^d(\theta_i; \kappa)\} > E\{W^o(\theta_i)\}$ for all κ. This completes the proof.

Notes

I am especially grateful to Patrick Bolton, Eric van Damme, Sanjeev Goyal, and Dan Kovenock for valuable discussions. I also thank the editor Jay Pil Choi, an anonymous referee, Marco Haan, Paul Heidhues, Johan Lagerlöf, Luca Lambertini, Pedro Perreira, Fréderic Pivetta, Dolf Talman, and seminar participants at CORE (Louvain-la-Neuve), IUI (Stockholm), UCM (Madrid), UAB (Barcelona), MERIT (Maastricht), and the CESifo Venice Summer Institute 2004 for helpful comments. The hospitality and support of MPSE (Université de Toulouse 1, France) and of the Department of Economics at Princeton University are gratefully acknowledged. Naturally, any errors are mine.

1. See, for example, Lopatka and Page 1995; Prentice 1996; Shapiro 1996; Shapiro and Varian 1999. An anecdotical report on Microsoft's strategies is presented in Wallace and Erickson 1993.

2. Another case in which some effects of product announcements were discussed occurred in the period 1987–1991, when shareholders of Apple Computer brought securities-fraud charges against the company. Apple's preannouncement of its Lisa computer and Twiggy disk drive and subsequent extensive delay in delivery were alleged to violate Section 10(b) and Rule 10b-5 of the 1934 U.S. Securities Exchange Act (e.g., see Prentice and Langmore 1994). The case was settled out of court.

3. Also, Bayus, Jain, and Rao 2001 discusses a signaling model of preannouncements. In contrast to Anton and Yao (2003, 2004) and this chapter, the innovative firm attempts to deter entry by sending costly messages, where the signal cost is exogenous.

4. For instance, Kühn and Vives 1995, Raith 1996, and Vives 1999 contain surveys. Jin 1995 studies the effects of precommitment to announcements about product quality.

5. For surveys of discretionary disclosure of proprietary information in the accounting literature, see for example Dye 2001 and Verrecchia 2001.

6. Alternatively, the profit result for firm n follows immediately from the fact that $\Pi_n^d(0) > \Pi_n^o$ for $\kappa = 0$, and $d\Pi_n^d(\kappa)/d\kappa > 0$ for all κ.

References

Anton, J. J., and D. A. Yao. 2003. "Patents, Invalidity, and the Strategic Transmission of Enabling Information." *Journal of Economics and Management Strategy* 12:151–178.

Anton, J. J., and D. A. Yao. 2004. "Little Patents and Big Secrets: Managing Intellectual Property." *RAND Journal of Economics* 35:1–22.

D'Aspremont, C., and A. Jacquemin. 1988. "Cooperative and Noncooperative R&D in Duopoly with Spillovers." *American Economic Review* 78:1133–1142.

Bayus, B. L., S. Jain, and A. G. Rao. 2001. "Truth or Consequences: An Analysis of Vaporware and New Product Announcements." *Journal of Marketing Research* 38:3–13.

Choi, J. P., E. G. Kristiansen, and J. Nahm. 2004. "Vaporware." Photocopy.

Dranove, D., and N. Gandal. 2003. "The DVD-vs.-DIVX Standard War: Empirical Evidence of Network Effects and Preannouncement Effects." *Journal of Economics and Management Strategy* 12:363–386.

Dye, R. A. 2001. "An Evaluation of 'Essays on Disclosure' and the Disclosure Literature in Accounting." *Journal of Accounting and Economics* 32:181–235.

Farrell, J., and G. Saloner. 1986. "Installed Base and Compatibility: Innovation, Product Preannouncements, and Predation." *American Economic Review* 76:940–955.

Fried, D. 1984. "Incentives for Information Production and Disclosure in a Duopolistic Environment." *Quarterly Journal of Economics* 99:367–381.

Gal-Or, E. 1986. "Information Transmission—Cournot and Bertrand Equilibria." *Review of Economic Studies* 53:85–92.

Gerlach, H. A. 2004. "Announcement, Entry, and Preemption When Consumers Have Switching Costs." *RAND Journal of Economics* 35:184–202.

Gertner, R. H. 1998. "Disclosure and Unraveling." In P. Newman ed., *The New Palgrave Dictionary of Economics and the Law.* London: Macmillan Press.

Gill, D. 2004. "Strategic Disclosure of Intermediate Research Results." Discussion Paper Series No. 211. Oxford: Department of Economics, University of Oxford.

Grossman, S. J. 1981. "The Informational Role of Warranties and Private Disclosure about Product Quality." *Journal of Law and Economics* 24:461–483.

Haan, M. A. 2003. "Vaporware as a Means of Entry Deterrence." *Journal of Industrial Economics* 51:345–358.

Jansen, J. 2005. "Strategic Information Revelation in an R&D Race with Spillovers." Photocopy.

Jansen, J. 2006. "Share to Scare: Technology Sharing Incentives in the Absence of Intellectual Property Rights." Photocopy.

Jin, J. Y. 1995. "Innovation Announcement with Vertical Differentiation." *Journal of Economic Behavior and Organization* 28:399–408.

Kamien, M. I., E. Muller, and I. Zang. 1992. "Research Joint Ventures and R&D Cartels." *American Economic Review* 82:1293–1306.

Katsoulacos, Y., and D. Ulph. 1998. "Endogenous Spillovers and the Performance of Research Joint Ventures." *Journal of Industrial Economics* 46:333–357.

Kühn, K.-U. 2001. "Fighting Collusion by Regulating Communication between Firms." *Economic Policy* 32:167–204.

Kühn, K.-U., and X. Vives. 1995. "Information Exchanges among Firms and Their Impact on Competition." *European Commission paper.* Luxembourg: Office for Official Publications of the European Communities.

Levy, S. M. 1997. "Should 'Vaporware' Be an Antitrust Concern?" *Antitrust Bulletin* 42:33–49.

Lopatka, J. E., and W. H. Page. 1995. "Microsoft, Monopolization, and Externalities: Some Uses and Abuses of Economic Theory in Antitrust Decision Making." *Antitrust Bulletin* 40:317–370.

Milgrom, P. R. 1981. "Good News and Bad News: Representation Theorems and Applications." *Bell Journal of Economics* 12:380–391.

Milgrom, P. R., and J. Roberts. 1986. "Relying on the Information of Interested Parties." *RAND Journal of Economics* 17:18–32.

Okuno-Fujiwara, M., A. Postlewaite, and K. Suzumura. 1990. "Strategic Information Revelation." *Review of Economic Studies* 57:25–47.

Ordover, J. A., and R. D. Willig. 1981. "An Economic Definition of Predation: Pricing and Product Innovation." *Yale Law Journal* 91:8–53.

Prentice, R. 1996. "Vaporware: Imaginary High-Tech Products and Real Antitrust Liability in a Post-Chicago World." *Ohio State Law Journal* 57:1163–1262.

Prentice, R. A., and J. H. Langmore. 1994. "Beware of Vaporware: Product Hype and the Securities Fraud Liability of High-Tech Companies." *Harvard Journal of Law and Technology* 8:1–74.

Raith, M. 1996. "A General Model of Information Sharing in Oligopoly." *Journal of Economic Theory* 71:260–288.

Scotchmer, S. 1991. "Standing on the Shoulder of Giants: Cumulative Research and Patent Law." *Journal of Economic Perspectives* 5:29–41.

Shapiro, C. 1986. "Exchange of Cost Information in Oligopoly." *Review of Economic Studies* 53:433–446.

Shapiro, C. 1996. "Antitrust in Network Industries." Address by Carl Shapiro, U.S. Department of Justice Antitrust Division, January 25.

Shapiro, C., and H. R. Varian. 1999. *Information Rules: A Strategic Guide to the Network Economy.* Boston: Harvard Business School Press.

United States v. Microsoft Corp. 1994–1995. Civil Action No. 94-1564.

Verrecchia, R. E. 2001. "Essays on Disclosure." *Journal of Accounting and Economics* 32:97–180.

Vives, X. 1999. *Oligopoly Pricing: Old Ideas and New Tools.* Cambridge, MA: MIT Press.

Wallace, J., and J. Erickson. 1993. "Hard Drive: Bill Gates and the Making of the Microsoft Empire." New York: Harper Business.

10 Ownership Structure of Cable Networks and Competition in Local Access

Duarte Brito and
Pedro Pereira

10.1 Introduction

A cable television network can be upgraded to offer telecommunications services and can therefore compete with a public switched telephone network. In this chapter, we discuss the role of cable television networks and their ownership structure in promoting competition in local access. Our objective is twofold. First, we investigate how the dual ownership of a telephone and a cable television network, compared with separate ownership, affects incentives to invest in upgrading the cable network.[1] We measure the incentives to upgrade the cable network by the resulting incremental profit and show, with a simple model, that there is no definite relationship between the incentives to upgrade and the ownership structure of the networks. Second, we argue that separate ownership of the two networks is important to promote competition in local access. We use our model to compare the equilibrium prices under the two ownership structures. Even if a firm that owns both networks upgrades its cable network, it should behave like a multiproduct monopolist, and it is unlikely that any meaningful competition between the two networks will emerge. Only an independently owned cable television firm will use its upgraded cable network to compete with the telecommunications incumbent.

To our knowledge, competition between cable television networks and public switched telephone networks has not been explicitly addressed in the literature. However, our chapter relates to the literature on the relative advantages of the various forms of entry in the telecommunications industry and to the literature on intermodal competition. Regarding the first literature strand, Faulhaber (2003) analyzes regulatory initiatives to open segments of the telecommunications market to competition and mentions cable networks as a viable alternative to the incumbents' local-access telecommunications network. Bourreau and Dogan (2004, 2005), using a dynamic model of technology adoption, study the incentives of an entrant to lease the incumbent's local loops and compete "service-based," or to build a more efficient infrastructure and compete "facility-based." They show that the incumbent can delay the entrant's adoption of new superior technology, by setting low rental prices for the local loops. Dessein (2004) considers competition between two established horizontally differentiated networks and shows how customer heterogeneity affects nonlinear pricing strategies. Regarding intermodal competition, Loomis and Swann (2005) develop and estimate a model of local competition. They find that there is substantial competition between incumbents and entrants using wireless and high-speed services.[2] Finally, note that although we use a model of a multiproduct monopolist, our setting has several nonstandard features, such as scope and coordination economies.

The remainder of the chapter is organized as follows. Section 10.2 presents the policy debate related to the ownership structure of cable networks. Section 10.3 presents the model and section 10.4 characterizes the equilibria. The analysis is conducted in section 10.5 and section 10.6 concludes. All proofs are in the appendix.

10.2 Policy Debate

In this section we provide an overview of the policy debates surrounding the ownership structure of cable television networks. First, we discuss the importance of facilities-based entry in promoting competition in local access. Second, we discuss the importance of cable television networks in promoting facilities-based entry. Third, we discuss the impact of the ownership structure on the incentives to upgrade the cable television network and on competition in local access.

10.2.1 Facilities-Based Entry and Competition in Local Access

In the United States, the Telecommunications Act of 1996 promoted the entry of new firms into the local-access market by two means in addition to own-facilities entry: the resale of the incumbent's services, and the unbundling of the incumbent's local loop.[3] This was a new and promising paradigm. The removal of high entry barriers to the local-access market, associated with scale, density, and scope economies, would give entrants time to develop their customer base and to build their own infrastructures.[4] The European Union experienced a similar process of liberalization.

Entry through resale and local-loop unbundling rely on the open-network principle, according to which all telecommunications firms should have access to the basic public telephone network, under the principles of nondiscrimination, transparency, and cost orientation.[5]

The open-network principle is part of the legislation of many countries—for example, the Access Directive 2002/19/EC. However, it is hard to enforce. The incumbent can resort to obstructionist tactics, which are hard to detect or prosecute. In addition, even if prosecution is feasible, due process takes time. In the 1974 antitrust suit against AT&T, the Antitrust Division of the U.S. Department of Justice asked for the divestiture of AT&T, on the basis of the argument that the sectorial regulator, the Federal Communications Commission, would not be able to stop AT&T from charging excessive prices and impeding its rivals' access to the local networks (Noll and Owen 1988).[6] In other words, the request for divestiture was based on the argument that the Federal Communications Commission would not be able to enforce the open-network provision. The process concluded in 1984 with the breakup of AT&T.[7]

Aside from leaving entrants dependent on the incumbent's infrastructures, the two alternative forms of entry constrain the entrants' marketing options. In particular, resale does not allow entrants much scope for product differentiation or innovation.

Either due to the incumbent's obstruction, or due to its intrinsic limitations, resale and the unbundling of the local loop have, so far, produced very modest results in both the United States and the European Union. As figure 10.1 illustrates, incumbents continue to dominate local access after six years of liberalization in the European Union. After all, it seems that these two forms of entry are no substitutes, even temporary, for facilities-based entry:

> In the end, unbundling is an unnatural act for a vertically integrated provider. . . . Realistically, a goal of perfect interconnection, or the complete absence of discriminatory treatment of affiliated and unaffiliated partners, is unattainable. The embedded local networks we have today were optimized for exclusive use by a monopoly carrier, not for wholesale supply of unbundled elements or other networks. (Woroch 2002, 709)[8]

A more benign interpretation of the current situation in the telecommunications markets is that entry takes more time than what was

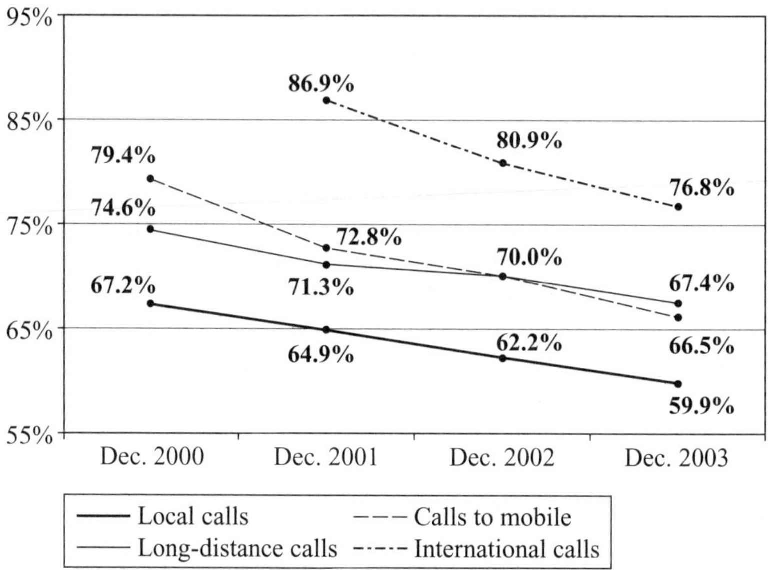

Figure 10.1
EU15 Incumbents' revenue market share on voice telephony
Source: European Telecoms Regulation and Markets 2004

initially anticipated. Geroski (1992) reports that for a wide range of industries, it takes entrants considerable time to accumulate a small market share. Given the complexity of the telecommunications industry, a slow entry process should come as no surprise.

10.2.2 Cable Networks and Competition in Local Access

Regarding the feasibility of facilities-based entry in promoting competition in local access, there is a clear dichotomy between the residential and the nonresidential markets.[9] Deploying a local-access network for nonresidential clients might not be a problem. Building a fixed wireless access for a large corporate client, or building a fiber-optic ring for a commercial business district, might be profitable investments.[10] However, the situation for most residential clients is different. Unless the network is used to provide other services, it might not be profitable to build. In this respect cable television networks can play an important role.

Among the various alternatives that provide local access to consumers, cable television networks have three special characteristics that allow them to compete in the short run with the public switched tele-

Table 10.1
Fixed-access lines and homes passed in the EU per 100 inhabitants

	Fixed access	Homes passed
Austria	*48.8*	*53*
Belgium	*50.1*	*100*
Denmark	*71.5*	*70*
Finland	*67.0*	*63*
France	*67.6*	*32*
Germany	*63.5*	*86*
Ireland	*48.5*	*50*
Luxembourg	*78.6*	*100*
Netherlands	*64.7*	*94*
Portugal	*43.5*	*47*
Sweden	*75.5*	*65*
United Kingdom	*58.9*	*51*

Source: OECD 2003.

phone network. The first characteristic is that they can be upgraded to offer telecommunications services. Cable television networks were originally designed to broadcast information—that is, to deliver a one-way signal.[11] However, they can be upgraded because fiber optics increases bandwidth, digitalization increases the quality and the range of services, bidirectional amplifiers allow carriage of a return signal, and switches enable circuit switching. An upgraded cable television network can offer a complete range of interactive services, such as fixed telephony, broadband access to the Internet through cable modem, and video on demand. The second special characteristic of cable networks is that upgrading an existing network to carry a return signal is faster and cheaper than deploying a new telecommunications network. Woroch 1997 puts the cost per household of upgrading the cable telephony in the range of $400–$900 and estimates a payback period of six years. See Hatfield Associates 1997 for other estimates.[12] The third special characteristic of cable networks, illustrated in table 10.1, is that in many countries, the cable infrastructure already deployed offers good coverage.[13]

10.2.2.1 The Case of the United Kingdom The example of the United Kingdom reveals the importance of cable television networks in promoting competition in local access. After seven years of legal duopoly, 1984–1991, Mercury, the rival of British Telecom, gained a 1 percent market share of voice services. Mercury resold lucrative services but did not invest in access lines. In 1991, with the publication of the 1990 Telecommunications Policy Review—the Duopoly Review—cable television firms were allowed to offer fixed telephony services.[14] Cable telephony rapidly overtook subscription television. Now there are more cable telephone subscribers than television subscribers. In the third quarter of 2003, NTL Home had 2,809,500 customers, of which 864,600 were broadband customers, 1,294,800 were digital television customers, 2,489,800 were telephony customers, and 55,100—that is, 1.96 percent—took all three services. In the same period, Telewest had 329,336 broadband customers, 911,191 digital television customers, and 1,588,358 telephony customers. In 1992, British Telecom had a revenue market share of 99.2 percent for UK geographic calls. In the second quarter of 2003, NTL and Telewest had jointly, a revenue market share of 13.4 percent for UK geographic calls and of 19.7 percent for residential calls, whereas British Telecom had 65.7 and 70.6 percent, respectively.[15] These numbers are remarkable since cable networks only pass around half of the households in the United Kingdom.

10.2.2.2 Other Cases The United States provides a less compelling case for the importance of cable television networks in promoting competition in local access.[16] In 2003, cable television firms supplied 2.5 million residential telephony lines, whereas there were 73.783 million basic cable customers and 102.900 million passed homes.[17] Comcast Cable Communications and Cox Communications were the largest providers with 63 and 31 percent market shares of cable telephony, respectively. In Germany, none of the firms that bought parts of Deutsche Telekom's cable television network have shown any interest in offering telephony services so far.[18]

Other alternative technologies give local access to consumers, like the wireless local loop,[19] or the combination of power-line communications[20] and voice over Internet protocol.[21] However, these alternatives are only starting to be deployed.

10.2.3 Ownership Structure, Incentives to Invest, and Competition

The U.S. Telecommunications Act of 1996 recognized the importance of the cable television networks for providing an alternative infrastructure to the incumbent's local-access network. It also recognized a potential conflict of interest. Section 302 of the 1996 Act imposes structural separation between firms that own local telecommunications networks and firms that own cable television networks.[22]

The legislation of the European Community, reflecting the political equilibrium between numerous parties, is ambiguous. Article 2 of Cable Directive 95/51/EC required firms that simultaneously offer telecommunications and cable television networks to put in place accounting separation between the two activities. However, it indicated a preference for the full structural separation of firms offering telecommunications and cable television networks.[23] In 1998, after the review of the measures taken in response to Directive 95/51/EC, the Commission concluded that accounting separation was insufficient to increase competition in the industry. In Communication 98/C 71/04, the Commission recommended that telecommunications and cable television activities should be legally separate, but added that the structural separation was preferable. Article 8 of Directive 2002/77/CE, however, imposed only legal separation.[24] Several European countries followed a more assertive approach, either forbidding ownership by the telecommunications incumbent of cable television networks or forcing the telecommunications incumbent to divest, totally or partially, its participation in the ownership of cable television networks.[25]

The basis for the Commission's preference for structural separation is the argument that a firm that owns both networks has no incentive to upgrade the cable network. A cable network endowed with bidirectionality can compete with the telephone network, in relation to both telephony services and broadband access to the Internet. It is unlikely that investment in the cable network will generate additional net revenues because it will merely redirect revenues. An independently owned cable television firm does not have the same conflict of interest. Telecommunications services attract new clients. Paragraph 10 of the preamble to Directive 99/64/EC states that

> where Member States have granted a special or exclusive right to build and operate cable TV networks, to a telecommunications organization in the same geographic area where it is dominant on the market for services using telecommunications infrastructure, that telecommunications organization has no incentive to upgrade both its public narrowband telecommunications network and its broadband cable TV network to an integrated broadband communications network ("full-service network") capable of delivering voice, data and images at high bandwidth. In other words, such an organization is placed in a situation whereby it has a conflict of interests, because any substantial improvement in either its telecommunications network or its cable TV network may

> lead to a loss of business for the other network. It would be desirable in those circumstances to separate the ownership of the two networks into two distinct companies since the joint ownership of the networks will lead those organizations to delay the emergence of new advanced communications services and will thus restrict technical progress at the expense of the users.

The OECD holds a similar position (OECD 1998).

Like the Commission, we favor structural separation. However, we disagree with the Commission's motivations for structural separation for two reasons. The first reason is that there is no simple relationship between ownership structure and incentives to upgrade a cable network. Dual ownership may or may not reduce incentives to upgrade the cable network. The self-cannibalization effect may reduce the incentives of a firm that owns both networks to upgrade the cable network. However, other factors can mitigate, or even overcome, the impact of this effect and give a firm that owns both networks more incentives to upgrade the cable network than an independently owned cable firm would have. These reasons include (1) coordination economies in the joint operation of the two networks, (2) differences in costs of upgrading the cable network between the two types of firms, (3) regulatory uncertainty, (4) regulatory arbitrage, and (5) attraction of new customers when networks are nonoverlapping. As seen in subsection 10.2.2, the example of Germany shows that structural separation is no guarantee that the cable network will be upgraded and used to provide telecommunications services.

The second and more important reason why we disagree with the Commission is that we think that the emphasis on the impact of the ownership structure on the incentives to upgrade the cable network is misplaced. We believe that the impact of the ownership structure in establishing competition in local-access is far more relevant. Even if a firm that owns both networks upgrades its cable network, it will have no incentive to make the cable network compete with the telecommunications network. Only an independently owned cable television firm will use the cable network to compete with the telecommunications firm.[26]

10.3 The Model

Since this is a policy-oriented discussion, we have developed a stylized model to make the analysis transparent. In section 10.6 we discuss several extensions.

There are two networks: (1) a public switched telephone network (PSTN), and (2) a cable network (CN). The PSTN belongs to the telecommunications company and provides fixed telephony services, denoted by f. The CN belongs to the cable company and provides subscription television services, denoted by t. If endowed with bidirectionality, the CN can also provide fixed telephony services bundled with subscription television, denoted by b. We index the products with subscript $j = f,t,b$. In subsection 10.6.2, we allow the cable company to offer fixed telephony services in a bundle as well as separately—that is, we allow the cable company to practice mixed bundling. There are two possible ownership structures for these companies: separate ownership and dual ownership, through a holding company. Denote by i the independently owned cable company and denote by h the cable company owned by the holding company. We index the two types of cable companies with superscript $k = i,h$.

The game has two stages, which unfold as follows under both ownership structures. In stage 1, the cable company decides whether to upgrade the CN. In stage 2, both companies choose prices simultaneously.

10.3.1 Firms

Upgrading the CN involves a fixed cost, $\varphi > 0$, independently of the ownership structure of the cable company. Marginal production costs are constant for the three products. Denote by c_f the marginal cost of telephony services. For subscription television and for the bundle, we distinguish between the marginal cost of an independently owned cable company and a cable company owned by the holding company. Denote by c_j^k, $j = t,b$, $k = i,h$, the marginal cost of product j, produced by cable company k.

We assume that there are coordination economies in the dual ownership of the two networks. Coordination economies stem from the cable company integrating its network with the telephone network, for example by sharing resources, if it is owned by the holding company.[27] This means that a cable company will have lower marginal costs if it is owned by the holding company than if it is owned independently. More specifically, $c_t^h := c_t^i - \delta_t$ and $c_b^h := c_b^i - \delta_b - \delta_t$. Parameter δ_t on $[0, c_t^i)$ captures coordination economies with respect to cable television services, and parameter δ_b on $[0, c_b^i - \delta_t)$ captures coordination economies with respect to the bundle.

We assume that there are economies of scope in the joint provision of subscription television services and fixed telephony services over the

Table 10.2
Unit costs under both ownership structures

	Fixed telephony	Cable	Bundle
Independent cable	—	c_t^i	$c_b^i = c_f + c_t^i - \gamma$
holding	c_f	$c_t^h = c_t^i - \delta_t$	$c_b^h = c_f + c_t^i - \gamma - \delta_t - \delta_b$

CN. Scope economies stem from joint marginal costs of offering multiple services over the same network.[28] This means that on the CN, the production cost of the bundle is no larger than the sum of the production costs of subscription television services and telephony services. More specifically, $c_b^i := c_f + c_t^i - \gamma$, where parameter γ on $[0, c_f + c_t^h - \delta_b)$ captures scope economies. Table 10.2 summarizes the cost structure.

We assume that the holding company behaves like a multiproduct monopolist and that firms do not engage in price discrimination—that is, firms charge all consumers the same price for identical services. The relevance of this assumption is discussed in note 34.

10.3.2 Consumers

There is a continuum of consumers, whose measure we normalize to 1. All consumers have access to both networks. Consumers come in two types, indexed by $\tau = 1,2$, which differ only in how they value the bundle. Denote by v_f and v_t the consumers' valuation for fixed telephony services and for subscription television services, respectively, and denote by $v_b^\tau := v_f + v_t + \theta^\tau$ the valuation of type τ consumers for the bundle, where θ^τ is a parameter on $\Re$ that measures the marginal valuation for the bundle. Type 1 consumers, a proportion β on (0, 1], have a high valuation for the bundle and type 2 consumers, a proportion $1 - \beta$, have a low valuation for the bundle—that is, $\theta^2 < \theta^1$. The high valuation for the bundle of type 1 consumers is due to the convenience of interacting with a single firm—signing one contract, paying one monthly bill, calling one maintenance service, and so on.[29] The low valuation of the bundle by type 2 consumers is due to some sort of consumer inertia that makes them reluctant to sign up for a new service. We assume that when consumers are indifferent as to whether or not to buy the bundle, they choose the former.

To close the model we make the following assumptions on the values of the parameters. Let $c_f < v_f$, $c_t^i < v_t$, and $\theta^2 < -(v_f - c_f) - (v_t - c_t^k) - \gamma < 0 \leq \theta^1$, $k = i,h$. These assumptions and the assumptions on the cost structure imply that $v_b^2 < c_b^h < c_b^i < v_b^1$.

We abstract from possible network effects since, typically, the PSTN has interconnection obligations.

10.4 Characterization of Equilibrium

In this section, we characterize the game's equilibria, which we solve by working backward for the two alternative ownership structures.

10.4.1 Stage 2: The Price Game

In this subsection, we characterize the equilibrium prices under the two ownership structures and for the cases in which the CN was, and was not, upgraded.

10.4.1.1 Nonupgraded CN Denote by p_j the price of product $j = f,t,b$. When the CN is not upgraded, the price equilibrium is simple and is the same under both ownership structures. The telecommunications and the cable companies are monopolists and charge their monopoly prices.[30] We present this observation in the next remark for future reference.

Remark 1 In equilibrium, if the CN was not upgraded, then the telecommunications and the cable companies charge, respectively: (i) $p_f = v_f$ and (ii) $p_t = v_t$.

To simplify notation, we define the monopoly profit margins for telephony and cable television as $\mu_f := v_f - c_f$ and $\mu_t^k := v_t - c_t^k$, $k = i,h$.

Using remark 1, the equilibrium profits of the telecommunications and the type k cable television companies when the CN was not upgraded are, respectively, μ_f and μ_t^k, $k = i,h$.

10.4.1.2 Upgraded CN with Dual Ownership The assumption that the holding company behaves like a multiproduct monopolist implies that it maximizes joint profits. Again the price equilibrium is simple.

Remark 2 In equilibrium, under dual ownership, if the CN was upgraded, then the holding company charges (i) $p_f = v_f$, (ii) $p_t = v_t$, and (iii) $p_b = v_b^1$.

The intuition of remark 2 is straightforward. The holding company faces a trade-off. It can sell the bundle to type 1 consumers through the cable company. Alternatively, it can sell telephony services and subscription television services separately through both networks to these consumers. Given that there are economies of scope in the supply of the bundle and that type 1 consumers have a higher valuation for the bundle, it is more profitable to sell the bundle than to sell both services separately: $v_b^1 - c_b^h = \mu_f + \mu_t^h + \theta^1 + \gamma + \delta_b > \mu_f + \mu_t^h$. The holding company is a monopolist with respect to the three services and sets prices accordingly. Monopoly prices allow the holding company not only to sell telephony and subscription television services to type 2 consumers, extracting all their surplus, but also to induce type 1 consumers to pay more for the bundle.

Using remark 2, the equilibrium profits of the holding company when the CN was upgraded are

$$\Pi^m = (1 - \beta)\,(\mu_f + \mu_t^h) + \beta(v_b^1 - c_b^h) - \varphi$$

10.4.1.3 Upgraded CN with Separate Ownership In this case, there exists no equilibrium in which the firms play pure pricing strategies with respect to all products. First, note that the cable company has a dominant strategy of charging the monopoly price for subscription television services, $p_t = v_t$.[31] At this price, the cable company sells subscription television services to type 2 consumers. Second, note that the cable company has no equilibrium pure strategy for the price of the bundle and the telecommunications company has no equilibrium pure strategy for the price of telephony services.[32] In subsection 10.6.3, we discuss how to modify the model so that all price equilibria are in pure strategies.

Next we construct the supports of the price distributions of telephony services and the bundle.[33] The telecommunications company may decide to sell only to consumers with a low valuation for the bundle, whose proportion is $1 - \beta$, at price v_f. Alternatively, the telecommunications company may charge a price lower than v_f, to try to undercut the cable company and also sell to consumers with a high valuation for the bundle. Let l_f be the lowest price the telecommunications company is willing to charge to sell to all consumers—that is,

$$(l_f - c_f) \equiv (1 - \beta)\mu_f$$

from which we obtain

$$l_f = c_f + (1 - \beta)\mu_f$$

Value l_f is decreasing in the proportion of consumers that have a high valuation for the bundle, β, and increasing in the monopoly profit margin for telephony services, μ_f. A larger β implies a smaller opportunity cost of charging a price lower than v_f to also sell to consumers with a high valuation for the bundle; a larger μ_f implies a larger opportunity cost of charging a price lower than v_f.

The cable company can sell subscription television services separately to consumers with a high valuation for the bundle, whose proportion is β, at price v_t. Alternatively, the cable company can sell the bundle to these consumers. Denote by l_b the lowest price the cable company is willing to charge for the bundle—that is,

$$\beta(l_b - c_b^i) \equiv \beta\mu_t^i$$

from which we obtain

$$l_b = c_b^i + \mu_t^i$$

Value l_b is decreasing in the cable company's monopoly profit margin for subscription television services, μ_t^i. A larger μ_t^i implies a larger opportunity cost of selling the bundle to consumers with a high valuation for the bundle.

The cable company sells the bundle to type 1 consumers, if

$$p_b \leq p_f + p_t + \theta^1 \tag{1}$$

As we argued at the beginning of this subsubsection, $p_t = v_t$. Replacing p_j by l_j, $j = f,b$, (1) becomes $l_b \leq l_f + v_t + \theta^1$. Thus, if the cable company charges $l_f + v_t + \theta^1$ for the bundle with probability 1, it sells the bundle to type 1 consumers and earns

$$\underline{\pi}_b^d = (l_f + \theta^1 + v_t - c_b^i)\beta = [(\theta^1 + \gamma) + (1 - \beta)\mu_f + \mu_t^i]\beta$$

Since

$$l_b - l_f - v_t - \theta^1 = -(\theta^1 + \gamma) - (1 - \beta)\mu_f < 0$$

this possibility is always feasible.

If the telecommunications company charges v_f with probability 1, it sells telephony services to type 2 consumers and earns

$$\underline{\pi}_f^d = (1 - \beta)\mu_f$$

Remark 3 In equilibrium, under separate ownership, if the *CN* was upgraded, then (i) the cable company charges for subscription television $p_t = v_t$ and (ii) the cable company plays a mixed strategy with respect to the price of the bundle whose support is $[l_f + \theta^1 + v_t, v_b^1]$ and the telecommunications company plays a mixed strategy with respect to the price of telephony services whose support is $[l_f, v_f]$.

The intuition of remark 3 is clear. The telecommunications and the cable companies compete for type 1 consumers. For the telecommunications company, charging a price lower than v_f entails both an expected marginal benefit, associated with more sales to type 1 consumers and a marginal loss, due to a smaller per-consumer profit on type 2 consumers. Similarly, for the cable company, charging a price lower than v_b^1 for the bundle also entails an expected marginal benefit, associated with more sales of the bundle to type 1 consumers and a marginal cost, associated with lower sales of subscription television services to type 1 consumers. Given that there are scope economies in the supply of the bundle and that type 1 consumers have a high marginal valuation for the bundle, the opportunity cost of charging lower prices for the bundle is smaller for the cable television company, than the opportunity cost of charging lower prices for telephony services for the telecommunications company: $l_b - l_f - \theta^1 - v_t < 0$. As a consequence, on average, the cable company succeeds in undercutting the telecommunications company and sells the bundle to type 1 consumers, earning $\underline{\pi}_b^d = (l_f + \theta^1 + v_t - c_b^i)\beta$. The telecommunications company charges $p_f = v_f$ with positive probability. Price $p_f = v_f$ can be interpreted as its regular price and lower prices can be viewed as discounts to attract type 1 consumers. In the appendix, we present the equilibrium cumulative price distributions for the bundle and telephony services.

When the CN was upgraded, using remark 3, the expected equilibrium profit of the telecommunications company is

$$\Pi_f^d = (1 - \beta)\mu_f$$

and the equilibrium profits of the independently owned cable company resulting from the sale of the bundle and of subscription television services are

$$\Pi_t^d + \Pi_b^d = (1 - \beta)\mu_t^i + [(\theta^1 + \gamma) + (1 - \beta)\mu_f + \mu_t^i]\beta - \varphi$$

10.4.2 Stage 1: The Investment Decision

In this subsection, we characterize the firms' equilibrium investment decisions under the two ownership structures.

The incremental profit of upgrading the CN for the holding company is

$$\Delta^{HC} := \Pi^m - \mu_f - \mu_t^h = \beta\theta^1 + \beta\gamma + \beta\delta_b - \varphi$$

The incremental benefit has three parts: first, the bundle-value effect, $\beta\theta^1$; second, the economies-of-scope effect, $\beta\gamma$; and third, the coordination-economies effect, $\beta\delta_b$.

The incremental profit of upgrading the CN for the independently owned cable company is

$$\Delta^{CC} := \Pi_t^d + \Pi_b^d - \mu_t^i = \beta\theta^1 + \beta\gamma + \beta(1-\beta)\mu_f - \varphi$$

The incremental benefit again has three parts: first, the bundle-value effect, $\beta\theta^1$; second, the economies-of-scope effect, $\beta\gamma$, and third, the business-stealing effect, $\beta(1-\beta)\mu_f$. Since $l_f = c_f + (1-\beta)\mu_f$ is the lowest price the telecommunications company is willing to charge, $l_f - c_f = (1-\beta)\mu_f$ is the minimum profit margin that it can earn with type 1 consumers. By introducing the bundle and successfully undercutting the telecommunications company, the cable company can steal this profit margin, $(1-\beta)\mu_f$, times the measure of type 1 consumers, β.[34]

10.5 Analysis

In this section, we first discuss the impact of the ownership structure on the firms' incentives to upgrade the CN, then turn to the impact of the ownership structure on competition.

10.5.1 Ownership Structure and Incentives to Upgrade the CN

We now show that the holding company may or may not have more incentives than the independently owned cable company to upgrade the CN. Note that $\Delta^{HC} - \Delta^{CC} = \beta[\delta_b - (1-\beta)\mu_f]$.

Proposition 1 (i) If either $\delta_b > \mu_f$, or $\delta_b < \mu_f$ and β is on $\left(1-\frac{\delta_b}{\mu_f}, 1\right)$, then the holding company has more incentives than the independently owned cable company to upgrade the *CN*. (ii) If $\delta_b < \mu_f$ and β is on $\left(0, 1-\frac{\delta_b}{\mu_f}\right)$, then the independently owned cable company has more incentives than the holding company to upgrade the *CN*.

As noted above, the investment in the upgrade of the cable network generates four effects. Two of the effects are common to both the holding company and the independently owned cable company. Both firms will benefit from consumers valuing the bundle and also from economies of scope. In addition, the holding company will benefit from coordination economies with respect to the bundle and the independently owned cable company will benefit from stealing business from the telecommunications company. The balance between the latter effects determines which type of firm has more incentives to upgrade. In addition, the net effect is potentially ambiguous.

There are three cases of interest. First, if all consumers have a high valuation for the bundle, $\beta = 1$, then the telecommunications company will have no captive consumers and will be prepared to price at marginal cost, $l_f = c_f$. This implies that the telecommunications company, on average, has zero profits, $\underline{\pi}_f^d = (1 - \beta)\mu_f = 0$, and therefore the business-stealing effect is null. Consequently, the holding company has more incentives than the independently owned cable company to upgrade the CN. Second, the profit margin for telephony services may be zero, $\mu_f = 0$, if either p_f is regulated, or the existence of an attractive outside option, such as mobile telephony, pushes v_f down. In either case, although the telecommunications company has captive consumers, the business-stealing effect is again null and the holding company has more incentives than the independently owned cable company to upgrade the CN. Third, in the absence of coordination economies for the bundle, $\delta_b = 0$, the independently owned cable company has more incentives than the dually owned cable company to upgrade the CN.[35]

10.5.2 Ownership Structure and Price Levels

In this subsection, we argue that dual ownership of the two networks leads to higher equilibrium prices than separate ownership.

Remark 4 If the *CN* is upgraded, then the prices of telephony services and the bundle are lower under separate ownership than under dual ownership.

Remark 4 follows trivially from remarks 2 and 3. The holding company should look out for the interests of both firms as a whole. This means behaving like a multiproduct monopolist and setting monopoly prices. Under separate ownership, the telecommunications company and the cable company compete for consumers that value the bundle. Consequently, the prices of telephony services and the bundle fall from their monopoly levels. Regardless of which ownership structure generates more incentives to upgrade the CN, separate ownership is important to promote competition in local access.

This perspective on the behavior of a holding company could be criticized on the grounds that perfect coordination among legally separate, dually owned firms may be hard to achieve. It is difficult to perfectly align the incentive schemes of the members of legally separated firms. Furthermore, price coordination among legally separated firms has to be done carefully, to avoid breaching competition law. However, casual empiricism suggests that some level of coordination among dually owned, legally separated firms is possible.[36] In addition, typically this level of coordination will be enough to ensure that these firms do not compete among themselves and will enable them to promote their common interests. Simple joint profit maximization may be an exaggeration, but assuming independent profit maximization by the telecommunications and cable firms would be even more inappropriate. Joint profit maximization is a simple way of capturing the idea that some coordination within the holding company is possible.

10.6 Concluding Remarks

In this chapter we discussed the role of cable television networks and their ownership structure in promoting competition in the local-access market. We showed that there is no simple relationship between the ownership structure and the incentives to upgrade the cable television network. We also argued that separate ownership of the two networks is important to promote competition in local access. To make the results transparent, we conducted the analysis with a very simple model. In the remainder of this section, we discuss several generalizations of the model in section 10.3.

10.6.1 Other Reasons

In this subsection, we discuss four additional reasons that might increase or decrease the firms' incentives to upgrade the CN.

First, if the holding company has easier access to financing than the independently owned cable company, perhaps because it is a larger firm, or because it has been in the market longer, it could bear a lower cost for upgrading the CN. In this case, the holding company could have, trivially, a larger incentive to upgrade the CN than the independently owned cable company.

Second, the holding company owns two potentially competing local-access networks. This may put the holding company under pressure from the sectorial regulator or the legislature to sell one of the networks, possibly the cable network. If the risk that the holding company is forced to sell the cable network increases significantly once the CN is upgraded, then the holding company has no incentive to upgrade the CN, independently of other technological or strategic considerations.

Third, there is typically some regulatory asymmetry between the PSTN and the CN. The PSTN is subject to the open-network provision, whereas the CN is not. For instance, broadband access to the Internet through DSL is regulated, whereas broadband access to the Internet through cable modem is not.[37] Evading regulatory obligations could be a motive for the holding company to upgrade the cable network.

Fourth, there is evidence of consumer substitution from fixed to mobile telephony (Barros and Cadima 2000; Rodini, Ward, and Woroch 2003). In several countries, like Denmark, Portugal, and Sweden, the penetration rate of fixed telephony has been falling, while the penetration rate of mobile telephony continues to rise. This implies that, potentially, there is a segment of consumers that do not buy telephony services from the incumbent telecommunications company, but buy subscription television services and might buy the bundle. The cable company will be a monopolist with respect to these consumers, independently of the ownership structure. However, in the absence of price discrimination, these consumers are more valuable to the holding company than to an independently owned cable company. The reason is that the holding company will be able to charge them monopoly prices, while the cable company has to take into account the fact that it faces competition with respect to type 1 consumers.

10.6.2 Mixed Bundling

Next, we discuss the implications of allowing the independently owned cable company to offer telephony services, both in a bundle and separately—that is, to practice mixed bundling. We show that if mixed bundling is allowed, it is still true that either of the two ownership structures can generate the largest incentives to invest in upgrading the CN.

Assume that consumers view telephony services offered through the PSTN and CN as perfect substitutes. Denote by $c_b^i + \gamma_{mb}$ the unit cost of producing subscription television and telephony services separately on the CN, where γ_{mb} on $(0, \gamma)$ is a parameter that measures the diseconomies of producing these two services separately instead of in a bundle. We assume that the cost of producing the bundle is lower than the cost of producing the two services separately through the cable network and that the latter is lower than the cost of producing the two services through different networks: $c_b^i < c_b^i + \gamma_{mb} < c_b^i + \gamma = c_f + c_t^i$. Producing subscription television and telephony services separately on the same network involves economies of scope, but of smaller magnitude than those of producing both services in a bundle. This is a reasonable assumption given that, if both services are produced separately, there will be a duplication of some of the activities required to produce the services.[38] Denote by p_ϕ the price of fixed telephony services provided through the CN.

The next remark describes the new price equilibrium.

Remark 5 In equilibrium, under separate ownership, if the *CN* was upgraded and there is mixed bundling, then the telecommunications and the cable companies charge (i) $p_f = c_f$, (ii) $p_t = v_t$, (iii) $p_b = c_f + v_t + \theta^1$, and (iv) $p_\phi = c_f - \varepsilon$, with $\varepsilon \to 0^+$.

Using remark 5, the equilibrium profits of the independently owned cable company, if the CN was upgraded and there is mixed bundling, are

$$\Pi_{mb}^d = \mu_t^i + \gamma + \beta\theta^1 - (1 - \beta)\gamma_{mb} - \varphi$$

Practicing mixed bundling is more profitable for the independently owned cable company than selling telephony services only in the bundle if, and only if, the profits obtained from selling fixed telephony separately above marginal cost to type 2 consumers is larger than the business-stealing effect: $(1 - \beta)(\gamma - \gamma_{mb}) > (1 - \beta)\mu_f\beta$.

With mixed bundling, the incremental profit of upgrading the CN for the independently owned cable company is

$$\Delta^{CC} = \beta\theta^1 + \gamma - (1 - \beta)\gamma_{mb} - \varphi$$

The expression of the incremental benefit differs in three respects relative to the expression of subsection 10.4.2. First, the business-stealing effect, $\beta(1 - \beta)\mu_f$, vanishes because the telecommunications company now prices at marginal cost. Second, all type 2 consumers are supplied through the same network, which allows the extension to all consumers of the economies-of-scope effect, γ. Third, type 2 consumers that purchase subscription television and telephony services separately through the CN are supplied at a higher cost than type 1 consumers, $(1 - \beta)\gamma_{mb}$.

Recalling the value Δ^{HC} from subsection 10.4.2, the difference in the incentives to upgrade the CN between the holding company and the independently owned cable company is

$$\Delta^{HC} - \Delta^{CC} = \beta\delta_b - (1 - \beta)(\gamma - \gamma_{mb})$$

The expression above can be positive or negative, depending on the relative strength of the coordination-economies effect, $\beta\delta_b$, which benefits the holding company, and the economies-of-scope effect, $(1 - \beta)(\gamma - \gamma_{mb})$, which benefits the independently owned cable company when selling telephony services separately to type 2 consumers. This implies that if mixed bundling is allowed, it is still true that either of the two ownership structures can generate the largest incentives to invest in upgrading the CN.

Finally, when mixed bundling is less profitable than only selling telephony services in the bundle, there is a prisoner's-dilemma type of commitment problem. The independently owned cable company would like to commit itself not to sell telephony services separately, because this ultimately decreases its profits. However, it may not be able to credibly commit to do so. If the telecommunications company sets a price above marginal cost, it is profitable for the cable company to undercut it and sell fixed telephony to type 2 consumers. Circumstances like product differentiation or the existence of residential and nonresidential consumer segments, which we ignored, would give additional incentives to the independently owned cable company to offer cable telephony outside the bundle.

10.6.3 Heterogeneous Type 1 Consumers

Next we discuss the implications of allowing type 1 consumers to be heterogeneous with respect to their valuation of the bundle, θ^1. The main consequence of this modification is that all price equilibria are in pure strategies. Consider the model of section 10.3, except that the valuation of the bundle of type 1 consumers, θ^1, is uniformly distributed on $[0, \Theta]$, with $0 < \Theta < +\infty$.

Now the cable company faces a downward sloping demand curve for the bundle. As a consequence, in remark 2 the cable company charges a price lower than the consumers' larger valuation of the bundle, $v_f + v_t + \Theta$, which implies that consumer surplus will be positive. Besides, when the CN is upgraded under separate ownership the price equilibrium is in pure strategies. Otherwise, this chapter's results continue to hold qualitatively. In particular, a version of proposition 1 and remark 4 continue to hold. Note, however, that the model with heterogeneous type 1 consumers involves a considerable expository cost, because the price-best response functions are kinked. See Brito and Pereira 2006 for the details.

Appendix

In the appendix we prove the results in the main text. The proofs of remarks 1, 2, 4, and 5 are obvious, and therefore omitted.

Remark 3 Denote by $G_i(.)$ the cumulative distribution of the prices charged for product *i*. Ignoring ties, the expected profit of the telecommunications company when it charges $p_f \leq v_f$ *is*

$$\pi_f^d(p) = (p - c_f)\{1 - \beta + \beta[1 - G_b(p + p_t + \theta^1)]\}$$

Similarly, the expected profit of the cable company with respect to the bundle when it charges $p_b \leq v_b^1$ is

$$\pi_b^d(p) = (p - c_b^i)\beta[1 - G_f(p - p_t - \theta^1)]$$

Equating for the two firms the expressions of the expected profits, $\pi_j^d(.)$, to the expressions of the equilibrium expected profits, $\underline{\pi}_j^d$, $j = f,b$, the equilibrium price distributions can be characterized as follows:

$$G_b(p)\begin{cases} 0 & \text{if } p < l_f + \theta^1 + v_t \\ 1 - \left(\dfrac{1-\beta}{\beta}\right)\left(\dfrac{v_b^1 - p}{p - v_t - \theta^1 - c_f}\right) & \text{if } l_f + \theta^1 + v_t \leq p < v_b^1 \\ 1 & \text{if } v_b^1 \leq p \end{cases}$$

$$G_f(p)\begin{cases} 0 & \text{if } p < l_f \\ 1 - \dfrac{(\theta^1 + \gamma) + (1-\beta)\mu_f + \mu_t^i}{p + v_t + \theta^1 - c_b^i} & \text{if } l_f \leq p < v_f \\ 1 & \text{if } v_f \leq p \end{cases}$$

Proposition 1 (i) A given ownership structure provides more incentives than the alternative ownership structure, if and only if it generates an incremental profit for upgrading the *CN* no smaller than the alternative ownership structure. Therefore, the holding company has more incentives than the independently owned cable company to upgrade the *CN* if and only if $\Delta^{HC} - \Delta^{CC} = \beta[\beta_b - (1 - \beta)\mu_f] \geq 0$. Because $0 < \beta \leq 1$, $\Delta^{HC} - \Delta^{CC} \geq 0 \Leftrightarrow \delta_b \geq (1 - \beta)\mu_f$.

Note that $\delta_b \geq \mu_f$ implies that $\delta_b \geq (1-\beta)\mu_f$. Also, if β is on $\left(1-\frac{\delta_b}{\mu_f}, 1\right)$, then $(1-\beta)\mu_f$ is on $(0, \delta_b]$, meaning that $(1-\beta)\mu_f \leq \delta_b$. (ii) Equally obvious.

Notes

We thank F. Dominguez, E. Sheehan, two anonymous referees, and Jay Pil Choi, the editor, for useful comments. The paper that provided the basis for this chapter was presented at the CES-IFO 2004 Venice Summer Institute "Recent Developments in Antitrust Analysis" and ITS 2004 Berlin. The opinions expressed in the chapter reflect only the authors' views and in no way bind the institutions to which they are affiliated.

1. Separate ownership means that there is no meaningful overlap between the shareholders of the individual companies. Dual ownership means that the companies are largely held by the same shareholders.

2. For a discussion of optimal pricing with intermodal competition, see Braeutigam 1979.

3. Local-access is the origin and termination of calls on local networks. In own-facilities entry, new firms build their own local loop, switches, and so on. This form of entry makes new firms independent of the incumbent's network, but requires time and large investments. In resale entry, new firms buy the incumbent's services at a lower price than that charged by the incumbent to its clients and the new firms resell these services to their own clients. This form of entry is fast and cheap. However, the arbitrage between the wholesale and the retail prices is the only profit opportunity. Entry through local-loop unbundling is a hybrid between the first and second forms of entry. New firms lease unbundled elements of the incumbent's local loop, and combine them with their own infrastructure.

4. The basic local telephone infrastructure consists of poles, conduits, and underground plants. To a large extent, this infrastructure is invariant to the number of circuits provided. In addition, the cost of this infrastructure constitutes more than a third of the total cost of the local basic telephone network. High-capacity transport is also subject to significant economies of scale. A denser and more even distribution of customers allows the construction of a more efficient transport network.

5. The existence of common costs makes the implementation of cost orientation hard. The legal battles in the United States, around the Telpak tariff in the 1960s, the ENFIA tariff in the 1970s, and the Telecommunications Act in the 1990s, illustrate these difficulties (Temin 2000). See Hausman 2003 for a discussion of cost orientation.

6. The suit alleged monopolization of the long-distance, local, and equipment markets.

7. Aside from an enforceability problem, the open-network provision also seems to have a legitimacy problem. In a recent judgment regarding Verizon v. Trinko (540 U. S. (2004)), the U.S. Supreme Court stated the following: "The 1996 Act is in an important respect much more ambitious than the antitrust laws. It attempts to eliminate the monopolies enjoyed by the inheritors of AT&T's local franchises. . . . Section 2 of the Sherman Act, by contrast, seeks merely to prevent unlawful monopolization. It would be a serious mistake to conflate the two goals. The Sherman Act is indeed the 'Magna Carta of free enterprise', . . . but it does not give judges carte blanche to insist that a monopolist

alter its way of doing business whenever some other approach might yield greater competition."

8. Crandall (2002) reports evidence that the building of their infrastructure was fundamental for the success of the firms that entered into the local-access market following the passage of the Telecommunications Act. Faulhaber (2003) predicts the failure of the current local-loop unbundling model.

9. Nonresidential and residential customers have different demand characteristics. Businesses often require high-capacity connections for data or the provision of private branch exchange trunks.

10. The fiber ring technology exhibits high fixed costs and negligible marginal costs. The high fixed costs limit the applicability of the technology to large-business customers or to areas with extremely high population densities, like multiunit residential buildings in urban areas. On the optimal pricing strategies for utilities with large customers who have attractive service options, see Einhorn 1987.

11. Cable television originated in the United States in 1948 to enhance poor reception of over-the-air television signals in mountainous or geographically remote areas. Community antennas were built on high points, and homes were connected to the antenna towers to receive the broadcast signals.

12. The cost of enabling the supply of telephony services varies depending on the state of the existing cable network. The traditional tree-and-branch architecture of cable networks is incompatible with telephony because cascading chains of amplifiers in the distribution network make two-way communication impossible. Such networks therefore have to be extensively overhauled. A recently built cable network may have replaced the coaxial cable in portions of the network with fiber optics in order to enhance cable quality, improve reliability, and increase capacity. In addition, it may have adopted a star-and-ring architecture, which is more conducive to two-way communications. A cable network built with a hybrid fiber coaxial cable network architecture, capable of supporting two-way communication, would need only minor additional upgrades. In the United Kingdom, firms followed a different technological approach by deploying networks in which a separate coaxial cable and copper wire pair were intertwined to form a single cable.

13. "Homes passed" is the expression used by the industry to designate homes covered by a network.

14. Cable operators were allowed to offer their own telephony services instead of merely reselling those of British Telecom or Mercury. In particular, they were allowed to deploy their own switches and to interconnect freely with other operators of adjacent cable franchises.

15. The data on NTL is from the firm's quarterly report, the data on Telewest is from ECCA's website, and the data on market shares is from OFCOM's "Market Information."

16. See Chandler, Kelley, and Nugent 2002 for a discussion of the inhibiting factors.

17. According to the National Cable & Telecommunications Association.

18. The German market has several idiosyncrasies. First, the sales pitch of digitalization has been premium programing and increased channel choice. However, analog, free-to-air, multichannel television, a substitute for cable television, is ubiquitous. This hinders the penetration of cable television. Second, the cable network is organized into four tiers,

which do not necessarily belong to the same party, even in a given geographic area. This reduces the firms' incentives to invest in upgrading their cable networks for telephony.

19. The wireless local loop is a set of technologies that connect subscribers to the public switched telephone network using radio signals as a substitute for copper for all or part of the connection between the subscriber and the switch. It includes cordless access systems, proprietary fixed radio access, and fixed cellular systems.

20. The digital powerline uses the existing electricity infrastructure to transmit low-frequency signals at 50 to 60 Hz and higher-frequency signals above 1 MHz. The lower-frequency signals carry power, while the higher-frequency signals can transmit data at a rate of 1 Mbps. A conditioning unit filters those separate signals, sending electricity to the outlets in the home and data signals to a service unit. The service unit provides multiple channels for data, voice, and so on. Base-station servers at local electricity substations connect to the Internet via fiber or broadband coaxial cable. The system is similar to a neighborhood local-area network.

21. Circuit-switched telephone networks establish a dedicated circuit between two end points for the duration of a call to avoid latency—that is, delays—in the transmission of data. However, latency control comes at the expense of wasted bandwidth. Although there are many periods during a telephone conversation where no data is transferred, a full 64-Kbps stream, on digital networks, is still required for the entire call. In packet-switched networks, instead of dedicated connections, network resources are shared and used only when data is sent or received in quick bursts. Using compression algorithms, telephone calls can be delivered at rates as low as 8 Kbps in a packet format, offering even more bandwidth efficiency.

22. Legal separation means that firms are different legal entities according to the principles of corporate law. Structural separation means that firms are legally separate, and in addition there is no meaningful cross-ownership between them.

23. Accounting separation of the activities of a dominant firm makes finance fluxes more transparent and helps to detect and avoid abusive practices by the dominant firm regarding price setting, for example. Legal separation of firms makes assets and costs more transparent. However, accounting and legal separation do not solve the fundamental conflict of interest. Two legally separate firms may be controlled by a third firm, with majority positions in both firms. The third firm will effectively control the assets of the other two firms.

24. Preambles cannot be relied on as such. However, they provide useful insights into the rationale of the directives. Paragraph 11 of the preamble to Directive 99/64/EC, which was amended by Directive 2002/77/CE, states that "in order to achieve this transparency, it is necessary that the networks be operated by separate legal entities which may, however, in principle be jointly owned. The requirement of legal separation would therefore be complied with if the cable TV operations of a telecommunications organization were transferred to a fully owned subsidiary of the telecommunications organization."

25. In the UK, Belgium, and Spain, the dominant firm offering telecommunications services was prohibited from offering cable television services. Holland took several measures to limit the dual ownership of the telecommunications and cable television networks by the telecommunications incumbent and to structurally separate the two activities. In 1997, KPN, the Dutch incumbent, was forced by the government to reduce its participation in the cable firm Casema from 100 to 20 percent. In the remaining coun-

tries, the pressure exerted by the sectorial regulators or antitrust authorities, combined with some financial difficulties, has led incumbents to divest their participation in firms that own cable networks. In December 1999, Swisscom, Siemens Schweiz, and Veba sold group Cablecom to NTL. In July 2002, following pressure from the European Commission, Deutsche Telekom divided its cable television firm, Kabel Deutschland, into nine regional firms that it has been progressively selling (Press Note of the Commission: IP/00637). In May 2002, the merger of Telia and Sonera—the telecommunications incumbents of Sweden and Finland, respectively—was approved by the Commission, subject to the condition, among other things, that Telia divest its cable television network.

26. Structural separation for the purpose of promoting competition in local access raises legitimacy problems similar to those discussed in note 7, regarding the open-network principle.

27. There is a duplication of resources between the two networks—for example, the local loops, switches, or backbone networks. If such resources are managed jointly, they can be used more efficiently. Besides, if both networks are digitalized, then—bandwidth considerations aside—either network can carry the two types of traffic. This allows the optimization of the traffic flow over the two networks.

28. According to Cluny 1996, for a multiple-services operator, about 10 percent of its operating costs are incremental to subscription television, 20 percent involve telephony, and 70 percent or more are nonattributable common costs. See also Woroch 1997 for a description of the technological advances that allow scope economies between video and voice services.

29. Cooper 2003 provides evidence that following the introduction of new advanced services, cable television firms were able to raise their fees by more than the increase in capital expenditures required to make these services available.

30. We assumed that a holding company that owns a nonupgraded network does not market the bundle for two reasons. First, it seems unlikely that two legally separated firms could offer consumers the benefits described above—that is, a unique contract, assistance, and payment. Second, by definition, there are no scope economies if each service is provided over a different network. Hence, bundling the services or selling them separately is exactly the same as far as consumer valuation and marginal costs are concerned.

31. Given that there are economies of scope and type 1 consumers value the bundle, the cable company would like to induce these consumers to buy the bundle. Thus, the cable company would never charge less than $p_b - p_f - \theta^1$ for subscription television services. This means that it will only sell subscription television services to type 2 consumers. However, since the cable company has monopoly power over these consumers, it charges the highest possible price of v_t.

32. Any price for telephony services, p_f, on $[c_f, \mathrm{v}_f]$ can be undercut by the cable company by setting $p_b = \mathrm{v}_t + p_f + \theta^1$. This is profitable for the cable company if and only if $(\mathrm{v}_t + p_f + \theta^1 - c_b^i)\beta + \mu_t^i(1 - \beta) > \mu_t^i$. Because this is equivalent to $p_f - c_f > -(\theta^1 + \gamma)$, which is always true, any price for telephony services will be undercut by the cable company. As for the bundle, any price p_b on $[c_b^i, \mathrm{v}_b^1]$ can be undercut by the telecommunications company by setting $p_f < p_b - \mathrm{v}_t - \theta^1$. Such a price is profitable for the telecommunications company if and only if $(p_f - c_f) > \mu_f(1 - \beta)$, or equivalently, if and only if $p_f > c_f + \mu_f(1 - \beta)$. Hence, undercutting is profitable if the interval $(c_f + \mu_f(1 - \beta), p_b - \mathrm{v}_t - \theta^1)$ is nonempty. This

happens if $p_b > v_b^1 - \mu_f\beta$. For $p_b \leq v_b^1 - \mu_f\beta$ the telecommunications company prefers to set $p_f = v_f$ rather than trying to sell to the type 1 consumers. But for $p_f = v_f$ the cable company prefers to set $p_b = v_t + v_f + \theta^1 = v_b^1$. Because $v_b^1 > v_b^1 - \mu_f\beta$, the telecommunications company would then undercut this price.

33. See Varian 1980 or Narasimhan 1988 for the details of the method we use.

34. Our assumption that firms do not price discriminate plays a crucial role here. First, note that it is unlikely that firms could identify the two types of consumers. However, if firms could set different prices for different types of consumers, the telecommunications company would be willing to lower its price for type 1 consumers until $p_f = c_f$. The cable company would then undercut this price, selling to all type 1 consumers at $p_b = v_t + \theta^1 + c_f$. The business-stealing effect would then be zero because the telecommunications company makes no profit.

35. As a monopolist, the holding company could suffer from productive inefficiency, due to some slack in cost control. This means that it could have higher production costs than the independently owned cable company: $\delta_b < 0$, $\delta_t < 0$. Alternatively, there could be a loss of coordination in operating two networks: $\delta_b < 0$. In either case, the holding company would have fewer incentives to upgrade the CN than the independently owned cable company would.

36. See Parker and Roller 1997 for evidence that cross-ownership affects the firms' pricing behavior.

37. See Sidak, Crandall, and Singer 2002 for a discussion of this particular asymmetry.

38. We assume that when the CN is upgraded, the holding company uses both networks to supply type 2 consumers. This allows the holding company to fully exploit coordination economies, but at the expense of not fully exploiting economies of scope. In a previous version of this chapter we considered the possibility that after upgrading the CN, the holding company shut down at least part of the PSTN and mainly used the CN to provide both services, even to consumers that do not purchase the bundle. This allowed the holding company to fully exploit economies of scope, but at the expense of foregoing at least part of the coordination economies. Again, it was unclear which ownership structure generates the largest incentives to upgrade the CN.

References

Barros, P., and N. Cadima. 2000. "The Impact of Mobile Phone Diffusion on the Fixed-Link Network." Discussion Paper 2598. London: Centre for Economic Policy Research.

Bourreau, M., and P. Dogan. 2004. "Service-Based vs. Facility-Based Competition in Local Access Networks." *Information Economics and Policy* 16:287–306.

Bourreau, M., and P. Dogan. 2005. "Unbundling the Local Loop." *European Economic Review* 49:173–199.

Braeutigam, R. 1979. "Optimal Pricing with Intermodal Competition." *American Economic Review* 69(1): 38–49.

Brito, D., and P. Pereira. 2006. "Some Investment and Competition Implications of the Ownership Structure of Overlapping Networks." Working paper 11, Lisbon: Autoridade da Concorrencia.

Chandler, R., D. Kelley, and D. Nugent. 2002. "The Technology and Economics of Cross-Platform Competition in Local Telecommunications Markets." HAI Report. Louisville, CO.: HAI Consulting, Inc.

Cluny, J. 1996. "Cable Telephony as a Business: The UK Experience." London: OFTEL.

Cooper, M. 2003. "Cable Mergers, Monopoly and Price Increases." Washington, D.C.: Consumer Federation of America.

Crandall, R. 2002. "An Assessment of the Competitive Local Exchange Carriers Five Years After the Passage of the Telecommunications Act." Washington, D.C.: Criterion Economics, L.L.C.

Dessein, W. 2004. "Network Competition with Heterogeneous Customers and Calling Patterns." *Information Economics and Policy* 16:323–345.

Einhorn, M. 1987. "Optimality and Sustainability: Regulation and Intermodel Competition in Telecommunications." *Rand Journal of Economics* 18(4): 550–563.

European Telecoms Regulation and Markets. 2003. "Ninth Report on the Implementation of the Telecommunications Regulatory Package." COM(2003) 715 final. European Commission.

European Telecoms Regulation and Markets. 2004. "Tenth Report on the Implementation of the Telecommunications Regulatory Package." COM(2004) 759 final. European Commission.

Faulhaber, G. R. 2003. "Policy-Induced Competition: The Telecommunications Experiments." *Information Economics and Policy* 15:73–97.

Geroski, P. 1992. *Market Dynamics and Entry*. Oxford: Blackwell.

Hatfield Associates. 1997. "The Enduring Local Bottleneck II." Louisville, CO: HAI Consulting, Inc.

Hausman, J. 2003. "Regulated Costs and Prices in Telecommunications." In G. Madden, ed., *International Handbook of Telecommunications, vol. 2, Economics: Emerging Telecommunications Networks*, 199–233. Cheltenham, UK: Edward Elgar.

Loomis, D. G., and C. M. Swann. 2005. "Intermodal Competition in Local Telecommunications Markets." *Information Economics and Policy* 17:97–113.

Narasimhan, C. 1988. "Competitive Promotional Strategies." *Journal of Business* 61:427–449.

Noll, R., and B. Owen. 1998. "The Anticompetitive Uses of Regulation: *United States v. AT&T* (1982)." In John E. Kwoka Jr. and Lawrence J. White, eds., *The Antitrust Revolution*. Glenview, IL: Scott, Foresman.

OECD. 1998. "Cross-Ownership and Convergence and Information Services Policies." DSTI/ICCP/TISP (98)3/FINAL. Paris: Organization for Economic Cooperation and Development.

OECD. 2003. "OECD Communications Outlook." Paris: Organization for Economic Cooperation and Development.

Parker, P. M., and L. Roller. 1997. "Collusive Conduct in Duopolies: Multimarket Contact and Cross-Ownership in the Mobile Telephone Industry." *Rand Journal of Economics* 28(2): 304–322.

Rodini, M., M. Ward, and G. Woroch. 2003. "Going Mobile: Substitution between Fixed and Mobile Access." *Telecommunications Policy* 27:457–476.

Sidak, J., R. Crandall, and H. Singer. 2002. "The Empirical Case against Asymmetric Regulation of Broadband Internet Access." *Berkeley Technology Law Journal* 17(3): 953–987.

Temin, P. 2000. *Continuing Confusion: Entry Prices in Telecommunications.* Cambridge, MA: MIT Press.

Varian, Hal. 1980. "A Model of Sales." *American Economic Review* 70:651–659.

Woroch, G. 1997. "Turning the Cables: Economic & Strategic Analysis of Cable Entry into Telecommunications." In E. Noam, ed., *Globalism and Localism in Telecommunications.* Amsterdam: Elsevier.

Woroch, G. 2002. "Local Network Competition." In M. Cave, S. Majumdar, and I. Vogelsang, eds., *Handbook of Telecommunications Economics.* Amsterdam: Elsevier.

Contributors

Mark Armstrong University College London

Francesca Barigozzi University of Bologna

Randy Brenkers Catholic University of Leuven

Duarte Brito Universidade Nova de Lisboa

Jay Pil Choi Michigan State University

David Evans LECG and University College London

Vivek Ghosal Georgia Institute of Technology

Jos Jansen Social Science Research Center Berlin (WZB)

Franco Mariuzzo Trinity College of Dublin, Ireland

Martin Peitz International University in Germany

Pedro Pereira Autoridade da Concorrencia

Michael Salinger Director of the Bureau of Economics at the Federal Trade Commission, on leave from Boston University

Frank Verboven Catholic University of Leuven

Michael Waldman Cornell University

Patrick Paul Walsh Trinity College of Dublin, Ireland

Ciara Whelan University College of Dublin, Ireland

Index